Ethical Leadership in Turbulent Times

Ethical Leadership in Turbulent Times

Modeling the Public Career of George C. Marshall

GERALD M. POPS

LEXINGTON BOOKS

A division of
ROWMAN & LITTLEFIELD PUBLISHERS, INC.
Lanham • Boulder • New York • Toronto • Plymouth, UK

LEXINGTON BOOKS

A division of Rowman & Littlefield Publishers, Inc.
A wholly owned subsidary of The Rowman & Littlefield Publishing Group, Inc.
4501 Forbes Boulevard, Suite 200
Lanham, MD 20706

Estover Road
Plymouth PL6 7PY
United Kingdom

British Library Cataloguing in Publication Information Available

Library of Congress Cataloging-in-Publication Data

Pops, Gerald M.
  Ethical leadership in turbulent times : modeling the public career of George C. Marshall
/ Gerald M. Pops.—1st ed.
    p. cm.
  Includes bibliographical references and index.
  ISBN 978-0-7391-2476-5 (cloth : alk. paper)
  ISBN 978-0-7391-3955-4 (electronic)
  1. Marshall, George C. (George Catlett), 1880–1959. 2. Leadership—Moral and ethical
aspects—United States—Case studies. 3. Generals—United States—Biography. 4.
Statesmen—United States—Biography. 5. United States. Army—Biography. I. Title.
  E745.M37P67 2009
  973.918092—dc22
  [B]   2009011100

Printed in the United States of America

⊖™ The paper used in this publication meets the minimum requirements of American
National Standard for Information Sciences—Permanence of Paper for Printed Library
Materials, ANSI/NISO Z39.48–1992.

In memory of Larry Bland, whose generous heart and love for learning inspired me, and with whom I share a desire to focus greater attention on Marshall's genius for ethical leadership.

CONTENTS

FOREWORD

Leadership has become a very popular topic these days. But while everyone seems to be impressed by good leadership and critical of bad leadership, few seem to be able to describe exactly what leadership is—much less describing what is good leadership and what is bad leadership. For some, leadership is merely about accomplishment, about getting things done. For others, leadership is about much more. It is about vision, inspiration, elevating the human spirit. In either case, the question of good leadership versus bad is inescapable.

Generally speaking, those trying to define good leadership pursue one of several paths. Some simply define good leadership as effective leadership: the good leader is one who brings about dramatic changes in his or her group, organization, or society. (This is the view through which some would say, using a classic illustration, that Hitler was a good leader.) Other definitions of good leadership are more thoroughly grounded in ethical considerations. Some focus on the leader's character: is the leader a virtuous person, a person of character, someone who exhibits honesty and integrity? Others focus on the objectives of leadership: is the leader seeking moral objectives or moral ends, the right policies or outcomes? Still others are concerned with the ethics of *how* leadership is exercised: does the act of leadership appreciably alter the values of the group in a positive way? (In these latter views, Hitler would not be seen as a good leader.)

Interestingly, these different approaches to leadership tend to reflect the context in which studies of leadership are carried out and perhaps even the disciplinary background of those who engage in these studies. For the most part, our scholarly understanding of leadership has been based in studies of business and industrial organizations and has been carried out by scholars with backgrounds in business management. Not surprisingly, such studies exhibit a distinctively managerial bias. Leadership, in this view, is seen as little more than enhanced management, the ability to set a direction and move people, groups, and organizations in that direction. In this view, good leadership is effective leadership, though hopefully leadership engaged in by ethical leaders.

With the exception of studies of presidential leadership, far fewer studies have been based in government and politics. But interestingly, where leadership studies in the political realm have occurred, they have expressed considerably more concern for the way in which ethics and values permeate the leadership process. Certainly James Macgregor Burns' monumental work, *Leadership,* stands as a dramatic example in this regard, suggesting as it does that leadership is not about power but involves a relationship between leaders and followers in which both are elevated or positively transformed by their interaction. In this view, good leadership is about more than good leaders. It is about ethical leadership.

In one sense, this heightened concern for ethical leadership in the realm of politics and government is not surprising given that the ethics of public service permeate everything that happens in that realm. Ethical leadership in the public service is never just about one's personal or self-interest. Instead, the public leader must always be cognizant of the demands of democratic accountability and responsiveness to the public will. An ethical public leader must constantly engage with followers—whether organizational subordinates, clients, or citizens generally—in a way that takes into account all points of view and, in Burns' words, elevates and transforms all who are involved.

What is most interesting is the suggestion that public leadership, thus defined, might become a model for ethical leadership wherever it occurs. Certainly it makes sense to say that, in a democratic society, the norms and standards of democracy should define leadership and governance at all levels. And in practice, from the leader on the playground to the leader in the boardroom to the leader in the Congress, the demands of democratic responsibility are always "in play." People want to participate, to have a say in the outcomes affecting them. They don't want to be managed; they want to engage. For this reason, I suspect that the model of public leadership will increasingly become a significant model for leadership generally. For this reason, the stories of those who have navigated the opportunities and perils of leadership in the public service will provide important lessons for leaders in all fields.

Gerald Pops has written just such a story. Pops' engaging and complete study of the background and career of George C. Marshall, told in the pages that follow, examines Marshall's life and legacy from each of the perspectives above. But what is special about Marshall's story is that it is told in terms of public service. What emerges is a picture of Marshall as not only a dedicated soldier and later peacemaker, one pursuing important goals, and doing so effectively, but also a virtuous person, attentive both to "doing the right things" and "doing things right." Even more important, as a distinguished public leader, Marshall is seen to understand the ethics of leadership—that leadership is not only about what you do but how you do it, that no act of the leader in relation to his or her followers is devoid of ethical implications, that leadership ultimately transforms both the leader and the follower.

While this study of George C. Marshall contains important biographical information and helps the reader understand the character and behavior of this remarkable public leader, what is distinctive about this study is the lens through which Marshall's life is examined. Pops has chosen to examine Marshall's life and times through the lens of ethical leadership, indeed ethical public leadership, and in doing so remarks not only on Marshall alone but on lessons of interest to potential leaders in many realms, including not only the military and political realms, those Marshall knew best, but those of business and society as well. What emerges is a case study, a biography, but one with a distinct slant or perspective, that of leadership in the public service. As such, this is a book that should be of interest to scholars interested in political leadership and administrative leadership in the public sector, but more broadly to those academics and practitioners seeking to understand the ethical commitments and practices required of leaders in all sectors. Hopefully, it will help many pursue the path of ethical leadership.

Robert B. Denhardt
ASU Regents Professor
Lincoln Professor of Leadership and Ethics
Director, ASU School of Public Affairs
Arizona State University

AUTHOR'S PREFACE

This book is the product of a six-year effort that grew from a single idea, that it was important to model the career of a great public administrator for students, administrators, and the general public to admire and emulate.

The inspiration to actually begin it arose from one observation and two accidents of geography. I noticed that there was no book published that drew a complete picture of a functioning public figure of great stature and achievement that could speak to my students from their own career experience about how to be an effective and ethical public administrator. Abstract concepts about leadership, management, and ethics that filled the textbooks seem to be pale substitutes for real people with an inspiring life experience.

One of the geographical accidents is that I live and teach in Morgantown, West Virginia, a scant twenty-five miles from Uniontown, Pennsylvania, the small city where George Catlett Marshall was born and raised. I learned about Marshall's origins in the mid-1990s in an essay by Hart and Hart (1992) from a book containing brief accounts of a number of exemplary public administrators and assigned it to my class in public ethics. I was intrigued and proud that such a man as Marshall was a product of our local culture. The second accident of geography is that the George C. Marshall Museum and Library in Lexington, Virginia was within a few hours from home via an idyllic drive through Appalachian mountain scenery on country roads. My first visit to Lexington began my exploration of Marshall's career in earnest.

Those who remember George Marshall usually do so in the context of his role as the father of the Marshall Plan of the late 1940s. Fewer are familiar with the monumental roles he played in Army history or in the world wars, or in China, or in leading the State and Defense Departments and the American Red Cross. Even those who do know that he filled these roles know nothing of his formidable skills as an organizer and leader of people.

These revelatory facts sparked my surprise and sadness that Marshall could be so little celebrated and appreciated by our people, particularly young Americans who could learn so much from him in choosing and pursuing a career of public leadership. It was important that a man whom Churchill called the "organizer of victory" in World War II and whom Truman believed to be the greatest American of the era should be made known to future leaders in terms they could understand and relate to, and that his ideas about service, management, and leadership should be clearly communicated to everyone. Since my belief is that more of our country's best and brightest ought to choose public service leadership careers, I thought that Marshall's example could help inspire them to do so. I also see telling his story as a useful step in righting the skewed perception we have in our society of the bureaucrat, a prototype unfairly maligned and denigrated in popular culture.

Given the man's great reputation and accomplishments, I realized there was a danger of writing a book too uncritically favorable. This is why I have gone to lengths to insert critical material in an attempt to present Marshall in a balanced way, as a whole person. Most importantly he emerges as a functioning public administrator: a person charged with responsibility for developing and carrying out public programs, usually with limited resources, someone who must make difficult choices on the public's behalf and in the presence of great uncertainty. Just how he achieved what he achieved engages the imagination and invites entry into his entire character.

Encouragement and assistance has been generously extended to me on this journey by many. I owe an especially great debt of gratitude to the director of the Marshall Papers Collection at the George C. Marshall research library in Lexington, Dr. Larry I. Bland. Larry confirmed on our very first meeting the need for such a book as I envisioned and shared my enthusiasm for the contribution it could make. He supported my every step along the way. His knowledge and insight into Marshall's career and character and his generosity in sharing his time, spirit, and insight into the military profession meant a great deal to me personally and to my growing sense that my mission was worthy. In the process he became a close friend. Larry died suddenly in November, 2007. At that time he was in the process of reading my chapters in near-final form and giving me feedback and technical suggestions. It is an agony to me that Larry will not be able to read the book to which he contributed so much.

My wife, Marcia Claire Pops, an accomplished public administrator herself, accompanied and assisted me on most of my research sorties and did the bulk of the editing. She came to share my excitement in exploring the extraordinary life and career of Marshall. A large share of the credit in supporting me and in shaping the final product belongs to her.

Deborah Koon, office manager in the Division of Public Administration at West Virginia University, was invaluable in supplying technical assistance, whether it be securing equipment which I could use in travel, transferring files, staying in contact with the publisher, printing and getting review copies to me, or rescuing me in ways too varied to recount. She never told me how much of this was done on her own time.

Herman Mertins, former chair of the Department of Public Administration and vice-president of finance and administration at West Virginia University made a unique contribution. Mert was both a teacher of leadership and an outstanding ethical educational leader who achieved much and influenced many university hands in a positive direction. He was an important role model to me and a person who reinforced many of the principles Marshall exemplified. During the writing of this book, he shared with me in interviews his personal philosophy on effective leadership which helped to inform my pursuit of the subject.

My good friend and near centenarian Benjamin Shames, who worked for Marshall at the State Department as head of the office of Economic Analysis, was an inspiration and confirmed many personal recollections of others about Marshall's management style and personality. My cousin, Martin Bader, added his cogent observations about both missteps and occasionally brilliant leadership within the bureaucracy of the Cleveland, Ohio school system, throwing light on the universality of the research. Martin and his daughter Lisa Rosenthal both offered helpful editorial comments that were incorporated into later drafts. My daughter Hillary Bhaskaran gave me editorial feedback as well. My son-in-law Randolph Wynne, a professor at Virginia Tech, helped by teaching me how to cut through much of the tedium of indexing.

The Marshall library's director of research, Joanne Hartog, was a great help to my wife and myself in our constant search for sources and bits of data that resided in the darkest corners of the library's holdings. Her welcoming demeanor and quiet competence quickened our return on a regular basis to do the planned research and to further widen our search. Thanks also go to library director Paul Barron, to library assistant Peggy Dillard, to former foundation presidents Harry Warner and Wesley Taylor, and to the current foundation president, Brian Shaw. Sharon Ritenour Stevens, who assisted Dr. Bland in compiling several volumes of the Marshall Papers, helped me to gather, caption, and reproduce photographs. In general, the warmth and sincere interest of the Marshall Museum and Library and foundation staff in advancing scholarly research belie the reputation for excessive formality and detachment that attach to some national archival centers. Valuable as well as helpful assistance was also received from the Truman and Eisenhower libraries in Independence, Missouri and Abilene, Kansas, respectively.

The George C. Marshall Foundation and its board graciously provided a $5,000 grant to assist with travel and related expense, greatly facilitating research. I am grateful for their assistance.

This work on Marshall, his career and contributions to ethical public leadership, draws upon a vast store of material. Doubtless, some factual errors have been unintentionally committed, and there will be interpretations of facts that may well clash with the interpretations of others. I accept responsibility for the former and am grateful for the latter that after all furnish the stuff of intellectual debate. I have done my best to complete my mission, just as I know General Marshall would have had me do.

CHAPTER ONE
THE SEARCH FOR IDEAL LEADERSHIP

Throughout my military career, I turned to Marshall often for inspiration and wisdom. And the better I understood the challenges he had to face, the better I understood what a giant he truly was. . . He never wrote a book to tell his story.
—Colin Powell
(Barber 1997, 25)

The story told in these pages is how the life, career, and character of George Catlett Marshall converged to make him an icon of ethical leadership. His resume contains the position titles of military cadet, army staff officer, dean of instruction of the army's elite infantry officer school, regional director of the Civilian Conservation Corps, U.S. Army chief of staff, special ambassador to China, secretary of state, president of the American Red Cross, and secretary of defense. However, his significance as a national and international leader cannot be appreciated from a bare listing of position titles. It is the goal of this book to describe and explain the nature of the ethical leadership he exhibited and modeled throughout a career of extraordinary length and range, all of it in service to the public's welfare.

His half century in this *potpourri* of leadership roles was almost uniformly successful, often spectacularly so. Its results included molding the greatest army in world history, shaping the education of a generation of military officers, blending the activities of American ground, naval, and air forces, harmonizing American armed forces with those of other nations, catalyzing the rebuilding of war-torn nations, and leaving behind a legacy of national leaders molded in his image.

This is a recounting which paints a portrait of one man's hugely successful career as a public administrator and as a statesman. The quality of his leadership on national and international stages for a full half-century was crucial to the survival of western democracies and European prosperity and cooperation. The recounting reaches beyond biography to inquire into the very nature of leadership, and in particular to the nature of ethical leadership. In doing so, it holds lessons for national and international students, managers, leaders, and citizens, particularly those who value democracy and constitutional governance.

This is also a story of how sterling character and virtues contribute to leadership. From its telling one can grasp hope that there is a vital connection between being an ethical person and being an effective administrator in a world that desperately needs both.

A Desire for Ethical Leadership

Although the nature of its conflicts and challenges have changed, America yet operates in dangerous times, as do many other nations. War in the middle east, civil conflict in Africa and Asia, an international financial crisis, and worldwide terrorist attacks enlarge the need for strong and competent leadership in all governments. In the United States scandals in corporate governance and the real estate mortgage industry, in the provision of military and reconstruction services in Iraq, in the financing of political campaigns, and in the clean-up activities associated with hurricane Katrina, just to cite a few examples, help make the case that self-interest and political patronage continue to threaten the public interest in the realm of both decision-making and administrative implementation of policy decisions.

The urgent and felt need for scandal-averse and effective government fuels a yearning for ethical leadership in all sectors—public, private, and nonprofit. Yet people seek different things when they express the need for ethical governance. Some want reformed decision making "systems" that employ new methods for breaking the powerful connection between money and elective leadership. Others wish to strengthen accountability for official actions or inactions. Still others press for more privatization and improving the quality of the contracting-out processes already being heavily relied upon by government. Regardless of the preferred ends, most place their hopes on finding superior people to serve—thus concentrating on identifying, electing, and appointing good candidates to office.

Many social scientists as well as popular writers and working or former executives have spoken out on the matter of leadership. Their models vary with their particular values. Few social science studies are explicitly based on real persons, events, and results although it is likely that much of the inspiration for them comes from observation. Audiences have little basis for drawing conclusions about the effectiveness and moral quality of differing leadership models other than compatibility with the values of those creating the models.

The attitudes and methods of those who are in leadership positions are rooted in the specific society and environment from which they spring. These conditions determine how they act and do not act, conflict and harmonize, inspire and disappoint, love and hate, and fail and succeed. Such terms as "attributes of leadership," "leadership traits and behaviors," "situational leadership" and "value-based leadership" are useful academic terms that contain insights potentially useful in organizational situations. Yet they are ultimately austere and bloodless *unless* we connect them to whole people and fully fleshed-out, real-world situations. The latter are invariably complex, usually stressful, and characterized by uncertainty and change.

Marshall as a Model

Marshall's career began at the dawn of America's emergence upon the international stage following the Spanish-American War. It extended through both world wars and bridged the beginning of the Cold War, the rebuilding of society in the face of colossal devastation, and the emergence of the United States as a nuclear and economic superpower. It is inseparable from the events and people that dominated the period, and lives in the memories and life experiences of many elders among us as well as the books and films that shape the images of people of all ages of the world in those times.

Most of the roles Marshall filled during this era gave him command authority over others. Many required that he coordinate the work of multiple units toward a common purpose or engage with persons from other organizations in joint planning and decision-making. Still others put him in the position of informing and advising national and world political leaders. All presented him with the opportunity to lead others. Always he labored within large, public organizations, but occasionally he operated in relative isolation in roles others regarded as thankless or unrelated to career advancement. His leadership in its totality swept across a wide range of public organizations.

Given Marshall's enormous influence on the events of the twentieth century, it is both surprising and disappointing that his life and administrative career are not more often the subject of academic and popular reflection. This is partially explained by the fact that his impact was played out on such a broad canvass of important and colorful events and personalities that his image is blurred. Nonetheless, virtually all Americans and Europeans who are old enough to have lived through WW II and its aftermath or know well their family history remember and honor the man in one context or another.

Yet the same absorbing history equips us with a set of hooks and anchors that may be used to better understand and assess Marshall's actions and contributions. Here is an illustrative list of names, places, and events (in no particular order) that draws us into his story: Dwight Eisenhower, Guadalcanal, Douglas MacArthur and his escape from Corregidor, MacArthur's removal from command in the Korean war, the pivotal Meuse-Argonne campaign of World War One (WW I), General John J. Pershing, the African-American 92nd Infantry Division fight against German troops in Italy, the WAAC's and the USO, the Enola Gay and Hiroshima, Patton and Montgomery and Bradley and the battles of the Bulge and the bridge at Remagen, de Gaulle and the French Resistance, Churchill and the Battle of Britain, the mobilization of the National Guard, the 101st Airborne Division at Normandy, Franklin Roosevelt and Harry Truman, the bombing of Germany by the 8th Air Force, lend-lease, the selective service system, the United Nations, the Civilian Conservation Corps, the Teheran and Casablanca and Yalta conferences, Joseph Stalin, the Marshall Plan, the Berlin airlift, George Kennan and containment policy, Harry Hopkins and Hans Morgenthau, and the North Atlantic Treaty Organization. The list is endless but it is its familiarity and evocation of images that drive home this point.

Long after his third and final retirement Marshall's opinions and actions continue to be raised in connection with national debates. Policy makers use "Marshall Plan" descriptors to gain support for their proposals. His views on military preparedness, the idea of a volunteer army, civil governance in occupied lands, and nation building have often been inserted into public debate, most recently during the Iraq war in connection with building civil governance and reconstruction. Many subsequent military chiefs of staff, cabinet and sub-cabinet officials, and other public leaders evoke his name as a mentor or as a source of inspiration: Maxwell Taylor, Oveta Culp Hobby, J. Lawton Collins, Matthew Ridgway, Dean Acheson, Robert Lovett, Frank Pace, Dean Rusk, and Colin Powell are but a few of these.

All of the personalities or events noted above had in common the fact that George Marshall himself placed them into recorded history or contributed to their significance or meaning in some tangible way. Taken as a whole, the only reasonable conclusion is that Marshall added greatly to our shared experience as a people. Thus, the telling of Marshall's story and his leadership are extracted from rich and fertile soil.

Marshall's career does honor to the millions of Americans who labor unselfishly to serve the public. Public servants all too often endure the derision of many of their fellow citizens, putdowns wrapped around the word "bureaucrat" intended to disparage their worth. This stereotyping causes pain and sometimes irreparable harm to many competent, well prepared, and selfless public servants. Perhaps more importantly, these expressions damage the general public from whom the disparagement comes. Through accepting and reinforcing the myth that public service is for the nonproductive, many talented and patriotic people are discouraged from entering public service where they are desperately needed, thus short-changing the nation. Marshall's career offers a contrasting and compelling, positive picture of the performance of public servants and the rewards and satisfactions of public service careers.

A society that today faces so many threats and challenges on so many fronts—terrorism and its threats to security and international stability, global warming and environmental pollution, financial systems melt down, unemployment and underemployment, the inability of many citizens to afford healthcare and education, systemic corruption and its undermining of government legitimacy—stands to gain much by studying and learning from its success stories. Lessons of good government and effective, ethical public leadership need to be preserved, cherished, and passed on.

Marshall, both the man and the leader, have the potential to inspire and to educate and in so doing create a powerful model for others to emulate. The neglect of his career in our educational institutions is regrettable but remediable. He is that rare public figure who, like George Washington, was renowned not only as a great soldier and military organizer but also as a statesman and civilian administrator. Although close to being an ideal type, he is rarely celebrated and studied within educational institutions in the fields of public administration and affairs, political science and public policy, business and non-profit organizations, and military administration and science. It is fitting and necessary that his administrative career and management and leadership attributes, methods, and ideas be studied in their full scope as a model of ethical leadership.

Outline of the Book

Telling the Marshall story in the way it may best serve as a model for leadership and management presents three challenges. The first is to properly set it within a framework of leadership theory. The second is to analyze his character, the special attributes of his personality and his system of values and virtues, and relate these elements to leadership theory. The third is to relate both the theory and the man to the environment and experiences that formed the world in which he acted. The uncertainty of the changing times that swirled about Marshall, creating new conditions that often rapidly altered the organizational and decision contexts in which he worked, affected the nature of the choices he faced and the manner in which his choices had to be carried out.

Addressing the first of these challenges begins in this introductory chapter with an overview of leadership theory. It will be abstract but will be kept short. The theory will be used from time to time throughout the book, especially in chapter eight which focuses on organizational theory, but each time this is done the relevance of Marshall to the theory is highlighted. The final chapter will include summary remarks about the special nature of Marshall's leadership and how it might be used to shape leadership theory in general.

Following the introductory chapter the book proceeds on roughly parallel tracks: (1) personality development, with special emphasis on values, virtues, and attributes of character that relate to management and leadership; and (2) historical description of roles and environment, featuring career experience and relationships with other public actors and institutions.

Personality development begins in chapter two with a description of Marshall's family and boyhood in Pennsylvania, followed by a presentation and analysis of the first forty years of his professional career. This very long period, although it covers more than half of his life, forms the basis upon which the unique latter stages of his leadership development depends. Early experiences in the military academy of the Virginia Military Institute (VMI), first duty assignments, intellectual growth in advanced military training, and command of state National Guard training maneuvers imparted the distinct flavor of his military professionalism and prepared him for the key role he was to play as a high-ranking staff officer on the battlefields of France in WW I.

There follows a recitation of numerous and far-ranging roles in the interregnum between the two great wars: his service at the side of General John J. Pershing; peace-keeping duty in China in charge of troops; a military education reformer; a major organizer of the Civilian Conservation Corps; service to the National Guard; and finally, his work in Washington with the General Staff of the War Department shortly before World War Two (WW II) erupted in Europe. This foundation, in and of itself, surpasses in achievement the whole career of almost any other military administrator and tells the story of the growth, achievements, and leadership qualities of a superb military administrator. However, for Marshall's ultimate place in leadership history, this period was but prelude to what came after.

By 1939 Marshall's character was well formed. The next two chapters, three and four, describe this character and give many examples of its facets and effects. They have somewhat different foci. Chapter three delves into those particular qualities of heart and mind that are associated in the literature with both ethical leadership and organizational effectiveness. Then, born of the belief that ethical leadership and effectiveness have much to do with character traits and virtues that go well beyond those conventionally labeled as related to managing and leading organizations, chapter four turns to other personality attributes and virtues. The latter, although not clearly identified in the literature as related to management and leadership, nonetheless bring about a clearer understanding of the man's philosophy and style and personality—all of which contributed to his reputation and his administrative successes. Collectively, chapters three and four are intended to explain those qualities that make Marshall memorable and worthy of study as an exemplar of ethical leadership.

Chapters five, six, and seven take the reader back onto the historical track of the Marshall career story. Chapter five focuses on his service as U.S. Army chief of staff from September 1, 1939, the day WW II began, until America's entry into the war on December 7, 1941. Here is told the story of that part of his career which was the most difficult, by his own account. He guides the Army through an extraordinarily difficult period that includes German and Japanese expansionism and public and Congressional opposition to preparing America to enter the war. The period presents an agonizing crucible of pressures and conflict, rapid learning, and personal growth in which Marshall was called on to make many decisions not only on how best to guide the Army, but also the Army's relationship to the Navy and air power. He was called upon to attend to relations with the western democracies who were not yet allies. He fought to build, train, and equip a massive army. He was pushed to the forefront of politics as Roosevelt's chief advocate of prepared-ness. In the process, he struggled with how to deal with a divided and often hostile Congress, a fearful public, the Army's old guard, and a sometimes quixotic president.

With the Japanese attack on Pearl Harbor came a distinctly new turn in Marshall's career and in the nature of the demands upon his leadership. Chapter six deals with yet a distinctly new set of environmental forces: the calamity and shock of initial military losses; moving to a total war footing; dealing with organizational dysfunctions in the Army and War Department; the demands of making cross-Atlantic military alliance effective; intense inter-service rivalries; and overseeing a multi-theater war. Finally, in the contemplation of final victory, came challenges in planning for the war's end, demobilizing, and occupying and governing conquered lands. Hidden within this most dramatic and triumphal period of the century were great challenges that involved harmonizing the interplay among enormous and conflicting forces and personalities.

Chapter seven takes the reader into the civilian stage of Marshall's career, one quite unlike any other through which he had previously passed. This relatively short, six-year period ran from November 1945 to September 1951 and is full of drama and historic crisis points. His first role during this era found him serving as

President Truman's special ambassador to China with the task of seeking peace and political accommodation between its two major political groups, the Nationalists and the Communists. He returned home to assume the position of secretary of state. At State, he was to involve himself in perhaps the furthest reaching initiatives in the history of American foreign policy. His second "retirement" led him into presiding over the American Red Cross prior to the outbreak of war in Korea, which brought him to his final role, that of secretary of defense. His performance at Defense offers yet further instruction on the nature of ethical leadership, as does the final period of his life following his final retirement from public service.

The content of chapters eight, nine, and ten demonstrates Marshall's thinking about managing public organizations and exercising ethical leadership by demonstrating just how he applied his management and leadership principles in practice. Chapter eight deals entirely with matters familiar to students and practitioners who manage organizations—principles and functions such as unity of command, coordination, planning, communication, and staffing—by focusing on how they were approached and practiced. How did Marshall think about organizations and their functioning? How did he go about structuring and managing them? How did he make decisions and how did he implement them? Of unique relevance to the public sector, there is a section on how he believed the administrative role ought to be influenced by the fact that it is carried out within a constitutional democracy.

Of supreme importance to the nature of leadership is the question of how organizations and governments respond and adapt to change. Chapter nine demonstrates Marshall's approach to change through its treatment of repeated reorganizations and organization building over the course of his career. These were huge and complex events with large consequences for governmental effectiveness. What drove his motivation to reorganize? How did he manage the reorganization process and its timing? How did he build organizational capacity and design effective decision processes? Exploring these questions yields insight into the practical side of managing change in organizations.

Managing people is the subject of chapter ten. The people to be managed are primarily organizational members but also extend to key political and public actors outside the organization. Marshall's abilities as an educator, talent scout, and motivator, and as a builder of organizational leadership are all taken up. How should people be selected, socialized, and developed for organizational roles? How ought they be motivated to act, and how should failure be handled? What degree of autonomy, trust, and responsibility should they be given, and how should their performance be measured and rewarded? How should organizational needs be balanced with human needs for recreation, physical and mental health, family, patriotism, grief, and service? Finally, what were Marshall's ideas about the nature of leadership and the preparation of leaders?

The final two chapters take up some broader concepts critical to ethical leadership in the public sector. Chapter eleven is about the fit between bureaucracy and democracy, especially in determining whether the principle of inclusiveness (of racial minorities and women) comes into conflict with the merit principle. To what extent should black troops be integrated with white troops? How much free speech should be allowed in wartime consistent with the need for military secrecy and national defense? Marshall's perspective on these confounding issues posed by the tension between democracy and bureaucracy and social pressures are explored.

The element of citizenship is considered at length. What role should it play in military and public organizations? What is the proper role of the military in civil governance and occupation within conquered territory? To what extent should the United States rely upon a citizen-based armed force for national security instead of a volunteer, career military?

The concluding chapter sums up Marshall's development as an ideal public, ethical leader. It also advances and debates his legacies—his views on the relationship of war-making to peace-keeping, the military use of nuclear energy, and the limits of military power. How does he speak to us in today's context of the war on terror; about America's obligations to other nations? Ultimately, the nature of his brand of public and ethical leadership must be assessed as a model to be used for the preparation of future leaders. The book ends by addressing the same pursuits that dominated the latter part of Marshall's administrative career: shaping leadership to define the great challenges of our times and mobilizing human and material resources to meet those challenges.

The Holy Grail of Leadership

The major purpose of this book is to gain insight into the nature of effective public and ethical leadership. The method is to study in detail the character and career of a singularly effective and ethical public leader—that is, modeling from an ideal type. This method departs from the way leadership is usually studied in academia or in business and government training programs.

In order to help draw lessons of ethical leadership from the study of Marshall's character and career, it is useful to begin by reviewing in broad outline how the subject has been approached to date. The first observation is that the literature is vast and reflects many approaches. Most of it comes from the private, business sector; only some of it translates to the public realm. The reality is that leadership in the public sector is not the same thing as leadership in the private sector. Much of the difference stems from the fact that being an effective leader in a democratic and pluralistic government regime depends on reaching a consensus among groups having differing values and interests and gaining inter-organizational cooperation. These aims are less often valued in the private sector.

The very large number of theories seeking to explain leadership reflect the writers' perspectives about how influence is exerted. Some look to the ability to effectively use group processes, while others focus on the personal attributes of the leader. Some stress the relationships between leaders and followers within their organizations, particularly those that help followers achieve their personal goals as well as further the organization's mission. Others focus on the relationships between leaders and significant persons and institutions external yet important to attaining the organization's mission (Northouse 2001, 2). Some theorists combine aspects of several perspectives (see, for example, Van Wart 2005). All have worked to spin out, label, and seek advocates for their formulations.

This mass of differing theories of leadership is grouped within three general categories: theories of *transactional* leadership, theories of *transformational* leadership, and theories of *ethical* leadership. Of course, these are not mutually exclusive categories because they have elements in common. It is well to stress the commonalities in leadership theories before putting them into categories and then distinguishing them. All share the idea that the phenomenon of leadership is mostly about *change*—inspiring, guiding, and managing it. All organizations must at least cope with it to survive, and those that embrace it in a measured, planned way will thrive. Change occurs both in the world surrounding the organization (for example, demography, technology, shifting political parameters, and social values are constantly changing) as well as within the organization and its people (interpersonal dynamics, relevant skill sets fluctuate constantly). It is a truism that the external world is not distinct from the internal organization itself. The so-called boundaries of the organization, particularly the public organization, are illusory. Especially in the public sector, the leader must be able to sense and react to opportunities in concert with other organizations, which are presented by political and social movements (Luke 1991). The leader uses these opportunities and circumstances to improve his or her organization's prospects for achieving its goals.

The phenomenon of change distinguishes the function of *leadership* from the function of *management*. Management focuses on the performance of specific functions including, in Luther Gulick's famous formulation: planning, organizing, staffing, directing, coordinating, reporting, and budgeting—POSDCoRB (Gulick 1937). The goals of management are organizational order, consistency, and stability, common striving toward the same goals, the efficient use of resources, acquiring the necessary skills, and increasing production (Northouse 2001, 8-10). Leadership, on the other hand, emphasizes goal-setting, gathering resources (material, human and knowledge), energizing people through inspiring, motivating, and encouraging creativity in the pursuit of the goals, and then revising and setting new goals and means for pursuing them in accord with the changing environment and what is required for the organization's survival and growth. But although management and leadership may be distinguished in theory, they cannot be separated in practice; the successful leader must be concerned about management.

Absolutely critical to bringing about needed change is the ability of public leaders to envision things in the long-term: what Richard Neustadt and Ernest May called "thinking in time streams," the essence of which "is imaging the future as it may be when it becomes the past" (1986, 253-254). Effective leadership involves visualizing both desirable and undesirable futures and constructing mental maps to enable getting to the desirable and avoiding the undesirable.

Transactional leadership theories focus on specific actions of those in positions of authority. Leadership is explained in terms of actions taken by the leader which in combination bring about the accomplishment of goals (using incentive pay in combination with overtime, for example). Among the many transactional theories (which include behavioral theories, path-goal theory, situational leadership theory, situational leadership theory, and leader-member exchange theories), is the one most familiar to the layman: trait theory. Trait theory relies on personal attributes of the leader alone and not on the nature of the followers. Certain traits are argued to lead to specific behaviors that move the organization forward. They are of universal application and possessing them is believed to enable the leader to bring about useful change. Although different writers offer differing lists of essential traits, the lists typically include self-confidence, sociability, intelligence, determination, and integrity (Northouse 2004, 15-24).

Trait theory assumes that having a set of natural personal attributes acquired through genetic inheritance and early nurturing sets the stage for the development of the leader. Added to this are the virtues gained through habitual practices, and the knowledge, values, and skills derived from a set of experiences gained in a series of organizational roles and in formal and informal education. Thus genetics, nurturing, virtues, and experience together impart the knowledge, skills, values, and practices that create the phenomenon known as leadership. One additional element may be added—there must exist the will to become a leader and exercise the power of leadership.

Situational leadership, another popular theory, entails fitting certain management "styles" to the needs and skills of followers. Effectiveness of leadership thus depends on whether there is a fit between leader style and follower needs and skills in the situation that leads to positive results, including the satisfaction and development of followers. From this perspective, one might reason that a folk music icon like Bob Dylan could influence a generation of young people to act in certain ways; for example, to oppose the war in Vietnam. Could a Dylan have been successful in getting young people to vote for a liberal candidate in the 1990s? Or oppose the war in Iraq in the first decade of the twenty-first century? The "situation" is very different in these latter two cases, but are the essential ingredients there (emotive communication, generational conflict, threat of being drafted, etc.)? Popular for many years, situational theory puts less stress than other leadership theories on personal character and virtues, values and ethics, vision, and competence (Van Wart 2005, 315-318). It is more important to have a certain type of person in the right place at the right time, so the theory goes, than to have a person with an ideal set of traits in the leadership position.

Transformational leadership theories are centered on the leader's role in changing the organization itself through altering its goals and objectives, structures and processes, the mix and skills of participants, and the culture of the organization. This kind of theory assumes a more fluid interaction between the leader's organization and its external environment (political, economic, and social). To make a major impact leaders must be perceived by others within and outside the organization as wise, involved, highly effective, and trustworthy; thus the element of reputation becomes important. Transformational theory assumes that change in the environment is constant, and that the leadership behavior that counts most is that concerned with gearing organizational dynamics to external and internal change factors and influencing "the right" people (Van Wart 2005, 335-338).

Transformational leadership is seen by its advocates as superior to transactional leadership since the transformational leader transforms the organization in a way that produces long-term results, rather than, as the transactional leader would do, simply succeed in getting improved results in a given situation (Bass 1985).

Moving further along the same line of reasoning, a yet more effective form of transformational leadership has been theorized. This would be a leadership that transforms *people* into carriers of the leader's visions and values, thus creating a new cadre of leaders that is able to sustain and extend relevant change (G. Fairholm 1991; M. Fairholm 2006). Such leadership:

> involves change but it is very different from changing actions and behaviors, culture, and mission. This leadership is intimate and is about changing who we are. It is about changing us for the better so that we will necessarily act and behave and perform in the ways that are valued because we value them ourselves; they are not forced, induced, incentivized, motivated, nor trained. They are rather inculcated through inspiration, reason, and freedom of choice (M. Fairholm 2006, 16).

According to this point of view, the best transformational leaders transform their organization, the people within it, and others outside the organization who interact with it. Denhardt (1993) closely examined persons acknowledged to be good leaders of public-purpose organizations with the goal of discovering the basis of their success. He came up with five leadership approaches which he argued capture the style of public leadership likely to be successful in modern American society: (1) a commitment to values; (2) concern for serving the public; (3) empowering others and sharing leadership; (4) pragmatic incrementalism (moving step by step; continuing in the same direction if it works); and (5) a dedication to public service. He found that these elements have the power to transform people. They also heavily depend upon ethical precepts and thus shade into a third type of leadership whose transformational qualities are heavily ethical in their nature—hence *ethical leadership.*

Ethical leadership is particularly suited to the public sector. It stresses democratic norms, human dignity, justice and fairness, and equality in addition to such general personal qualities as trust, courage, integrity, and compassion. The focus is more often on leader values and the means of leadership rather than on the results achieved, with organizational effectiveness assumed or taken on faith. The question of whether ethical leadership is also *effective* leadership is a continuing question of great importance.

Marshall's Search for Leadership

Marshall himself was absorbed throughout his life with the phenomenon of leadership. In the latter part of his career he cared enough to institutionalize leadership training within the organizations he served. His thinking about the subject began in his boyhood, entering into his consciousness through his parents and friends and rumination about historical events. Much more came to him as a professional soldier from people whom he modeled as his mentors: General Pershing, Secretary of War Newton D. Baker, and presidential assistant Harry Hopkins were among the most important. Perhaps most of his ideas on the subject came from his powers of logic, instinctual reactions to opportunity and threat, a willingness to learn from trial and error, and from that mysterious source labeled, simply, "intuition."

Many have come along who have succeeded in positions of leadership. But Marshall is among the very few who persevered, who was able to reinvent himself and continue to successfully lead over a great length of time in a variety of organizational contexts. Self-education and growth were essential to this process along with an innate ability to scan both the internal and external environments of the organization in which he worked. When virtually all of his contemporaries from WW II were retired, infirm, or dead, Marshall ascended to and mastered still another set of leadership challenges, the last devoted to the pursuit of world harmony and peace rather than the building of successful military organizations.

Although aided by good fortune, his progress up the leadership ladder was by no means accidental. He was forever curious about the nature of leadership and coveted the role of leader. At VMI he discovered that he not only possessed the capacity to lead others but was humbled by the responsibility it placed upon him. By 1940 the awesome responsibility would fall largely to him to select and prepare others who themselves would become the elite leadership core of the Army, a group that would largely determine by their qualities and decisions the fate of America and its allies in WW II.

As we seek to extract leadership lessons from his career it is important to remember that he was quintessentially a man of action. We must look to his actions rather than his words to discern and flesh out both his concepts and practices relative to ethical leadership. No "little red book" of Marshall's aphorisms or axioms about organizational practices has been left behind. However, he did speak occasionally on the subject, as he did not hesitate to attempt to imprint on his charges his own understanding of leadership and its importance. Relative to the command of troops, he reflected late in the war:

> Aggressive and determined leadership, from the purely military point of view, is the final determining factor in warfare. Genuine discipline, sound training, suitable munitions and adequate numbers are essentials, but they will be ineffective without the dominating influence of strong leadership. Deficiencies are made good by leadership. Difficulties are overcome by leadership. Military victories depend upon leadership.[1]

The story recounting Marshall's career as a warrior and as a statesman is filled with lessons on leadership and management principles. As these are encountered, there will be no attempt to point out where Marshall "fits" among the many theories of leadership. Rather, the intent is to move in the opposite direction—using Marshall to point the way to improved theory. Until now no systematic work focusing on how he operated as an organizational leader has been attempted—such an effort is being made in this book.[2]

Using Marshall's career as an ideal type of ethical leadership is not without its risks. Being only human, he cannot by himself constitute an ideal type any more than can some highly respected organization be used by itself to demonstrate an "ideal-type bureaucracy" in the spirit of Max Weber's classic model (Gerth and Mills, 1947). But Marshall's brand of leadership can and does concentrate attention on an approach to leadership that is demonstrably effective. An additional point is that its highly ethical content may impart understanding of how ethical factors contribute to leadership effectiveness.

Sources in the Search for Marshall's Leadership

Marshall wrote well but he did little writing reflecting on matters of leadership, organizational functioning, and management methods. During the period of 1919-1923 he wrote memoirs of his WW I experiences with the American Expeditionary Forces in France (Marshall 1976). Whether this was accomplished from memory or from notes made during the war is not made clear. In any event, this manuscript gives us a window on his mind at a relatively early point in his career. He never wrote such a collection of his thoughts again. In fact, he had decided not to publish even that set of memoirs, directing instead that they be destroyed (and this was done faithfully by his widow). Fortunately for future scholarship his step-daughter, Molly Pender Winn, discovered a carbon copy after his death and frustrated Marshall's intent by securing its publication (Bland 1991, 10).

Historian Douglas Southall Freeman suggested to General Marshall in 1942 that he keep memoranda or a diary of important daily events. Marshall refused, stating that doing so "tends to cultivate a state of mind unduly concerned with possible investigations, rather than a complete concentration on the business of victory." Although he conceded that he would "probably be embarrassed" at some future time by lack of evidence or notes to support some position or decision he had taken, he believed that keeping a self-conscious record "would inevitably affect the clarity of logic of my daily approach to the changing situation" (Bland 1991, vii). In other words, he feared that his ability to focus on the effects of change would be compromised by tangential and relatively self-serving considerations (Pogue 1963, xiii).

Another reason he gave for not publishing his memoirs was that he did not wish to be unfair to anyone by putting an unkind remark in print. He supported this view steadfastly by almost always refusing to speak negatively of American and foreign leaders, public figures, and military colleagues. Consistent with this desire, he refrained also from claiming the responsibility for proposals or actions leading to ultimately successful developments. He preferred instead to leave the writing of his story and the assessment of the quality of his leadership to historians (Bland 1991, 5, 12-13; Bryden 1958, 36). This lack of a desire to look good and to avoid making others look bad persisted as a striking virtue in the man.

Modesty, the priority placed upon the need to keep from being distracted, and the desire to be kind to people, however admirable these motives are from a moral point of view, came at a high cost to both Marshall personally and to those who attempt to study his thinking and actions from his perspective. When he reached retirement he spurned an offer of one million dollars to produce memoirs of WW II and the post-war years. He had never earned an annual salary above fifteen thousand and his retirement, while not uncomfortable, was modest. He would have benefitted greatly from the proceeds and given his widow greater financial security. However, as he often said, service to the nation is a privilege and should not be used as a source of personal enrichment. The loss is primarily ours.[3]

Finally, in 1956, upon the urging of a former aide and after the George C. Marshall Research Foundation had been founded with Dr. Forrest C. Pogue as its director, the general consented to a series of interviews with Pogue. Pogue was a professional historian who had compiled the official history of the European Theater Command at the end of WW II. Consent was conditioned upon the understanding that profits from any book based on the material obtained from the interviews would not go to Marshall or his family or estate, but be used for research. Pogue's historic interviews began in late 1956 and continued until the general's health made their continuance impossible in April 1957.

The major project emerging from the Pogue-Marshall interviews was the volume, *George C. Marshall: Interviews and Reminiscences for Forrest C. Pogue,* edited by Dr. Larry I. Bland and published in 1991. This work contains many of the thoughts and words of General Marshall and contributed importantly to the writing of this book.[4] The other major work on Marshall's career is Pogue's exhaustive four-volume biography of Marshall compiled from many interviews with Marshall contemporaries and intimate coworkers, and other research (Pogue 1963; Pogue 1966; Pogue 1973; and Pogue 1987).

In the personal remembrances that he shared with Pogue and occasionally with other correspondents or interviewers, Marshall is rarely negative in his evaluation of the role or actions of others (Bland 1991, 12) and often kinder than is perhaps warranted. The temptation to gossip—enormous for many mortals in the same position given the many colorful and outsized personalities of the day—either did not arise in his thoughts or was squelched on principle.

Certain aides and associates who worked closely with Marshall have been relied upon heavily in the writing of this book. Their observations are contained in the extensive interviews recorded by Pogue from 1956 to 1962 (with the two exceptions of William Heffner and Merrill Pasco, who were interviewed in 1995 and 1997 respectively). Their insights have the special advantage of conveying many of the nuances of Marshall's organizational practices and habits, virtues and faults, from the perspective of close and frequent observers at various points in his career. Their names, with biographical descriptions especially relevant to their service with Marshall, follow:

Thomas T. Handy—served as assistant chief of staff for operations (June 1942-October 1944) and deputy chief of staff (October 1944-November 1945) in the War Department, under Marshall.

Frank McCarthy—assistant secretary and secretary of the General Staff of the War Department through most of WW II and immediately after WW II.

Charles Bolte—instructed under Marshall at Ft. Benning Infantry Officer School in 1930; chief of staff of U.S. Forces in Great Britain in 1942 and commanded the 34th Infantry Division in Italy in 1943-1944; rose to the position of Army vice-chief of staff, 1953-1955.

John Hilldring—instructor at Fort Benning under Marshall; assistant chief of staff, Personnel Section of the General Staff, 1939-41; assistant chief of staff, Office of Civil Affairs of the General Staff, 1943-45; assistant secretary of state, 1947-51.

John Deane—with Marshall at Fort Benning; assistant secretary, General Staff, during attack on Pearl Harbor, December 7, 1941; made secretary of General Staff soon thereafter.

Frederick Osborn—chair of Army Committee on Welfare and Recreation, 1940; chief of Morale Branch, War Department, 1941.

Matthew Ridgway—student under Marshall at Ft. Benning, 1929-31; assigned to War Plans Division early in WW II; commanded 8th Army in Korea, 1951; commanded UN forces in Korea, 1951; commanded Supreme Allied Command in Europe, 1952; U.S. Army chief of staff, 1952-1955.

Walter Bedell "Beetle" Smith—served Marshall as assistant secretary and secretary of the General Staff in the War Department; secretary to Combined Chiefs of Staff, 1939-1942; ambassador to the Soviet Union; director of Central Intelligence Agency, 1950-1953; undersecretary of State Department, 1953-54.

George Kennan—headed Office of Planning and Policy, Department of State under Marshall, 1947-1949; ambassador to the Soviet Union and Yugoslavia; diplomat, political scientist and historian.

Merrill Pasco—assistant secretary and secretary of the General Staff in the War Department, throughout WW II.

There are many others whose observations are used. Where appropriate, these will be identified as they are introduced.

The author of a book about Marshall and ethical leadership can take no better direction as a compass setting than that set by General Marshall himself in the instruction of young officers: keep your eye on the purpose and not let go, do the best that you are able, and be thorough and accurate with the facts. The purpose of this book is to tell the story about how he came to the leadership roles he so much valued, how he changed them and himself in the course of fulfilling them, how his concepts of leadership and managerial style sustained and guided him, and how all of these lessons might help to guide the lives and careers of the rest of us.

Notes

1.   Marshall, quoted in a letter sent by his aide, Merrill Pasco, to Mr. Enit Kaufman, on March 13, 1944.

2.   Two books which deal with Marshall's leadership are in print (Uldrich 2005; Husted 2007), but do not undertake systematic treatment of the subject.

3.   An editorial in the Nashville Tennessean on March 25, 1950 commented: "His motives are entitled to the highest respect, denoting as they do a modesty that is entirely refreshing. But the fact remains that he could make a valuable contribution to the history of the greatest war. His entire career bespeaks a sincerity that would remove all doubt that his views and factual reports were presented factually and with as little bias as possible (Correspondence, Box 167, File 21, GCMRL).

4.   All references to this source will be cited "Bland 1991."

CHAPTER TWO
GROWTH OF A LEADER

Leaders teach. Abraham Lincoln in his second inaugural address provided an extraordinary example of the leader as teacher. Teaching and leading are distinguishable occupations, but every great leader is clearly teaching—and every great teacher is leading.
            —John W. Gardner, former Secretary of Health,
                    Education, and Welfare, 1965-1968 (Gardner 1986, 19)

Two things stand out for those trying to follow Marshall's development. On the one hand the insatiable desire to learn, to know, to understand, and on the other hand his keen and wide-awake interest in the individual soldier, his indefatigable work for the welfare of the soldier.
                    —Carl Joachim Hambro
        (Presentation speech, 1953 Nobel Peace Prize Award ceremonies)

Family and Boyhood

George Catlett Marshall was the third and last child born to a stern, middle-class businessman and a warm-hearted community-conscious woman in Uniontown, Pennsylvania on the very last day of 1880. His father, the first in the family to be christened George Catlett Marshall and hereinafter referred to as George senior, was born in 1845 and raised in Augusta, Kentucky. Although George senior's family was loyal to the confederacy and he was old enough to serve, he engaged with neither side in the conflict. Young George's mother, born Laura Bradford, was of a family hailing from both Kentucky and Virginia.

Laura's father was a doctor of considerable distinction and public spiritedness who was well known for having developed the saline injection for cholera (Bland 1991, 103). Her uncle was an Episcopalian minister and an abolitionist, a pursuit consistent with a Bradford family loyalty that lay with the union, the Republican party, and Abe Lincoln. There was such enmity between the Marshall and Bradford clans that George senior and Laura "had to wait until one or the other of their fathers had died before they could dare to marry" (Bland 1991, 103-104).

It is perhaps of more than passing interest that John Marshall, the famed chief justice of the early United States Supreme Court who played a large role in developing that institution, was a part of his father's ancestry. The senior Marshall highly esteemed this relationship.[1]

After the birth of Stuart and Marie in Kentucky, George senior took advantage of the post-Civil War boom in coal production to move his family to southwestern Pennsylvania not long before George was born. There, he opened a coke production plant and engaged in a coal mining equipment production operation.

Not much is known about young George's boyhood days in Uniontown and the forces which formed his personality.[2] General Marshall late in life recalled a mostly happy youth. The family settled on the western edge of town on Main Street, the famous National Pike federal road. Uniontown was a small settlement of about three thousand five hundred people located thirty miles south of Pittsburgh. The prospering coal industry entrepreneur was able to rent a two-story brick house with a broad verandah for his family. This solid structure surrounded by fruit trees stood between the road and a creek. The town itself was part of a rural landscape in a beautiful valley bordered by some large hills and low-lying mountains to the east.

To their house came many invited visitors, particularly young businessmen, whom the Marshalls would entertain at dinner (Bland 1991, 54). The natural setting, the family's hospitality, and the peacefulness of the environment also attracted many children to the Marshall home, allowing George abundant opportunity for play and the freedom to roam the area and to interact with most of the "kindly" (as Marshall described them) townspeople (Bland 1991, 20-21, 52).

The Uniontown area was rich in early American history, a fact that encouraged the boy's awareness and development. During the French and Indian War George Washington had commanded British-led American troops just to the east of Uniontown at Fort Necessity. Nearby, Washington had stood and fought with the ill-fated British general, Edward Braddock, in a major battle in which Braddock was fatally wounded. The senior Marshall's accounts of the battle were a source of inspiration for a young boy and opened his eyes to what was to become a lifetime fascination with both local history and national destinies (Bland 1991, 29-31).

George was quiet and shy, an unusually serious boy with an altogether reserved manner. Despite this quality, he possessed the happy facility of regularly making friends with both adults and children. Among the adults were an African-American barber (his name could not be recalled) to whom he could speak freely and to whose shop he went frequently to listen in on adult conversation, and a young Episcopal pastor, the Reverend John R. Wightman. He recalled Reverend Wightman being far more liberal than could be tolerated by his congregation. They took long walks and shared many observations of life. George was much influenced by the young clergyman (Gallagher 1962, 51; Bland 1991, 72). These relationships helped to compensate for the distance that existed between the boy and his father, who was often severe with him and often engendered fear. Nonetheless, young George cherished the times they spent together, particularly their fishing trips and their excursions to Fort Necessity.

George's brother Stuart preceded him by six years. Stuart had little liking for his younger brother and caused him to feel inadequate. His sister Marie, younger than Stuart, thought him a pest and a barbarian, particularly as she reached her teen years. George would intentionally discourage her male callers. He recalled dropping a water bomb on one of them from an upstairs window as the young admirer stood waiting at the front door. On another occasion he was barred from attending his sister's party given for a visiting schoolmate, the governor's daughter. George went to his friend's house across the road and the two literally stirred up a bee's nest for sport. A bee chased George across the street, through the Marshall house, and stung the guest of honor (Bland 1991, 56). As an adult George was to become close to Marie but he never did bridge the divide with his brother.

Easily, the most important person in George's life was his mother. He cherished and confided in her, and it was this relationship that had the largest impact on his development and character. Laura was a quiet and dignified person possessed of a fine sense of humor. She doted on George and took great amusement in his adventures. Always patient and sympathetic, she conspired to keep unpleasant things concerning George from her husband. She managed to convey to George that he was the center of her existence. As a consequence he never felt deprived of love and came to think well of himself, he recalled (Bland 1991, 37-39).

At the neighborhood Episcopalian church George was responsible for pumping the organ. Once he failed to perform the task because he was reading a novel, and was dismissed from his job by the lady organist (Bland 1991, 54-55). Inattention was also paid to his private tutors at home. George was a poor student except in history and geography. He and his inseparable pal Andy Thompson built a tiny canal to parallel the stream behind the Marshall home and filled it with matchstick boats which they called "the great white fleet" and showed off to other boys in the neighborhood (Bland 1991, 20-21).

Later in their youth George and Andy got help from a local store owner in building a real flat-bottomed boat with which they could navigate the stream, and the boys pressed it into ferry service. They printed and sold tickets mostly to young girls who boarded the boat on their way to and from school. One day the girls rebelled; they boarded but refused to surrender their tickets to George, and they laughed along with Andy at his protests. Marshall recalled:

> Just then my eye fastened on a cork in the floor of the boat which was utilized in draining it. With the inspiration of the moment, I pulled the cork. . . . All the girls screamed and I sank the boat in the middle of the stream. They all had to wade ashore. I never forgot that because I had to do something and I had to think quickly. What I did set me up again as the temporary master of the situation (Bland 1991, 22).

There were many other business adventures, including a makeshift restaurant, flower basket design, greenhouse tomatoes, a root beer bar, and fighting game chickens. Most were intended to turn a profit; whether they did was secondary to the fact that they dominated his spare time and imagination (Bland 1991, 22-27). Later, in his teens, he took a job as an assistant on a surveying crew.

The Marshall family's prosperity and reputation suffered a severe downturn in the early 1890s when his father experienced economic reverses resulting from unwise financial speculation in Virginia real estate (Bland 1991, 69-70). The resulting semi-poverty led to striking changes in life style. General Marshall recalled how he had to beg for scrap meat from a local hotel and carry it home; he found the experience "painful and humiliating."

Still, there was a positive side to family decline. His father had more time to engage in politics, from which George was able to learn. The senior Marshall, although a Democrat, had scant sympathy for miners and workers in the the famous Homestead Steel strike. His partner was targeted for murder by a secret society among the miners, the Molly Maguires. He testified in the criminal trial despite himself being threatened with assassination and helped to convict many of those responsible. General Marshall recalled: "The whole Molly Maguire business appealed to me very strongly, and I was quite thrilled by the procedure which led to the conviction of so many of them. . . ." (Bland 1991, 106).

Genteel poverty conferred other benefits. George learned frugality and developed a passion for solvency, instincts clearly influencing his future administrative life. The second benefit was the change in his educational circumstances. Lacking funds to continue his private education (which by all accounts was inferior to begin with), he was forced into a public school. He later came to believe that this accident turned out to be a good preparation for living in a democracy (Bland 1991, 44).

In sum, George Marshall began life rather in the style of Mark Twain's Tom Sawyer: adventurous and free, unspoiled, middle-class with small town values, living among caring and engaged people, fueling his imagination and contemplating a useful and productive life. Throughout his conversations with Pogue, Marshall vividly and with great good humor demonstrated mostly fond memories of his youth (Bland 1991).

The VMI Experience

General Marshall could never recount how he came to think about becoming a soldier. His parents were not opposed to the idea on principle. Stuart had been sent to the Virginia Military Institute (VMI) in Lexington, Virginia and had performed well there. George was not as good a student as Stuart, and some embarrassment played into the reluctance of their father to send his second son to the same school. Though George wanted military education, West Point was out of the question—he lacked the grades and the family lacked the political influence to secure a position there for him. Also, he had a physical disability (a damaged right elbow) that doubtless would have disqualified him even if his father had been a Republican.

When George announced his intention to go to VMI, Stuart opposed the idea. Acting like a beacon in Marshall's memory was a chance event involving Stuart that steeled his resolve and impelled his decision to attend VMI:

But when I was begging to go to VMI, I overheard Stuart talking to my mother. He was trying to persuade her not to let me go, because he thought I would disgrace the family name. Well, that made more impression on me than all instructors, parental pressures, or anything else, and I decided right then that I was going to . . . 'wipe his eye'. . . . [T]he urging came from overhearing this conversation, and it had quite a psychological effect on my career (Bland 1991, 39-40).

Persuaded to act by both his son and his wife, the senior Marshall grudgingly wrote a letter to superintendent General Scott Shipp at VMI and in it exaggerated George's academic abilities. General Shipp replied enthusiastically. With money raised by Mrs. Marshall from the sale of some land she inherited in Tennessee and a lot in Uniontown upon which she had hoped to someday build a house of her own, the money was found to send George to VMI. The fateful decision to attend VMI was thus made through the combination of a boy's determination and a mother's sacrifice.

George took to Lexington and VMI with great zeal. Although he arrived in Lexington weakened by the effects of typhoid fever and was subjected immediately to the taunts of classmates because of his southwestern Pennsylvania "Yankee twang," he embraced the institution's disciplinary philosophy (Superintendent Shipp believed that VMI taught life-discipline rather than prepared boys for military careers) and eagerly sought to conform to the rigid standards of the cadet training program. Such enthusiasm carried him through his second week on campus when he was seriously injured in a hazing incident. He was ordered by senior classmates, in violation of the institution's rules, to squat on school grounds over a fixed bayonet for an extended period of time. Weakened by the typhoid, he fell upon the bayonet and sustained a deep gash in his buttock. Keeping the identity of his tormentors a secret gained him an important measure of respect and ended the harassment.

Like other cadets, he lived a Spartan existence at VMI. Forced to sleep with the windows open, he often awoke with snow on his blanket. Food was of poor quality and the hours of instruction and drill long; little time was left for recreation.[3] He remained calm and serious and attended closely to both the letter and spirit of the rules. He was fortunate to draw supportive and compassionate roommates. One was Leonard ("Nick) Nicholson, heir to the *Times-Picayune* newspaper owners in New Orleans.

He found the scholastic side at VMI to be not so positive. He was to conclude later that academic education there had to be compensated for later in his career. He remained a mediocre student, although his grades improved in his engineering classes. He graduated fifteenth advanced to fifth (fifth among engineering graduates) but graduated without any sort of academic distinction or honors and was not invited to speak at the graduation ceremonies. An unofficial bonus allowed him to read voraciously his last year and a half: Nick received barrels of books from the *Times-Picayune* and shared them with his roommates (Bland 1991, 95).

Cadet Marshall did excel in one area. He welcomed "being disciplined, and . . . learning discipline," and was given increasingly greater responsibility as he ascended in rank. In each year beyond the first he was honored as VMI's top cadet in the training program: he became "first corporal" in his sophomore year; "first sergeant" in his junior year; and "first captain" and headed the whole cadet corps as a senior. He believed that his steady progression up the cadet line of authority was facilitated by his being exacting in all military duties through a combination of great effort and an appreciation of tradition (Bland 1991, 97, 99, 119):[4]

> What I learned most at the V.M.I. was self-control, discipline, so it was ground in, and the problem of managing men which fell to the cadet noncommissioned officer and cadet officer. He was very severely judged by his classmates if he was slack (Bland 1991, 98).

In a revealing anecdote Marshall told about how he handled a mutinous incident in the mess hall when he was responsible for the behavior of the whole cadet corps. The students in normal course were expected to engage in conversation over dinner, but drawing upon an incident at West Point, they conspired to be silent for the purpose of testing their cadet chief. When Marshall sensed what was happening he abruptly interrupted the rare strawberry dessert they were enjoying and ordered the cadets out of the mess hall to form ranks outside, effectively denying them the treat (Bland 1991, 97-98). He had acted instinctively. After the fact, he had been in awe of the responsibility the leadership role carried with it to exercise authority in such a way as not to cause resentment (Bland 1991, 118).

On campus one day he was stopped in his tracks by the piano music coming from a house at the edge of the campus. The musician turned out to be a young woman who was regarded by the cadets as a local beauty. Attracted by her charm and the fact that her musical ability reminded him of his mother, George was immediately infatuated (Bland 1991, 82). Her name was Elizabeth Carter "Lily" Coles, the daughter of an old Virginia family. After repeated visits to her home, which lay just yards off-limits to cadets, her folks came to tolerate his presence although they sniffed at his Yankee accent and "common" background (they incorrectly assumed that Lexington was older and its social standing more prestigious than Uniontown's). Lily, who was more than five years older than her suitor, was an independent sort and did not allow her family's treatment of him to affect their relationship in the least. The courtship proceeded quickly, she accepted his proposal, and they set the marriage date after graduation and after he could obtain a military commission or secure other employment.

In 1901 most VMI graduates did not choose to enter military service. Marshall had his sights fixed on a military officer's career since the day when, during his second summer home from VMI in 1899, he stood transfixed watching a Spanish-American war veterans parade in Uniontown. Although his goal was clear, it was not yet clear to him just how he would go about achieving it (Bland 1991, 115). He was aided in his quest by Superintendent Shipp and by his partially financially rehabilitated father, who used his political connections to gain letters from prominent politicians commending George to attorney general Philander C. Knox.

The greatest assistance came from his own straightforward courage. He made an impulsive visit to the White House two months before his graduation to see President McKinley to seek permission to take an examination for a commission in the army officers corps. Presenting himself at the White House without an appointment, he was told firmly by an attendant responsible for screening and admitting visitors that there was no chance to spend even one moment with the president. Persevering, he waited in the visitor room and when the opportunity presented itself, attached himself to a large party that was being shown into the president's office, enduring the withering look of the attendant. He remained after the others left the room and when the president asked him his business Marshall stated his case. It is more than likely, according to McKinley, that from that meeting flowed the authority to take the commissioning examination (Bland 1991, 85-86).

Whether by dint of his brash initiative or his father's influence or a combination of the two, or subsequent letters from both Pennsylvania senators, Marshall was allowed to take the examination and passed it easily. The critical variable now became the number of commissions available. Fortunately for Marshall, the insurrection in the Philippine Islands begun in 1899 in the aftermath of the Spanish-American war had led Congress to enlarge the Army by twelve hundred new officer positions, with one-fifth of these to be filled by examination. Marshall requested artillery duty. He was offered a commission in the infantry service, accepted, and formally signed on February 3, 1902 (although it was backdated to February 2, 1901). He thereupon entered the United States Army as a second lieutenant.

The marriage of George and Lily followed the signing by a scant eight days. The ceremony was held at Lily's family home on the edge of the VMI campus and at its conclusion the couple walked out on the parade ground at VMI, an appropriate first step in an active military career that was to last nearly forty-four years. He left for his first active duty assignment with the 30th Infantry in the Philippine Islands ten days later.

Duty in the Philippines

It is a fitting irony that at the moment he arrived in Manilla the commander of US forces in the islands was General Arthur MacArthur, the father of future Army chief of staff and five-star general Douglas MacArthur. William Howard Taft, who became president in 1909, was poised to become the first American civilian governor of the islands a few months later. Despite Spain's capitulation to the United States, the doomed rebellion was continuing; it was a struggle destined to take about forty-two hundred American lives by 1902.

Lieutenant Marshall hopped an inter-island freighter to make his way to his duty station on the island of Mindoro. *En route*, the small boat was caught in a typhoon and came close to capsizing. When the captain of the ship deserted his post, Marshall and another American junior officer used their weapons to force the frightened crew to stay at their posts in the engine room while the ship continued on its perilous voyage (Pogue 1963, 71-72).

On Mindoro the new officer was confronted with yet two more challenges: a cholera epidemic and boredom among the enlisted men. Marshall and military doctor Fletcher Gardner, his roommate, set about enforcing the regulations ensuring meticulous cleanliness in the camp. He also helped Dr. Gardner treat the ill at the native village two miles away from the army camp. Treatment of cholera at the time was primitive, and nearly all of the natives who became ill died. Because of the hygiene enforced on post by Gardner and Marshall, no American became ill. Marshall's training at VMI in precisely following procedure now served him and his charges well. He later recalled:

> The men were confined to their barracks and not allowed out at all. Everything had to be boiled. The fingernails had to be cleaned, the hands had to be washed in hot water. Their mess kits had to be washed in two or three runs of hot water. You had to enforce these things very carefully or they would skimp them. A very little skimping would cost you your life (Bland 1991, 126).

A gala party with entertainment and sporting contests was scheduled to celebrate the end of the epidemic. As the junior officer Marshall was assigned to handle arrangements. The enlisted men, described by Marshall as "about the wildest crowd I've ever seen before or since" disliked the post commander and sulked, not buying into the whole idea (Pogue 1963, 74). Activity was to begin with the hundred-yard dash and only two men entered. Marshall divided the whole prize money for the event among the two instead of giving them two of the four shares that had been allocated. Now others were induced to enter into the other events. For the evening Marshall had a talented soldier released from the guardhouse to supply musical entertainment. The party was a great success and was an early indication of Marshall's willingness to change the rules in order to get a better result.

Later in the tour Marshall found himself filling in for an absent company commander at Mangarin and became the *de facto* governor in the absence of civil authority. The assignment lasted two months. The pattern of being the man in charge in the absence of another was to recur frequently throughout his career and afford him copious command experience without benefit of authority or rank. He delegated many duties to two seasoned non-commissioned officers, improvised his own forms, established a close friendship with the local native leader, and conducted search patrols for *ladrones* (armed insurrectionists). In these ways he gained responsibility and was to cultivate a talent crucial to an unseasoned officer—the ability to think quickly under pressure and to learn how to trust able, experienced subordinates (Pogue 1963, 76-77).

It was at Mangarin that he marched his patrol through a river his men believed, from local rumor, to be crocodile-infested. They broke ranks when they heard a splash and in their panic trampled Marshall into the mud in an effort to reach the stream bank. Gathering his dignity, he arose from the muck, climbed up on the bank, commanded his men to regroup, and then with a simple command marched them across the stream and then back again without once uttering an angry word or raising his voice. He had instinctively regained his dignity and maintained control (Pogue 1963, 77-78).

In late 1902 Marshall moved to pleasant garrison life in Manilla and there learned to handle and ride horses. Thus began a lifetime love affair with horseback riding. When a horse fell on him he volunteered to help the headquarters inspector examine property accounts of officers as part of a clearance process preparatory to sending them home. The duty allowed him to gain proficiency in financial regulations and military accounting. He was next assigned to guard military prisoners and lead a prison unit when its commander left. He worked under terrible conditions and found the assignment depressing, but persevered.

Marshall learned a great deal in this first duty tour. Of particular long-term interest to him were his reflections about the large struggle he was witnessing and the Army's strategies and techniques for occupying a land of alien, though mostly peaceful, people. He found an uncomfortable tension between the dual roles of using military control to facilitate native government and working to reestablish civil government under native administrators. Sometimes the very people that were capable of self-government were treated as savages by army regulars, and the sight of army brutality sickened him. He deplored a senseless incident in which a combination cathedral-library was burned down and troops mocked the priests. But he also sympathized with the Army's need to uproot and control insurgents. He felt native civil officials went too far too fast and understood the frustration of American soldiers who suffered as a result. He appreciated the reasons for the tough army attitude, and understood but did not condone the excesses of reprisals and the harsh methods of making insurrectionists talk.

In short, he concluded that taking a one-sided American or Filipino approach to the conflict was wrong, and he learned the importance of the principle of reestablishing civil control quickly (Pogue 1963, 81-82). What was needed, he concluded, was some form of working synthesis based on trust.

This learning took clearer form a decade later when, returning to the Philippines, he read on his own initiative official reports and a comprehensive history of the Philippine experience he had lived through. He sought out the causes of the Spanish-American war and the factors leading to the insurrection. Questions of occupation and civil governance would resonate in his thoughts the rest of his career, challenging him to formulate notions about how occupation administration and treatment of conquered peoples should be managed. It is doubtful that Second Lieutenant Marshall had these larger issues on his mind during this first tour of duty, yet awareness was dawning and a new maturity was settling upon him. New and complicated thoughts began to gestate in the mind of the young officer; he began to think about his career in terms other than imposed discipline, compliance with regulations, and legalized coercion.

His many experiences and adventures in the Philippines were formative. Rather than confronting combat or the rigors of battle, he wrestled with the everyday problems of morale, standards of living, interaction with a native population, and improvising to meet unforseen circumstances, especially the sudden descent of command responsibility. These unforseen events and urgencies, together with his already formed self-discipline, allowed Marshall to grow and learn at an accelerated pace.

Fort Reno

The tiny, quiet frontier post of Fort Reno in the Oklahoma Territory was his next duty station, a quiet diversion where he would serve from 1904 to 1906. This remote duty put him under the command of a spit and polish regimen and formal rules, again with no hint of combat.

The most significant experience during this period was a special assignment to Rio Grande desert country in south Texas. He was assigned the task of commanding a small group of men and pack mules in the mapping of two thousand square miles of wilderness. The task became a survival test. Moving over wild, roadless terrain in heat sometimes reaching one hundred and thirty degrees, he and his charges suffered extraordinary hardship, much of it due to the gross negligence of the supply authority that failed to deliver agreed-upon provisions to agreed-upon pick-up sites at specific times. The incompetence threatened the very lives of the men as they often went without food or water. When Marshall finally reported back to an unconcerned Captain Malin Craig (a future Army chief of staff) at Fort Clark, he was virtually ignored. He did receive a warm welcome from Captain George Van Horn Moseley,[5] who deemed his map the best and only complete one produced by the several mapping teams employed.

Returning to Fort Reno, Marshall served as ranking officer at the post. Noting the pitiful condition of family housing quarters, he suggested to the wife of a soldier that if she cleaned up her cluttered, unsightly yard, he would return and have the house painted in whatever colors she chose. She agreed and he made good on his promise. Other women followed suit, resulting in a much-improved appearance and morale on the post (Pogue 1963, 91-92).

Learning to Learn and to Teach

Marshall's first big career break came with his acceptance to the Infantry and Cavalry School at Fort Leavenworth, Kansas in the summer of 1906. The school was in effect the first postgraduate professional training program in the Army, progressive and designed for officers expected to achieve high command levels. It had been installed under the reforms of Secretary of War Elihu Root earlier in the decade. Acceptance barely preceded an order limiting program enrollment to officers of captain rank or above, a status as yet unrealized by the second lieutenant. He resolved at once that he would rank first among his talented schoolmates.

His exemplary performance (he did indeed finish first among his peers) earned him a place the following year in the Army Staff College at Fort Leavenworth, the goal of every aspiring young army officer (Pogue 1963, 93-96). It also brought him to the attention of the school commander, General J. Franklin Bell, who was slated to become Army chief of staff later that year. In this year Marshall took and passed a promotional examination and received his first increase in rank, to that of First Lieutenant (Pogue 1963, 97).

Through pure resolve and punishing hard work Marshall had made himself into a first-rate student for the first time in his life. The course of study at the Army Staff College consisted mainly of committing facts and formulae to memory. Its time demands forced Marshall to a new level of efficiency and focus (Pogue 1963, 97-98). His greatest satisfaction in this difficult year was his exposure to a gifted teacher of tactics, Major John F. Morrison, who used a teaching method that downplayed technique in favor of principles demonstrated through action.

> Simplicity and dispersion became fixed quantities in my mind, never to be forgotten.... He (Morrison) spoke a tactical language I had never heard from any other officer. He was self-educated, reading constantly and creating and solving problems for himself. He taught me all I have ever known of tactics (Pogue 1963, 99).

Solving operational problems as he had in the Philippines now became the very essence of Marshall's thought process. The stimulus of learning in the heady atmosphere of Fort Leavenworth meant everything to the young officer:

> I learned how to learn. . . . I began to develop along more stable lines. Leavenworth was immensely instructive, not so much because the course was perfect—because it was not—but the association with the officers, the reading we did and the discussion and the leadership . . . of a man like Morrison had a tremendous effect, certainly on me (Pogue 1963, 101).

The intense competition among the Army's best was much to his liking. He strove not just for excellence but to be the best among the best. When complaints about the severity and rigor of the program eventually caused a cutback in the requirements in Fort Leavenworth's program, he thought it a great mistake.

> If you were going to compete, you had to be near perfection in the particular subjects, and that's what made it so hard. However, it was invaluable to me as a matter of training because I learnt a thoroughness which stood me in good stead through . . . the war (Bland 1991, 153, 160).

After completing his year as a student in the Army Staff College Marshall was appointed by special permission of General Bell as an instructor at Fort Leavenworth. Here he was called on to instruct officers who outranked him. By adopting many of Morrison's techniques he was able to instruct, evaluate, impress, and get to know many of the officers who were to lead the Army in the following years (Bland 1991, 153, 157-58).[6]

Experimenting with Troop Movements

Bell, now Army chief of staff and the highest ranking officer in the Army, secured a summer assignment for Marshall in the instruction of Pennsylvania national guardsmen while maintaining his permanent duty station at Leavenworth. This was to be the first in a long series of similar formative experiences for Marshall throughout his career, covering multiple National Guard, Reserve, and Regular Army units.

The training took the form of organizing and participating in large-scale troop maneuvers. The many units rapidly brought together, many of them poorly trained, had to be quickly organized and given goals to pursue and problems to solve. The success of their efforts had to be critiqued generally within the space of a single week. In effect they were experimental laboratories in which Marshall learned and taught tactical warfare and especially the art and science of logistics. Surprising as it may seem as judged by early twenty-first century standards, he was permitted to run a major military exercise from the lowly position of a lieutenant staff officer:

> The National Guard camps were immensely valuable to me. They were an experimental value, too, because I was able to do things there with a regiment where I wouldn't be able to get a command of a company on a post (Bland 1991, 160-61).

He could do things "pretty much any way I wanted, and I wasn't being criticized. I was being accepted with enthusiasm and that was a great stimulant" (Bland 1991, 163). In such an environment, much could be learned, confidence could be gained, and leadership nurtured.

Experimentation as a value became a dominant motif in Marshall's military organizational philosophy. As a formulator of maneuvers he had the luxury of changing format or tactical problems at will, and to see how these changes might affect both operations and outcomes. In this he valued *learning as much from failure as from success*—the very essence of experimentation. He was storing lessons for campaigns yet to come and developing the facility for planning and reacting to the unforseen exigencies of war which could frustrate plans almost as fast as they were made.

Marshall was gloriously happy in his four years at Leavenworth with summers in the field with state National Guard units. He and Lily blossomed socially. He bought a horse and trained it, acquired hunting dogs, and enjoyed a reputation and gained confidence as a fine teacher and organizer of large-scale military maneuvers (Pogue 1963, 104-105). Not the least of his gains were the many officers he befriended or became acquainted with at the school who were destined to play important roles in both world wars: John McAuley Palmer, Billy Mitchell, Walter Krueger, and Douglas MacArthur, to name just a few.

1910 to 1913

Following his tour at Leavenworth Marshall used his accumulated leave to take Lily to Europe for the extended honeymoon they had never had. He returned to a series of short tours in the states in Watertown, New York; San Antonio; Boston; Little Rock; and Galveston, Texas, serving mostly under officers he had known at Leavenworth. The new Army chief of staff, General Leonard Wood, was then engaged in reorganizing and consolidating the service's widely scattered troops of battalion size or less by bringing them together in joint maneuvers in regiment or division strength. Because of his experience with National Guard exercises, Marshall was singled out to participate in these efforts. He now worked with large-scale Regular Army troop maneuvers as well as continuing to lead National Guard maneuvers (Pogue 1963, 110-119).

In these assignments he was exposed to innovations in warfare technology, particularly in communications. At San Antonio he organized a communications center and was present at the first experiments employing the radio in large-scale maneuvers. He read the very first radio message that was received at a military headquarters: "I am just west of the manure pile." It was also at San Antonio that the first military observation airplanes were used (Pogue 1963, 113). With these changes came a new reality in battle command—the separation of the commander from the line.

Return to the Philippines

In May, 1913 Lieutenant Marshall was assigned to the 13th Infantry Regiment at Fort McKinley in Manilla, again as a staff officer. He was attached to a small unit under the command of a captain who had been a student and friend of his at Leavenworth, a circumstance that could not have pleased him. His slow rise in rank, due largely to being caught up in the jumble of new officers entering service after the Spanish-American War, had been further impaired by serving in staff positions. Moving up in rank in the U.S. Army during this period required holding command positions. Despite having been evaluated as highly capable of leading men, he had been denied these.

Despite his stalled career advance, he became deeply involved in yet another activity that promoted his development as a field tactician and coordinator of the efforts of multiple organizations. With Japan vaguely seen to be threatening American interests in the Pacific, General Bell, now commanding the Philippine Department, designed a massive war game involving troops throughout the islands. Because Bell viewed Marshall's commanding officer as ineffective, he named Marshall acting chief of staff of the white force and gave him *de facto* command of almost five thousand troops in the maneuvers.

Marshall faced great obstacles in organizing the maneuvers. The worst among these were getting supplies and finding ways of moving troops while competing against men who outranked him. To get what he needed, he spoke bluntly to the quartermaster and had to rely on General Bell's support. The exercise was in fact less complex than many of the war games Marshall had already designed and carried out in training state guard units.

His performance in the war games gave rise to a reputation that was to stick to him for life. Rumor had it that General Bell said to his staff about Marshall, "This, gentlemen, is the greatest military genius since Stonewall Jackson." Whether he said it or not, the rumor was enough: Marshall's reputation as the "wizard of tactics" was born (Pogue 1963, 121-124).

Verified, on the other hand, is Lieutenant Henry H. ("Hap") Arnold's description, in a letter to his wife, of a man he told her was destined to become a future Army chief of staff. In his letter Arnold drew an image of Lieutenant Marshall lying in a bamboo clump studying a map and dictating precise field orders for a successful advance (Arnold 1949, 44).

Still, the games had a serious downside. Marshall drove himself so hard that the strain brought on a mental breakdown, the second of his life (the first had occurred in 1913). It was a blessing in disguise. Granted two months sick leave by General Bell, and extending that with two months of regular leave, George and Lily spent time in Japan, and George toured Manchuria and Korea by himself. Rather than simply relaxing and playing the tourist, Lieutenant Marshall befriended officials and military leaders and engaged them in candid discussions on military tactics. From what he was told and what he observed by being privileged to watch Japanese troop exercises, and putting these together with his study of the Russo-Japanese war, he schooled himself on Japanese field tactics. He admired their skillful use of the bayonet in close-order combat, noted their extensive training with hand grenades, and learned of their proficiency in night attacks.

Horseback riding and daily hikes had returned him to good health. Fit and re-energized, he reported his findings on Japanese military tactics to the adjutant general on his return and lectured on the subject to officers at Fort McKinley (Pogue 1963, 124-125). Marshall had learned the importance of pacing himself and now was resolved to ride, play tennis, relax each day before and after work, and arrive home early. This now became his behavioral regimen from this time forward. He would push the same model for those under his command—take vacations, lead balanced lives, and recreate. With more leisure time at Fort McKinley he would join the children as they played baseball at post housing in the lazy tropical afternoons, go on long automobile rides with Lily in the countryside, and take an engine apart just to learn how it was done (Pogue 1963, 125-127).

The rest of his time in the islands was spent touring, studying the history of recent warfare in the Philippines, and contemplating what he had learned in his travels in Japan and Korea. He concluded from the island terrain that if the Japanese were to attack the Philippines they would be successful. Not long before leaving the islands he was reassigned as an aide to Brigadier General Hunter Liggett. Liggett had known him at Leavenworth and from training maneuvers in Connecticut, and he was convinced that in the event of war he wanted Marshall under his command.

Marshall was at a crossroads. He had become dissatisfied with the Army because of low rank and the minor scope of duties that low rank entitled him to perform. He desired desperately to do something of value for country or society and was no longer sure this could be achieved in a military career. In late 1915, still a first lieutenant and nearing thirty-five years of age, he wrote to his friend, General W. E. Nichols, superintendent at VMI, that he would leave the Army "as soon as business conditions improve." He told Nichols, "I do not feel it right to waste all my best years in the vain struggle against insurmountable difficulties" (Pogue 1963, 129-130). Nichols, to his eternal credit, advised Marshall against such a move. He envisioned an expansion of the military because of the growth of the world's trouble spots and helped to clarify for Marshall the opportunities for promotion and challenge in such an environment.

Preparing Others for Battle

The staff assignments continued. On his return from the Philippines in the summer of 1916 Marshall was assigned as *aide-de-camp* to General Bell, who now commanded a National Guard that had been federalized after the break in diplomatic relations with Germany. Again, Marshall had reason to be dissatisfied with a career-adverse staff position. Added to his burden was that although respecting the fighting abilities of General Bell, Marshall rated him a poor administrator. He had found him to be ineffective as US Army chief of staff because: "[h]e tried to handle things too much by personal association and by letters" (Bland 1991, 183).

Marshall served Bell at training camps at the Presidio in San Francisco and in Monterrey, California. The junior officer was given the responsibility for finding and curing the ills in the National Guard training program at Monterrey. Commanded by General William L. Sibert, the Monterrey camp was staffed mostly by retired officers recalled to duty to fill in for Army regulars ordered to service on the troubled Mexican border. The camp's troops were drawn from San Francisco's elite class. Bell had cautioned Sibert not to be too severe with these men, a point of view Marshall did not share:

> I thought a large number of things were wrong, but I say a good bit of that grew out of first, the fact they were all retired officers; next that the drill regulations had changed before a good many of them came (back) in; and next that the instructors had been cautioned to be very easy on them and they were dealing with a very lively, sporty lot. I don't mean sporty in the way of dissipated, but I mean sporty in the way of polo and football and this and that, and Rolls Royce cars and all that. All their wives or their sweeties and all had come down there with them, so that was quite a set-up (Bland 1991, 179).

Marshall made it a priority to get to know the men. His opportunity came as he unpacked his bedroll in his tent, in plain sight of the officers en route to the hotel dining room:

> When I got the roll opened, the first thing on top, of course, was my saddle. But the next thing, under the saddle, were two of Mrs. Marshall's nightgowns that had been packed at the last minute, and then a whole string of stuff of hers which

didn't look like anything like a bedding roll arrangement for the field. That amused them greatly. . . . So they came back from the hotel to escort me over to have dinner, and with speeches and all as to my field equipment, I came to know them all very quickly that same night (Bland 1991, 179).

On his first day of inspection he discovered many violations and decided to take these matters up with General Sibert and his adjutant directly, rather than report them to General Bell as he had been instructed. He forthrightly told General Sibert his orders from Bell but told Sibert he preferred to do things this way because he was "in a very embarrassing position." The general immediately issued orders to change most of the defects but the adjutant, a colonel, was furious with Marshall, a mere lieutenant. Lieutenant Marshall went through the same procedure the next day, finding fewer problems, and General Sibert again dictated changes to the adjutant. This time, Marshall complimented both the general and the adjutant on their progress and stated he would not submit criticisms to General Bell, and Sibert accepted the suggestion (Bland 1991, 179-180).

The adjutant, perhaps maliciously, sent the list of uncorrected items forward and in addition requested Bell's headquarters to have Marshall detailed to the camp. He then put Marshall in command of a different company each day, a strenuous assignment because Marshall would not be able to gain control of a company before he had to move on to the next. Marshall did not protest. On the first afternoon, with the men sleepy after an enjoyable lunch under the trees with their ladies, Marshall ordered a tough close-order drill and then bawled them out for their ineffectiveness, and had them do it again.

So we had a very strenuous drill and they were very much humiliated by this talk I gave them. Then they turned around and gave me a big dinner that night at the hotel. I remember at the time I was called "Dynamite" Marshall, but it was really quite a funny thing, and all of them became my friends and I continued these friendships through a good many years after that (Bland 1991, 181).

This story is told in detail because it throws light on a management style that Marshall had been developing. It combined unflinching maintenance of focus on the goal (in this case, training the troops), flexibility in dealing with rules (he downplayed the outmoded ones), a lack of personal malice or desire to retaliate (he avoided embarrassing the camp commander in the eyes of his superior), and compassion for the organization's rank and file (the reservist officer trainees). It is no accident that when Marshall went to war in France in 1917, General Sibert asked that Marshall be assigned to serve on his staff (Bland 1991, 188).

Reassigned with Bell from San Francisco to Governors Island, New York, Captain[7] Marshall arrived in May, 1917 with the extremely important task of setting up the first of twenty officer training camps spread around the country with an eye to service in the world war (labeled the "Plattsburgh Plan"). Each camp was to have 2,500 men. General Bell, caused to be absent by the flu, assigned Marshall the task of running a number of the camps in his name and with his delegated authority. Marshall thus commanded about fifteen senior colonels, none too happy to be responding to a junior officer's direction. Pressures came from the outside in the form of a flood of mail, telegrams, and personal calls from persons of influence in New York City seeking admission to the camp for favored sons.[8] Marshall survived this period by "following a fixed policy of noninterference with the regularly prescribed method of selection" (Marshall 1976, 2). He treated them all alike (Bland 1991, 182).

Serious conflict developed over supplies and ordnance. Older staff officers in the quartermaster's offices were certain that supplies were sufficient and rebuffed Marshall's attempts to get more. However, he accepted the complaints coming from the men in the camps as true. He asked an aide of Bell's to visit the camps with the supply lists and check them against what was actually found on the sites. Serious shortages were found—blankets, mattresses, pillows, and so forth. Armed with the new list, he returned to the quartermaster and secured rapid delivery of new supplies over their objections about the special delivery expense.

The difficulty in finding provisions for the forty thousand men due to arrive at the camps was, to him, "an impressive demonstration of our complete state of unpreparedness" (Marshall 1976, 2-3). The example was to be multiplied many times over in the months to come as America went to war.

War Comes: The Complete Staff Officer

Marshall's view of WW I probably covered a larger spectrum than that of virtually any other American officer. He arrived with the first American troops and stayed until well beyond the end of fighting. He occupied roles at all levels of command and interacted with all major French and some British commands.

Embarking with the initial American combat units in June, 1917, he stood with the commander of the Port of Embarkation in New York City watching an endless column of infantry moving across the docks and into troop carriers refitted from fruit boats. Marshall remarked on how the men seemed very solemn. "Of course they are," replied the embarkation chief. "We are watching the harvest of death" (Marshall 1976, 5-6).

General Sibert had selected him as his assistant chief of staff for operations in the First Infantry Division, the first American combat unit to arrive on French soil. Marshall was thus positioned to watch the whole American army operation (called the American Expeditionary Forces or AEF) in its earliest fumbling unpreparedness and through the struggles it endured to develop into an effective fighting force. It came essentially untrained and had to take its training on French soil. It was dependent on the French for much of its equipment. He would later ascend from the division to the (First) Army Corps level and then to headquarters level toward the end of the war. To be effective in each of these roles he had to work closely and continually with French and British counterparts. He drafted or helped draft the orders of battle for both the first American raid and for the first general offensive as well as for the last great battle and then for the cessation of hostilities.

Problems of Staff Work in Wartime

Pre-war service in the role of a non-command officer concerned with staff functions (supply, intelligence, operations, and personnel) and as a planner for simulated battles now made Marshall invaluable. He could see clearly the difficulties involved in executing these functions in a war zone. Staff officers needed to adjust in three ways to altered conditions. First, he noted the long delays experienced in preparing, distributing, and following complicated orders. Staff officers, he cautioned, must recognize that speed is more important than technique and that orders must be flexible enough to permit them to be simplified and improvised as demanded by rapidly changing battlefield conditions (Bland and Hadsel 1981, 205). A second problem was the maddening frequency with which orders are of necessity changed in the field. He cautioned that the good staff officer must understand that in large operations frequent changes are the norm. A third difficulty, one that demoralized and irritated many staff officers, was the obligation to vigorously implement a plan with which the staff officer does not fully agree. The officer must embrace orders and instructions loyally and enthusiastically even if he finds them to be wrong-headed (Bland and Hadsel 1981, 215-216).[9]

He watched as the AEF grew from a single division into a force numbering in the millions. In his *Memoirs of My Services in the World War* (1976), he reflected on the differences in moving from a staff position in a single army division to a staff position in AEF headquarters:

> In the First Division we had struggled with the concrete proposition of feeding, clothing, training, marching, and fighting the men. Their health and morale was a daily issue; their dead and wounded a daily tragedy. . . . Huge projects for the future made no appeal to us. . . . Each man was living in his own little world, ignorant to a surprising degree of all that occurred elsewhere (Marshall 1976, 121).

The view from the top as a member of Pershing's headquarters team contrasted sharply. The concern was with shipping, ports of debarkation, dock construction, capacity for unloading cargo, methods for the training of new divisions, production and securing of weaponry, and relating to British and French command needs. This was the stuff of the staff's waking day. He observed that individual officers in the line, particularly older officers of the Regular Army, were often viewed contemptuously by these headquarters staff people because they were "slowing down the machinery." Field officers were seen as "victims of lifelong routine, whose view was decidedly local and frequently personal," and thus obstacles to planning because they encouraged adjustments detracting from overall effectiveness (Marshall 1976, 142-143).

Marshall was of two opinions concerning these contrasting mind sets. On one hand, he sympathized with the macro-perspective of the headquarters staff man:

Our office was continuously flooded with a stream of officers, mostly from the divisions gathering for the conflict. They usually urged some minor change in their orders which they considered entirely reasonable, without thought of how each alteration complicated the interlocking of the parts in the huge machine. The freedom of action . . . enjoyed by the small, scattered units of our old Regular army had been conducive to a state of mind in its officers which made them slow to realize the rigidity of arrangements imposed by the massing of immense numbers of troops (Marshall 1976, 133).

At the same time he was acutely aware of the view from the bottom and his sympathies tended to lay with the foot-soldier:

[A conversation at the top] might result in some seemingly insignificant amendment to the general plan, but it usually resulted in a wide disturbance in the lower echelons. An inch at the top became a mile at the bottom; and a division which had just marched up a hill might find itself reversed and ordered back to its starting point. These changes are unavoidable in making combinations among large armies, though they arouse the ire of the humble soldier, particularly the American with his characteristics of independent thought and action (Marshall 1976, 133-134).

A sympathetic understanding between staff officers and troops must be sought because harmony and unity are critical. The staff officer loses contact with the organization below when he sits in headquarters. He becomes impersonal because he is not tested by daily needs and results as he would be if he were in the thick of a campaign. No matter how difficult, the "most important function of the general staff is to promote a spirit of harmony, cooperation, and understanding throughout the Army. If it doesn't accomplish this, nine-tenths of its value is lost" (Bland and Hadsel 1981, 217).

From observing commanding generals and top staff officers operating under the most trying of circumstances, he formed strong opinions about the requirements of effective leadership. Some around Pershing attempted to imitate the stern and severe style of the man but did not share the latter's talent or basic compassion for those under his command:

Their requirements for the troops were unduly difficult, I thought. No complaint was tolerated. Well, I think this did a great deal of harm, allowing a man with that state of mind, that personality, to be in a commanding position, a control position. . . . What the High Command had to do, and which unfrequently [sic] they were very loathe to do, was to see if his generals did their job (Bland 1991, 240-241).

It was Marshall's gift to be able to appreciate both the "big picture" and the needs of the little guy in the field, and to harmonize and incorporate these in his decision calculus. Finding the balance was difficult but to tilt totally in favor of the high command view endangered morale and undermined confidence of the rank and file in their leadership; to focus solely on the needs of dispersed field commanders, was to endanger the success of the overall mission. To be sensitive to both and to make the effort to deal with both was essential. His effort and ability to do both underlay much of his developing organizational philosophy.

Working With the French

Marshall was shaken by the state of unpreparedness and lack of training among American troops at the war's beginning. The officers, the choice of the litter from each of the twenty officer training camps in the U.S., were meeting each other for the first time aboard the troop ships bound for France. No one in command had any idea of the nature of the campaign they were entering or of the organization and weaponry that was their life-or-death business to learn. The French population that watched them on their arrival found them very willing and affable but inept and unsoldierly. Intensive training in the most elementary aspects of soldiering was needed. This task consumed the whole of the next six months (Marshall 1976, 13-19).

As it developed, the major disagreement between French and American commanders was over what use was to be made of American forces. The French, assuming the Americans to be highly trained regulars (despite their disarray upon arrival), demanded that Americans be inserted in small units into French units under French command. The Americans insisted that their own troops be kept together, rigorously trained, and then committed as entire units under American command to fight on their own. Given the greenness of the troops, submitting to the French plan would have been disastrous (Marshall 1976, 19). Marshall observed that the American soldier was more adaptable than the French soldier and that French training methods were too rigid. To some extent the Americans adopted some of the rigidity to placate the French, further hindering the task of reaching combat readiness.

St.-Mihiel to the Meuse-Argonne

The greatest personal trial (and greatest achievement) of Marshall during the war was the successful planning and execution of the redeployment of a huge American force from the St.-Mihiel front to the Meuse-Argonne front in the midst of an offensive action. Marshall wrote not long after these events:

> I could not recall an incident in history where the fighting of one battle [the battle of Saint Mihiel] had been preceded by the plans for a later battle [Meuse-Argonne] to be fought by the same army on a different front, and involving the issuing of orders for the movement of troops already destined to participate in the first battle, directing their transfer to the new field of action (Marshall 1976, 137-138).

It fell to Marshall, assisted by Colonel Walter S. Grant, to make all of this happen. The task was hugely complex and beset by appalling obstacles: bombed-out roads; lack of enough vehicles and horses to move men, supplies and artillery;

coordinating all movements with French operations and needs in the same area; and the inexperience of the fresh troops. During the period between September 16 and September 25 his assignment was to plan and oversee the execution of the transfer of about six hundred thousand men and two thousand seven hundred artillery pieces over three roads. All depended upon his succeeding. He wrote that this was a daunting challenge and "the most trying mental ordeal" he had ever faced, and that the plan he produced and the implementing actions he took "represented my best contribution to the war" (Bland and Hadsel 1981, 160-161).

The redeployment came off without a noticeable hitch. Marshall's planning has been described as "a logistical feat of unprecedented proportions" (Stoler 1989, 40) and "the most magnificent staff operation of the war" (Frye 1947, 160). The operation cemented Marshall's reputation as a genius of logistics without peer. In the battle of Meuse-Argonne, the French, with massive infusions of American troops, went on to roll back the German lines and win the decisive battle of the war.

Even if Marshall never achieved anything else of value in his entire career, his reputation as a military legend had been secured. Still, much was expected of him in the future, for which more training and varied experience would be required.

Pershing's Right Hand

A few months after the armistice was signed, Marshall was chosen by Pershing to serve as one of his *aide-de-camps* (Curtin 1958, 1), ushering in a new career phase. His education was to be of another sort and the range of his associations greatly widened. He came to serve as Pershing's *alter ego*, his right-hand man.

As Pershing's aide, Marshall traveled with the general throughout Europe, interacting with royalty and state leaders and sharing in the outpouring of tribute heaped upon the AEF and its commander. The speeches, lavish parties, parades, dinners and dances in the capital cities of Europe had to have their effect on the handsome, personable and yet highly correct young man who was now rebounding from the fatigue and trauma of the battlefield.

A close working relationship was forged between the two men which continued for five full years and influenced the rest of their lives. After Pershing's tumultuous return to the states in 1919 to a tickertape parade in New York City on horseback, Pershing was dispatched with Marshall in tow to military encampments around the U.S. to take stock of military needs and preparedness and report back to Congress. In 1921 Pershing was appointed Army chief of staff and he took Marshall with him to the War Department to serve as his chief assistant and advisor.

The time spent together in these roles was a virtual post-graduate education in military policy and politics at the highest levels. Together, they fought the battle in Congress for an effective peacetime army. The fight shaped up as a contest between General Peyton C. March, who advocated for a large standing army, and Pershing, who did not believe a large force was politically feasible and so favored a smaller, more professional army. In the course of the battle Marshall went once with Pershing to visit President Harding in the White House, and more often to meet with Charles Dawes, director of the Budget Bureau. Dawes would speak at great length about insider politics at the highest levels. Pershing won the fight in Congress and succeeded in getting a permanent army of two hundred and eighty thousand authorized.

Part of what Marshall learned in these years were some of the general's personal leadership traits. Pershing had lost his wife and three young daughters in a tragic house fire in 1915.[10] He coped with the tragedy by throwing himself fully into his work and career and remaking himself into an outwardly austere and inwardly disciplined man. This drive caused him to be humorless and impersonal during the workday, but approachable and genial in off-hours. As they traveled and shared the everyday chores and activities of life a mutual appreciation and admiration arose between them.

Despite Pershing's congressional victory the Army's funding consistently decreased in succeeding years. By 1935 a force of just one hundred and twenty-five thousand men existed and that force was being starved of new equipment. Although the Air Corps was growing in number of planes and personnel, it was being outfitted at the expense of the infantry, artillery, engineering, and signal corps units, which were being reduced below levels needed for minimum operations (Watson 1950, 24-26). The Army's deterioration depressed Marshall, but its long-term effect was to provide him with experience and motivation he would need in the attempt to counter the trend as WW II approached. What he said in a letter to a congressman in 1940 closely parallels what he was thinking in the 1920s:

> We will be seriously handicapped in our problem of developing skill in handling large units, and keeping them properly supplied in the field, until we are able to organize again at least a limited number of the essential control, supply, and communications units of corps and army troops. Furthermore, and of equal or greater importance, is the pressing necessity for a certain minimum of seasoned, trained units immediately available for service (Watson 1950, 26).

The crises in the 1920s and later were in part caused by a congressional and public distaste for involving America in Europe's conflicts and in part by budget-saving motives. Cuts in funding and manpower were exacerbated in the depression era. These were supported by the policies dictating that armed forces be committed only to defensive purposes and to arms limitation treaties. Such policies had a repressive psychological effect on the Army itself, for example by discouraging it from supporting the development of long-range bomber units.[11]

While Marshall's rank and status had improved sharply under Pershing (he had been promoted to major in 1921 and lieutenant colonel in 1923), the prevailing practice of reserving the highest ranks for commanders of troops still worked against him. He yearned for troop duty and the opportunity to go abroad to take on responsibility and experience personal growth. Thus he requested Pershing's help in getting assigned abroad.

Keeping the Peace in China

With Pershing's blessing, Lieutenant Colonel Marshall arrived in August of 1924 with his wife Lily at Tientsin, China, a large city near Beijing (Peking) containing a small U.S. compound (among other, larger compounds and concessions).[12] There, he took up the post of executive officer of the Fifteenth Infantry Division. The Fifteenth was charged with keeping segments of the Mukden-Peking railway lines to the coast free and with protecting American citizens and interests in the region. Although second in command, Marshall took advantage of a leadership vacuum to put his stamp on how the post was run. While Lily enjoyed the social activity and perquisites of living on a foreign post with abundant domestic labor, her husband poured himself into reviewing and reforming every aspect of training, compound life, mission focus and operations.

Complicating the mission was the fact that the compound was integrated within a large urban community with all its vices and influences. Gambling, opium dens, and prostitution were easily accessible and wide-spread. Venereal disease was rampant. Marshall launched an ambitious recreation program to promote the well-being and morale of the troops and fundamentally alter the social life of the compound for every man, woman, and child. Musical shows, track meets, horse competitions, hockey, and intramural athletics featuring competition and prizes were instituted. Officers were required to be instructors in these pursuits and every soldier had to participate in at least one activity.

Animals were not exempted. American mules had been shipped in with carts to work the local roads but the carts were unsatisfactory because the width of their axles did not fit the road ruts. Marshall had the carts modified and found the funds needed to buy small, local Mongolian ponies to pull them, and gave the surplus mules to the Chinese. Horse shows and a polo competition were organized with the ponies and a mounted scout troop was drawn and outfitted from among the post's children. Marshall's enthusiasm and energy seemed boundless (Gallagher 1962, 19-20).

Some officers thought it odd when Marshall personally took on training the troops in small groups because they felt it was undignified duty for a man of his rank. He not only persisted in doing so but broadened the training to include atypical skills, most notably the study of conversational Chinese. Taking the idea from his own study of the Mandarin language and customs, he ordered similar training for troops. His reason for doing so was to improve the capacity of the military forces that were on hand to control Chinese warlord armies that posed a potential threat to American and other western concessions within the city. The plan was to set up kitchens and feed the warlord armies, use interpreters to persuade them to move to the native part of the city, and leave the concessions undisturbed. They would only be allowed to come into the concessions if they laid down their arms.

Using their new skills and a show of arms, Marshall's troops used threats, entreaties, and bluffs to keep the peace. The positive effects of teaching language skills to his officers and troops were great. Competing warlords at any time could create conditions that would necessitate the immediate protection of Americans in the area of the concessions and lead to bloodshed. Communicating with their armies was the best way to detect and head off growing tension among them (Barrett[13] 1959, 8-10). The Fifteenth succeeded by negotiating with and pacifying the three warlord armies of the region to keep the peace.

Return to the US and Personal Crisis

Marshall's personally satisfying tour in Tientsin came to an end with his reassignment in July of 1927 to teach at the Army War College in Washington, D.C. This was to prove the worst time of his life. His job as an instructor at the War College left him dissatisfied and frustrated. He was away from troops. He was distanced from the arc of events that was determining the future of the Army and the nation. And then tragedy struck. Lily, always in delicate health because of her weakened heart and suffering with a diseased thyroid gland, died suddenly and unexpectedly shortly after undergoing minor surgery at Walter Reed Hospital. Marshall, who had been devoted to her, protective of her welfare, and by her side constantly when she fell ill, was plunged into deep depression and feelings of guilt (Pogue 1963, 245-246).

He wrote to Pershing expressing his vulnerability:

> The truth is, the thought of all you had endured gave me hope. But twenty-six years of most intimate companionship, something I have known since I was a mere boy, leaves me lost in my best effort to adjust myself to future prospects in life. If I had been given to club life or other intimacies with men outside of athletic diversions, of if there was a campaign or other pressing duty demanding a concentrated effort, then I think I should do better. However, I will find a way (Pogue 1963, 246).

Aware of his protege's ambition and the depth of his depression, the old soldier performed an act of mercy by responding to this expression of despair by his young friend and protégé. A transfer was arranged for Marshall to an educational leadership position at the Infantry Officer School at Fort Benning, Georgia. The move redeemed Marshall's spirit and redirected his career.

Revolutionizing Army Officer Training

Marshall arrived at Fort Benning in the fall of 1927 and moved into a small house on its spacious grounds. He was assigned to duty as assistant commandant of the Infantry School and head of its academic department. He was given free rein by successive commandants (with whom he had previously served) to conduct and alter the officer training program as he saw fit. His predecessor, Colonel Frank S. Cocheu, had already built a well-developed curriculum and a good faculty (J. Collins 1958, 2), but the program was routinized and academic (Bull 1959, 1). Marshall immediately set out to change the school according to his lights, escaping into his work with demonic energy and new purpose. In the evenings, away from the classrooms, he sat alone at a small dinner table on his porch, book in hand, attended by an elderly black woman who cared and cooked for him (Gallagher, 1962, 41).

He had come to Benning with a vision of how to go about preparing all Army officers, not just infantry officers, for the next war. The idea was to make training extremely practical, to cause officers to think originally, and to instill the need for coordination among different types of units (artillery, armor, air, ordnance and supply, communication, and infantry). He would urge his charges to study the first six months of the next war, not the last war or the classic campaigns of the past.

He assembled at Benning a corps of teachers and students he thought to be capable and innovative. Then he watched them for signs of an ability to lead. The number of potential leaders he studied was large, some two hundred of the army's top-ranking officers whom he termed "the most brilliant, interesting and thoroughly competent collection of men I have ever been associated with." Here he observed, taught, and interacted with men who were destined to become the core of WW II's general officers: Omar Bradley, Walter Bedell "Beetle" Smith, Courtney Hodges, J. Lawton Collins, "Vinegar" Joe Stilwell, Matthew Ridgway, and many others (Stoler 1989, 55-56).

At the end of each academic year, infantry school students were given a chance to command regular troops who were brought from the Atlanta area at great expense and against considerable political opposition. In the first part of the exercises troops were commanded by their own officers with the students as observers. In the second, they were commanded by advanced students using exercises designed by the faculty. Supply system problems were introduced and tied together with issues of troop strength and deployment (Bull 1959, 13; Collins 1958, 4).

Ridgway gave glowing testimony to the ultimate impact of Marshall's reformulation of officer training at Fort Benning:

> [He] just remade the Infantry School there . . . he revitalized and reoriented the tactical courses . . . I think any officer who had the benefit of the Infantry School from then on found the instruction there of almost incalculable benefit in his later career. . . . The debt that the American people owe to the Army school system is something that is very little appreciated—we couldn't have expanded our armies the way we did, with the skill and professional touch which characterized the American armies in both World War I and World War II. It would have been utterly impossible without these years and years to teach the mental preparation . . . particularly young troops, the stresses which they could expect to encounter on the battlefield (Ridgway 1959, 2, 4).

Marshall continued the cultural and personal expansion of officers that he had begun at Tientsin. Monthly sessions conducted at his Benning residence featured individual reading and reporting by officers on many topics and books—mostly drawing on sociology, applied psychology, and history (Gallagher 1962, 41). The officer would present a synopsis; evaluation and discussion would follow. The sessions stimulated and broadened instructor perspectives (J. Collins 1958, 3-4).

Another achievement of Marshall at Benning was meeting, wooing, and wedding Katherine Tupper Brown. Widowed by the murder of her first husband, Katherine and her three children, Clifton, Allen, and Molly, were to become an important key to Marshall's future stability and approach to life.

In sum, the transfer to Fort Benning and the five years he spent there not only proved pivotal to Marshall's rehabilitation, they were of crucial importance to the long-term quality of the Army's officer corps and the waging of WW II.

Champion of the CCC and the Citizen-Soldier

Substantial involvement with state national guard units and reservists prior to WW I had sparked Marshall's interest in the "citizen-soldier" concept. By 1923, as the Regular Army's strength dwindled, he had concluded that the nation's defense had to rely in part on a citizen army and state National Guard units. It was necessary to embrace the opportunity under the 1920 Act to "enroll and train the framework of a citizen army, with officers prepared for their work and thus not to be left at the mercy of chance" (Pogue 1963, 221).

The Regular Army officer corps was very small. In the event of a new war most of it would necessarily become involved in training National Guard units, the major source of military manpower, leaving the country without any effective fighting units for at least the first year of such a war. Essential military skills would have to be imparted to guardsmen in order to allow them to serve effectively in combat or as trainers of new troops. This would require Regular Army personnel to change their attitudes toward the National Guard. Civilian soldiers must be won over, socialized to army ways, properly trained and, most importantly, made to feel an integral and valued part of the defense force. Unfortunately, much of the Regular Army resisted such ideas (Bland and Hadsel 1981, 240-243).

Yet a new wrinkle in Army-civilian relations was added in 1933 with Congress's creation of the Civilian Conservation Corps (CCC). Although the legislation was intended to respond to the huge increase in the number of unemployed young men during the Great Depression, President Roosevelt asked General Douglas MacArthur, then Army chief of staff, to take over the planning and operation of the CCC from the Labor Department. MacArthur reluctantly accepted but objected on the ground that putting young, unemployed males to work in federal land area camps to build federal infrastructure bore no relationship to the Army's fighting mission. Although displeased with MacArthur's attitude, Roosevelt concluded that his instinct to protect the professional soldiering corps was natural (Hilldring 1959, 61-62).

Marshall's view of the Army-CCC relationship was strikingly different. Assigned to assist in developing the CCC in the southeast region in his new Fort Screven, Georgia command and then in a larger region which included the Screven assignment from his base at Fort Moultrie, South Carolina, he gladly embraced the project. Seeing a natural relationship between the Army and the CCC mission, he became a strong advocate of the CCC and its purpose. With the War Department's call-up of reserve officers to help run the program, two hundred and fifty thousand CCC trainees were nationally moved into work campsites by July of 1933. Marshall handed over operation of the normal military duties at Fort Screven to reserve officers and devoted himself to putting the CCC camps within his multi-state district into operation, which included the housing, feeding, clothing, training, and educating of the young trainees (Pogue 1963, 275-276).

Marshall knew that the officers he was sending out to run the camps were going to encounter new and unfamiliar challenges. He told them, only half in jest: "I'll be out to see you soon and if I find you doing something, I will help you, but if I find you doing nothing, only God will help you" (Pogue 1963, 278). He took great pleasure and pride in watching most of the young corpsmen acquire discipline and skills. With his newly granted rank, Colonel Marshall displayed the camps to visitors and encouraged nearby communities, especially Charleston, South Carolina, to support the CCC as a valuable social experiment (Pogue 1963, 278-280).

It is possible that MacArthur resented Marshall's embrace of the CCC program. Or, he may have feared that Marshall's ascendancy in the military hierarchy and in the president's good graces would challenge his own ambitions. In any event, he used Marshall's impressive CCC performance as a basis for making Marshall's next assignment an unfavorable one. General Roy D. Keehn, the politically influential commander of the 33rd Division of the Illinois National Guard headquartered in Chicago, had asked for a regular officer to serve as senior advisor to deal with the division's complicated community relations problems. MacArthur recommended Marshall for the job. The move was clearly unfavorable, perhaps fatal, to Colonel Marshall's career, in that it was another staff job that would not help him achieve promotion to brigadier general and, worse, would run the clock and make promotion to general status during his career unlikely.

Friends of Marshall, including famed commander General Fox Conner of the First Army in France in WW I, wrote to MacArthur to express their opposition to his decision (Bolte 1958, 37; Buchanan 1958, 9). MacArthur defended the assignment on the grounds that Marshall's background perfectly fit the need to deal with politically sensitive labor and race relations problems (Butler 1960, 1). Some who knew both MacArthur and Marshall were of the opinion that there was no malice in MacArthurs's action (Herron 1958, 12-13; Hilldring 1959). However, there is some reason to doubt MacArthur's protest that he was simply responding to the urgent demands coming to him from General Keehn. MacArthur was known to be prejudiced against "the Pershing men" from his WW I experience (Buchanan 1958, 2-3). There is no evidence that Marshall ever harbored any ill-feeling toward MacArthur for the assignment.

The fact is that Marshall was ideal for the assignment and up to the challenge. If the post was a lemon career-wise, he would turn it into lemonade. He brought to it the same enthusiasm for civilian-military relations that he had shown in all his earlier posts. Forewarned about unrest in the Chicago area which might prompt use of the National Guard, he delved into labor relations law under the new National

Labor Relations Act. He developed a thoroughgoing understanding of labor relations processes as well as greater empathy for the labor perspective, something that he had until that time known little about (Buchanan 1958, 4) or for which he had little sympathy (given his father's experience with militant strike leaders). His sophistication and balanced approach proved popular with all sides in the controversy and from this experience he gained some knowledge of diplomacy (Buchanan 1958, 9).

Marshall's work with the Illinois 33rd Division brought him back to his long-standing association with state guard units. He even returned to his pre-WW I role of leading large-scale field maneuvers. According to Ridgway, he remade the division into an effective military unit (1959, 8). In the process the officers and rank-and-file members of the Illinois guard developed great affection and respect for him. He never hesitated to be critical but always did so in such a way as not to demean or demoralize (Buchanan 1958, 16). In his almost non-existent spare time he worked to improve the public's perception of the Guard by personally editing the *Illinois Guardsman*, a magazine devoted to Guard affairs, without once mentioning his own role within the journal.

Serving with the Guard also gave him the opportunity to work on methods for training large numbers of citizen-soldiers in minimal time, shortcutting many of the procedures and regulations Regular Army personnel were expected to learn (Ridgway 1959, 8). The activity aided Marshall in developing patterns of thought about how to facilitate the rapid buildup of the Army, which became crucial in the early stages of WW II.

Still, Marshall was not happy in Chicago. He disliked living in a big city and having to give up his daily horseback ride. The assignment to the Guard did in fact delay promotion to brigadier general and cloud prospects of reaching high Army position. Although there is no evidence that Marshall suppressed his traditional revulsion to asking for favors or exerting pressure, it is true that Pershing tried to help.[14]

Vancouver Barracks

A new assignment to Vancouver Barracks in southwestern Washington state in the summer of 1936 revived Marshall's spirits and put him back on the elite career track. He was placed in command of the Fifth Brigade of the Third Division. Living in the northwest brought both Marshalls instant happiness. He was back in his favorite role of commanding troops, his promotion to brigadier general was made on October 1, and he was living in close proximity to a fishing and hunting wonderland. His interests now extended to everything around him—to the community, to building up the post chapel and its activities, and especially to the CCC operation within the area of his command, which included all of Washington and Oregon.

It was into the CCC that he again poured most of his energy and passion. His responsibility extended to the education, housing and feeding, recreating, and welfare of the young men and adolescent boys who lived in twenty-seven camps.

They came from every part of the country and from every background, often from pasts that were underprivileged and troubled. The military staff assigned to administer the regional CCC was attached to brigade headquarters (Poch 1960, 26, 30; Pogue 1963, 308-311).

Leaving the bulk of managing the brigade to a trusted assistant commander,[15] Marshall devoted himself to the needs of the trainees. As at Screven and Moultrie, he set out to convince the citizens of Vancouver and Portland, Oregon, its near-neighbor across the Columbia River, that these young men were "wholly dependable," efficient, and of good character, as he stated in "Comments for the CCC District Review on Camp Inspections" in June, 1937 (Bland and Hadsel 1981, 543-544). His enthusiasm for this new role is palpable in the following letter he wrote to a friend, Leo Farrell, in March, 1938:

> I have several thousand from the southeast—many from Georgia—and I am struggling to force their education, academic or vocational, to the point where they will be on the road to really useful citizenship by the time they return to their homes. I have done over my corps of civilian educators, and their methods, until I think we really have something supremely practical. To me it has been a fascinating side line, though it really takes the major portion of my time (Bland and Hadsel 1981, 586).

Marshall conceived of his CCC role as (1) seeing how the men under him performed in the field; (2) monitoring the results of the work that was going on, and (3) taking corrective action as needed. Eschewing paperwork and protecting his officers from having to respond to requests for reports, he empowered his camp commanders and their staffs with wide discretion in demanding high standards from the men and backed their requests for supplies, new instructors, and anything else that in their judgment they might need. Marshall told his staff:

> We in headquarters live and have our being in order that the people in the field may carry out their mission. If they [the camp commanders and their staffs] ask for anything, regardless of its nature, give it to them. If I find out later that their judgment was faulty I will handle the situation (Pogue 1963, 310).[16]

The educational part of the program was seen as central to the mission of the CCC. Creativity was often called for in finding jobs for corpsmen. The Portland Chamber of Commerce was lobbied through presentations by selected trainees to set a generally favorable tone. Community leaders were induced to discover how the organization worked and to witness some of its successes, and then to spread the word generally throughout the community (Pogue 1963, 310-311).

Marshall directed corpsmen trained in farm accounting to approach large-scale farmers in the district and tell them that part of their training had been to work with farmers and not to say they knew anything about farm accounting, but simply that they wished to learn. Marshall separately requested of the farmers that they take in the boys and help train them. In this way the boys would not be oversold and farmers could take satisfaction in helping to train them. In many cases the boys were later hired by the farmers as farm accountants (Osborn 1959, 1-2).

A wholly fortuitous event occurred at Vancouver Barracks on June 20, 1937 with the unexpected arrival of three Soviet pilots who were completing an exploratory flight over the North Pole. Planning to land in Oakland, California, low fuel forced the plane down at Pearson Field in Vancouver quite near to Marshall's post residence. When Marshall received word that the pilots had landed, he ordered they be brought directly to his home. He found an interpreter, had them bathe, eat, and sleep, and outfitted them with comfortable clothing. At the same time, he kept reporters and curious observers at a distance. His considerate treatment of these Soviet heroes earned him an outpouring of affection from Stalin and Soviet military brass as well as the Soviet public.

The value of what Marshall gained from his CCC and National Guard experiences can hardly be overstated. The chief lessons centered around the training of civilians for military and national service. When war came, much of what he learned from turning CCC trainees into productive adults was applied to building an army of over eight million conscripts and enlistees drawn from every ethnic group, race, and corner of America, some wishing to serve and others resisting.

Return to the Capital and Top Leadership

The path now wide open to top army leadership posts, Marshall was brought back to Washington, DC in 1938 as assistant chief of the War Plans Division (WPD) of the General Staff of the War Department. He began by taking on as a matter of the highest priority the task of orienting himself to the realities of air power, including its growth and organization. In doing so, he was seeking to plug a large gap in his education. Although he had early experience before and during WW I with using the airplane tactically as an adjunct to ground forces, he wished to learn as much as possible about the burgeoning technology and potential uses of air power, unlike many of his Regular Army contemporaries.

Hap Arnold, his old friend from his Philippines service in 1913, was in place as the Army Air Corps' top ranking officer. Along with the extremely able Colonel Frank M. Andrews, commander at nearby Langley Field, Virginia, Marshall's interests were embraced and his education begun. Marshall and Andrews teamed on a cross-country tour of airfields and aircraft plants to both investigate technological matters and explore the conflicts dividing Air Corps from traditional army personnel. With Andrews' tutelage, Marshall came to see that the General Staff had little respect for the Air Corps and had treated it unfairly (Dahlquist 1958, 9; Pogue 1966, 84-85).

It was also during this period that Marshall and President Roosevelt had their first meeting of consequence.[17] At a November, 1938 session at the White House Marshall voiced a fundamental disagreement with a proposal the president was making to supply ten thousand aircraft to the British and French. Their interaction at the meeting had a dramatic effect in terms of how each man was to perceive and approach the other.[18]

At first their relationship was strained. Roosevelt's informality clashed with Marshall's sense of propriety and seriousness about the decision-making process. Marshall resolved to find third parties that would help him better understand and communicate with Roosevelt. To gain greater access and get across his thinking, Marshall approached presidential advisor Harry Hopkins in late 1938. Because Hopkins was perhaps Roosevelt's closest confidant, and because Hopkins and Marshall had a high regard for each other, Marshall reasoned that Hopkins could help him bridge the gap he felt he had with the president. The two worked together to arrange for committing some of the Work Projects Administration budget to the production of munitions and small arms, an idea welcomed by Roosevelt.[19]

Marshall's elevation to the job of US Army chief of staff was neither predestined nor simple. The current chief of staff, General Malin Craig, had already announced his intention to step down but had not endorsed anyone to replace him, although he had shown his confidence in Marshall by moving him to the position of deputy chief of staff in October, 1938. Craig's silence was in part prompted by the fact that many generals outranked Marshall and the tradition was that the most senior general with sufficient time left to serve before retirement would accede to the top job. Ultimately, of course, the choice was the president's to make.

Five men with at least four years left to serve (the usual span of the chief of staff's tenure) outranked Marshall, and Roosevelt was also free to go down the list of brigadier generals below Marshall to make his decision. Eventually the list was boiled down to just two men, Marshall and Lieutenant General Hugh Drum. Drum had served as Pershing's chief of staff in the AEF and for a brief time had been Marshall's superior in WW I. He actively lobbied for the position through political friends while Marshall carried on no such campaign (Gerow 1958, 39). As it happened, Roosevelt resented Drum's incessant politicking[20] and listened to the many who argued that Marshall was the more competent man.

The president also sought the opinion of Pershing, who knew both men intimately. Pershing weighed in on Marshall's side. The other players in the competition were Secretary of War Harry Woodring and Assistant Secretary of War Louis Johnson. While both supported Marshall, the fact of each man's support was carefully hidden from the other man by Marshall, so great was the enmity between the two men. Following discussion with Hopkins at the president's Warm Springs retreat in early April, Roosevelt privately chose Marshall as his next Army chief of staff (Black, 2003, 499).

With the choice made, Marshall was made acting chief of staff on July 1 and then notified of the promotion to chief of staff in August, with the swearing-in set for the White House on September 1, 1939. It did not occur at that place because on that day Hitler's forces stormed across the Polish border to begin the second great world war. The ceremony was moved to the War Department because of the emergency. There Marshall was administered the oath in a brief session conducted by Secretary of War Woodring.

Summary

The period 1897 to 1938 had seen the rise of the United States from a provincial republic just emerging as a player on the international stage to a major world power looked to by European nations for support in repulsing Nazi aggression. The pace of social and technological change during this time was far greater than in any period of world history. It was a simple truism that for America to grow and prosper during this period successive waves of new leadership would have to emerge to meet the demands of its population for applied science, mass communications and transportation, social protection and economic opportunities for an increasingly urbanized society.

No single person could be expected to grow and change steadily in knowledge, sensitivity, and skills so as to be equipped to lead complex organizations through those changing times. Yet, George Marshall did precisely that. He was superbly, perhaps uniquely, prepared to lead the Army in whatever military emergencies lay ahead. As a young man in his early twenties in the army of the Philippines he had been thrust by circumstance into positions of responsibility. Self-reliance and "inner-directedness"[21] were the consequences. Aided by chance but owing principally to his own driving ambition and self-discipline first acquired at VMI, he secured a place among the Army's elite at Fort Leavenworth and thus came under the approving eye of the future chief of staff, General Bell, who was to advance the young and talented officer's opportunities and challenges.

Cultivating his physical and mental resources through self-discipline and extraordinary effort, he earned a reputation for excellence as a staff officer, educator, and innovator in military maneuvers in his early assignments. His reputation as a superior staff officer brought him into prominence in WW I and under the influence and direct tutelage of the foremost military leader and hero of the day, General John J. Pershing. Through a passion for learning and clarity of thought, and the good fortune to find himself in a position of military academic leadership, he became a paragon of military professionalism and was introduced to the best and brightest of military leadership at Fort Benning. Through the exigencies of the national nightmare of the Great Depression, he had also been exposed to and embraced the citizen-soldier culture in the form of the National Guard and the CCC.

Thus in 1939, at the age of fifty-eight, he had arrived at a high state of preparation in his career that few military figures in history, at least military history, could match. He had served with distinction and success in a great variety of posts under conditions that ran from the rule book to the totally unpredictable. He had served with small and large units, within the US and in foreign lands, and in places both remote and very near to the epicenter of power. He had endured extraordinary pressures and had survived to draw lessons from them. He had retained exceptional vigor. Not least of all, he was eager for continued duty in the service of his country.

The tools Marshall had brought to the doorstep of WW II and his new position at the top of the Army hierarchy were truly impressive. Not only had he come to know at a personal level virtually every high ranking officer in the Army, he had much to do with how some of them came to be where they were and thus commanded their loyalty as well as their admiration. He had studied and mastered the weaponry and technologies and military organizational patterns that were likely to be used in the next war. Perhaps better than any man, he understood the logistics of acquiring, training, equipping, and shipping troops, and of deploying and supporting them in the field. Moreover, he had worked extensively with officers and leaders and the ordinary people of other nations and cultures—French, British, Chinese, and Filipino, as well as Americans of all kinds and classes, and had coordinated the affairs of all of them.

No one was better prepared than General Marshall to lead the American military in the event of its entry into a new war. And no one, not even Marshall, could have foreseen what that involvement would entail and require of him.

Notes

1.   General Marshall himself was uninterested in his ancestry. He was in fact embarrassed by his father's insistence on stressing the relationship. "I thought the continued harking on the name of John Marshall was kind of poor business. It was about time for somebody to swim for the family again, though he was only a collateral relative" (Bland 1991, 86).

2.   What is known is formed mostly from what General Marshall himself described to his biographer, Forrest C. Pogue, in his last years (Bland 1991), plus the recollections of a few boyhood friends.

3.   He later concluded that the lack of vacations was on the whole not a good thing. "There was a great deal of time we gained in one sense, but I think we got so stale that we would have done very much better if we had had a breather here and there" (Bland 1991, 117).

4.   Marshall was much influenced by the traditions at VMI involving General Robert E. Lee, who presided in Lexington at Washington College (now Washington and Lee University), and General Stonewall Jackson, who taught at VMI.

5.   Moseley became a student of Marshall's at Fort Leavenworth a few years later, and went on to serve as General Pershing's chief of staff, deputy chief of staff, and chief of supply in WW I, reaching the rank of major general.

6.   This included twenty-six or twenty-seven of the twenty-nine combat division commanders who saw action in WW I.

7.   Promotion occurred in July, 1916.

8.   Two examples: former President Taft and financial titan J.P. Morgan.

9.   The reason he must accept the "wrong" order is because the larger picture of the entire field of engagement over the entire front is not available to him.

10.   Pershing's only son, Warren, survived.

11.   While the Air Corps strongly supported strategic bombing units, they were kept in restraint not only by the Regular army types but also by the fact that operations over water were still considered to be within the Navy's jurisdiction.

12.   Other nations represented, as a result of the concessions granted following the Boxer Rebellion, were Great Britain, France, Japan, and Belgium.

13. David Dean Barrett (1892-1977), assigned to the 15th, was an American soldier, diplomat, and an old Army China hand. Most of his 35 years in the US Army were served in China.

14. Roosevelt, at Pershing's request, asked Secretary of War Dern to promote Marshall to brigadier general in 1935 (Black 2003, 496).

15. The first of these was Col. Walton H. Walker, later famed as commander of the XX Corps in WW II and of the Eighth Army in Korea.

16. Pogue is quoting from a 1960 (month and day not given) interview with Brig. Gen. Barnhard A. Johnson.

17. Roosevelt and Marshall had met perfunctorily at Mount Hood, Oregon, in September, 1937.

18. The interchange is described in detail in chapter 3.

19. Ultimately, this transfer was judged to have greatly advanced US preparedness (Black 2003, 466, 498).

20. FDR was quoted by Life magazine, June 16, 1941 as saying, "Drum, Drum, I wish he would stop beating his own drum!" (Pogue 1963, 408).

21. "Inner-directedness" is the predisposition to act on judgment and conscience rather than calculations of external approval (Riesman 1950).

CHAPTER THREE
CORE ETHICAL ATTRIBUTES OF LEADERSHIP

For I believe you know that ever since I was one of your elderly pupils at Leavenworth I have considered you one of the real leaders of progress in the army. I know nobody in whom endowments of intellect, character, courage and rare tact are more abundantly provided and more perfectly balanced.
—John McAuley Palmer
Historian and Chief of the Demobilization Task Force, Joint Chiefs of Staff, 1943-1945 (Bland and Hadsel 1981, 210)

Marshall's character had matured into its quintessential form by 1939, perhaps much earlier. In his late fifties and tempered in the oven of conflict and career progression, his virtues were known and his values formed by the time he was sworn in as Army chief of staff on September 1, 1939. He was now in a position of such crucial gravity that whatever qualities of leadership he possessed would be of great moment to the nation's defense and world influence.

Before plunging ahead into the story of WW II, the matter of Marshall's character as it stood in 1939 will be dissected and assessed. In this and the next chapter the focus will be on discovering just what and who George Marshall was by looking more deeply into his values, his traits and virtues, his behavioral and moral faults, his learned practices of behavior, and his reactions to stress and his consistency and sturdiness over time.

Is There an Ethical Basis of Public Leadership?

There is a set of values, traits, and behaviors (collectively referred to here as "attributes") that are argued to be related to public leadership and increase the likelihood that leadership will be both effective and ethical. This and the next chapter will identify a set of personal attributes that have an ethical or normative base. A caveat is necessary: the word "ethical" is somewhat ambiguous since conclusions about how people and organizations *ought to* behave and decide will differ with the values and mores held within a given society. For example, special knowledge (such as that pertaining to military protocol and tactics) may be seen by many as a *cognitive* attribute rather than as an *ethical* attribute. However, if in that social grouping such knowledge has a moral value, such that members of that organization believe they *ought* to have such knowledge, then a disciplined effort to acquire that type of knowledge becomes an ethical matter.

51

The attributes discussed in this chapter relate to those normally found to be relevant to ethical leadership in the public realm. They include constitutional legitimacy, optimism and flexibility of mind, extraordinary courage, fairness, professionalism, loyalty to goal first and to people second, integrity and honesty, and decisiveness and the principle of action. These attributes may be termed *core* ethical leadership attributes and clearly relate to the achievement of public policy goals. In the next chapter other attributes that are not usually highlighted in the leadership literature will be the center of attention. They are referred to as *ancillary* (or "other") ethical attributes which *may be related* to public leadership, and in Marshall's case clearly add to the style of his leadership.

Discovering and describing these attributes in Marshall's case is not so difficult a task. The observations of many creditable people who worked closely with him in both the military and civilian phases of his careers have been captured and are easily accessible.[1] Many have noted or have inferred certain traits and virtues. When a particular attribute is confirmed by creditable sources without dissent, it may be reliably assumed. Inferences about the degree to which certain attributes are held may also be drawn from Marshall's own words in his correspondence, memoranda, and speeches.[2]

Lastly, inferences may be drawn directly from his decisions and actions while acting in his official capacity as an administrator. These are abundant due to the length of the general's career and also because of the spotlight put on many of them by historians, political scientists, sociologists, and journalists. An argument can be made that it is practice and action that best indicate both character and intent. After all, there is a tendency in human nature to project socially favorable images that may or may not be backed up in practice. In contrast, Marshall was far more concerned with practice and action than with self-promotion.[3]

Role legitimacy is the starting point of ethical leadership in the public sector. That is to say, public officials in democratic societies are expected to behave and express themselves in ways that are consistent with expectations of the broader society. This idea may also be conveyed by saying that public authority should be exercised in conformity with constitutional and statutory law, augmented by social customs and oaths of office. While acting consistent with legitimate roles does not in and of itself define ethical public behavior, it does appear to be a necessary precondition. To truly lead in the ethical sense, high standards of conduct, recognized best practices, and widely accepted cultural norms must be added to role legitimacy. In American society these include optimism, courage, fairness, professionalism, democratic values, and humaneness.

Acting Within the Bounds of the Constitution

When we inquire into just whose expectations it is necessary for public officials to consult, three reference groups become relevant: (1) the lawmakers, (2) the citizenry, and (3) members of the official's own organization. To the lawmakers (the legitimate political authority of the state which includes legislatures, elected executives, and courts) is owed the obligation to embrace and pursue the policies and rules that are rendered into law through constitutionally legitimate process. To the public at large (the citizenry) is owed the obligation to strive to deliver the law's intended benefits and sanctions. To the leader's organization and its members two obligations are owing: first, providing the tools that will allow them to deliver to the citizenry those benefits promised by the law; and second, to do so in ways that promote and preserve dignity, respect, and justice for both public beneficiaries and public servants (Pops and Pavlak 1991).

Moral Qualities of the Ethical Leader

In a seminal essay Stephen Bailey, dean of Syracuse University's Maxwell School of Citizenship and Public Affairs from 1961-1969, identified three essential moral qualities of the ethical administrator: optimism, courage, and fairness tempered by charity. *Optimism*, in Bailey's words, "is the capacity to settle with some consistency on the sunnier side of doubt." Without optimism, there is no incentive to better the condition of mankind. Optimism must be cultivated as a life-style, that is to say, as a virtue which inculcates faith in taking reasonable risks and allows one "to see the possibilities for good in the uncertain" (Bailey 1964, 240). *Courage* means acting in the face of adversity or in opposition to popular or expert opinion, and thus taking on additional risk regarding one's life, safety, status and reputation, or career. However, courage "is of no value unless it results in just and charitable actions and attitudes." It follows that a most important moral quality of ethical leadership is to exercise power fairly and compassionately. *Fairness* is critical and basic to public leadership; yet it must be accompanied by *charity*, "the virtue which compensates for inadequate information and for the subtle importunities of self in the making of judgments designed to be fair" (Bailey 1964, 242-243).

Optimism and Flexibility of Mind

The future may be thought about with optimism or with pessimism. The ability to think flexibly allows us to see *more* obstacles as well as *more* opportunities, and to see them in greater complexity. The willingness to move ahead into the realm of future-oriented action and to deal with these contingencies is consistent with an optimistic predisposition, as well as with the quality of resilience. Marshall was essentially an optimist. "He said if we could get to the morale of (our) soldiers, we can beat the Germans." . . . "I think he had concerns . . . but . . . in a reserved, quiet way" was convinced that "it was going to get done" (Pasco 1997, 19, 21).

Marshall's mind leaped quickly to the future and embraced the necessity of change. He was more than willing to enter into thinking about the future with all its complexity, problems, and necessity for change. His tendency was to start by grasping the possibilities before imagining the obstacles. Thus, unlike most of his army contemporaries, he studied the dynamics of the new technology of air power and became its champion prior to the outbreak of WW II. He was credited by one highly placed airman with "having a natural inclination toward innovation and the acceptance of the unusual" (Hansell 1959, 16).

Convinced that there was a need to consider the contingency of all-out involvement of the US in a European war as early as 1938, Marshall made a concentrated effort to learn the intricacies of large-scale production of war materiel and equipment. Although not trained as a modern engineer (although he graduated from VMI as a civil engineer) or in machine production, he was immediately able to grasp the importance of the time dimension involved in producing weapons and military vehicles and equipment. He called in military industrialists to relate the problems and met them with charts and descriptions presenting the army's strengths, weaknesses, and needs; that is, he played the role of a willing collaborator. The importance of machine tool design as a first step in the manufacturing of weapons and the time required for the design was explained to him, and the importance of ramping up the entire machine tool industry to run at a pace many times its peacetime level was also explained (Geier 1959, 4).

> What impressed me about General Marshall was that his mind did not run along purely military lines. He had an immediate grasp of the industrial and prepared-ness problems, which were not understood by some other people in Washington. They didn't realize that you just can't go out and buy something and have it overnight. In some cases, you had to design machines to build things, and you had to tune those machines up and you had a long cycle. . . . General Marshall seemed to have a plastic mind where he could grasp some of those things that were completely foreign to the line of experience he had before (Geier 1959, 6).

Optimism in battle had been gained at Pershing's side. His mentor had taught him that thinking positively about the outcome of battle was of crucial importance. Both subordinate staff and the troops had to be convinced that their commander truly believed that victory, or at least a positive outcome to the fight, was achievable and that he knew the best path to achieve it. Marshall told the House Committee on Military Affairs in 1940:

> You have to lead men in war by bringing them along to endure and to display qualities of fortitude that are beyond the average man's thought of what he should be expected to do. You have to inspire them when they are hungry and exhausted and desperately uncomfortable and in great danger; and only a man of positive characteristics of leadership, with the physical stamina that goes with it, can function under those conditions (Pogue 1966, 97).

Courage

Courage may take on many forms in public administration. For example, it "is needed to ensure that degree of impersonality without which friendship leads to inequities and special favors" (Bailey 1964, 241). Courage is needed to also face down pressures brought to bear on the decision maker by popular majorities and expert opinion. It involves standing up for what one believes to be important despite the personal cost. It includes the readiness to take responsibility for one's decisions and actions (Eisenhower 1962, 22).

When, in 1940, Marshall undertook a policy of restricting field command positions to younger men to insure their physical vigor, many of those who were removed or not appointed due to their greater age petitioned him directly. They exerted leverage based on prior combat records, personal friendship, or past relationship or a combination of these. Often their pleas were buttressed by congressmen and other influential persons. Marshall persisted in demanding evidence of *present* vigor as justification for the award of a command position. This, as he later told Pogue, was among the most difficult burdens he ever had to bear, as many of these men had been comrades he had fought with. In the end, he used but a single criterion: the capacity for effective leadership *in the coming war*. Most took the career-damning decision quietly; many appealed to others; a few were left embittered by the experience. Marshall bore the huge personal cost rather than compromise the quality of the officer corps.

The story was told of Marshall's confrontation, as chief of operations of the First Infantry Division with the rank of major, in his first meeting in France with General Pershing during WW I. Pershing, Marshall, and General Sibert, Marshall's superior and commander of the First Infantry Division, and other officers were gathered to watch a review of division troops on parade. Pershing directed criticism at Sibert for what he saw as faulty parade procedure. Pershing's remarks struck Marshall as unfair and led him to vigorously defend Sibert on the spot by telling Pershing that much of the blame was attributable to faulty directives from Pershing's staff as well as harsh field conditions. Pershing muttered that he had his own problems, but Marshall persisted, saying "Yes, I know you do, General, but ours are immediate and every day and have to be solved before night" (Uldrich 2005, 102).

Following this outburst his fellow officers quietly expressed their farewells to Marshall, expecting an imminent career setback for the brash major. Marshall responded by saying he did what he knew was right and his forwardness was called for, although he later allowed as how he had "gotten into it up to my neck." The result surprised many. Pershing so much appreciated Marshall's courageous honesty that he began thereafter to ask Marshall's opinions and later called him to Chaumont to serve as chief of operations of his headquarters staff (Pogue 1963, 151-153).

Another example of extraordinary courage is Marshall's first working meeting with President Roosevelt at the White House in the capacity of deputy chief of staff in 1938. The president called together military and civilian officials to discuss his (the president's) plan to ask Congress for $500 million for the production of 10,000 fighter planes to be supplied to the British and French for use against the German air force. Marshall was a secondary participant at the meeting but came armed with knowledge about air power he had gained from Frank Andrews and Hap Arnold as well as his own considerable Washington experience. Roosevelt asked those present if they agreed with his proposal.

> Most of them agreed with him entirely, had very little to say, and were very soothing in their comments. . . . He finally came around to me. . . . I remember he

called me "George"— I don't think he ever did it again. Well, anyway, that rather irritated me because I didn't know him on that basis. . . . So he turned to me at the end of this general outlining, in which he had done much of the talking, and said, "Don't you think so, George?" I replied, "Mr. President, I am sorry, but I don't agree with that at all" (Bland 1991, 108-109).

Marshall went on to explain that the number of planes must be considered in connection not only with the cost of their manufacture, but also in terms of logistics, the training of pilots and technicians, securing bases, and ammunition stores. Thus, the cost of building the planes vastly understated the total costs and difficulties.

I know that ended the conference. The president gave me a very startled look, and when I went out they all bade me goodbye and said my tour in Washington was over. But I want to say in compliment to the president that that didn't antagonize him at all (Bland 1991, 108-109).

It is reasonable to speculate that Marshall either did not think about or chose to ignore the fact that the president had in his grasp Marshall's future and lifelong goal to serve as Army chief of staff. Instinctively, he did what he thought was right. Doing so probably helped establish a healthier long-term relationship with Roosevelt, although Marshall could not have known that at the time.

In serving General Bell prior to WW I Marshall told Bell forthrightly that his speeches were long and boring and undermined his leadership. Marshall later explained his action:

I made it plain that I thought he was making a great mistake in making these speeches. Mrs. Bell was shocked. . . . But I was convinced that that was the trouble and I thought that was my duty to tell him, and if he didn't like that he could relieve me as an aide, because I wasn't after that kind of a job (Bland 1991, 184).[4]

As secretary of state in the spring of 1948, Marshall led a large contingent to Bogota, Columbia for a conference of the Organization of American States (OAS). No sooner had the conference started than a national rebellion erupted. The killing of a political opposition leader threw the nation and the conference into pandemonium. As many nations' delegations prepared to leave the country, Marshall rallied them, stating to the assemblage that the attack had occurred as a result of the OAS meeting and that all of the nations' representatives had an obligation to stay, absorb the risk, and back the threatened government of Columbia. He succeeded. Threatened with his own assassination, and with some eighty delegates from twenty-one countries penned up in two buildings without food or water, Marshall, acting more as a defense secretary than a secretary of state,[5] arranged for troops to be brought in from the lowlands of Columbia and supplies flown in from the US and Panama in order to defend and feed many of the delegates (Pawley 1962, 4-7). The conference continued.

The Uncertain Line Between Courage and Temper

As the Pershing and Roosevelt anecdotes suggest, an issue exists as to when anger, whether motivated by good intentions or not, may become counter-productive to the organization (Pershing could have ordered another parade; Roosevelt could have appointed a lesser chief of staff). In releasing anger there is a danger of losing one's poise. The heart of the solution is a proper analysis by the actor of whether the pretext of the confrontational behavior is the need to protect or further an important organizational objective.

Marshall recognized the peril posed by his anger: allowing it to rise within him clouded judgment and handicapped capacity for rational action, thus reducing the effectiveness of decision-making. He expressed this fear to others and told them that it was important for him to keep his temper under control. Still, he needed to be clear and forceful on matters of principle and in defense of organizational goals he considered to be important. Wherever possible, he believed that persuasion should replace heat. Passion should be channeled into persistence in finding and presenting facts with persuasive force and sincerity and not be subverted into anger.

Fairness

According to Bailey, fairness is the premier ethical attribute of leadership. General Sexton, an assistant secretary of the General Staff serving the chief of staff during much of WW II, gave an often voiced assessment of George Marshall: he is "the fairest man I believe I have ever encountered" (Sexton 1958, 20).

Marshall always insisted that anyone with a legitimate stake in a decision be allowed the opportunity to be heard and the chance to present views and evidence. Accordingly, he went to great lengths to provide a forum for the air forces to have a voice in military planning and decision-making equal to the Army and Navy in deliberations. General Ira Eaker, who commanded the US Army Air Forces in the Mediterranean during WW II, stated that Marshall had a "judicial temperament, [an] innate sense of fairness" and gave everyone the "feeling that they all had a fair, square shake" (Eaker 1959, 4, 6, 25).

He bore few grudges and did not act on those he may have harbored. General Herron recalls two officers coming up for promotion who had, when they were younger, grievously offended the general. When Herron submitted their paper work, Marshall signed his name without comment. "That's the way he did business. He bore malice alright, I feel sure, but it did not interfere with his duty" (Herron 1958, 15).

It is true that on occasion he allowed gratitude to alter the practice of striving for strict fairness. He had a special fondness for some of those, especially of lower rank, who served him personally as orderlies and drivers or in other service roles. He made a special point of keeping some of these people with him if they showed an interest in staying. Sergeant Powder, his chauffeur, had performed heroically in protecting Mrs. Marshall and her daughter in a hurricane at Fire Island, New York when they were vacationing and the general had to be in Washington. Marshall offered Powder a commission, which Powder refused, pleading that his lack of education could embarrass the general (Powder 1959, 4).[6]

Another case involved a very small girl he had met when he sought drinking water at a farmhouse in West Virginia during a Pennsylvania National Guard maneuver in 1908. He had been grateful for the family's kindness and was charmed by the girl, and had then kept in touch with the family through Christmas greetings over the years. Over thirty years later, when a vacancy developed in the chief of staff's office, she was hired as his receptionist.[7] He also hired as a confidential secretary General Bell's daughter who had been abandoned by her husband, an army general, because he sympathized with her predicament (Sexton 1958, 13-14).[8]

Typically, he had no time or patience for special pleaders. His personal files are studded with polite but firm (sometimes curt) refusals to intervene in requests for assignments, promotions, or favorable official decisions. It was well known that in the officer corps it never helped to be the general's close friend (Hilldring 1959, 2). His reaction to even being approached by someone seeking special treatment was visceral, almost always to the detriment of the requester (Devers 1958, 19-20). He gave no special treatment to or even took notice of whether an officer had been attached to a military unit for which Marshall served, such as the First Infantry Division in WW I or the Fifteenth Infantry Regiment at Tientsin. Likewise, it scarcely mattered to him whether an officer had attended his alma mater at VMI (Bolte 1958, 36; Gerow 1958, 33).[9]

Two examples give this particular trait added flavor. He would not intercede to gain a military assignment on behalf of his wife Katherine's brother, a well-respected officer (Devers 1958, 9). He would not allow the fact that his stepsons Allen and Clifton (both bore the last name Brown) were related to him to be made known. When invited by the commanding general of the armored forces school to speak to the graduating class in June of 1943, he refused because his stepson Allen was in it. Marshall was concerned that the relationship not be disclosed to school personnel or classmates lest Allen get special preference and receive honors he had not earned on his own. In a curt letter to Major General Gillem declining the invitation, he wrote:

> I ask you now to see that his graduation bears no comment on his connection with me. The fact that it is known that he is my stepson denies him a good bit of the credit for earning his own way and I am distressed that it has become public (Bland and Stevens 1996, 9).

The above examples are somewhat contradicted by the fact that he was quick to assist both stepsons by getting them into combat faster than they could have on their own. He facilitated an immediate assignment for Allen to an armored division in North Africa (including air passage home to visit his mother en route). Also, he granted Clifton's plea to be allowed to serve overseas despite a bad foot that would have otherwise kept him out (Pogue 1973, 221). This seeming inconsistency may have been on his mind and prompted him to tell General Devers, "I don't mind intervening to get a man into combat when he wouldn't normally go, but I won't bring a man out because he is kin to me or anything else" (Devers 1958, 19-20, quotation at 20).[10]

Even the appearance of favoritism was not to be permitted. Men too long in the field should be returned stateside. Men serving stateside should be properly trained and see their share of combat. On his way to the Pentagon from his home in Leesburg, Virginia and dressed in civilian garb, Marshall picked up a hitchhiker in uniform who did not recognize him. He discovered from questioning the young man that he was a trained anti-aircraft artilleryman who had been in the service for thirty-three months but had been attached to the Washington military district for most of that period without ever serving overseas, and further that his case was not unusual. Marshall immediately demanded an explanation from the district commander as to why young men were being held so long in the states without seeing duty overseas (Bland and Stevens 1996, 150).

In yet another case, Marshall risked President Roosevelt's displeasure by asking that a lieutenant colonel who was in charge of the map room in the White House, a Roosevelt favorite, be released so that he could be sent overseas, for the reason that he was young and had seen "very little duty with troops" (Bland and Stevens 1996, 157). It was important, Marshall thought, that men in combat overseas not get the impression that staff officers in Washington assignments were being favored. This was also the reason he ordered that distinguished service medals and legions of merit not be awarded to men stationed at the War Department or on American soil (Bland and Stevens 1996, 14).

Marshall rarely intervened in a personnel decision nominally within the purview of a field commander. The few instances in which he did seemed to be confined to situations when allegations were made which, if true, would present clear instances of injustice. In these cases the intervening action was framed in the spirit of a request to look into the matter. He made such a request to General Krueger in Australia to keep a watch on a Major Salisbury within his command. Salisbury, who had served under Marshall a decade earlier, had written directly to Marshall telling him he had been overlooked for promotion. Salisbury claimed, accurately, that he had led a rescue party onto a burning ammunition ship assisted by two other men. The two assistants were awarded the silver star but he himself had been ignored. Marshall wrote to Kreuger in 1943, enclosing Salisbury's letter to Marshall:

> I wish you would find out whether or not the vicissitudes described in his letter were due to his incompetence, or more or less the hard luck of having been superseded by men who had gotten rapid promotions. I hope you will not visit on him your wrath for having written me directly; but if I know the man, this is the first time in his life he has ever spoken out of turn. . . . Don't trouble to answer this. . . . I seldom touch these unless I have reason to feel that it may be a case of genuine injustice (Bland and Stevens 1996, 119-120).

Not everyone credits Marshall with having been fair-minded; he had some detractors on this score. Most of the criticism relates to application of the 1940 policy on appointment to command positions favoring younger men, discussed earlier in this chapter. Complaints and external pressures came from some of the men who felt the policy was either unfair on its face or misapplied in their particular case (Pogue 1966, 92-98). Stung by the complaints and resentful of the leveraging of influence on behalf of the complainants, Marshall was led to wonder whether he, also, was too old for continued service as Army chief of staff. He thus wrote to Roosevelt requesting that he be replaced by a younger man. The president took no action. Marshall asked again, this time through Harry Hopkins. Again, the president did not respond (Pogue 1966, 98-99).

A few observed that Marshall could occasionally be unfair when making a promotion or assignment decision if he had formed, at a prior time, a very strong opinion (positive or negative) about an officer's worth. The argument went that he could trust his intuition too much and get an idea about a man's worth so fixed in his mind it was extremely difficult for someone to muster the courage to dislodge it. "Well, he was right about 85 percent of the time and maybe that's as high a score as anybody" (Bolte 1958, 20-21, 24).

Two of his more famous critics were General Douglas MacArthur and White House counsel Clark Clifford. Both quarreled with him on matters of policy and referred to Marshall as unfairly biased. MacArthur faulted Marshall for what the Southwest Pacific commander regarded as Marshall's European bias in the allocation of troops, weapons, and supplies; a criticism that attacked the wisdom of the "Europe-first" policy favored by not only Marshall but the president, the secretary of war, and the British allies.

Clifford quarreled sharply with Marshall over the latter's opposition to the partition of Palestine and immediate recognition of a Jewish state in 1947. Clifford found Marshall to be unfair, unapproachable, and stubborn (Clifford and Holbrooke 1991). This opinion may have been more a reaction to Marshall's resentment of the role the young Clifford played in the decision process than revulsion for the general's policy views on Jewish statehood.[11] There is no hint in anyone's account of the episode or in Marshall's communications to suggest that the general had a negative view of the Jewish state or the American Jewish lobby.

Professionalism

Much of Marshall's influence lay in his acknowledged mastery of military matters and in the related ability to rapidly absorb new knowledge. He exuded self-confidence in his professional knowledge of Army affairs. The sources of this knowledge had come from about two decades of staff work at many levels and exposed him to tactical warfare, logistics, official protocol, accounting and record-keeping, budgeting, and communication skills both within the US Army and internationally. He had acquired through self-study and active curiosity a passion for the study of culture, language, and military history. Further, he had imparted these skills and interests as a teacher to many of the army's elite officers (Clark 1959, 57).

Behind it all was an intense drive to master any situation associated with his official role, which he typically defined broadly.

> I don't think his mind was ever inactive. The point was, he had such high standards of performance of duty, of perfection in performance of anything connected with the military . . . that he just saw things that had to be done, and other people would go along and maybe they would do them and maybe they wouldn't. But he would tear into the damn thing, and he had so many irons in the fire that he might have appeared to be under a strain (Gallagher 1962, 47).

Not only did his mastery of the military craft command the respect of others, it added greatly to his poise and self-assurance. "Nobody ever questioned his ability. They just looked on him as the law of the land" said Kenneth Buchanan, deputy chief of staff to Marshall in 1939-1940 (1958, 17). "I know of no one who had a greater or more thorough grasp of the situation and the ability to analyze it, and also the ability to come up with remedial measures that would correct situations" (Buchanan 1958, 46). "He appeared to know more than anybody else about what was going on, and he had no compunction about the fact that he was in the right place, that he was the best man to run the Army" (Pasco 1997, 18-19). He was effective with Congress because they knew he was right when he stated the cost to accomplish something. Competence went hand in hand with trust and honesty; he was "all gold, and he was accepted on that basis by everybody who had any contact with him" (Buchanan 1958, 47).

He brought a fresh outlook to each situation.

> He would look at each problem individually, and if it required action at that time, then precedence could go hang. This was to be taken care of on its own merits, and he was quick to see the merits (Poch 1960, 13).

Rules below the dignity of laws were subordinated to purposes; if a thing was needed it would just have to be done whether there was a rule against it or not. If the rule did not serve the larger purposes of the organization it could not be allowed to stand in the way. Regulations were for the mediocre officer and useless paper work could infuriate him (Poch 1960, 25).

Even with such credentials he could not do everything himself, of course. Nor did he try to give that impression. He simply created the feeling that things would be organized so that the task could be done. He wouldn't purposely pass over anything. If he lacked time to tend to something himself, he would see that a staff member would do it (Buchanan 1958, 19). No observer seems to have used the expression, "fell in the cracks" or a similar phrase, when they reviewed the results of a Marshall operation. He was entirely on top of his subject and would never put forward "a flat argument—all his points were clear" (Wilson 1961, 18).

Loyalty to Goal First, to People Second

Loyalty may be given to a superior, to an organization or to a unit within an organization, to a cause or to a goal, to the public, or to an ideal. In public administration there ought to be a high degree of consonance among these objects of loyalty. Ideally, the chief officers within every organization should embrace public policy goals as central to their motivation. They should not be seeking to promote a cause that is personal or designed to enlarge the power and prestige of the organization for its own sake. In this way loyalty to those superiors who hold public policy goals dear becomes the same as loyalty to the public interest and to organizational leadership.

The same reasoning applies to where loyalties should lie within the organization. If an organization is well led and managed, the various units of the organization will be coordinated in directing their energies to achieving the overall goals of the entire organization instead of being focused on aggrandizing the power of just one of its units.

Unfortunately, there is all too often a lack of harmony among these potential objects of loyalty. Loyalty to political or organizational leaders for the purpose of keeping them in power regardless of whether they are serving legitimate public policy goals is a kind of perversion of the public interest. Similarly, if the object of the loyalty is to enhance the power of an organization without reference to broader public policy goals, this brand of loyalty is hardly an ethical virtue in a public official.

It is a common practice for people in public organizations to assume that if they are loyal to their organization they will be serving the public in the process. They are justified in doing so *if* the organizational leadership is devoted to achieving legitimate public policy goals. All too often, however, such loyalty is misplaced. The ethical actor must draw a broad line between loyalty to leaders who wish to hold and exercise power simply for its own sake, and leaders who wish to hold and exercise power in order to meet policy and public objectives.

This is the choice that has faced every leader ascending to a position of high authority, as George Marshall did on becoming US Army chief of staff. His superior, the commander-in-chief and president, though personally inclined to come to the aid of our European allies, was at the same time politically committed to keeping the United States out of a European war. Already planning a run for an unprecedented third term of office, he knew he would be facing an electorate that was opposed to entering or even preparing for a foreign war.

Marshall conceived his role to be the preparation of the Army to enter a major war which, were it to be fought, would threaten vital American interests (Stark 1959, 27).[12] He had seen the disastrous effects of unpreparedness in WW I and knew that a protracted period of time would be required to prepare the country for another great war. He had witnessed in the Philippines and in China the threat posed by Japan and the likelihood of a war there that would make a world war far more difficult strategically, tactically, and logistically than the last one. Both his attention and loyalties were focused upon the nation's *future* welfare, public policy, and actions.

This definition of role meant that his loyalty related principally to the goal of building a strong national defense, and only secondarily to the person of the president. It was nonetheless true that, as a military career man, he had been trained to give absolute loyalty to his superior. If he felt conflict, he placed hope in his belief that the president and members of the Congress were at base reasonable people who loved their country and would eventually come to see that solid preparation for a possible global war was essential to survival. He thus set himself to working to achieve two integrated goals: (1) preparation for global war, and (2) persuasion of his political superiors of the need for preparation. He held steadfast to his conviction that military preparedness was of the utmost importance to the national interest, but he proved his loyalty to this goal in a way that did not sacrifice his loyalty to the president or Congress. He understood that both must be persuaded if he was to gain their undivided support.

He proceeded toward achieving these related goals in a very consistent fashion. If he felt strongly about taking a particular course of action, like the choice of a best strategy for preparation or the pace of build-up, he argued forcefully for it with his political superiors without displaying personal rancor. He took great care to assemble the relevant facts and then used his considerable powers of persuasion to convince others of both their accuracy and implications. This approach normally carried the day. When it did not and his superiors reached a conclusion not to his liking, he would simply accept the decision and work wholeheartedly to implement it in the most effective way possible in the direction of achieving the goal. He didn't grouse, he didn't continue the fight beyond the making of the decision, and he never sabotaged or delayed executing a decision once it was made.

Neither was Marshall tolerant of others who did not wholeheartedly accept and work to implement a decision with which they did not agree. If he asked an officer to assume a new duty or position, and the officer did not respond favorably or dragged his feet, that officer's career was in trouble. For example, when setting up the Joint Chiefs of Staff (JCS) he was permitted to recommend a secretary for it. He turned to a colonel who was present and designated that man as his choice. The officer interjected that he had hoped to have a combat command instead. Marshall summarily rejected the man from consideration, and he was never thereafter promoted (Hilldring 1959, 25-26).

Therefore Marshall squelched the temptation to make a quiet deal with Congress when its leadership finally indicated that it was prepared to move faster than the president could politically tolerate. He continued to argue his case urgently and as persuasively as he could to the president without being contentious (Pogue 1966, 22-23). He even resisted efforts by the president to add troops or weaponry in ways that were not orderly and would create imbalances in military administration. A large military with great resources was not the primary need; rather, an effective military capable of defending American interests over the long run was the guiding objective.

This insistence on being loyal to the public interest in military preparation, while at the same time being unwilling to play off one political superior against another to reach the goal more quickly, exemplified a key Marshall virtue. It was to be manifested time and time again throughout his career.

Integrity and Honesty

"Integrity" comes from the Latin adjective *integer* (in mathematics, a whole number), meaning "whole." A "person of integrity" is one whose life reveals a certain wholeness—that is, an internal consistency, a steadiness, a firmness of character. If a man is a loving father, an upright citizen, a supportive husband, and a fair employer but takes delight in torturing animals, we may conclude that he may be a moral and ethical being in some ways but lacks moral "wholeness" because of an evil flaw. Likewise, integrity includes a disdain for speaking falsely and an unwillingness to act as another person's pawn (Pogue 1966, 16).

Integrity is an individual virtue having to do with the extent to which espoused values and principles actually determine behavior and are consistent with it (Frankena 1973). It is the penultimate virtue in the sense and to the degree that we judge the moral worth of persons by their actions more than their words. No aspect of Marshall's character is more frequently noted than his integrity. As Dean Acheson, undersecretary of state to Marshall and later secretary of state in his own right, said: "The thing that stands out in everybody's recollection of General Marshall is the immensity of his integrity, the loftiness and beauty of his character" (Acheson 1957, 1). Robert Lovett, Marshall's number two man at both the Departments of State and Defense, was describing Marshall's integrity when he said: "You knew perfectly well that there was no pressure which could be put on General Marshall or Colonel Stimson which would make them do something that wasn't proper" (Lovett 1973, 67).

Honesty, or telling the truth, is a virtue that typically accompanies integrity. Truth-telling is a necessary yet not sufficient condition for integrity. President Truman said about Marshall:

> People not only thought he was telling them the truth, he did tell them the truth. He always told me the truth when I was President of the United States (Mosley 1982, 401).

To Lord Ismay, chief of staff to Churchill, Marshall was

> like a rock, something that was so absolutely trustworthy; something that couldn't be broken; something on which everyone could rely; something that was so completely selfless, so truthful. You felt that if he gave his word, you were absolutely safe. If he said he would do a thing—. . . there was no need, no cause for worry—it was as good as a bond. You knew that he was a most faithful servant not only of his own country but of the allies. . . . He was not only thinking in terms of America, he was thinking in terms of world citizenship (Ismay 1960, 12).

Part of honesty is not making a pretense of knowing more than one actually knows or knowingly allow a false impression to continue in another's mind. Marshall would not go beyond what he knew for certain or reasonably could conclude were the facts. His preference for speaking in simple language and backing all his statements with the best factual information he could gather from his background and staff made him a great favorite of congressmen. He would turn frequently to his staff, when questioned, and ask for information in the plain hearing of the committee. There was no pretense or posturing about making it appear that he knew the answer when he did not (Smith 1958, 3).

Coupled with being honest with others is the insistence that others be honest in return. He demonstrated this dramatically in his instructions to the new secretary of the General Staff, Colonel John Deane, immediately after Pearl Harbor. He told Deane that every paper that would reach him (Marshall) would first come to Deane. He wanted Deane to be prepared to tell him what the paper was about; and that if he, Marshall, wanted his secretary's opinion on it, that opinion must be his honest opinion. "And, that if he ever thought that I was saying something because I thought it was what he wanted to hear, then my usefulness to him would be finished" (Deane 1960, 6).

If others surprised him by speaking candidly, he responded with something resembling gratitude. Lewis Douglas, for example, who was working with the War Shipping Administration at the War Department, decided to redirect a ship bound to the Aleutian Islands to Guadalcanal in the South Pacific. Marshall was angry with the decision and found his way to Douglas when he learned that he was the source. When Douglas forthrightly explained the reasons for the decision and told him he was entirely responsible for it, Marshall told him, "Douglas, I like that, at least you are absolutely honest" (Douglas 1962, 21-22).[13]

Decisiveness and the Principle of Action

"Don't agonize over the problem, solve it." These words, famously and frequently uttered by Marshall, point to another important leadership attribute, the ability to initiate action, make decisions, and undertake their implementation without delay. From childhood on he knew the value of taking charge of situations. He had both the passion for command and the willingness to accept the consequences of his actions. Once the facts were before him he moved quickly (Bryden 1958, 14).

Two examples suffice to convey the flavor of this particular virtue. In 1933 he told army officers supervising CCC camps that he would support them if they took the initiative: "I'll be out to see you soon and if I find you doing something, I will help you, but if I find you doing nothing, only God will help you" (Pogue 1963, 278). In 1941 he told graduates of the Army's Officer Candidate School: "Passive inactivity, because you have not been given specific instructions to do this or to do that, is a serious deficiency" (Uldrich 2005, 60).

Pogue asked Admiral of the Fleet Lord Cunningham in 1961 whether Marshall kept his promises. The distinguished British admiral answered in these terms: "Absolutely. Mind you, he wasn't given to promising much. His promises usually took the form of action, probably before he even gave his orders. He believed in action, yes" (Cunningham 1961, 15).

In his interviews with Marshall, Pogue noted the general's indifference to explaining or defending why a particular action was taken or not taken. He would just say, "Well, this is just what we thought best at the time," and let it go at that. This approach may complicate the historian's search for motives but clearly demonstrates a penchant for moving forward and putting aside (which is not the same as forgetting) what is done and finished. He simply found it counterproductive to agonize over decisions once they were made. Major General Charles Bolte, who commanded troops in Italy and later was vice chief of staff of the US Army, made the same point in this way:

> I think his—if not the most outstanding characteristic—certainly one, is his complete avoidance of equivocation. In other words, he has the characteristics of a high military commander, a high leader, of arriving at a clear-cut decision and sticking to that decision (1958, 61).

Marshall's regard for "offensive-mindedness" as a key quality of leadership to be sought in military officer selection led him to demonstrate an appreciation of people who took initiative rather than waiting to be told what to do. When WW II began and as the cost of inaction rose, he showed a particular affinity for men and women of action. He relied heavily on General Brehon Somervell during the reorganization of the War Department in late 1941 to early 1942 because of the latter's dedication to the principle of action. Somervell was rough, insensitive, persistent, ambitious, and interested in acquiring control and power. He was disliked heartily by much of the General Staff and by supply services people in the field, but Marshall defended him:

> I depended on him very, very heavily. His handling of things awakened . . . the hostility of the staff departments. . . . Actually, he was one of the most efficient officers I have ever seen. . . . Whenever I asked him for something, he did it and he got it. He was very forcible. He reformed . . . the Adjutant General's Department and others. He found conditions there were just intolerable and, naturally, they were all bitterly against him. . . . If I went into control in another war, I would start out looking for another General Somervell the very first thing I did, and so would anybody else who went through that struggle on this side (Bland 1991, 445).

Offensive-mindedness is clearly relevant to military organizations and command. How suitable did Marshall find the principle of action in the more contemplative environment of the State Department? It seems fair to say that although he tempered his judgment about how much hostility and disagreement could be tolerated in an organization, the need for deciding and acting once the relevant information was collected and considered remained firm.

A Terse Appraisal by a Wise Man[14]

Scholar-diplomat George Kennan summed up what he thought to be Marshall's virtues as an administrator:

> Monumental integrity first of all, his courage, his orderliness and deliberateness of procedure, his great dignity and real elevation of character which impressed everyone who met him. . . . He was not a brilliant man but he was immensely conscientious. . . . [He] was more aware of the political angles of his job. . . . I respected also his complete fairness as a chief and his cheeriness with praise and his avoidance of . . . light good-fellowship with anyone who worked under him. . . . And when he made up his mind, after the best advice he could get, he made his decision and he went home and slept well at night (1959, 18-19).

Notes

1. Most are collected and catalogued at the George C. Marshall Research Library in Lexington, Virginia.
2. These are also maintained at the Marshall Library in Lexington. See, in particular, the complete record of Pogue's personal interviews with Marshall that have been edited and presented in Bland (1991).
3. These "secondary sources" are found in books, journals, magazines, and newspapers available in many libraries and electronic data banks: see especially Pogue and Harrison 1963; Pogue 1966, 1973, 1987; Stoler 1989; Bland 1998; Cray 1990; Sherwood 1948; Acheson 1969; Neustadt and May 1986; Parrish 1989; and Barber 1997.
4. Marshall continued: "But we got along. Mrs. Bell didn't like me at all at first and afterwards we became devoted friends."
5. When Marshall became secretary of defense four years later, the bills for this operation were shunted over to Defense from the State Department for him to consider paying.
6. Powder later served as one of the pallbearers, by Marshall's request.
7. The girl, Cora Thomas, was by then a mature and competent woman (Thomas 1961).
8. By all accounts, both of these women performed well within his office.
9. He was typically unconcerned with, and often forgot, where officers had gone to school.
10. Both Katherine Marshall and Devers felt that the general carried this ethic of "being correct" too far (Devers 1958, 20).
11. Marshall believed that Clifford was exceeding his expertise and authority in speaking for President Truman and resented his intrusion into the decision process.
12. Admiral Stark, Chief of Naval Operations, said in his interview with Pogue: "We started out both of us with so very little compared to what we needed if we were to get into the war, and while we hoped we wouldn't, there was only one safe assumption and that was to assume the worst and to get ready for it."
13. Later, with President Truman's blessing, Marshall secured Douglas's appointment to London as Ambassador to the United Kingdom, where he served with distinction from 1947 until 1951.

14. The use of the descriptor, "wise man," is a reference to Kennan's inclusion as one of six wise men in a book titled *The Wise Men*, by Walter Isaacson and Evan Thomas. The other wise men were Dean Acheson, Charles "Chip" Bohlen, Averell Harriman, Robert Lovett, and John McCloy.

CHAPTER FOUR
ADDITIONAL ETHICAL ATTRIBUTES

It is what Marshall was, and not what he did, that lingers in the mind—his goodness seemed to put ambition out of countenance.
—Lord Moran[1] (1966, 597)

In this chapter are collected and reported other aspects of Marshall's character. These are not so clearly linked to leadership in the literature, but they are nevertheless part of the man and reflect the style and atmosphere he created in the organizations he led. Taken up in this chapter are both strengths and perceived shortcomings of the manner in which he approached and carried out his various roles, particularly that of chief of staff.

"Menschenkeit": Greatness of Soul

An important quality of a hero is "greatness of soul" (Gibbon 2002, 13). What is this quality? The concept is best expressed by the Yiddish-German word "mensch." *Mensch* refers to a certain presence, bearing, humanity, dignity, humility, and calmness, all acting together to produce a person who is at the same time admirable and unforgettable.

The quality of *presence*—an aura of stature, command, *gravitas*, an ability to attract attention without trying to—arises frequently as a descriptor to describe Marshall. General Maxwell Taylor, serving on the General Staff under Marshall before the war and himself a future Army chief of staff, recalled vividly the day Marshall spoke to mark opening day of the War College in 1939:

> What he said that day I do not remember, but the way he said it, I do. General Marshall never spoke anywhere without receiving the undivided attention of every listener to the words of a man who obviously knew what he was talking about. One could never imagine questioning the accuracy of his facts or challenging the soundness of his conclusions on any subject he undertook to discuss. He did not give the impression of great brilliance of mind, as General MacArthur did, but of calm strength and unshakeable will (Taylor 1972, 36-37).

Robert Lovett, Marshall's second-in-command in his two cabinet posts, and someone who also interacted with him at the War Department during WW II, addressed the matter of presence directly:

General Marshall had a peculiar thing which I think on a stage they call presence. . . . You were aware of the fact that he was there whether he opened his mouth or not and that had an impact on any group of people. . . . It was very impressive to watch. Part of it was the magnetism, what I suppose the boys today writing would call charisma, but whatever it was he had it, in ample perhaps surplus supply (Lovett 1973, 66-67).

Marshall's personality had a favorable effect upon the British. At every meeting he was accepted by British leadership as the leader of America's war team. Anthony Eden reported to Churchill on his first meeting with General Marshall: "He seems to me a modern edition of Robert E. Lee" (Eden 1961, 9). His words were accepted as representing the final American position (Smith 1958, 7). Lord Ismay added his opinion that, taken as a whole, Marshall stood first in stature among all the personalities of WW II, a "completely selfless" man, "absolutely straight" (Ismay 1960, 8-9).

It is revealing that part of his ability to dominate any interaction lay in the trust he generated by trying *not* to dominate. He spoke infrequently and listened intently to others (Smith 1958, 7; and McCloy 1959, 1), "but when he saw something was going off the track, he could take it away from the President or Mr. Churchill or anybody else that was present" (McCloy 1959, 1). He would only assert himself when confident in his information.

His presence was derived in part from his elegant physical appearance. This in turn was based on his neat but simple dress, rectitude, and an aura of dignity. Standing just below six feet and of medium weight, he stood and sat erectly but not stiffly. He looked to be fit, perhaps even athletic, despite the arm partially disabled by a childhood injury. He dressed neatly and without unnecessary decoration or flamboyant flourishes. This simplicity set him apart from many military personalities of his time (for example, Patton with his jodhpurs and spurs; MacArthur with his frayed hats).[2] Edward R. Murrow observed:

Marshall is a man who held himself erect, but with a loose rein, the most completely self-contained man I have ever known, capable of sitting through a long speech or a committee hearing without moving a muscle, but at the same time there was no tension about him (CBS, September 12, 1951).

The personal attributes contributing most strongly to *menschenkeit*, in Marshall's case, included civility, compassion and kindness, a penchant for direct and simple speech, humility, ability to accept change and keep cool in a crisis, capacity for friendship, a sense of order and propriety, and accessibility and openness. Undoubtedly, his reputation for integrity, honesty, optimism, fairness, and courage, discussed in the preceding chapter, also contributed. For all of these traits, as well as for his professional competence, he was universally admired. Reflecting on these traits, Lovett spoke from the heart shortly after the general's death:

Much has been said of General Marshall as a great public figure but not nearly enough about him as a very great human being. . . . His eminence in leadership, it seems to me, was a talent bestowed by a divine Providence and heightened by use and experience. . . . His greatness, however, was enriched by personal traits which, like ardor, spring from the heart. He was a man of extraordinary compassion, of most sensitive and discriminating instinct, and there was an air of natural elegance about him which was unassuming and added enormously to his calm dignity. . . . There were two qualities which seemed to me to have had deep, perhaps even controlling, influence in lifting him to the heights of true greatness: first, his sincere concern for others; and secondly, his acceptance of change as a law of nature (Lovett 1960).

Compassion and exceptional kindness remained constant features of his character throughout his career; yet his extreme reserve and sense of correctness often served to hide his interest in the welfare of others (Hilldring 1959, 3). Wrapping up his duties at the San Francisco Presidio in 1916, he dictated a note of thanks to a telephone operator, noting her efficiency in reaching people for him at all hours. While revisiting the site in the early 1920s with General Pershing, he mentioned the woman to Pershing and the base commander and his wife. The commander's wife wanted to meet the woman, who was still there, and arranged a three-way meeting with Marshall. The woman told them that in her long service, receiving his earlier note was the first time she had ever been thanked.

One of Marshall's fondest memories was a pre-WWI Christmas party he put on for children at a post near Little Rock, Arkansas. Five days before Christmas he discovered that no celebration had been planned for the children and brought this to the attention of the post commander, who promptly gave Marshall the task. He collected money, talked Little Rock merchants into supplying toys at bargain prices, recruited a Santa Claus and convinced him to build a chimney in the post gymnasium, and got some army prisoners to volunteer to decorate the gymnasium. He rewarded the volunteers by allowing them to give out the presents to the children on Christmas morning. Later that day, he found the prisoners gathered in the guardhouse. Their spokesman said that only one of them had ever celebrated Christmas at home—now Lieutenant Marshall had given Christmas to them all. If ever he called upon any one of them to do anything, he was told, they would come if they could (Pogue 1963, 117-118).

Marshall was not a man who spoke ill of others (Bland 1991, 12; Eisenhower 1962, 3-4; Gerow 1958, 56) or felt animus towards those who may have slighted or worked against him. When Lieutenant General Drum was passed over for chief of staff by Roosevelt in favor of Marshall, he (Drum) issued a report critical of Army policy in areas of training and organization. He did so perhaps out of pique but clearly outside the bounds of his authority. Instead of admonishing him "Marshall leaned over backwards . . . to back him up without contradicting him. . . . In my estimation, it was a great example of a great man not trying to take on somebody that is now temporarily beneath him and embarrass him" (Buchanan 1958, 10-11).

Although Marshall did not allow others to criticize his subordinates (Gerow 1958, 56) and looked after certain of their needs (such as comfortable accommodations), it was clear he did not coddle them (Bryden 1958,5). Indeed, he showed a decided preference for the morale of the common soldier over that of the officer. He could be oblivious to how hard the officers around him were working (Gallagher 1962, 46-47; Groves 1970). Once, waiting on an airfield tarmac on a very hot day with several uniformed officers for the arrival of the secretary of war, he was asked whether the officers must be kept standing in the sun. He said, "Those officers have kept more GI's waiting in the sun for more years. It is about time they waited in the sun" (Bundy 1959, 33).

This preference for the common person was a constant. On his frequent visits to military posts and other travels he would go out of his way to speak with common soldiers, young boys considering military service, a farmer standing in a field, a crowd waiting at the wrong train gate to greet him, a cook in a kitchen (Geier 1959, 7; Bundy 1959, 30). General Deane, secretary to the General Staff at the beginning of WW II, talked about Marshall's style: "He was a very kindly man but he hated people to catch him at [it]." Deane recalled the time that an old black man named Henderson, head of the janitorial service for the Office of the Chief of Staff, was retiring. Deane interrupted a high-level meeting just prior to a scheduled departure in order to get Marshall's signature on a congratulatory letter. When he bent to tell Marshall the reason for the interruption the general pardoned himself, went to the outer office to get and sign a photograph, "signed the letter, got Henderson in, told him what a wonderful job he had done, shook hands with him, gave him the photograph" and said goodbye, never expecting to see him again (Deane 1960, 6).

Occasionally the kindness had an instrumental purpose. When Prime Minister Churchill threatened to reassign Marshall's close friend and confidant, Field Marshal Sir John Dill from his post in Washington to India, Marshall went to extraordinary lengths to have Yale University bestow honors upon Dill. This attention convinced Churchill to retain Dill in Washington to the relief of the American chiefs of staff. Another case of purposeful kindness involved General MacArthur, who had done Marshall's career no favors. When Marshall reached MacArthur on Corregidor in early 1942 with the message that he should be rescued with his family and chief aides, MacArthur replied impertinently, saying he would get out but only when he was ready. Marshall persisted, arranging both for the escape of MacArthur's family and chief aides to Australia and his appointment as supreme commander of the Pacific Southwest Theater of operations. Marshall's compassion in this case is best explained by his assessment of MacArthur as a great field general whose services would advance the war effort (Sexton 1958, 29-30).[3]

As already noted, Marshall disliked attention being called to his person. While chief of staff, he suppressed or discouraged awards, honors, publicity, and special events intended to honor him. His staff was instructed to convey these instructions in preparation of his visits to military bases, graduation ceremonies, public speaking engagements, and the like (Memorandum to General Osborn, March 23, 1944; Bland and Stevens 1996, 368).[5] When Churchill sent a tribute for Marshall to

Secretary of War Henry Stimson, Marshall managed to suppress its distribution throughout the department, claiming it would embarrass him (Bland and Stevens 1991). Still, he could not totally avoid spontaneous expressions of gratitude. In the twilight of his career, as he and General Bradley walked down the aisle at Westminster Abbey prior to Queen Elizabeth's coronation procession, row after row of prominent people rose to their feet. "Who are they rising for?" whispered Marshall to Bradley. "You," Bradley answered (Lubetkin 1989, 7).

According to one of his closest aides, Marshall was offended when officers were given too much credit for the achievements of their organizations. He called the practice of claiming personal credit "self-advertising." Conversely, recognizing and giving others credit in the form of medals, letters of commendation, or assigning more responsibility to signal their competence were all part of his management style (Pasco 1997, 21).

In a real sense the concept of credit was irrelevant to him. Real achievement lay in doing a good job in cooperation with others in moving toward accomplishing measurable goals. The achievement itself should constitute the bulk of the credit and honor and should not depend on currying public gratitude. Identifying the major actors in gaining positive results is necessary, because the people with relevant skills must continue to be used to achieve other national and public objectives. It followed that he took a dim view of those under his command that indulged themselves in self-promotion or credit-grabbing and held such behavior against them in making decisions about career advancement.

When Congress moved, at the Navy's urging, to create the five-star rank during the war in order to give King, Leahy, Marshall, and Eisenhower status equal to the highest-ranking military officers in other nations (British and Soviet "marshals" had five stars, and the French awarded a sixth), Marshall opposed the proposal. The Navy was a bit miffed. He argued that he did not wish personal recognition and did not need more rank to do his job (Heffner 1995, 19). Only after Roosevelt and Pershing threw in their support did he relent, and then only under two conditions. First, the special rank should be extended to include Generals MacArthur and Arnold and Admiral Nimitz. Second, the title should be changed to "General of the Army" and thus not compete with Pershing's existing designation as "General of the Armies" (Uldrich 2005, 89).

Selflessness was evident in Marshall's character at every stage of his career. Edward Bowditch, who served with him in WW I, recalled:

> He was utterly unselfish in his feeling toward other officers. . . . There are certain officers who are rather selfish and who get things because they use all the strings. George . . . never used any strings on anybody, but just stood on his own feet and got his promotions through hard work and results (Bowditch 1959, 10).

In that war Marshall was offered a temporary field promotion from lieutenant colonel to brigadier general and refused it. When asked why he would take such an unusual step, he is reported to have answered that he did not wish to be promoted over many colonels who were his seniors. "If, later on, they want to make me a general, I'll be glad to accept it" (Coulter 1960, 3a). General Herron found him to be "one of the few men I've ever known who I felt was wholly without guile" (Herron 1958, 27).

It is entirely in keeping with his view on the role of self that in his famous reports to the nation on the progress of the war, for which he wrote the texts, there was not a single usage of the word "I" (*Time* 1944).

Publicity, he believed, should be reserved for situations where it might advance an important military or national objective, such as the sale of war bonds or public support for feeding the hungry or rebuilding Europe's economy. Calling attention to self or one's organization only distracted from the need to concentrate upon mission accomplishment (Hart and Hart 1992). Indeed, publicity could have serious negative effects on the organization's mission, especially if it was being generated by news sources without a full command of the facts or the context on which they were reporting. Worse, too much personal publicity was likely to engender irritation or jealousy in other parts of the government.

Marshall knew how information could be manipulated and used unfairly. Prior to the pivotal Meuse-Argonne campaign of October-November 1918, the general plan put together in September by American commanders and staff, including Marshall, called for covertly redeploying vast numbers of troops and supplies from the St-Mihiel part of the front. This unique maneuver had to be accomplished within a finite time over ground best described as a no-man's land of devastation and shell craters. Engineers had virtually no time to reconstruct roads over a battleground that had become part of the rear in the wake of the rapid advance (Marshall 1976, 162-164). To the military mind, such difficulties were simply what the Army does when fighting over ravaged land and were seen "merely as something which must be overcome, and that speedily, and [we] had no thought that we had tied ourselves up." But to the naive observer the seeming chaos, vehicle losses, and delays in movement of the wounded to care stations in the rear and movement of supplies and replacements to the front were bewildering. The novice observers reported to their readers what appeared to them incompetence and chaos, an impression pushed by the British perhaps to weaken President Wilson in the peace talks. Marshall contemptuously traced the effects:

> At the moment the army was accomplishing a miracle of achievement, these broadcasters furnished all the fuel possible . . . to subdivide our army and utilize its divisions after their own fashion. . . . The propaganda built out of this incident grew by leaps and bounds. Its poisonous touch reached even the President of the United States, and like a snowball it continued to gather weight and size after the Armistice, apparently with the object of depreciating the American effort in order to weaken Mr. Wilson's powerful position at the opening of the Peace Conference in Paris (Marshall 1976, 163)[4]

Despite his aversion to the limelight, his service as the administration's congressional point man after 1939 on virtually all national security policy issues put him there routinely. The adulation his Congressional and media appearances prompted may have embarrassed him but did not induce him to withdraw from the role.

The ability to stay calm under pressure and a sense of propriety were other Marshall trademarks. Former President Truman called him "a man you couldn't ruffle. . . . When they were cussing him out in Congress, like Jenner (Republican senator from Indiana), calling him every name in the book that they could think of, he never lost his temper, and he never answered back. He wouldn't take the time" (Miller 1974, 227-28). General Brereton noted "a quiet mannerism and a method of never making you feel there was pressure on you" (1962, 29).

Dean Acheson, with reference to the Korean war of 1950, called him a "towering figure of strength in times of disaster." Marshall, along with Generals Bradley and Collins, remained perfectly calm in the Fall of 1950 when the Chinese intervened and smashed up many UN units. This allowed Acheson and other administration officials, including President Truman, to be "perfectly sure in their minds that disasters predicted by General MacArthur would not occur, and enabled us all to come through this thing" (Acheson 1957, 4).

Marshall's calm demeanor owed much to his conviction that a person cannot allow himself to worry about things he can do nothing to change. It is probable that this wisdom was gained from severe experience and disaster—including mental breakdowns, death and chaos on the battlefield, and his first wife's unexpected death. When General Lee, his chief of intelligence, went on sick leave in 1943 for extreme anxiety, he wrote to Mrs. Lee that, at least for himself, "I have been able to go along and do my best and not give much of a damn beyond that." Still, he recognized that "the hardest job is to prevail upon certain individuals to stop worrying" and that if "one starts to worry it does not help much even to realize it is bad to worry" (letter to Mrs. Raymond E. Lee, July 13, 1943; Bland and Stevens 1996, 58-59). His inner calm helped stabilize the environments in which he worked and led others to focus on the task at hand and do their best.

Concern with protocol and amenities contributed to a sense of order. Anthony Eden enthused about Marshall's role at the several great wartime conferences: "I never once, on these many occasions, saw Marshall other than courteous and patient. That is why, I think, all of us on the British side felt for him the utmost respect and admiration" (Eden 1961, 10). He was rarely profane, apologized when he was, and did not raise his voice or bawl out soldiers, officers, or staff (Gallagher 1962, 52).

Persuasiveness

Sometimes included as an essential trait of leadership, persuasiveness places great stress on factual accuracy and careful preparation. It played a major part in his role as an effective advocate. Assistant Secretary of War Harvey Bundy remarked on Marshall's clarity of expression and a facility for persuasive advocacy that was linked to his well-known mastery of military professional knowledge (Bundy 1959, 30). He was seen in Congress as a most convincing speaker, always prepared, and with an air of sincerity that carried conviction. He excelled in his ability to get huge appropriations from Congress. One reason for his success was that he was seen as being above expressing a partisan view or engaging in politics (Senator James Byrnes 1959, 1-2).

Frederick Osborn, who represented the US on the UN Atomic Energy Commission and worked for Marshall during WW II, stressed the effect of the general's passion on his ability to be persuasive:

> General Marshall was a very, very powerful and moving speaker. I heard Woodrow Wilson at his best. I heard William Jennings Bryan at almost his best, but none of them could hold a candle to General Marshall when he wanted to make people do things. When he got through speaking . . . you said, "Yes." When he came to the conclusion that something should be done, he said it with such a firmness and with such solidity, that you just agreed with him. You knew he was right (Osborn 1959, 7-8).

Accepting Criticism

One of the lessons that Marshall learned from Pershing was Pershing's unusual practice of receiving criticism without seeming irritation, so long as the criticism related to the effectiveness of his military organization (Bland 1991, 111-112). Their first encounter involved Marshall criticizing Pershing's headquarters procedures for the conduct of formal troop review. Instead of being hurt or angry, Pershing had responded by listening, then turning to the younger officer for more analysis and criticism. Marshall was to mirror this behavior in his own career.

Not only did Marshall accept criticism, he sometimes asked for it. After Bradley's first week working as an assistant for the Secretariat of the General Staff under the chief of staff, Marshall admonished him and the other assistants. "I'm disappointed in all of you. You have not disagreed with anything I've done all week." Several days later, the secretariat staff attacked a General Staff study in their presentation. Marshall responded:

> Now, that's what I want. Unless I hear all the arguments for or against an action I am about to take, I don't know whether or not I'm right. If I hear all the arguments against some action and still find in favor of it, I'm *sure* I'm right" (Bradley and Blair 1983, 84; emphasis is the author's).

In one of his first meetings with Dean Acheson after appointing Acheson undersecretary of state, Marshall urged Acheson always to be candid and outspoken with him and brutally frank. Acheson need not worry about hurting his feelings. "I have no feelings except those I reserve for Mrs. Marshall" (Mosley 1982, 401-402).

Allegations surfaced in the wake of the attack on Pearl Harbor that Marshall had not properly informed the command at Pearl of the danger of attack, and that he intentionally had made himself difficult to find on the morning of the attack. A thorough Congressional investigation was delayed until the end of the war. A man who was expected to be criticized could have been expected to talk to other principals during the war in order to prepare a defense. Marshall would not do so.

He did not regard it as proper to avoid criticism if it was to come (memorandum to Cordell Hull, December 14, 1945; Bland and Stevens 2003, 392).

Nor would Marshall keep a diary or write defensive memoirs. When he heard after the fact that General Lucas had kept a diary during the campaign at Anzio, Marshall told his informant: "the primary job of the commander was the successful conduct of these operations, not keeping a record of them. He should have his mind on the future (operations), and not on the past" (Marshall 1949, 22).

Humility

Marshall Carter served General Marshall as an aide at the end of WW II and again as an executive assistant in the latter's assignments as secretary of the Departments of State and Defense. He observed that Marshall genuinely believed he was not special:

> Possibly the most astounding personal quality in this man who held three of the most powerful jobs in the world was his humility. When, during his last years, people would recognize him and burst into spontaneous applause, he would invariably turn around to see who was being applauded (Carter 1972, 6).

Soon after the Joint Chiefs of Staff came into being in 1942, chief of naval operations Admiral Ernest King, a man very aware and protective of his status, was unintentionally kept waiting in the general's outer office. King stalked off. Marshall, after discovering the situation, grabbed his hat and ran next door on Constitution Avenue to King's office to make amends. King's feelings were still ruffled when Marshall arrived. Marshall told Deane when he returned:

> I went in and saw King and I impressed on him in no uncertain terms that if we were going to fight a war together we had to do it as men and not children and that as a matter of fact the reason I was late is that I was trying to keep some Guatemalans off of his back" (Deane 1960, 13).[5]

Marshall had understood King's weakness of vanity and compensated for it by humbling himself in the interest of building a relationship critical to mission achievement.

Discipline and Self-Discipline

Marshall's ideas about discipline were not typical of the military leadership of his day. The concept of discipline he had learned as a student at VMI and that was in vogue in many of the posts in which he served was a discipline that was externally imposed and aimed at securing rote obedience. In contrast, he preached that the best type of discipline was internally developed. Self-discipline was particularly appropriate for the type of citizen-soldier he envisaged, a person rooted in the civilian world but who must be trained to be an effective soldier.

Civilian-soldiers, he reasoned, were most effective if they had a high degree of independence and were allowed to question the purposes and means of their service. Such an approach breeds initiative instead of rote obedience. Obedience, particularly in combat, was crucial, but in Marshall's words, "the staying power, the spirit which endures to the end—the will to win" was based on reason and seeing the need to follow orders and to contribute. The "new discipline," he continued in his speech at Trinity College in Hartford, Connecticut in June 1941, was based on:

> . . . replacing force of habit of body with force of habit of mind. We are basing the discipline of the individual on respect rather than on fear . . . ; on the effect of good example given by officers; on the intelligent comprehension by all ranks of why an order has to be and why it must be carried out; on a sense of duty, on *esprit de corps* (de Weerd 1945, 123-124).

It was better "to direct men by trying to make them see the way to go" rather than telling them; he applied this philosophy to civilians and army officers alike (Stoler 1989, 25). In other words, it is preferable to have people ask themselves what behaviors they should adopt and what virtues they should inculcate than to have an external source impose correction.

He did not believe in punishment. His actions in response to improper conduct were normally confined to keeping persons out of decision-making roles or from exercising authority over others. It was more important to take an action that would convey clear meaning and resolve. General Patton's comment when he was brought into planning talks for the North Africa landing was that he "would take the Goddamn landing craft and run it right up the Germans' asses," and if he encountered any difficulties with the US Navy he "would just kick them overboard" (Handy 1956, 1). On the same visit he asked Marshall for the command of an Army Corps rather than the smaller division which Marshall had offered. Marshall's telegraphic response to Patton's request was to assign Patton back to the Desert Training Center near Palm Springs, California to train tank corpsmen without reprimand or even so much as a comment. Patton replied, apologizing humbly and stating that he wanted to serve in any way he could be most useful. Marshall then sent him to Africa to lead the entire Western Task Force (more than one-third of the entire invasion force). Patton served there and later on in Italy and France with great effect.

Self-discipline is directed at oneself, and as a result Marshall learned to demand at least as much of himself as others. He had learned self-control and responsibility at VMI. Being the student cadet on the top of each class had an important effect upon him: "in my job as First Captain [I] had to exercise authority all the time and I had to do it in such a way that didn't create resentment" (Bland 1991, 118). When he was forced to impose discipline, he directed it at whole units rather than individuals and without anger.

Openness and Accessibility

In the part of his career already presented Marshall was not only approachable but went out of his way to create incentives for social activity, discussion, the expression of unconventional ideas, and even dissent. At Tientsin and Fort Benning, for example, he was constantly organizing sports activities, book discussions, horse-mounted fox and treasure hunts, and cultural and social events for officers and their families, where he was available for conversation and consultation. Opportunities for interaction were plentiful in these and other pre-WW II assignments (Gallagher 1962; Bull 1959, 19).

Beginning with his ascendancy in 1939 to chief of staff the situation changed in several ways. The engaged, softer personality of earlier days was replaced by a sternness brought on by the rigors of crushing responsibility and extraordinary demands upon time and energy. A thorough-going reorganization of the General Staff (see Chapter Nine) limited the number of officers who had the right to report to him from sixty-odd to just six, in order to create clear lines of authority and speed communications.[6] Then too, he developed a style that tended to put off more junior subordinates while he remained open to immediate staff and outside visitors. All of this contributed to a growing reputation for "aloofness."

Colonel David Barrett, who became reacquainted with Marshall in China in 1946, twenty years after their association at Tientsin, spoke frankly to Pogue in 1959 about the change he saw in the man he so much admired. Unlike the 1920s at Tientsin, Marshall rarely showed his gift for kindness in the workplace or while engaged in official duties:

> Carrying that heavy burden, it would tend to divest him—he couldn't afford to be soft in any way, . . . had to be right on the beam every single second, and any tendency to be kindly or something like that, might have led him into doing something that would have had an effect on the course of history (Barrett 1959, 19).

Chief Deputy General T. T. Handy thought him "probably the busiest man in Washington" who "always had time enough to do everything, but no spare time." Handy said that his time was so precious that he lacked patience with people who did not come quickly to the point or who did not state their needs or requests clearly. Under this pressure, those who spoke to him could become inarticulate or ramble. At such times, he turned his attention to other matters on his desk and left them standing uncomfortably (Handy 1959, 28-30).

The same mixture of being accessible but not wishing to suffer from the hesitancy of others showed itself in the notice posted on his office door. "Once you open this door, WALK IN, no matter what is going on inside." The tentative soul who might back out annoyed him mightily (K. T. Marshall 1947, 59).

This style in dealing with subordinates contrasted sharply with the receptivity shown to the press. He would share information with them that his staff felt he should not disclose. He took the newsmen into his confidence by telling them that there was something he wanted them to know for background purposes, something secret perhaps, but that they should understand it was not for publication. A good example of his knack for walking the line between his innate desire for openness and the need for wartime secrecy is shown by a technique he used in the midst of rapidly building up the air and ground defenses of the Philippine Islands in November, 1941. He was concerned lest leakage of information about this redirection of resources led the Japanese to conclude that it was in their interest to attack the Philippines before the American buildup was far along. The movement of supplies and personnel was of such magnitude that it was only a matter of time before a perceptive reporter would break the story. To prevent this, he called in a group of responsible news leaders (representatives of the New York Times, New York Herald Tribune, *Time*, *Newsweek*, and the major wire services were invited) to an early Saturday morning briefing.

As they sat in his office looking at maps of the Pacific theater, its airbases and the range of aircraft stationed there, Marshall explained that what he had to tell them was to remain secret. If this was unacceptable they were free to leave. They all stayed. He went on to say that war with Japan was imminent, laid out the Philippine strategy (without details) and the administration's hope that if the buildup could be completed and only then revealed to the Japanese, enemy aggression could be avoided or in the very least delayed until the US could reach a higher state of preparedness (Pogue 1966, 201-202).

He listened with intensity and without arguing. Walter Robertson, the number two man in the Marshall Mission in China in 1945-46, stated:

> . . . he listened very attentively and almost impassively to what you had to say to him. I've never known him to . . . try to argue you out of your position. . . . I didn't mean he didn't discuss things with you but he always impressed me as being very objective in trying to find out what the realities were without trying to prove anything. I think he had absolute selfless objectivity in doing what he set out to do (1962, 6).

Dividing Work and Personal Time

Pershing's influence also lay at the core of Marshall's practice of separating work from off-duty time. The two would socialize like two good friends off the job, "[b]ut when I came to the office . . . it was just business as though we hadn't been together before" (Bland 1991, 110-11). Those who worked with Marshall, especially later in his career, made the same observation about him. As chief of staff his demeanor at the office remained all business and he became even more direct and humorless.

Even people who had worked in close proximity to him at Fort Benning and other posts reported that when they went to work for the General Staff and came in for the first time to Marshall's office, he did not acknowledge their relationship even though it was certain that he knew them (Deane 1960, 4). "But you might have been just a perfect stranger to him as far as his ever having seen you. He would look right through you" (Gallagher 1962, 52).

At the workplace he discouraged familiarity, addressed others by only their last name or rank, and signed his personal correspondence in the same impersonal manner, as "Marshall" or "GCM." Robert Lovett, Marshall's closest associate at the Departments of State and Defense and a close friend, was invariably called "Lovett." Marshall even made it clear to President Roosevelt to address him, and more importantly to think of him, as "General" and not "George."

He saw a close relationship between being impersonal on the job and being fair, a cardinal virtue of ethical leadership. He believed that personalities and interpersonal relations should never influence matters of policy or organization and that feelings about people detracted from sound judgment. The distance he created undoubtedly helped him psychologically to make decisions, such as those concerning appointments to field commands and promotions in rank (Rusk 1990, 133).

This practice led to the perception that the general was aloof and austere. However, it seems likely that this perception is more an observation on his management style than proof of an innate personality trait. What was perceived as aloofness was instead the combination of a natural reserve plus an attitude that effective organizational functioning required an impersonal approach.

Subordinates tried with mixed success to follow their chief's example. Dean Rusk, chief of the UN desk at the Department of State under Marshall, reflected on the general's admonition not to mix work and friendship after he tried to follow the general's example as President Kennedy's secretary of state. He felt its only result was that he "developed a reputation for being aloof and enigmatic" (Rusk 1990, 133).

Away from work, as it had been with Pershing, it was another story. Marshall was relaxed, easily approached, friendly and informal, "a very humble sort of man" (Geier 1959, 8). He was warm and unfailingly kind and demonstrated an appealing sense of humor (Pasco 1997, 4, 7). Even at work, the basic warmth of the man would occasionally creep in, particularly into his correspondence which he typically filled with gracious notes and considerate gestures to friends, associates, and their families.

Recreation and Time Off

One criticism that Marshall had about his cadet days at VMI was the lack of vacation time. The additional time gained for duty, he felt, only led to staleness and reduced effectiveness (Bland 1991, 116-17). He would constantly urge his subordinates and commanders to take time off for family and to recreate, and backed up these personal exhortations by fashioning policies for rotation, forced rest and relaxation leaves, and time away from combat.

His routine during WW II sharply separated official and personal time (Bryden 1958, 14). Except for times of great urgency, he insisted upon leaving the office at five o'clock and rarely took his work home with him. An associate in the chief of staff's office recalled that he asked Marshall to sign a document as he was reaching for his hat to leave for the day. Marshall replied, "If I must sign it now, I should have signed it at 9 o'clock this morning. I'll be back at that time tomorrow. Good day, gentlemen," and walked out (Brooks 1964, 21).

On a typical workday, even during WW II, he rode his horse in the early morning, departed the office at noon to have lunch with his wife at home, and often followed lunch with a brief nap, all a tonic to his sense of well-being. He treasured the quiet routine of his home life, his garden, his family and friendships, casual reading, and frequent movies with his wife. Always there were great pressures but he felt he could perform much better with a fresh mind, broad interests, and his sense of humor intact. He was once asked why he spent so much time in his garden:

> Well, my answer is simple. First, it's a pause, it gives me relaxation. It's a form of exercise that I enjoy and there's an end product which I enjoy at my table. But I suppose the most important part is —the hoe can't talk (Pratt and George 1962, 11).

He typically counseled subordinates to do likewise. A surprising letter to an executive officer at a domestic post that he had just promoted to brigadier general illustrates his philosophy:

> Dear Magruder:
> . . . out of my deep regard for you and your future, I want to make a few and very confidential, personal comments on . . . being a brigadier general. You have always worked too hard; you have done too many other people's work. This all but cost you your promotion. . . . Now I counsel you to make a studied business of relaxing and taking things easy, getting to the office late, taking trips, and making everybody else work like hell. It is pretty hard for a leopard to change its spots, but you must cloak your new rank with a deliberate effort to be quite casual. . . . I woke up at about thirty-three to the fact that I was working myself to death, to my superior's advantage, and that I was acquiring the reputation of being merely a pick and shovel man. From that time on I made it a business to avoid, so far as possible, detail work, and to relax as completely as I could manage in a pleasurable fashion. . . . I have finally gotten to the point where I sometimes think I am too casual about things; but I think I have reaped a greater advantage than this other possible disadvantage. Please take me very seriously. You have wonderful qualities, but you are too conscientious. I will be delighted to find that you have decided to take leave and do a little traveling before you report for duty, and I would be even more pleased if I had to write you later on and tell you that you were absenting yourself too frequently from your duties. With my most sincere regard for your future,
> Faithfully yours, G.C.M.

The pattern continued after the war. Rusk thought that one of the things that made Marshall so effective in the State Department was that he did only those things which the secretary of state could do, went home at four-thirty or five o'clock each day, and trusted the rest to his subordinates (Rusk 1990, 534).

Recreation played an important role in his vision of work. He told his people to get out of the workplace anytime they had caught up on their tasks, and to hunt, go riding, or play tennis. "There is no law against your thinking, but do it out there. You can see things and do things that are of permanent value to you." When it came to horses, more than recreation was probably intended. For Marshall, horsemanship related not only to physical condition and sociability but to military training as well; caring for and riding horses built character and vaulting over jumps and getting thrown toughened people. Horse-mounted hunts at Benning (opened also to spouses and children) not only promoted competition but, more importantly, offered training in reading maps, following directions, pursuing missions, using compasses, finding one's way in the dark, and exploring different types of terrain—woodlands, swamps, bridges, and streams. Learning teamwork was central to it all (Bull 1959, 20-21).

Memory

Like many leaders, George Marshall was known for his memory. He would remember practically every detail of long briefings and retain them for weeks (Handy 1956, 2). He remembered any paper he had seen and would become irritated if the Office of the Secretariat, which had problems with filing and access up until the war began, couldn't find it immediately (Deane 1960, 7).

As a student at Fort Leavenworth he had worked hard to train his memory. He tried to remember at least one fact about everyone he met—an officer's wound, a secretary's child, a special task well done by an aide. He would say, "this is something I must remember and he sticks it in a pigeon hole [in his mind] and there it stays" (Betts 1958, 1). Frequently, when talking to a group of fifteen or twenty reporters, he would elicit their verbal questions without answering, and then proceed to answer each question while looking directly at the reporter who had asked the question (Brooks 1964, 24).

Humor

Sometimes on the job, but mostly away from it, Marshall saw the advantage of levity and light-heartedness. Humor and good-natured kidding, he believed, were particularly important in the management of stress. At the height of enormous strain in preparing for the battle of St. Mihiel, Marshall cavorted with his friend and colleague:

> Colonel Grant was one of those unusually capable men with initiative and a highly developed sense of responsibility, who at the same time enjoyed the relaxation of a little frivolous badinage to lessen the strain. The more serious the situation, the more absurdities we usually indulged in, for our own private amusement, and even after our duties separated us we usually employed the telephone for a short time each day to exchange the latest story and offer a few words of cheer and encouragement. While this may seem incongruous in connection with the conduct

of a battle, yet it played an important part in promoting optimism, and I find it has left me with many delightful recollections (Marshall 1976, 129).[7]

Frugality

The semi-poverty of Marshall's boyhood taught him the hard lesson of making do with what he had and was applied in the workplace. Putting the needs of the Army into a larger context, he "consistently urged his colleagues in the Pentagon to be practical in their budget demands and to consider the impact of these demands on the economy as a whole." Economy also helps to explain his support for the policy of universal military training. He believed this approach would convince the world of America's resolve, yet at a reasonable price. "It also explains his consistent opposition to [Secretary of Defense] Forrestal's efforts to inflate the defense budget" (Hogan 1998, 104).

Frugality also helped to forge his exceptionally close relationship with Congress and Senator Harry S. Truman (then chairman of the Senate's Special Committee to Investigate the National Defense Program). Marshall was not the least bit defensive as Truman and his colleagues searched for waste and fraud in military spending. He whole-heartedly facilitated the committee's inquiries, an action that endeared him to Truman and launched their exceptionally close relationship.

During the war he found himself weighing expense against human life. He seemed to be of two minds. On one hand, it was better to buy new equipment and have abundant supplies in readiness in order to keep casualties down and ensure success in operations, even though the action must ultimately end up leaving the nation with unexpended stores of surplus weapons, ordnance, and supplies. On the other hand, he believed that a cavalier attitude toward the budget would result in two negatives: (1) loss of confidence of the legislature and perhaps the public, who needed the funds for other public purposes in addition to defense and making war; and (2) an unbalancing of military forces through favoring one arm too much over another, leading to demoralization and internal bickering.

Expecting Ethical Conduct of Others

Ethics may be thought of as the broad category of principles and practices related to the aims and behaviors of society, organizations, communities, and nations. The particulars vary with the societies in which they operate and also with time. In an important sense this description is an academic one—in lay terms, ethics is about goodness. George Marshall did not fret over whether he was doing good—his practices of virtue were so settled and consistent that goodness was, for him, implicit in his actions. What did matter to him was that those in the organizations he served and led (the Army, the State Department, the American Red Cross, the Defense Department) were professional, were good people, and gave their full efforts to the nation they served.

He believed that people should be clear about the roles and obligations that were settled upon them by the law, policy, and their employer. Decisions must be based on what is best for the nation and what will achieve the legitimate mission of the organization. They should not be premised on what best serves the organization itself or its members, and certainly not on what might be advantageous to an individual's career. Once decisions had cranked their way through the democratic lawmaking process and had become policy, public servants were obliged to carry them out as well as they were capable of doing. Doing so was a natural reflex to the trust placed in a public servant by one's employer, commander, or nation.

The quest for excellence began with himself. He conducted himself in a manner that set a clear model for others to emulate (Douglas 1962, 22).[8] He possessed a strong moral code honoring marital fidelity and avoiding fraternization with foreign nationals, honest dealing and thrift, acquiring knowledge relevant to his duties, and following through on promises. Nowhere in his letters and memoranda, the recollections of others, or in his associations with others is there a hint of indiscretion, a dishonest act, or a knowing misrepresentation. The faults that may be ascribed to him seem to have been relatively trivial.

These qualities, far from making him a bloodless crusader for righteousness, shaped him as a gentle nurturer of common decency who had respect for others and an expectation of their good-faith performance and humane behavior. Both by example and design, Marshall projected his own values onto those in the organizations he led. He expected the most from officers entrusted with the greatest responsibility. They should strive for excellence for themselves as well as bring forth excellence in those they led. He said in a speech to a group of officers:

> Never for an instant can you divest yourselves of the fact that you are officers. On the athletic field, at the club, in civilian clothes, or even at home on leave, the fact that you are a commissioned officer in the Army imposes a constant obligation to higher standards than might ordinarily seem normal or necessary for your personal guidance (Fitton 1991, 303).

Shortcomings and Human Failings

As with any human being, Marshall had weaknesses. Although none of them can be described accurately as ethical lapses, a few of them relate to management style. They involve mechanical skills or mental functioning, self-control, and interpersonal skills. The "defects" noted are not consistent over time and observers might even disagree on whether they exist at all. Some may be argued to be strengths as well as weaknesses.

At the level of mechanics, some observers found Marshall to be a poor orator, possessed of a monotonous voice which by itself rarely inspired enthusiasm. It was also said that he was not charismatic; and that he lacked a lively sense of humor that could be used to enliven speeches and punctuate conversation (though a dry wit was occasionally remarked upon even by these critics).[9]

Despite his generally fine memory, Marshall was inexplicably plagued by forgetting names, even the names of the people with whom he worked. His long-time and faithful personal secretary, Mona Nason, was destined to be called Miss Mason regardless of how many times her boss was corrected. He could not get the last name of his chief aide and good friend for many years, Frank McCarthy, calling him McCartney or McArthur—reluctantly, he retreated to referring to him by his first name (Taylor 1972, 40). In the interviews with Forrest Pogue he could not recall Pogue's name and so hid behind the title of "doctor." Pogue noted that in the very same interviews he would remember something that Churchill said, instantly locate the book, and quickly find the passage (Bland 1991, 474, 606).[10]

At the level of personality, he was seen later in his career as aloof and stiff, distant, even forbidding. At a minimum, his manner was always reserved and he was rarely expressive about his feelings (Ismay 1960, 8-9; Buchanan 1958, 18; Haislip 1959, 26). He was criticized early in his career for being too much of a military martinet, too concerned with spit and polish, too unforgiving if rules were not strictly followed. This type of criticism faded and did not recur beginning with his time at Fort Benning.

His natural reserve was a problem for President Roosevelt. Harry Hopkins, the president's closest confidant and adviser, asked Beetle Smith, then in Marshall's office, to help bring the president and Marshall closer together on a personal, more intimate level. Roosevelt wanted Marshall to drop by the White House to share a scotch and a quiet conversation after dinner. Smith repeated the request to Marshall and recalls him thinking carefully and then responding:

> I'm at the president's disposal and he knows it, twenty-four hours of the day, but if I attempted to step out of character, then it would be artificial, and I just don't think that I can or should do it (Smith 1958, 3).

There is disagreement about whether he had the capacity to draw close to others. He rarely left his office in the War or State Department to visit staff offices (Hilldring 1959, 15-16). Yet, it is unlikely that this was rooted in a desire to be distant from other people. A close aide found him to be "as terse as anybody that you ever saw" (in official conversations), and "just as considerate and kindly and friendly as anybody that you want, too" (Buchanan 1958, 18). The warmth of his correspondence and gracious actions toward his associates and their families abundantly support Buchanan's contention.

As WW II intensified, and as his responsibilities weighed more heavily upon him, Marshall became more withdrawn and impatient. "I think he realized he had a responsibility there, not enough hours in the day to get them [sic] all done, and he didn't have any time for foolishness" (Gerow 1958, 56). But his constant editing of the letters of subordinates seemed like a great waste of time to some of his staff (Bradley and Blair 1983, 84).

Eisenhower shared the view that officers in the WPD of the General Staff were afraid of Marshall. Brigadier General Robert Crawford was "a brilliant man with an unlimited future," in Eisenhower's opinion, but became tongue-tied in Marshall's presence. As a result, his talents were never sufficiently utilized (Ambrose 1983, 136).

Maxwell Taylor, a future chairman of the Joint Chiefs of Staff, agreed. "If George Marshall had a fault it was that his strong personality had such an unnerving effect on officers around him that it adversely affected the quality of their work," he said (1952, 40). Even Omar Bradley, who had worked closely with Marshall at Fort Benning and knew that his judgment and professionalism were valued by Marshall "was still in awe and some fear of the man" (Bradley and Blair 1983, 83).

A more serious complaint related to Marshall's judgment on strategic matters. The primary critic was Field Marshall Alan Brooke (Sir Alanbrooke), Chief of the Imperial General Staff and himself a considerable intellect. Brooke reckoned Marshall to be of average intelligence and lacking in vision and strategic sense. In his diaries Brooke expressed the view that "his (Marshall's) thoughts revolve around the creation of forces and not on their employment" (Black 2003, 800-801). Brooke and other British defense chiefs, including Churchill, were critics of the cross-channel assault plan highly preferred by Marshall and supported by most of the allied military chiefs. Their major complaint was Marshall's desire to implement that plan in 1943. Had he succeeded in forcing that date American and British forces may well have been overwhelmed.

Further evidence advanced to demonstrate strategic misjudgment was Marshall's belief that the naval and air bases at Pearl Harbor were impregnable. Stimson recalled: "Marshall felt that with our heavy bombers and our new fine pursuit planes, the land force could put up such a defense that the Japs wouldn't dare attack Hawaii, particularly such a long distance from home" (Pogue 1966, 135).

George Kennan, a stalwart defender of Marshall's administrative prowess, echoed Brooke and other British critics in stating that Marshall was overly moved by purely military aspects of strategy and betrayed impatience with anything seeming to be a diversion from military goals. Part of this distorted vision was caused, he argued, by a capitulation in policy making to the political branches during WW II (Kennan 1959, 22). Partially balancing this view is the opinion of such notables as Acheson, Eleanor Roosevelt, and Marshall Carter, all of whom found in Marshall an extraordinary ability to make the leap to "non-military" thought processes when serving as secretary of state. It seems reasonable to believe that Marshall himself would have argued that it was his role more than his thinking that changed after his time as chief of staff. As secretary of state he had become the president's advisor on foreign policy, a political role, and had left behind the essentially administrative role of leader and manager of a two-front war with clear goals of victory and minimization of human and capital losses.

Marshall was prone to outbursts of temper, often fierce, which he freely recognized and deplored in his own behavior. Lovett said Marshall "could burn the paint off the wall" even without raising his voice. The anger would normally take the form of a look, "icy cold and withdrawn," and then pass quickly (Bradley and Blair 1983, 84). There seemed to be three major triggers associated with the outbursts: impatience resulting from incompetence or unwillingness of others to take action; unjust criticism of the Army (Pasco 1997, 20); and people who put their self-interest before that of the nation.

He would become impatient if some important detail were overlooked that delayed action (Gallagher 1962, 45; Gerow 1958, 40-41). In this impatience lay a possible and uncomfortable contradiction. Although he was justly respected for his attention to detail (as in the editing of reports and communications) and demanded the same from others, he was often not disposed to hear all the details that others might lay out in the effort to fully inform him. This tendency contributed to the fear some had of him (Pasco 1997, 18).

An example of anger aimed at legislative obtuseness crept into a speech delivered to the American Legion in September 1941, a few days after the razor-close House of Representatives vote on the extension of the draft which came perilously close to derailing the Army's rebuilding. "It is impossible to develop an efficient army if decisions purely of a military nature are continuously subjected to investigation, cross-examination, debate, ridicule, and public discussion," he stormed, his respect for democratic process for the moment running thin (Cray 1990, 235).

Fortunately, his self-discipline generally trumped his temper, allowing him to maintain a considerable measure of control. His rational self understood that giving in to his emotional side invited major negative effects: cloudy thinking, less rational decisions, and a waste of valuable time and energy. He expressed regret when he gave into it and struggled successfully to correct it. In his doctor's opinion, his knowledge that he had a somewhat frail heart, detected at the time he was at Vancouver Barracks in the late 1930s, aided him in exerting self-control over anger that caused his blood pressure to rise (Stayer 1960, 7).

Eisenhower, who had a great deal of interaction with Marshall on matters of profound importance and delicacy, observed that Marshall became angrier at stupidity than anyone he had ever seen. "Yet the outburst is so fleeting, he returns so quickly to complete 'normalcy' that I'm certain he does it for effect" (Ambrose 1983, 143). One method he devised to assist him in controlling the effects of anger was to get a top aide in the office of the Secretary of the General Staff to review his correspondence for intemperate language. Given a second chance, he would normally remove it.

Marshall made enough progress on controlling his temper that by the time of his post-war service many were noting in him an unusual capacity for patience. The meeting of foreign ministers in Moscow in 1947 would have tested the patience of Job because of the stone-walling, repetitiousness, rudeness, and bluster of Molotov, the Soviet foreign minister, and the transparent duplicity of Stalin. Both were intent on blocking progress of any sort on postwar peace treaties, reparations, or occupation arrangements. Marshall somehow persevered and remained civil over a period of several weeks until the meetings were mercifully terminated.

Eleanor Roosevelt, who worked often with Marshall during WW II and also served as a delegate to the UN when Marshall was at State, recognized him as "a magnificent presiding officer" with "an extraordinary quality of patience" who took the time to hear everybody's point of view (E. Roosevelt 1958, 3).

Marshall could be inconsiderate. Katherine Marshall, in remembering her husband, said the general would say that it took him no time at all to prepare for a trip, neglecting to notice how his wife and orderly had struggled to pack for him (K. Marshall 1947). He could remain out of sorts for extended periods of time to people who irritated him (Eaker 1959, 25).

Despite what has been said about his distaste for honors and awards, a recognized although mild Marshall fault was a certain vanity. Bolte noted that Marshall "loves to have a story, but he's got to be the hero of it . . . anything that tends to reflect on his dignity is to be carefully avoided . . . anybody that thinks he is a modest, shy, retiring, humble individual, is wrong, in my opinion" (Bolte 1958, 29-30). Acheson remarked on the same quality: "He had a pleasant vanity—he liked to be praised for doing things that he thought were good, but," he added reverently, "there was no conceit . . . the important thing is that his ego never got between him and the goal" (Acheson 1957, 1).

Marshall's tendency toward vanity may at times have blunted the willingness of others to speak frankly to him. As Bernard Baruch and Marshall rode together to visit Pershing at Walter Reed hospital, Baruch criticized the speech Marshall had made the day before as being too political, and told him he should stay in character as a military expert and not trespass into the president's arena. Marshall reddened and became sullen and silent for a period lasting through the hospital visit and partway through the return ride. Finally, he offered a delayed reply: "you know a true friend will tell you when you are doing wrong, you don't wait for your enemies to do it," and then said, "I'm sorry I got angry . . . that was an act of real friendship" (Baruch 1961, 20).

Some amateur psychological analysis is tempting. Was it personal affection that Marshall craved in these exchanges? A longing for *camaraderie?* Public adoration was something he never sought and purposely kept at a distance. Was he looking for validation of himself and his actions from people with whom he shared a certain intimacy and whom he knew took their value from fighting; a would-be warrior who was not allowed to fight? In the total mix of things, character flaws such as these seem only to mark him merely as touchingly human.

Relationship of Character to Leadership

Is good character positively related to effective public leadership? Closer study of the wide-ranging, combined military-diplomatic-cabinet level public administrative career of Marshall adds to greater understanding of the power and role of ethics in public leadership. It does this by focusing attention upon a set of personal attributes and practices that are not only associated with sterling moral character but also contribute to getting things done and inspiring others to deepen and extend their own performance.

In the case of Marshall, there is virtually unanimous agreement on both his effectiveness and the existence of his remarkable virtues and practices. Just how these attributes affected the organizations he led are played out in the outcomes described in the next few chapters.

Notes

1. Lord Moran (Charles McMoran Wilson) was Churchill's wartime physician.

2. Paul Fussell, in his humorous yet serious book, groups military professionals with others in the lower middle class in the manner of their wearing of civilian clothes, which he termed awkward. But then he added: "Although there's always the example of General George C. Marshall, who, after a lifetime of appearing in uniform, managed in mufti to wear the three-button, three-piece suit as if to the class manner born" (1983, 62).

3. General Sexton summed up his admiration of the general's characteristic compassion: "I feel that General Marshall is just one notch below Jesus Christ . . . the many kindnesses that he did to people" (Sexton 1958, 28).

4. The lesson was to stay with him. In WW II efforts were made to control the access of non-essential and uninformed persons to battle zones.

5. King was mollified and apologized.

6. He reorganized the State Department in the same way in 1947.

7. His definition of humor did not extend to the telling of off-color stories (Harding 1958, 47).

8. Lewis Douglas said of Marshall's expectations of others: "But he demands massive, monolithic integrity and character" (Douglas 1962).

9. Lord Hastings Ismay, Churchill's chief of staff, said that "he (Marshall) had a delicious sense of humor" (Ismay 1960, 9).

10. Marshall owned up to this shortcoming. He said to Pogue: "Well, that name problem is almost entirely one of a certain habit that one has when they start to mention a person's name and they have in their mind one minute and they have lost in the next—which I have always had, and I still have, and maybe in a little bit greater degree than formerly" (Bland 1991, 474).

CHAPTER FIVE
DARK PASSAGE: PREPARING THE NATION FOR WAR

During the period depicted here the Chief of Staff built so well and so strongly that the tragedy of Pearl Harbor did not shake the confidence of the nation.
—Maj. Gen. Orlando Ward, Secretary of the General Staff, 1939-1941 (Watson 1950, foreword)

The Nation's Perspective as World War II Begins

The invasion of Poland by Germany triggered interlocking treaties that brought the United Kingdom and France into the widening war on the side of Poland. However, the shock of the Nazi aggression did not galvanize American public opinion in the direction of joining or even assisting in the conflict. Had this occurred, George Marshall's task of building a strong army would have been greatly eased. Rather, something of the opposite nature occurred. President Roosevelt, fearing the reaction of an isolationist Congress and a public left wounded from the great war of 1917-1918, refrained from any public declaration that the United States would involve itself militarily in European conflicts. Thus, the public and its government were encouraged to think, hope, or pretend that the war would not reach across the Atlantic.

The Army's state of readiness was abysmal. It was rated as the globe's seventeenth strongest army, just behind Romania. The National Defense Act of 1920 (NDA) limited the size of the Army to two hundred and fifty-five thousand but the Army numbered only one hundred and thirty thousand including some seventeen thousand air personnel. It was poorly supplied (its weaponry was largely left over from WW I) and it lacked adequate training resources. Adding to the inadequacy was the Neutrality Act which prevented the US from actively coming to the aid of its natural friends, the western democracies.

The War Department, the administrative center of the Army, was struggling under a top-heavy administrative system designed around the conditions existing in the first decade of the twentieth century. Authority was decentralized and badly fragmented. The structure put a heavy strain on the Office of Chief of Staff (COS) by putting its leader in a direct supervisory position for scores of units but with little authority to command and follow through. The working relationship between the president and the chief of staff, his chief advisor for ground and air forces, was clouded by the obligation owed by the chief of staff to top War Department officials above him in the hierarchy, especially during peacetime.

Secretary of War Woodring was an uncompromising anti-interventionist and was opposed to significant military increases. His influence with the president had been undermined by his open power feud with Assistant Secretary Louis Johnson. Johnson, for his part, was a strong advocate for increased air power but saw no urgent need to expand ground forces. In short, Marshall could expect no help or guidance from either in his efforts to obtain help from congress or the president. Wisely, he had good personal relations with both men and stayed clear of their battles, which allowed him to keep the Army functional during a period of potential discord (Cray 1990, 146, 148-149).

The Army's small size, its inadequate training, its obsolescent equipment, its virtually nonexistent military industrial base, its underdeveloped air forces, and the dysfunctional War Department organization in which it was set made the task of preparing the Army for war monumental (Nelsen 1993). Marshall's special qualities of character and personality, would be sorely tested under these circumstances.

Would he be resilient and adaptive enough to lead? Would he be able to enlist and motivate the talent and skills that would be required? Would he find the reserves of energy and optimism in himself he would need to be successful? And, would he be adept enough to weather the political vicissitudes of the capital city?

This and the following two chapters will move through the roles Marshall held during and after WW II. How he perceived and then handled each new role and how each prepared him to deal with the next will be the major focus. His views and uses of intra- and inter-organizational phenomena are crucial to this inquiry.

Building Blocks of Public Leadership

Some critical building blocks in Marshall's thought processes were already in place. First, he held strongly to the view that the proper role of a military chief officer under the US Constitution required being accountable to political leadership. A second piece in his behavior was the habit of looking ahead to put in place the kinds of methods, people, and weaponry needed to meet the foreseeable needs of a future war. A third was his belief that dignity and respect was to be accorded to the people and officials of other nations and cultures. This view was linked to the value placed on preparation for war in Marshall's mind because he saw multi-national and multi-cultural approaches as critical to military outcomes.

All political leaders (including presidents, prime ministers, kings, and dictators) attempt to satisfy, mollify, put off, build consensus among, or otherwise manipulate multiple constituencies in order to build the political resources they need to remain in power and to succeed, or at least appear to be successful. This is also true of high-ranking American public administrators, but to a lesser extent. They must also be responsive to influential or potentially influential political figures in their executive hierarchies and in the Congress. They must also build trust and support among powerful political interest groups as well as professional reference groups and the general public. Like politicians, they are expected to nurture their constituencies, build a favorable public image, and leverage these to maximize their budgets and increase their political influence. At the same time they must keep harmony within their own ranks.

Marshall believed that the only justification for the use of power by public executives is to advance the public interest. His oft-stated view that military and administrative arms of the state must subordinate themselves to the constitutional, civilian authority of the state is clearly within this spirit (Rusk 1990, 134). It is the duty of a military administrator to follow policy and to make maximum effort to realize the goals of such policy, and not to make policy. Yet it is the duty of the highest ranking officers, cabinet members as well as chiefs of staff, to be a part of the policy-making process through giving advice to those charged by the constitution to make political decisions, while not usurping the right to make such decisions themselves.[1] Finally, it followed from the principle of constitutional subordination that administrators, particularly military administrators, should not engage in partisan or elective politics. He had given this advice to General Pershing in the 1920s, and he repeated it to a close aide almost twenty years later:

> You know, any military man who aspires to the presidency is making a very foolish mistake. All our training is contrary to the development of the abilities, political abilities that a man needs for the presidency, and he can't but make a failure at it. Any military man ought to know this, ought not to consider the job (Osborn 1959, 8).[2]

Dealing with policy is a complicated matter for an administrator such as a chief of staff. A professional application of an existing policy may actually constitute new policy when it gives to that policy a new spin or meaning. Marshall had strong views about professional military matters as well as on military organizational structure and process. He believed his position required him to be forceful and persuasive on policy recommendations in order to advance these views. He never hesitated to argue vigorously with congressional or White House people for new policy he believed was necessary *for professional reasons*, since he felt it vital that policy makers have both the context and the logic that his professional expertise afforded. Ultimately, he accepted the principle that it was the politicians' rightful burden to make the final decision.

Once policy was adopted by his political superior, he made a distinct role shift from vigorous advocate to faithful supporter. Lewis Douglas said that he witnessed occasions on which Marshall would argue with Roosevelt "with as much persuasion as he could muster and mobilize on the particular point at issue" and then, "if he failed, he would carry out Roosevelt's or Stimson's order with complete and unimpeachable faith" (Douglas 1962, 5). The principle followed was to be a powerful advocate up until the time the decision was made and then be an enthusiastic team player from that time on.

Entry to the Dark Passage

It is a striking accident of history that the very matters that concerned Marshall on August 31, 1939, took on different form the very next day. He was dragged immediately into the vortex of events set in motion by Germany's attack on Poland. His first act, even before his swearing-in at the War Department, was to put all army military personnel on war alert (Black 2003, 528). The spotlight shifted quickly to two crucial concerns. The first was whether and to what extent the United States could aid its natural allies in this dark hour—particularly Great Britain, France, the Netherlands, and Norway. The second was the increased urgency to rebuild the Army and Army Air Forces numerically, equip and supply them properly, and train them.

Taking action on these matters was made difficult, for the president as well as for the chief of staff, by some huge legal and political obstacles. The Neutrality Act, the National Defense Act (NDA), isolationism, and the urgent economic and social needs generated by the Great Depression all stood in the way of military preparation. The NDA's imposed ceiling of two hundred and fifty-five thousand Regular Army members was not immediately critical because a growth potential of one hundred and twenty-five thousand regulars plus many more in the state National Guard units could be realized before the act became a constraint. Still, funding for the additional troops would have to be found as well as the money to arm, train, and supply them.

The Army's problem was compounded by a general bias in favor of air and naval forces over ground forces. The media and the public, and most politicians, were far more impressed by the glamour of naval and air weaponry and life styles (Bland 1991, 259-260). Serving in the ground forces was by contrast dull, traditional, underpaid, and considered more dangerous. Roosevelt himself reinforced the bias by virtue of his naval background and his naive hope that the best way to avoid American entry into the war was to produce warplanes for the UK and France.

One of Marshall's first initiatives was to strengthen the air forces through a series of steps. He began by promoting Colonel Frank Andrews to brigadier general and bringing him onto the General Staff as chief of the operations division (Brett 1962, 26). This was part of his effort to ensure that air perspectives and concerns were articulated in Army staff meetings and promoted in decision making. He then approved a proposal from the air chiefs to expand the Army Air Corps to fifty-four air groups, not only approving the request in full but also inquiring why more units were not sought (Pogue 1966, 86). The proposal included the acquisition of heavy bombers along with aircraft capable of providing direct support to ground troops (Bland 1991, 448-449). Perhaps most importantly, he gave *de facto* authority to air officers to take the major role in making decisions on the design and production of aircraft.

Proceeding cautiously, he was unwilling to appear to be acting for a president eager for war. He resisted the call of a powerful group of senators who, sharing the sense of urgency, begged him to take the lead in insisting on the rapid growth of ground forces. His instinct was instead to tread softly in awakening the public consciousness to the need for military expansion. Too forceful an effort could lead to a complete rejection of his views and a dramatic reduction of his influence, to the ultimate impairment of the entire rearmament effort (Bland 1991, 301-302; Watson 1950, 181).

Marshall stayed for the moment with matters of Army structure. His first priority here was stimulating industrial production of the goods and materiel needed to clothe, shelter, feed, equip, and put modern weaponry into the hands of the troops on hand and provide a reserve to serve expected future mobilization. Lead time was necessary to get these things to the troops, and thus production design, planning, and scheduling had to be the first order of business. It would take at least a year before troops had these items in sufficient quantity for meaningful training. Marshall repeatedly emphasized that any orderly, balanced mobilization required the necessary equipment to be on hand before men could form new units and train properly. The massive equipment shortages existing at the start of WW I haunted him (Frye 1947, 262-264).

He carried out his long-contemplated reorganization of the Regular Army "division" structure. The traditional "square division" of four large regiments, which he regarded as cumbersome, was replaced by a "triangular division" structure of three, smaller, more mobile regiments. He used congressional funding permitting a modest seventeen thousand man increase in the Regular Army plus the additional manpower generated by the move to the smaller division format to create five fully manned divisions of the new type. In addition, he created a host of specialized units to serve as support troops to build the new "corps" structure (combat units supported by military police, engineers, logistical elements, air defense units, field artillery units, and signal corps or communications units).

The training of state national guard and Army Reserve units was revamped to make it more compatible with Regular Army training, and brought closer to the vision of the type of training appropriate to a citizen army. He then moved quickly to federalize these units and get them into the field as part of a new "combined-arms" team approach.

Corps and division maneuvers were scheduled for the spring of 1940. At the same time planning was proceeding for an unprecedented joint amphibious operation with the Navy (Frye 1947, 271-272; Bland, Ritenour and Wunderlin 1986, 85).

In the midst of undertaking this increase in the scope of his chief of staff duties, Marshall fought to improve the quality of the General Staff and its capacity to function effectively. The machinery he had inherited was not in good health. It had to function within the archaic and inefficient structure of the overall Department of War as well as the outdated processes imposed on the COS itself. Marshall was forced to fight conservative forces within the Army and the War Department. The immediate effect of Andrews' promotion to the General Staff was violent opposition from ground officers who had long held the prejudice that airmen were neither qualified nor mainstream enough to serve in top Army staff positions (Brett 1962, 26; Parton 1986, 116, 125-126). Opposition to the Andrews appointment came not only from traditional army men, but also from Woodring, Johnson, and former chief of staff Malin Craig. To reinforce the policy and blunt the criticism, Marshall created a new position of deputy chief of staff for air and appointed Arnold to fill it (Pogue 1966, 86).

Mounting Pressures on the Chief of Staff

All the while, external pressures were coming from democratic nations desperately battling for survival against German forces, as well as from political forces that were either working for or against giving these nations greater assistance or to prepare the US military for war. The pressures were compounded by the indirect political influence of semi-autonomous army units exerted upon congress which made reorganization exceedingly difficult. In this climate, Marshall was unmercifully put upon. A lesser man could have been expected to go through the motions and wait to be relieved. Instead, he enlarged the scope of his responsibilities.

Although the need for reorganization of the War Department was becoming obvious there was no real opportunity for undertaking it. The politics of the task were daunting. Congressional opposition to reorganization was certain. Moreover, seeking the changes contemplated would be divisive and explosive within the War Department and the Army and thus set back the various reforms Marshall had already set in motion.

It might have helped had Marshall had the unflagging support of the president. But here too, all was not well. Marshall had initially found Roosevelt's breezy, discursive, self-indulgent manner of conducting meetings to be superficial and off-putting. Roosevelt used informality with cabinet members and advisors to create an environment in which he had the upper hand in fending off thoughtful advice. Marshall sought a relationship based on mutual respect. He refused to "drop in" at the White House, his discussions focused strictly on business, and he even deliberately refused to laugh at the President's jokes (Pogue 1963, 324; Bland 1991, 282, 417; Cray 1990, 144; Frye 1947, 310-311). For his part, Roosevelt was clearly uncomfortable with Marshall's serious demeanor.

All these circumstances were in place shortly into Marshall's tenure as US Army chief of staff. As a consequence, they made for the most difficult period of Marshall's professional and administrative career. The challenge was to severely test his character, his endurance and health, and the resilience of his spirit. No less than the security of the nation, generally unrecognized and underappreciated, depended on how he would perform in his new leadership role. For George Marshall as well as for America, it was to be a dark passage.

Managing the War Department

In the same spirit that he had led at command posts such as Tientsin and Vancouver Barracks, Marshall preferred working with small staffs on a personal basis. His standard operating mode had been to assign whole jobs to individuals rather than piecing together a project by coordinating the work of several persons and separate offices. This pattern was what he was familiar with and what had worked well for him. His new job called for him to work with a great number of General Staff officers reporting to him, some of whom were weak performers and some of whom were excellent. The General Staff had been designed and selected for an earlier, peacetime era. It was stodgy and entrenched, organized for giving advice to the chief of staff but not for action, and unduly preoccupied with personal concerns about rank and status.

In this climate, the General Staff could not be used to good advantage. The head of the personnel division of the General Staff (G-1), General Wade Haislip, was aware that information relevant to the manpower needs of an entire army came from many sources and had to be coordinated by a central secretariat. Individuals were not up to performing assigned tasks of large scope, thus confounding Marshall's expectations and habitual working pattern (Haislip 1959, 2-3, 6).

Marshall was fated to become aware of the difficulties and possible reforms only through frustratingly hard work and frequent system breakdowns. Awareness came to him before it came to most others, but there was scant opportunity for reorganizing either the COS or the War Department as a whole, since doing either required law change and overcoming entrenched political opposition. Many and various Army units had developed their own public constituencies and congressional allies and would seek to retain the *status quo* regardless of the wishes of either the president or the chief of staff.

For the present Marshall could only hope to conserve his energy and health and to cope. He was in the midst of learning to master, in quick-time, not a single new role but several new roles: advocate for preparedness, army builder, and internationalist. These developments would necessitate delaying many of the internal tasks of organization, despite their importance.

Advocate and Army Builder

The roles of advocate for preparedness and army builder are discussed together because they are so closely interrelated. Recognizing and accepting the delicate path that the president himself was on, Marshall came grudgingly but philosophically to accept Roosevelt's cautionary approach to preparedness. Soon after Germany invaded Poland Marshall had this insight:

> I had early made up my mind that . . . it was far more important in the long run that I be well established as a member of the [political and military] team and try to do my convincing within that team, rather than to take action publicly contrary to the desires of the president and certain members of Congress. There was a certain group of senators at this time who were very intent on going ahead much more rapidly than the administration was willing to do, and their pressure on me at all times was very great. But . . . I foresaw that it was going to be very important for me to establish the fact that I would not run off to a public appeal, but rather, I would try my level best to deal within the team of which the president was the head (Bland 1991, 297).

Fortunately, Roosevelt shared with Marshall the desire to prepare for possible global conflict. Due to his official position as the president's top military adviser and his genuine commitment to Roosevelt's political team, and because of the growing respect in which he was held by members of the Congress, Marshall was chosen by Roosevelt to be the point man for the administration in the gaining of defense-related authorizations and appropriations from the Congress.

From the very beginning of his frequent visits to the capitol to testify Marshall became a great favorite of legislators of both parties. They were virtually unanimous in their praise of his professionalism, his penchant for careful development of factual bases for recommendations, a gift for clear presentation, his logical mind, his honesty and integrity, and for his passionate belief in the cause of military preparedness.

Events intervened to greatly strengthen Marshall's hand with the Congress. First, there was a rapid succession of invasions by Germany of Denmark, Norway, the Netherlands, Belgium, and France in the spring of 1940 that quickly converted democracies into Nazi-dominated fascist states. This had an important effect in turning public opinion, and thus Congressional opinion, toward the growing need for mobilization of the armed forces.

The second event, more gradual, was the transformation of the relationship existing between the president and his chief of staff. Marshall's business-like approach began to have the desired effect—it set a tone of dignity and respect in their relations. Marshall gradually detected that Roosevelt was a man of strength, purpose, and, when required, courage. There began to develop between them a relationship sufficiently relaxed that Roosevelt dispensed with "tactical circumlocution" (as Marshall called it) and Marshall stopped taking offense from the president's informality (Black 2003, 499). Gradually, mutual respect replaced the cautious circling that had characterized their dealings. The relationship remained cordial and businesslike but strong mutual trust began to evolve, eventually giving Marshall great influence with Roosevelt.

The third event came in the summer of 1940 when Roosevelt appointed Henry Lewis Stimson to the cabinet as secretary of war. Stimson was a strong advocate of military preparedness and alliance with western European countries. A Republican, his appointment helped to blunt partisan opposition to war preparation. He was well respected as a two-time, former cabinet member.[3] By chance, Stimson and Marshall had met in 1918 in France and Stimson had been much impressed by the crack staff officer. In 1927, as Stimson was set to depart for the Philippines to assume the role of Governor-General, he invited Marshall to accompany him with the promise of giving him a staff position with the rank of brigadier general. Marshall declined because he was eager to escape staff duty, but he much respected Stimson and had been flattered by the offer (Bland 1991, 202, 230). Their relationship at the War Department was destined to become a warm partnership and an important source of political and moral support for Marshall.

Germany's western European aggression coincided with the budget season of 1940. Marshall moved cautiously, focusing on voluntary recruitment as the preferred means to meet the newly authorized manpower ceiling for the Regular

Army. He intended to use the additional men to bring all active divisions up to full manpower limits under the combined arms team model. Funding was to be focused on training and the equipment and weaponry necessary not only for these troops but also to build up a reserve for the manpower expansion expected in the future. Adopting a draft system at this point would disrupt this process by absorbing many Regular Army personnel in the training of inductees rather than in preparing effective combat units (Cray 1990, 166-168).

For Marshall, the key to Army growth was balance and concentration on building effective units rather than simply adding people. Advocates of a more rapid expansion were urging the type of crash officer training (the Plattsburgh program) that had occurred in 1917,[4] a type of officer training Marshall regarded as having been made "wholly unacceptable" by the conditions of the "next war" (Bland 1991, 298-300):

> I wanted to go ahead as fast as we were able to manage the thing. That was all ignored. They just wanted what I call numbers, the number racket, which I wouldn't accept at all. So we had a very hard time and particularly with Mr. Stimson at this time, because he was against the way we were going. . . . We were opposed to these large training camps they wanted to have because we had no instructors. And we couldn't tear apart what little we did have all to pieces in order to produce a half-baked organization (Bland 1991, 300).

Poorly planned and badly executed mobilization before a war could be as harmful as rapid demobilization following a war. A too rapid build-up of troops and planes could outstrip the Army's ability to train, equip, house, and transport forces. It was urgent that the Army be able to put on the field at least a few effective fighting units should these be needed immediately, and this would be impossible if these units were cannibalized in order to provide instructors for new troops.

Marshall keenly appreciated the role that events and timing play in acquiring resources. In considering the military appropriation bill for the coming year, he had remarked to his staff: "It will react to our advantage if our bill is acted on at the latest possible date. It is probable that events in Europe will develop in such a way as to affect Congressional action." He was demonstrating a very refined sense of measuring the mood of Congress (Cray 1990, 165; Watson 1950, 164).

He thus waited until early June before deciding to support a draft lottery measure, the Selective Training and Service Act (STSA), even with its consequence of an overly rapid buildup of new soldiers that would have to be trained. Support was given discretely. Fearing an anti-military backlash with adverse effects for future mobilization efforts, he wanted to see the bill introduced as a civilian initiative, which did occur.[5] With the President's blessing, Marshall sent members of his staff to help write the legislation and quietly lobbied for the bill (Stoler 1989, 75-76; Bland 1991, 305). Once the bill was introduced, he enthusiastically supported its passage. However, he had to compromise on one key point to ensure its passage—limiting National Guard federal service to twelve months.

In late summer, at Marshall's urging, Congress enacted in rapid succession a call-up to federal duty of the National Guard and the Army Reserves, to accompany the draft measure. This burst of legislation forced Marshall to break up existing Regular Army units in order to mobilize the seasoned personnel needed to train the rapidly growing army of conscripts, guardsmen, and reservists. As feared, the opportunity for deliberate and balanced growth of forces had been badly compromised, but Marshall judged it was necessary in order to adjust to the new reality brought on by events.

By the end of 1940, eight-hundred thousand men were undergoing intensive field training. The net gain in Army strength over the previous three months had been nearly two-hundred thousand men, a number larger than the total size of the Regular Army when Marshall became Acting Chief of Staff in 1939. By Christmas, these soldiers were manning eighteen of the new, more mobile divisions, with nine more soon to appear. The passage of the STSA, in effect, authorized a Regular Army of five-hundred thousand men, a National Guard of two hundred and seventy thousand, and an inductee population of six hundred and thirty thousand, an aggregate strength of one million, four-hundred thousand (Bland, Ritenour, and Wunderlin 1986, 323, 355-356).

A seemingly impossible log jam of work loomed—building and organizing basic training camps for draftees, removing Regular Army personnel from existing fighting units and using reservists and more seasoned national guardsmen to train inductees, shuffling remaining units around to keep at least some effective forces in the field, and equipping all of them. The scope of these tasks was colossal, and it had to be accomplished with an inadequate administrative system. Most of Marshall's time from September 1940 to June 1941 was spent in managing this enormous expansion through erecting facilities, planning maneuvers, providing recreational services, and procuring and distributing equipment.

That all of these things happened is a tribute to Marshall, who must alone be credited with their being undertaken and accomplished (Nelsen 1993). That they happened along with achieving a marked increase in the number of divisions being trained for combat is mind-boggling. He drove the preparations and personally overcame almost every major obstacle (Nelsen 1993; Pogue 1966, 89-90). He created the corps as a complete Army unit; before training had always been done in scattered battalions. He thus took a long stride toward his vision of a holistic, complementary force of combined-arms elements working in coordinated teams, adequately equipped and trained in a coordinated fashion.

Simultaneously, attention had to be directed to creating a general headquarters (GHQ) as the operations center of a Europe-based, expeditionary fighting force in the event of war, after the model used in WW I and prescribed by law. Marshall selected the much-respected Lieutenant General Lesley J. McNair to be brought in to organize the GHQ. It was assumed that if and when war came Marshall would take command of GHQ in Europe much as Pershing had done in WW I and would probably keep McNair on as his chief of staff. This development would have the unwelcome side effect of siphoning off some of the best and badly needed General Staff people in Washington for service in Europe (Bradley and Blair 1983, 91-92).

As Japan expanded the scope of its aggression in the western Pacific, the WW I organizational model began to seem oddly quaint. Where would an overseas GHQ be established? How would resources be allocated in the event of a two-ocean war? Marshall's decision was to give up on the GHQ model and bring McNair home to take over the giant task of overseeing the training of the Army's new soldiers. Having the senior and capable McNair take over this role proved to be an astute staffing decision based entirely on merit. Marshall was a great admirer of McNair. The two men had a warm professional and personal relationship dating back to 1917 when they shared a stateroom on the first WW I troop ship to France. McNair was too old for troop command duty under new eligibility standards that Marshall was setting in place, and so no damage was being done to his career (Pasco 1997, 25).

Personnel Issues

As Nazi aggression, particularly the bombing of Great Britain, continued in Europe, funding for the buildup of the army Marshall envisioned had ceased to be a problem. However, the problems associated with the expansion were great and growing larger. Finding sufficient numbers of experienced Regular Army instructors to train the new troops had torn apart effective Regular Army units and ensured that the Army would remain an inadequate fighting force for at least a year. Existing command and control of specialized units would likewise be diluted or even destroyed by the redeployment of seasoned personnel (Bland 1991, 251-254).

Despite the pressures, Marshall continued to insist on as reasoned, incremental, and balanced an approach to the buildup as could be managed. He pointed out that, with so many new troops, an effective military professional force would be absent in the short term. Huge appropriations were needed not only to run the camps and train the troops but also to secure equipment, housing, transport, and airplanes in amounts never before attempted.

As the expansion of the officer corps continued in 1940-1941 in order to keep pace with total Army growth, Marshall faced the crucial question of how to select men to fill the rapidly growing demand for troop command positions, absolutely crucial to effectiveness in war. Predictably, contemporaries of Marshall with command experience in WW I or since that time were eagerly seeking promotion to top assignments. They at least expected to keep the command positions they had.

To their great surprise and consternation, Marshall's new policy contained an age limitation effectively cutting off command positions for men of ages of fifty and older. It was then applied to eliminate them from gaining new or even keeping existing troop commands. The basic problem he observed was that they had reached an age at which their physical vitality would be more easily exhausted under the stress of battle and war conditions than that of younger officers. His new officer selection policy stipulated that a man's previous record would not be considered and only an assessment of the officer's *present value* to the service would be relevant (Herron 1958, 28).

The new policy was uniformly and rigidly enforced with the result that many seasoned commanders of established reputation were either passed over for promotion or not retained in their current commands. Pleas and recriminations from old friends and associates denied troop command duty were numerous and deeply painful to Marshall (Pogue 1966, 92-97).

The age limitation policy evoked controversy even among those not directly affected by it. Marshall aide and deputy General Kenneth Buchanan argued that age had such variable effects in different human beings that to rigidly apply a strict age policy would be arbitrary and unfair so long as physical testing and performance ("efficiency") reports were available (Buchanan 1958, 47). To depersonalize the process and to make it as fair as possible, Marshall decided upon two courses of action. First, the near-automatic disqualification from command positions based on age was changed to a rebuttable presumption which permitted the possibility of an exception if the officer was able to demonstrate unusual current vigor (equal to that of a much younger man) coupled with high promise. Such an exception was applied to George Patton, for example.[6]

As a second step, a "plucking board" was established to review the chief of staff's decision, manned by six retired officers and headed by former chief of staff Malin Craig. Although Marshall was removed from the hot seat of decision-maker, the criterion for retention remained the same—present value to the Army and not the officer's past record. A field command post was not to become a reward for positive past performance that an officer was no longer capable of repeating (Pogue 1966, 97-98). This seemed an overly tough standard to many, but Marshall was preparing an army for war and felt that the selection of those who could lead in battle was a duty owed to the nation and especially to the troops who would be putting their lives on the line (Pogue 1966, 95).

It was also important to assure younger persons of talent that the road to permanent career advancement was open. In conjunction with the age limitation policy Marshall sought and got legislation, with the help of Senator James Byrnes of South Carolina, that permitted younger officers of exceptional talent to be upgraded rapidly and to leap-frog over more senior but less promising officers. Included in the initial group that was put on the fast track to higher command were such stand-outs as Dwight D. Eisenhower, Mark Clark, George Kenney, Ira Eaker, and Carl "Tooey" Spaatz (Pogue 1966, 98).

Political Problems Surface

This recitation of steps dealing with the problems of the growth of the Army leaves out some important elements. Great pressure was being exerted by Roosevelt, Churchill and the British, the French, and the Chinese to give what could be spared in weaponry, ordnance, and supplies to the allies. The main connection of these demands to Army growth and preparation, of course, was that whatever could be found and supplied to the allies would necessarily reduce what remained to support the American buildup and would be resisted by those Army units already in great need—in short, all of them. Moreover, any assistance given had to meet the terms of the Neutrality Act and would face scrutiny and probably opposition by isolationists.

In addition, the explosive growth of the Army[7] was hatching severe domestic issues. Construction of new training facilities, rapid movement of troops and facilities into communities, and the politics of the economics of war production were the primary underlying causes. Questions of quality and fraud emerged in the construction of army housing. Racial tensions arose between black and white troops and these expanded to bedevil relations between army bases and communities. Rising crime, only some of it related to race relations, was generally experienced in the impacted communities. These disputes led to heated complaints from politicians and local leaders and calls for corrective measures. In turn, pressures to remedy the problems were heaped upon the Army command structure.

A greater political threat surfaced in the summer of 1941. The draft law enacted by congress in September, 1940 was due to expire in September, 1941 because of the extreme political caution that had been exercised by both the president and the congress in framing the measure. Length of service was limited to just twelve months for both draftees and National Guard members, and the place of their service was confined to the US and its territories. Isolationists, set back on their heels by the ferociousness of Nazi aggression in the previous year, had found stronger voices in the summer of 1941 because Germany's invasion of the USSR had taken pressure off western Europe and had bought time for Great Britain to strengthen its defenses.

Political timidity ruled the day. Few legislators, particularly in the House of Representatives, were brave enough to openly support the extensions, fearing the loss of their seats. Roosevelt had the authority to extend the term of service by executive order but shrank from taking the responsibility for doing so. In mid-June, with time running out, Marshall urged the president to ask congress to extend the terms of service. Roosevelt, however, shied away from making the request himself and suggested Marshall take the lead. As Marshall later commented on the difficulty of taking the initiative: "the trouble was we were undertaking very severe war measures and we were not at war" (Cray 1990, 204-206; Bland 1991, 307-308).

Deeply concerned, Marshall took a bold step. With the president's approval, he wrote a nonpolitical, formal report to the congress as chief of staff, and in forty pages of plain language explained the direness of the situation. But distrust of Roosevelt's motives ran deep, and neutralists and isolationists portrayed extension of time and lifting the ban against location of the use of drafted soldiers as tantamount to giving Roosevelt a "green light" to lead the United States into war. It became obvious that some compromise was in order. With the President's approval, Marshall accepted an amendment which limited term extensions to a maximum individual service of eighteen months. This move made the whole issue more palatable to the public and greatly improved the promise of the bill's passage, although Marshall had earlier opposed this restriction most vehemently (Cray 1990, 206-208).

Sam Rayburn, the powerful Democratic Speaker of the House, stated the basis for the president's decision to place the entire burden on Marshall:

Marshall was simple, able, candid. He laid it on the line. He would tell the truth
even if it hurt his cause. Congress always respected him. They would give him
things they would give no one else (Pogue 1973, 131).

Marshall testified before the Senate and House Committees on Military Affairs
in July of 1941. He spoke with cold passion to a Congress, that would rather have
not wanted to hear it, of the effect that failure to extend the draft would have: "the
complete destruction . . . of the fabric of the army that we had built up." His words
were freighted with awful weight:

> In view of the international situation and its rapidly increasing threat to our
> security, I submit, on the basis of cold logic, that the virtual disbandment or
> immobilization of two-thirds of our enlisted strength and three-fourths of our
> trained officer personnel at this time might well involve a national tragedy (de
> Weerd 1945, 129-130, 133, 146-167).

Isolationists and anti-Roosevelt Democrats in both houses were not intimidated. They appealed to those who could not see why it was necessary for
American boys to fight to save Great Britain. Cries of "OHIO" ("over the hill in
October") were being trumpeted by anti-war and right-wing opponents and
supported by Henry Luce and his popular *Life* magazine. Marshall was aided by
a small group of legislative leaders, including Republican James W. Wadsworth of
the House and Democrat senate majority leader Byrnes (Bland 1991, 286; Cray
1990, 209).

Converts to extension were steadily gained as Marshall spoke to small groups
of legislators in both formal and informal settings. After one presentation to a group
of forty Republicans, one of them told the general that although he had put the case
well, he, the Congressman, would not support the president. Marshall, stunned, shot
back with uncharacteristic anger: "You are going to let plain hatred of the
personality dictate to you to do something that you realize is very harmful to the
interest of the country" (Cray 1990, 208-209).

On August 12, amidst a frenzy of last-minute lobbying efforts, the House of
Representatives voted to extend the terms of draftees and guardsmen service by a
single vote. The Senate's anticlimactic vote, not nearly so close, came later (Cray
1990, 210). Catastrophe in the cause of preparation as well as in the matter of
Marshall's career driving force had been narrowly averted.

Military historian John T. Nelsen, II summarized the whole affair with insight:

> Marshall's role in this whole episode was pivotal. Faced with a serious situation
> most politicians wanted to avoid, he forced the issue into the open public forum.
> He did so by the brilliant and creative maneuver of issuing a biennial report when
> all other doors of formal communication seemed closed. Despite some missteps
> surrounding the report's issuance, he made a rapid recovery. He alone shouldered
> the administration's burden of arguing for the term extensions before Congress,
> transforming a no-win situation into a winning one. He did so by striking a series
> of convincing themes, which gave congressmen enough solid ground to justify

voting for the extensions. He also executed a superb, behind-the-scenes lobbying effort and demonstrated impressive skills at striking timely compromises. His growing circle of civilian, and especially congressional, contacts also played a key role. Important to note, Marshall's persuasive talents were not applied manipulatively; he never sought to mislead or deceive. What he said, he meant fully from the mind or from the heart. When he appealed on altruistic grounds, he acted from altruistic motives. This approach gave him a moral high ground and a strength of character which greatly deepened the respect which Congress already had for him. If he was the architect of the Army as it existed in July 1941, he was the savior of that Army as it continued to exist beyond September. His will and his efforts had made the difference (Nelsen, 1993).

One major political threat to the Army's future still remained, as late as three months before Pearl Harbor. President Roosevelt was close to accepting a proposal, advanced by the Navy, to reduce the strength of Army ground forces in favor of increased support for naval and air power, along with providing more aid for the allies. Marshall believed this serious, orchestrated political effort was wrongheaded on two grounds. It was based on an unrealistic understanding of the nature of warfare; and it played on the appeal to the public of technological superiority of air and naval power. Marshall persuaded the president to drop the idea:

> In this situation he had all the pressures from the outside and against what I was putting forward . . . , and it required a great deal of wear and tear before I could make an understanding of this clear to his satisfaction (Bland 1991, 282).

Becoming an Internationalist

Playing a leadership role in a global war required a change in world-view. Reacting rapidly to changing alliances and altered power relationships on a world-wide basis was not common fare for US military leaders. There was no policy manual to draw upon for guidance. Marshall's job, until September 1, 1939, was admittedly difficult politically and operationally, but it had at least been focused on a single objective, that of preparing the Army, including its air arm, for a potential war. In this pursuit he worked at the same things he had always worked on, only at a higher level. With Germany's invasion of Poland bringing forth a broader war involving many nations and power blocs, the world had drastically changed in character.

Marshall had a head-start in the realm of working internationally. His lengthy service in the Philippines and China, his touring of Japan and Korea, and especially his close liaison with the French and British in WW I all were of benefit. He had interacted with heads of state and royalty. He had kept the peace among contentious Chinese warlords. He had schooled himself in French and Chinese culture and languages. He had charmed Soviet leaders by giving safe harbor to heroic Russian pilots at Vancouver Barracks. Such extensive and colorful experience had made it easy in the spring of 1939 for President Roosevelt to select deputy chief of staff Marshall to lead a diplomatic mission to Brazil to counteract a German initiative to talk the Brazilians into building bases on South American soil to use strategically against the allies. He had, on that visit, made a highly favorable impression on the Brazilian people and its military elite (Ridgway 1959, 11-13).

The desperate fighting raging in Europe not only leant urgency to the need for building an effective American army against the possibility of German aggression against the US; it also created a pressing need to assist our threatened western European friends. The latter need flowed from different though interrelated perspectives: bolstering western democracies against fascist aggression in general (a noble but general objective); and propping up Britain and France as the first line of an American defense in the struggle against the Nazis (a more self-serving objective).

At the administration's urging Congress passed the Lend-Lease Act in March, 1941, obligating the US to participate as a supplier of war-related goods to the allies. Marshall supported its passage despite the fact it would make war preparation for the US Army more difficult in the short run by shifting stores of war goods overseas.

The Soviets presented a threat to the west by virtue of its 1939 non-aggression pact with Hitler. The purpose of the agreement was the partitioning of Poland and thus made the USSR a functioning part of the Axis bloc. When, in the spring of 1941, Germany betrayed the alliance and turned its forces on the USSR, a situation was created in which the US had to rethink its policies and alter its military planning models. The effects of Hitler's gamble were both good and bad for America, mostly good. In order to achieve its goal of scoring a quick knockout of the Soviet Union, the Nazis concentrated their forces on their eastern front. Strong Soviet resistance would mean an attenuation of German military strength, thus buying western Europe time and breathing space. Although many in the west hoped that the Nazi and communist regimes would kill each other off, Roosevelt and Marshall saw the need for long-term Soviet help in a continuing war.

The bad news for US planners and policy-makers was that the Soviet Union now joined the British, the French, and the Chinese as supplicants for US aid. They competed against each other and, implicitly, against using US-produced war goods to rebuild the American military. With scarce resources to go around, Marshall was thrown into a kind of "Hobson's Choice" in which he had to balance directing war goods to the growing American army against providing aid to the hard-pressed allies. Simultaneously, he had to lobby Congress for resources in order to be able to prepare to fight a war without knowing if America would enter the war directly or fight it by proxy.

A period was dawning which included an important new role for him, but that role was undefined and he would have to play a part in defining it. Being the stalwart leader of a strengthened US Army continued to be at the center of his official role. Practically, in the interest of national defense, the speed of the expansion had to be weighed against serving the fighting needs of our allies (Pogue 1966, 46-79). Their survival was essential. Putting up a stronger defense via ramparts manned by its allies would put off the day that America would have to enter the fighting. Struggling with this dilemma had a profound effect on Marshall:

In this forcing house of international chaos he quickly grew in national stature and his mental horizons expanded to embrace the globe. In 1940 and early 1941 he made the great transition from the role of an able soldier intent on making an efficient force of United States troops and fliers to that of a planner and leader charged with considering the problems of armies and strategies other than his own (Pogue 1966, 47).

As difficult as these calculations were, they grew even more complicated in the summer of 1941. American opposition to Japanese military and economic expansionism in the southwestern Pacific and China took the form of denying to it certain natural resources in order to contain its war-making power. These efforts escalated Japanese resentment and provoked threats of military action. Gradually, the possibility of a Japanese attack ripened into a probability and caused military planners to take actions to anticipate its military action and to take steps to reinforce American possessions where that action might occur.

The basic policy of concentrating on Europe first and attending to a Pacific war secondarily had already been decided upon by the president, the War Department, and the Navy. Still, with an actual attack expected in the Pacific, attention had to be refocused to a great extent on bolstering American defenses there, in Panama, and in the Far East, particularly the Philippine Islands. Sending troops, ships, airplanes, and supplies west, and particularly to the Philippines, came to be regarded as an urgent priority in order to discourage a Japanese attack and to respond if one came.

The Europe-first priority was based on analysis and probability estimates, and it had to take into account a real shooting war going on between Allied and Axis powers in Europe and Africa. As a result of the planning and preparation processes, Marshall was inexorably drawn into the center of heated debates over technical matters involving weaponry and ammunition, production schedules, shipping capacity, shipping loss projections from enemy submarine activity, equipment innovations, and a host of other matters.

His role as Roosevelt's advocate for preparedness accordingly increased. Marshall's voice had become the single voice on matters of war and preparation trusted above all others within the US The calm and professional soldier-administrator with all the facts at his command was in constant demand by congressional committees. It was his task to make the case for appropriations for the War Department, greater discretionary powers, and troops; to answer the myriad questions relating to the building of Army training bases and related consequences; to explain delays in new housing construction; to give advice on supply production and dispersion problems; and to address manpower, training, and officer promotion issues. He had, in short, taken on the role of America's major spokesman on security matters.

Bridging the Atlantic

The Anglo-American relationship in the mid-twentieth century has been described as "remarkably close and yet particularly strained" (Thorne 1978). Americans were divided roughly into two camps in their opinions of their British allies. In the first camp were those that felt the Brits were arrogant and looked down on the Yanks as unsophisticated and lacking in the ability to wage war. Some of these were fearful that the British would act selfishly to direct American resources toward British war aims. In the second camp were those with a strong affinity for the British based on common language and a history that places Great Britain as the originating source of American governmental and legal institutions. This latter group saw the UK and the US sharing common interests and a common destiny, and believed that these would dominate the relationship. They admired Churchill's appeals to traditional partnership and believed that America's support of British war aims should be unstinting.

Marshall stood in the second camp while many of his staff were in the first. As a WW I staff officer he had coordinated battle campaigns with them and had been the guest of British officers at the end of the war. In Pershing's company, he was feted by British royalty in London, and had been escorted about by Churchill (Marshall 1976). Experience also reflected more recent contacts made as chief of staff following President Roosevelt's lead in providing as much material aid as he could within the legal and practical limits of the Neutrality Act and the staggering demands of his own army. Marshall regarded the British as intelligent and patriotic, admired their fighting spirit, and cherished the pluck they demonstrated in weathering the brutal German bombings in 1940.

In a stroke of rare good luck, he had befriended the chief of the British Imperial General Staff, Sir John Dill. The first meeting with the dignified and soldierly Dill came at the British-American meetings aboard the H.M.S. Prince of Wales off Argentia, Newfoundland in the summer of 1941. They were kindred souls with WW I backgrounds in infantry and a deep love for professional army training. They bonded instantly and a close friendship formed between them.

Most of the British, with the major exception of Field Marshal Brooke (who was to succeed Dill in early 1942), were well pleased that so much of their working relationship with the Americans would be in Marshall's hands. This relationship would soon be reinforced at the Arcadia conference following on the heels of the attack on Pearl Harbor.

At the End of the Tunnel

Although it had become obvious through the summer and fall of 1941 that the Japanese would attack, it was anything but obvious where the blow would fall. Military analysts tilted toward the Philippine Islands as the most logical site because their conquest or neutralization would clear the sea lanes for Japanese expansion in southeast Asia and the southwestern Pacific. Pearl Harbor seemed less likely because it was heavily defended and at much greater distance from Japan's base of operations. Also believed to be at risk because of its strategic value was the Panama Canal, which could be struck by German or Japanese forces with the purpose of crippling America's ability to conduct a two-ocean war.

Marshall himself tilted toward the exceptionally vulnerable Philippines. He ordered vigorous, even frenetic, shoring up of defenses there. He drove the General Staff to push training, housing, aircraft design and testing, and shipping related to defense of the islands, and special attention was given to getting pilots, aircraft, and equipment to the islands (Gerow 1958, 43). The obstacles were daunting and time was of the essence. Just as quantity production was approaching the point of making a substantial contribution to the islands' defense, delivery was largely cut off by the Japanese capture of Dutch air bases in the southwest Pacific (Bland 1991, 292-93).

On November 26, 1941, a mere eleven days before the attack on Pearl Harbor, Marshall cabled all overseas command posts that war was imminent. The Hawaiian command and its commander, General Walter Short, were on the list and received the same message. Vigorous disagreement existed then and later about what exactly was said and the sequence of message dispatches and receipts, wording, and the reasonable inferences which could be drawn from these. It is not the purpose here to analyze or debate the adequacy of the communication or its interpretation. It is relevant only that Pearl Harbor was struck on December 7 and that the attack came as a surprise to those manning the naval and army military bases in Hawaii and their superiors in Washington.

The thoroughness and honesty of Marshall's testimony and reports to Congress and his strenuous efforts during his tenure as chief of staff to man, supply, and defend all potential American bases that could be attacked left no doubt that he would keep both his command and the confidence of the congress and the president in the wake of the attack. The nation had passed from the realm of denial, delay, and obstruction into an actual state of war on a global scale. The passage had been run.

Notes

1. Marshall was later to apply this principle to himself as a cabinet officer.
2. Marshall applied this advice to himself as well. To discourage a movement by some senators that he should be considered as a presidential nominee in 1944 to replace the physically failing President Roosevelt, he sent a confidential note to Secretary Stimson suggesting that he, Stimson, announce at a press conference that talk of this sort was harmful to the war effort and personally embarrassing to the chief of staff (Bland and Stevens 1996, 184-185).
3. Stimson was secretary of war under Taft and secretary of state during Hoover's administration.
4. To Marshall's argument that providing instructors for a large increase in officer training camps would cripple other constructive work of the Army, Assistant Secretaries of War Patterson and McCloy argued to Stimson (in Marshall's

absence) that "the Army's opposition (to increasing the number of camps) is simply a mark of incompetence and narrow-mindedness on the part of the Army" (Stimson 3/27/41, XXXI: 118).

5.   The bill was introduced in the House of Representatives and was signed into law on September 16, 1940. Conscription was done by lottery. If drafted, a man served for twelve months. Drafted soldiers had to remain in the US or its possessions or territories. Not more than nine-hundred thousand men were to be in training at any one time. Service was limited to twelve months.

6.   Marshall was moved to offer his own resignation to Roosevelt in view of his own age (59): "I would forfeit my career in the effort to make it possible to do this (enforce retirement from command positions) by a younger chief of staff and not stir up too much of turmoil and damage to morale." He visited Roosevelt twice and twice made the offer, "but the issue died there and my efforts to resign were defeated" (Bland 1991, 477-478).

7.   By the time America entered the war, the Army had grown to be eight times the size it had been in September, 1939. It would grow to sixty times its September 1939 size by early 1944, to over eight million.

CHAPTER SIX
ORGANIZER OF VICTORY

Pray . . . give . . . [General Marshall] my warmest congratulations on the magnificent fighting and conduct of the American and Allied Armies under General Eisenhower, and say what a joy it must be to him to see how the armies he called into being by his own genius have won immortal renown. He is the true "organizer of victory."
—Prime Minister Churchill to Dr. Henry Maitland Wilson, March 30, 1945
(GCMRL: 5, 114)

Crisis and Response

On Sunday morning, December 7, 1941, General Marshall went out for his daily recreational horseback ride near his home at Fort Meyers, accompanied by his faithful Dalmation dog Flash. He was thus not immediately available when news of the Japanese air attack on Pearl Harbor arrived; he had to be found on the trail to be given the message.

Despite the fact that an attack, somewhere, was expected, Marshall's outward calm on the "day of infamy" was a source of wonder to his staff. Perhaps his composure had come from having been under fire in WW I, or remembering General Pershing's specific admonition never to allow oneself, when leading others, to appear downcast, lest it be discouraging to staff and troops. His chief of personnel recalled:

> That afternoon and night and the next day, I don't think I left my office, and saw General Marshall a dozen times in that fifteen or sixteen hours. He was as calm and collected as a man could be. I saw him. He had many things to attend to. He wasn't the least bit ruffled or excited, didn't raise his voice, and didn't seem to be particularly hurried (Hilldring 1959, Parts 2, 3).

Despite the expectation of American and British leaders that the US would be drawn into a two-ocean war, there was in place no grand strategy beyond the general decision, reached in the Rainbow exercises, to make the war in Europe the first priority. There were no manuals or guidebooks or even a very relevant history on hand to be used as a point of departure. All the guiding theory and strategy were yet to emerge and had to be crafted anew out of the imagination and inter-workings of the people on hand and a set of structures and processes not then in place.

111

Looking back, the evolution from non-involvement to full-scale engagement looks natural and predestined, as though the United States and its allies were confidently at the controls of a giant productive machine undergoing gradual conversion from peacetime to wartime. The image is appealing but wholly false. The reality was a situation charged with uncertainty, internal conflict, and learning by doing.

Formation of the Grand Alliance

Less than three weeks after the attack on Pearl Harbor, British and American political and military leaders met in Washington at a conference that came to be labeled Arcadia. Churchill brought his closest military advisors and staff people and he himself took up residence in the White House and meetings with Roosevelt and American military staff began. The purpose of Arcadia was to reach agreement on basic war strategy and to put together the allied administrative machinery needed to carry it out.

British and American military teams were wary of each other. The Americans knew full well the desperate fight the British had been waging and expected the British would be aggressive in insisting on taking the leading role in the decision process, and were resolved not to allow the British to dictate war strategy to them. The bargaining power of the two sides was asymmetric; Churchill was prepared and forceful, Roosevelt unprepared and vacillating. To be sure, there was already agreement on some matters, much worked out in the Argentia meetings in the previous summer, particularly on ways the Americans could support British operations in the Atlantic against Germany's submarine fleet and supply the British across the north Atlantic. Little had been decided beyond that (Pogue 1966, 266-267).

Under these circumstances it is remarkable that Marshall dominated the conference, in the process making an indelible impression on the British in general and US Navy chiefs in particular. In brief outline he introduced two major organizing concepts and strongly supported a third, British proposal. All were adopted. His proposals were: (1) creating a joint command structure and a division of the world war into distinct theaters of operation with a distinct command structure; and (2) making the allocation of war production goods subject to the joint decision-making of the military chiefs of both nations. The British proposal was to establish a combined, permanent board of British and American military chiefs to guide strategic and tactical war decisions, a body referred to thereafter as the Combined Chiefs of Staff (CCOS). All three proposals became fundamental aspects of wartime decision-making. After Arcadia, Marshall, with the President's consent, created the Joint Chiefs of Staff (JCS) to further unify the American Military Chiefs.

Marshall prevailed at Arcadia because of his forceful presentation, persuasiveness, and passion for the principles he believed in. Beyond establishing his personal leadership, he increased the overall military role in the decision-making process. The major holdout to Marshall's leadership was the chief of the British Imperial

General Staff, Field Marshal Brooke. In this, Brooke's opinion differed sharply from every other British military leader.[1]

Churchill, although a rapid convert to Marshall's military leadership, continued to oppose him on some key strategy matters. In April, 1942, Marshall traveled to London to seek Churchill's agreement to strategic plans that had been worked out in the Operations Division (OPD had replaced WPD) and reflected the work of Eisenhower, Gerow, and Marshall, and bore the approval of the president and Hopkins. The essence of the plan (code-named BOLERO) was a massive build-up of allied forces in the British Isles preparatory to a cross-channel attack tentatively planned to take place in 1943. An auxiliary plan to launch an attack in France in 1942 ("SLEDGEMAMMER") was also advanced but was contingent upon a collapse of the Soviet defense on the eastern front. Its purpose would be to draw German divisions away from the eastern front to prevent the fall of the USSR. Marshall insisted to Churchill that project success would be impossible without whole-hearted British cooperation: "lukewarm acquiescence was not enough" (Davis 1952, 296).

The two spent leisurely hours together at Churchill's country home at Chequers, and their relationship tightened. Marshall admired Churchill's wit and intelligence, his knowledge of history, his unparalleled gift for language, and his courage. There was a negative impression, as well. He was concerned with how rapidly the prime minister could change his mind or mood and demonstrate disregard for important details of military operations (Pogue 1966, 312-313). Their styles were different. Marshall's persistence, calm reason and habit of remaining focused contrasted sharply with Churchill's emotionality, mercurial passion, brilliant insight, and restless search for more variables to bring into any discussion.

There was also duplicity in Churchill's nature, although Marshall did not see it on this visit. He allowed Marshall to assume that he, Churchill, had been convinced of the value of the American war strategy and had accepted in principle Marshall's major points, when in fact he harbored major reservations (Davis 1952, 296). Churchill secretly favored a pro-empire, Mediterranean and Middle East strategy which he fervently hoped to convince Roosevelt to adopt (Pogue 166, 314-319). His failure to make this thinking explicit to Marshall early on would lead to sharp clashes later in the war.

Each deferred to the other. Churchill believed that Marshall was the preeminent organizing force of the allied effort and resolved not to go around him on matters of organization. Marshall, for his part, was sensitive to Churchill's preferences for leadership positions and would only send Americans to serve in Britain that Churchill favored (these included Generals Eisenhower and Eaker).

Marshall was using his growing knowledge of British ways to both political and administrative advantage. He learned from Dill that the British military chiefs were so well indoctrinated in the democratic process and in hewing to the approved government policy that it was necessary to wait for a decision of the war cabinet (which Churchill led) before speaking to any military chief respecting some specific line of action (Marshall 1949, 2). To gain even greater insight into British positions and the strength with which they were held, he very much depended on his special relationship with Dill (Danchev, 1986).

The Continuing Battle Over European Strategy

Major strategic disagreements dogged the allies during the first eighteen months of the war. The principal debate centered on whether Germany should be directly confronted in Western Europe or more indirectly through campaigns in Africa, Italy, and the eastern Mediterranean. The Americans favored the former, the British differed in their views but often followed Churchill's lead in backing the latter.

Among the Americans there was additional disagreement between the Europe-first and the Pacific-first advocates, generally reflecting the different world-views of the Army and the Navy respectively. The Army and its air arm (receiving important aid from Navy Admirals Stark and Leahy, Roosevelt's naval aide) supported the earlier decisions of the war planners to place greater priority on the war against Germany. Although Admiral King, naval chief of operations, was constrained to at least formally support the adopted policy as a member of the JCS, he shared the Navy's general preference to emphasize the Pacific conflict (Pasco 1997, 35). The Navy received support from General MacArthur and his Southwest Pacific theater command. Despite the adoption of the Europe-first policy, there was a continuing need to strike a balance between the two camps.

In the early stages of the war, heavy losses and lack of success in the Pacific and Southwest Pacific theaters of operation (in the Solomon Islands and in New Guinea, respectively) created great pressure to shift resources to the Pacific at the expense of mounting an offensive on the European front. Marshall was confronted by a strategic dilemma:

> My struggle was to see that the main show (the war in Europe) went on and the later show (the war against Japan) was not washed out. But the Pacific people were Pacific, and you might say they were not interested at all in the Atlantic (Bland 1991, 352).

Marshall had come to worry on a constant basis that Churchill would be able to persuade Roosevelt that the first action of combined British and American ground forces in the European theater should not be launched on the European continent. Churchill and some of his military chiefs reasoned that US troops were not yet sufficiently assembled and were untested in battle. Thus a continental attack, if it were to be made, would have to be led by the British, in which case Churchill feared a catastrophe at the hands of massive German forces entrenched on the continent. British military planners were looking for an alternative holding a greater opportunity of success and also one that could buy time for US forces to gain combat experience and amass greater troop and materiel strength. They settled upon a campaign in North Africa as holding a greater chance of success and buy time before the heart of the German forces would have to be confronted in Europe.

Despite Marshall's pleas to the president that the US concentrate its efforts on building an assault capacity in western Europe for 1943, Roosevelt was persuaded by Churchill and perhaps by domestic political considerations (the need to show military success before the mid-term 1942 congressional elections) to take on a campaign in North Africa before turning to Europe. He correctly reasoned that the American public was growing impatient for success and was thus turned away from Marshall's arguments for a more orderly and efficient approach to the use of American forces.

Before the final decision was made, Marshall made his opposition to TORCH (code-name for the North African campaign) and his support for a buildup in Great Britain of joint forces for a cross-channel invasion in 1943 as clear as he possibly could. Exasperated by Churchill's ability to maneuver Roosevelt toward what he believed was a wasteful diversion in North Africa, and fearing also that a victorious campaign would strengthen Churchill's hand in advocating for his favored Mediterranean strategy, Marshall gambled on a maneuver. He convinced the JCS to propose that the bulk of US forces be shifted to the Pacific theater, judging that such an initiative would induce the British to agree to the western European strategy over the North African strategy. The idea was enthusiastically supported by King, who hoped the result of the tactic would be a permanent switch to a Pacific priority. As finally presented to Roosevelt, the JCS proposal stated that unless the British committed to a 1943 cross-channel invasion, America should change its primary focus to the Pacific war (Black 2003, 751).

Roosevelt wisely observed that Marshall's gambit risked creating a breach between the allies. He thus quashed the initiative and followed up by dispatching Marshall and King to London along with Hopkins, acting as Roosevelt's *alter ego*, with instructions to arrive at some form of joint plan to bring US troops into large-scale combat operations in the European-African theater (Black 2003, 751).

Marshall's uncharacteristic gamesmanship exposed the depth of his anxiety that TORCH would divert and waste US war-making resources. Roosevelt had detected Marshall's exasperation and deftly turned his tactic in the direction of purposeful negotiation. Marshall himself came to appreciate the president's judgment. The result of the Marshall-Churchill-King-Hopkins talks in London was an agreement to launch TORCH in late 1942 and follow it with a cross-channel assault which the Americans hoped would come in 1943. Once this decision was made Marshall leant his whole-hearted support to TORCH. With Churchill, he agreed that Eisenhower would lead the operation.

In retrospect, mounting operation TORCH appears to have been a sound decision. It had the advantage of committing the US in its first WW II land engagement to action mostly against the Vichy French rather than seasoned German troops. American troops without battle history would be tested and allowed to gain experience and confidence. Practice in organizing joint amphibious landings, so critical to future European operations, could also be gained (Black 2003, 760). British pride would also be restored (referring back to its ejection from the continent at Dunkirk) as Rommel's and other German forces were defeated. Finally, and perhaps most importantly, time would be purchased for the amassing of manpower, materiel, and training, so necessary to the war-waging capacity of US forces in other theaters.

TORCH was set to begin no later than October 30, 1942, days before the mid-term elections. Marshall, Stimson, and Eisenhower, fearful that disaster might befall the risky venture, were gloomy. For purely military reasons Marshall and Eisenhower rescheduled the invasion to start after the elections, which curried some disfavor at the White House. Solid support was given to Eisenhower throughout the planning phase and the War Department and the COS refused to second-guess him. Roosevelt, although he must have been disappointed because of the rescheduling, did not press for an earlier beginning of the assault. Marshall showed his gratitude for this by asking Eisenhower to highlight in the media US contributions to TORCH so as to better credit the president (Pogue 1966, 399-419).

Despite the agreement they had reached at Chequers, Marshall felt that he could not trust Churchill's promise to follow up the North African campaign with the cross-channel assault. He was ever wary that Roosevelt could fall prey to the prime minister's beguiling powers of persuasion. It was true that Roosevelt had gone on record agreeing with the joint chiefs on a cross-channel strategy, but this did not preclude his committing Americans to Churchill's plan through "loose talk." As Marshall later would put the matter: "When President Roosevelt began waving his cigarette holder you never knew where you were going" (Marshall 1949, 21).

Marshall's fears were well founded. As the North African campaign appeared headed toward a successful conclusion, Churchill began to push for an invasion of the Balkans and Italy. One certain result of such a strategy would be to again defer the cross-channel invasion. The argument made by Churchill in favor of a Mediterranean strategy was that an allied force should be interposed between Soviet and German forces, with two goals in mind. The first objective was to prevent Soviet forces from overrunning eastern and central Europe and reaching Germany first, thus decreasing the USSR's post-war influence. The second goal, mostly unstated, was to put the British in a better position to protect its imperial interests in the Middle East. Churchill may well have been prescient in his desire to protect eastern and central Europe from long-term Soviet expansion.[2]

Churchill partially succeeded. He was able to get Roosevelt to commit first to an invasion of Sicily and Italy with the goal of taking Italy out of the war. However, pushed by his war chiefs, Roosevelt insisted that plans proceed for the massive buildup in Great Britain for a cross-channel operation against the main concentration of German armed forces in the west. Roosevelt's decision to press for a cross-channel attack had two consequences, much welcomed by Marshall. The Mediterranean strategy of interposition opposed by both American and British military chiefs was probably dead, and the build-up for the cross-channel invasion was now finally underway.

Marshall's strategic view of Europe and opposition to a Mediterranean campaign were heavily based on the importance he attached to logistics. Shipping troops and supplies to the eastern Mediterranean was more expensive, time-consuming, and risky than shipping the same to American and British staging areas in West European beachheads and ports. It would also seriously drain American capacity to fight elsewhere, particularly in the Pacific, thereby extending the war.[3] His ability to keep the president and the British military chiefs in line on opposing the prime minister's strategy, and his steadfastness on pursuing the cross-channel strategy undoubtedly brought an earlier end to the war.

Put another way, the debate was between Marshall's focus on logistical and tactical factors (which favored the cross-channel invasion) and Churchill's preoccupation with geopolitical factors with the twin goals of maintaining the British Empire and reducing post-war Soviet influence in Europe and the Middle East. True to his sense of mission and role, Marshall supported the strategy that promised to win the war against both Germany and Japan as quickly and with as little loss of life as possible. Had Roosevelt, or later Truman, decided as a matter of national policy to support Churchill, Marshall would have changed his focus and complied. Neither president did so, and thus Marshall was able to hold his ground.

Brokering Competing Personalities and Demands

General Douglas MacArthur was among the most talented and difficult persons under Marshall's command. The son of a *bona fide* civil war hero who had also been a one-time commander of US forces in the Philippines, he had served his country valiantly in WW I. A brilliant military strategist, he was supported by both Marshall and the War Department because of his generalship. These traits had caused Marshall to initiate the proposal to award MacArthur the Congressional Medal of Honor when the latter was under siege at Corregidor in the first few months of the war, and to order his rescue and that of his family and his chief aides. While en route on his escape to a triumphant arrival in Australia, Marshall arranged to have him installed as supreme commander of the newly constituted Southwest Pacific Theater (James 1975, 32).[4]

MacArthur's shortcomings were also great. An obstinate belief in the superiority of his own reasoning often led him to turn away from collaborating with other military leaders. WW I had left him with a contempt for "Pershing men," and he had counted Marshall among them. When MacArthur was US Army chief of staff in the mid-1930s, his assignment of Marshall as an advisor to the Illinois National Guard was at least insensitive to and perhaps intentionally hostile to Marshall's career prospects for top Army command. Despite this, Marshall did not bear him any malice, at least as measured by his later actions.

MacArthur's vanity caused him to surround himself with less than competent staff who would not challenge him.[5] He characteristically viewed his own theater of command as strategically the most important on the worldwide stage, both militarily and politically. He believed that the Army was superior to the Navy in its ability to lead joint operations and he frequently antagonized Navy leaders by provoking quarrels with them (Handy 1956, 3).

The relationship between the two generals was strained. In MacArthur's view the judgment of the theater commander was superior to the judgment of those in Washington. Marshall saw the qualities of "verbosity, arrogance, and self-importance" in his Southwest Theater commander and summed up his assessment of MacArthur by stating that "he was very difficult—very, very difficult at times" (Bland 1991, 244). In the relative privacy of his office, he had referred to "that fellow MacArthur," interpreted by his staff as a Marshall epithet equivalent to "son of a bitch" (Pasco 1997, 29).

Complicating Marshall's attempts to manage MacArthur was the fact that Roosevelt also disliked MacArthur. As chief of staff in 1932 during the Hoover administration, MacArthur had harshly put down a demonstration by WW I veterans held on federal property in the District of Columbia. The men had camped and marched illegally on the mall in Washington seeking additional compensation for their war service in order to blunt the economic hardships they were suffering. Roosevelt had been appalled at the brutal manner in which the demonstration was terminated by MacArthur's order. Shortly after Roosevelt's election, MacArthur, still serving as chief of staff, was critical of Roosevelt's plan to have the Army oversee the Civilian Conservation Corps on the grounds that this was not the type of duty the Army had been trained to perform. Roosevelt later demonstrated his enmity by opposing promotions and awards for MacArthur even though they had been recommended by the War Department and had Marshall's approval. Marshall inserted himself into the gulf between the two men in order to mollify egos in the interest of prosecuting the war.

A quarrel over scarce resources erupted in 1942 between Admiral Nimitz of the South Pacific Theater command (engaged in a protracted battle in the Solomon Islands), and MacArthur's Southwest Pacific Theater command (itself threatened in New Guinea and Australia). The Navy claimed it was getting insufficient help from MacArthur. MacArthur countered that the Navy was mishandling the Solomon Islands campaign and in any case resources were more desperately needed to defend what he believed to be the more strategically important areas of New Guinea and Australia. Marshall found himself drawn into the middle of what he called "a war of personalities—a very vicious war" (Bland 1991, 365). Although acknowledging that he had little in the way of supplies, weaponry, and men to send to MacArthur:

> I supported him through thick and thin on most of the questions. . . . But he had a great many prejudices and intense feelings. All of this was arrangeable if the two commanders wanted to get together. But their approaches, particularly on MacArthur's side, were so filled with deep prejudice that it was very hard to go about it . . . (Bland 1991, 376).

Air Chief of Staff Arnold was of the opinion, contrary to that of naval chief King, that air combat forces already in the Pacific region were sufficient to service both theaters and that additional forces should not be diverted from their current use in Africa. Arnold saw two factors contributing to the situation: (1) air resources were being misused through poor naval administrative and logistics decisions; and (2) MacArthur was not harmonizing his actions in New Guinea in a way that would lend more support to the operations in the Solomons. Marshall decided to send Arnold to the Pacific to get a closer reading. As Arnold prepared to leave, and knowing that Arnold's views would not be popular with those he would meet on his trip, Marshall advised him to "let the other fellow tell his story first," and "don't get mad" (Pogue 1966, 388).

The dispute had become a political quagmire. Pacific-first advocates were accusing Roosevelt and Churchill of neglecting US forces on that front. Some of the many political and press friends of the highly popular MacArthur were accusing the Navy and political leaders, including the president and Marshall, of favoring the Solomons battle over the more important New Guinea front because they were afraid of MacArthur as a potential presidential candidate. MacArthur did little or nothing to stop the expression of these views by members of his own command (Bland and Stevens 1991, 413-415).[6] Marshall sent a sharply worded telegram to MacArthur admonishing him for "this editorial through the medium of press releases emanating from your headquarters" alleging neglect of the Southwest Pacific theater by the CCOS (GCMRL: Box 74, Folder 49).

MacArthur's squabbles with the Navy and Nimitz did not stop at disagreement over whether the Solomons or New Guinea should have the greater support. MacArthur had little respect for either King or Nimitz (although he worked well with Admiral Halsey, who in late 1942 was appointed commander of the Pacific fleet under Nimitz). Some of this feeling was no doubt related to the overriding service rivalries that afflicted many in the traditional services; but much of it had to do with MacArthur's view of his own personal status regardless of the fact that he was outranked by the JCS, CCOS, President, and Congress. The war plan that the CCOS had adopted simply exacerbated the conflict for him: MacArthur never accepted the national strategy to concentrate the major effort in Europe (Pogue 1966, 377-378).

The conflict over competing priorities became so severe in mid-1942 that King advised Nimitz to prepare an offensive in the Pacific and to assume that the Army's support would be unnecessary. At this point Marshall interjected himself into the breach, objecting directly to King's preference to "go it alone." He admonished MacArthur that it was more important for the two services to use their full efforts on the enemy rather than on each other (Pogue 1966, 380-381). By continual urging and firm efforts at negotiation, the crisis passed.

Marshall also struggled with the Navy but at the highest levels was able to ensure a modicum of cooperation. The primary meeting ground was the JCS. Marshall had wisely balanced JCS membership by adding, with the president's approval, a fourth member and chair to the body in the person of Admiral Leahy. This move gave the Navy two voices (Leahy and King) to match the two voices of the Army (Marshall and Arnold) and thus avoided the charge that Marshall sought to dominate JCS decision-making. Although he was able to get Leahy and King to agree on the Europe-first strategy, frequent clashes erupted on specific questions of how resources were to be allocated between the two fronts (Marshall 1949, 22).

King was a rigid and doctrinal navy man, but he was also an able leader. Both he and Marshall worked together effectively to present a united front to the president. Still, they were unable to generate solid staff cooperation below the deputy chief of staff level, and so the four-member JCS meetings continued to be of the greatest importance in gaining coordinated planning and operations. All army intelligence was shared with the Navy except that which came via Eisenhower's private and direct line to Marshall, and the Navy reciprocated (Pasco 1997, 35-37). Because Marshall was looked to by others as the natural leader of the military chiefs he was able to coordinate JCS decision-making despite the fact that Leahy was formally its chair, and to do it gently through insisting on reaching consensus on decisions (Wilson 1961, 17).

More positive was the constant harmony and common strategy formulation that existed between Marshall and his air generals. On his first wartime visit to England he said to General Eaker, "I don't believe we'll ever successfully invade the continent . . . unless we first defeat the Luftwaffe" and agreed with Eaker that the way to get the Luftwaffe into the air was to launch a strategic heavy bomber offensive against German war industry on German soil. Their bargain became one of the central and most successful American strategies of the war (Parton 1986, 148).

American-British relations were to be sorely tested over two issues involving Eaker's and Spaatz's Eighth Air Force. Should it be moved from England to North Africa as part of operation TORCH? The Americans opposed the move and the British supported it. Should it engage in daytime bombing (which the Americans favored) or perform only nighttime bombing (favored by the British)? Although heavily pressured by Churchill, Marshall, with help from British Air Marshal Portal, was able to keep the Eighth Air Force in Britain (Parton 1986, 183) and promote the highly successful daytime bombing which ultimately destroyed the German war industry. Also, Marshall joined with his European-based air commanders to resist massive relocation of air units to the Pacific.

Conflict Over China Policy

Another bone of contention dividing the allies was the conflict over the role China should play in the China-Burma-India theater. US policy, worked out at the presidential level, called for getting China directly into the war against Japan by supplying it with military goods and training Chiang Kai-Shek's army. British policy placed less emphasis on China and Chiang, preferring instead to focus on protecting India, a part of the British Commonwealth.

There were two specific issues. The US wished to supply the Chinese by air from India (flying over the "Burma hump") and to use amphibious landing craft in the region to capture the air bases needed to carry on these operations. This preference conflicted with the British desire to reserve the landing craft for possible use in the Mediterranean. The policy gap crystallized on a second dispute, that being who should be named supreme commander of the China theater—Archibald Wavell, the British general, or the American general, Joseph "Vinegar Joe" Stilwell?

The British wanted their own man appointed. Wavell was an able administrator who was generally cool to the Burma-China operation and more interested in India. Marshall backed General Stilwell, a "Marshall man" who had been a superior instructor under his command at Fort Benning. Stilwell spoke fluent Chinese, had great fighting spirit, and had already proven his talent in the training of Chinese troops. His great failing was that he lacked diplomatic tact and could not abide the Chinese nationalists or their leader, Chiang Kai-Shek. Chiang preferred to let Mao Zedong's communist troops do most of the fighting against the Japanese and to keep his own troops in reserve and stockpile US military support with an eye to doing battle against the communists once the Japanese were defeated. Chiang demanded Stillwell's removal from his role heading Chinese troop training and preparation (Bland 1991, 366).

A compromise was reached when Lord Mountbatten finally emerged as the new supreme commander by the unanimous agreement of the CCOS. Stilwell was assigned to serve under Mountbatten with the continued responsibility to train Chinese troops, insuring continuation of the Stilwell-Chiang feud. The issue of the scope of the Chinese war effort was never adequately resolved.

Some Principles in Managing Conflict

As some of these conflicts demonstrate, Marshall often called on others to fight the battles so as not to diminish his own currency. To succeed at this strategy he had to have a very good understanding of the people with whom he was dealing as well as their values and views. His choice of intermediaries was crucial—individuals he knew intimately and admired: Dill, Arnold, Eisenhower, Hopkins, Baruch, Morgenthau, and Portal, to cite the most obvious. Robert Lovett, another intimate associate, described Marshall's method:

> Whenever the Chiefs of Staff got together and started to make things tough for Marshall, Hap [Arnold] would rush in as a running guard and blast out interference for him (Parton 1986, 226).

Where the British were deeply involved, Marshall could rely on Portal and Dill to run the interference. Leahy was valuable as a go-between in dealing with the Navy.

Unlikely to insinuate himself into a policy role, Marshall was yet peculiarly suited to deal with both conflict and cooperation, the essence of policymaking, and thus found himself constantly consulted by policy makers. There is but a shade of difference between conflict and cooperation. Conflict was typically fueled during the war by a mixture of differing world-views and strategic theories, or by sharp personality clashes, or by differing approaches to arrive at a shared end, or some combination of these. In these climates his integrity and fairness of mind could be counted upon. If he lost a battle on a strategy issue or on a personnel selection matter he would turn immediately to support the decision vigorously and without rancor or equivocation, just as he had done on operation TORCH.

In managing relations among key personalities Marshall demonstrated a remarkably refined and subtle touch. He began by creating a dignified climate by according respect to others. He was prepared to give on matters that he did not believe were critical to the central objective. Focusing on goal achievement (such as winning the war while minimizing casualties) helped him to ease tensions by gaining common ground and reminding the parties of their similar interests.

In terms of process, this meant that everyone should state their views, the various consequences should be foreseen as far as possible, and their costs and outputs evaluated in terms of their influence on shared objectives. The person who is in the best position to know the facts (if the decision has to do with which means to select to best implement a policy objective, given time as a serious constraint) or the person with constitutional authority acting with complete or near-complete information (if the decision is one of policy) should make the decision. During wartime, the parties usually had so much going on at one time that there was little time for complex process and arguments; efficiency thus was essential as it was important to move quickly and get beyond the conflict. Acceptance of the decision, if it was to be made by Marshall, was furthered by the fact that he was known to be unconcerned with credit for a decision; thus his ego was not a complicating factor in the situation (Pasco 1997, 46).

Care in building a decision process compatible with organizational structure and knowledge was another factor in the reduction of unnecessary conflict. Good examples are found in the cross-channel invasion: making preparations for D-Day, the timing of the decision to go, the logistics of landing operations, and the buildup necessary to break out from Normandy were tactical decisions all delegated to Eisenhower, who in turn delegated duties to the major commanders: Bradley, Montgomery, Patton, Alexander, Clark, and others. To be sure, Eisenhower had conflicts (especially with Montgomery), but Marshall supported Eisenhower absolutely. Recalling his visit to Montgomery's headquarters in Holland after the Battle of the Bulge, in which the British general had been openly critical of Eisenhower, Marshall admitted that he had come "pretty near to blowing off":

> And then I thought, now this is Eisenhower's business and not mine, and I had better not meddle, though it was very hard for me to restrain myself because I didn't think there was any logic in what he [Montgomery] said, but overwhelming egotism (Bland 1991, 345).

Even when American forces were surprised by the German counter-attack in the Battle of the Bulge, leading to heavy losses on both sides and exerting great pressures for counter-reactive tactics, Marshall did not intervene. He instructed his staff to send no messages requiring things like special reports from Eisenhower's staff, thus demonstrating his confidence and removing extra pressure on the field command structure (Hilldring 1959, Part 2, 3).

Who Should Lead the Cross-Channel Invasion?

The supreme personal goal of Marshall's career was to command American field forces in Europe much as General Pershing had done in WW I. The opportunity presented itself in late 1943 as the question arose as to who would lead operation Overlord, the cross-channel invasion of France and Western Europe. Marshall had virtually willed the climactic confrontation between the huge German and American-British armies through his constant pursuit of the strategy. He knew that the landing in France and the subsequent drive directly into the German heartland would be the defining campaign of the war and determine the outcome of the greatest struggle in the history of warfare. The chief commander of a successful invasion would be remembered forever. This role would be "the culmination of all his efforts between 1939 and 1944 and, in a sense, the climax to which all his career had been directed" (Pogue 1973, 320).

Assignment to this role could easily have been his for the asking. No one in power wished to deny to him what was widely accepted as being his right to claim. What ultimately kept him from making the claim was an ethical premise that had always guided him: his belief that in a constitutional democracy, a public servant must leave political judgments to those with the constitutional authority to make them. He truly believed that he should play no part in selecting the supreme commander of Overlord. His behavior during the process of choosing the commander suggests that it may not have even occurred to him to attempt to influence the decision, despite its enormous personal import to him.

Pogue observed that Marshall "would not have the command if he had to ask for it or even to reach out his hand" (1973, 320). Historian and biographer Mark Stoler amplifies why the assignment was neither offered nor requested:

> . . . Roosevelt could figure out no sound arrangement whereby Marshall could function as both chief of staff and Overlord commander. Still, his respect for the army chief had become so enormous, and his desire to make him "the Pershing of the second World War" so great, that he was willing to give him the command and make Eisenhower chief of staff provided Marshall requested such a change. . . . This Marshall would not do. He desperately wanted the Overlord command, but his sense of honor and duty precluded any expressions of personal preference. The president, he insisted, would have to decide what was best for the country, not for George Marshall (1989, 108).

Roosevelt was under great pressure both to give Marshall the command and to withhold it. Secretary of War Stimson and Admiral Leahy were among many who urged that Marshall was clearly the man for the job. Roosevelt himself was influenced by his own sense that no one was more deserving. But to move in this direction he would have to find a substitute for Marshall as US Army chief of staff and *de facto* leader of the allied forces worldwide. The folly of doing this was reinforced by Pershing himself, who wrote to the president that none other than Marshall could harmonize the multiple parts of the American military, let alone lead the combined chiefs of staff and the military establishments of the various nations within the grand alliance. And this was only possible from his current position. The British also weighed in on the issue, supporting Marshall for the command but regretting his potential loss as leader of the CCOS.

In an effort to discover General Marshall's thoughts on the subject, Roosevelt dispatched Harry Hopkins to sound him out. Marshall gave Hopkins no hint of his feelings and insisted that Roosevelt make the decision and that the decision be made according to what the national interest required. Hopkins, who himself was strongly in favor of giving Marshall the assignment, reported back to the president.

Now becoming anxious about the cost of uncertainty and delay in this most important business, Marshall directed his operations chief, General Handy, and air chief of staff Arnold, to work out a solution. As Handy later recalled:

> He (Marshall) definitely and specifically ordered that the solution be based on our own ideas of what we considered sound and that we were not to be influenced in any way whatsoever by the fact that he was involved personally in the matter (Bland and Stevens 1996, 178).

Digesting feedback from Hopkins, Pershing, Stimson, the British, and the Handy-Arnold recommendations, Roosevelt finally met with Marshall and asked directly for his, Marshall's, advice on the assignment. As Marshall later wrote to Sherwood:

> I recalled saying that I would not attempt to estimate my capabilities; the President would have to do that; I merely wished to make clear that whatever the decision, I would go along with it wholeheartedly; that the issue was too great for any personal feeling to be considered. I did not discuss the pros and cons of the matter. If I recall, the President stated in completing our conversation, "I feel I could not sleep at night with you out of the country" (Sherwood 1948, 803).

Recounting the event to Pogue at a later date, he added:

> I was determined that I should not embarrass the President one way or the other—that he must be able to deal in this matter with a perfectly free hand in whatever he felt was the best interest [of the country]. . . . I was utterly sincere in the desire to avoid what had happened so much in other wars—the consideration of the feelings of the individual rather than the good of the country (Pogue 1973, 321).

Ultimately, it was Marshall's sense of role as well as his selflessness that allowed the president to make the choice that was his to make. It is probable that Roosevelt made the right decision in keeping his chief of staff in Washington to harmonize and oversee the large-scale war efforts then going on in multiple theaters, rather than allowing his best soldier to submerge himself in a single theater.[7] Arnold, Handy, and Pershing had similarly reasoned the matter.

The Turn Toward Peace

As battle successes turned the tide in both Europe and the Pacific, three new types of demands grew rapidly. First, differences between the US and USSR arose which begged resolution. Second, the conquered territories, ravaged by five years of war, had to be governed by the allies until they could be returned to the sovereignty of liberated or conquered nations. Third, pressures were mounting for disengagement of the troops, transporting them home, and discharging them from service—processes collectively known as demobilization. These issues not only had relevance and importance for the conduct of the final stages of the war, they also had critical ramifications for the post-war world and America's role in that world.

What Policy to Adopt Toward the Soviets?

In early 1945, as Soviet forces advanced from the east, British forces from the northwest, and American forces from the west and southwest, converging on a vanishing German state, the political as well as the military strategic climate changed markedly. War still raged in the Pacific against a powerful and determined foe committed to continuing the conflict until its homeland was overrun. The atom bomb was untested and of uncertain value. The American people were tired of sacrifice and dreading the final campaigns in the Pacific and Asia and desperate to return to peacetime normalcy. A power vacuum now in central and eastern Europe needed to be filled. All of these factors pointed toward the wisdom of maintaining amicable relations with the Soviets and working out an effective global order to keep the peace and promote recovery and democracy in the postwar era. This had been the view of Roosevelt and it had been the premise for most decisions and arrangements reached at the Teheran and Yalta summit meetings. Truman, replacing Roosevelt in April of 1945, continued on the path of his predecessor.

Other factors dictated a much different approach to relations with the USSR. Stalin's intention to dominate eastern and central European, and to play a larger role in western Europe, was becoming apparent. This aim was coupled with the desire to permanently cripple Germany's economy and industrial potential by exacting reparations and making rearmament impossible. Trust in its western allies had never been strong and was fading further.

How to handle the Soviet Union became a divisive issue among the allies. On one hand, American policy makers were firm in their belief that gaining Soviet participation in the war against Japan would save many lives and be a useful prelude to post-war cooperation. The Soviets would be inclined to go to war with Japan in order to secure its eastern borders and settle damaged interests left over from the Sino-Soviet War of 1905. Such action would also cement its place in the new world order alongside the United States in the United Nations.

Churchill and the British were far less optimistic. He distrusted Stalin and did not share Roosevelt's view that the United Nations would help blunt Soviet designs in eastern and central Europe. Such matters dominated the shadows during the Yalta talks. Marshall was present but avoided taking part because of his conviction that it was Roosevelt's constitutional role to take the lead. After Roosevelt's death in April of 1945 Marshall characteristically waited for Truman and his political advisors to fill the political decision vacuum.

As history now makes clear, Churchill was the better judge of Soviet intentions at this crucial juncture. A world organization might even play into its hands because its autonomy to act was not diminished by the UN or by regional arrangements. It was even then engaged in a *sub rosa* effort to establish strong, Soviet-influenced communist parties in Central and Western Europe which would further serve to strengthen its strategic position in the post-war era. Joining with America in the war against Japan was deemed a tactical plus to furthering its objectives of stability and expansion.

Political factors often dominated discussions of the American joint chiefs. For example, they discussed issues of occupation of European countries at length. The chiefs preferred to think that political considerations did not affect their decisions, and they did not discuss politics with their British counterparts. They wished not to be seen to arrogate to themselves decisions belonging to heads of state (Bland 1991, 414-415). In the absence of political direction, the central military objective remained—that of successfully concluding the war against Japan. Politically, anything other than total victory and an unconditional surrender was not an option. The best means to accomplish total victory necessitated rapid redeployment of forces to the Pacific theater and bringing Soviet arms to bear on Japan.

Thus Eisenhower held back from sending his armies to Berlin and Prague before the Soviet army reached them, and Marshall supported him in this decision. They would not move aggressively without a political directive from the president, and that did not come. Whatever the wisdom of an aggressive Soviet-blocking strategy might have been, Marshall felt strongly that this was not his or Eisenhower's call to make. As always, the military course of action they selected was carefully designed to serve the goals of shortening the war in Europe and saving lives (Pogue 1973, 574-78).

Re-instituting Government in the Conquered Territories

The need to reestablish functioning governments in conquered and liberated territories brought to the armies of the allies and their governments a new set of challenges. The dimensions of the enterprise began to take shape in the North African campaign as American and British forces overwhelmed German forces in Tunisia. General Eisenhower, the supreme allied commander in the theater who was already heavily burdened with the continuing fighting and the planning for future campaigns, could not afford to be distracted by the difficult and mostly non-military tasks of governance. These tasks included the care and feeding of native populations, the maintenance of security, the rebuilding of homes and industry and providing employment—all required the creation of management and implementation systems.

Eisenhower and Beetle Smith, his administrative chief, turned to Marshall for assistance and guidance. It was Marshall's hope that the State Department, the president, and the cabinet would take the lead in fashioning American policy concerning civil governance. In his view, the Army had an obligation to initially occupy areas overrun by its forces, to stabilize security in these zones, and to initially organize the systems needed to provide on a temporary basis for meeting the essential needs of residents—clean water, the fair distribution of food, and furnishing of basic medical supplies. However, beyond meeting these basic needs, the Army should not be put in the position of having to develop more permanent systems of civil governance. Not only would such activity drain resources from its continuing military objectives, it would likely set in motion mechanisms incompatible with the long-term governance systems of the reemerging nations and their local government components.

Marshall had anticipated early in the war, in May of 1942 to be precise, the need for planning to prepare military and civilian officers to serve as civil administrators to manage the villages, cities and towns of Africa and Europe that would eventually come to be occupied. He thus created a planning group and charged it with determining how thousands of highly skilled people from civilian and military life, including mayors and ex-governors, bank and corporation presidents, engineers, and health officials would be recruited, trained, and assigned. The group's efforts led to the establishment of a new School of Military Government at the University of Virginia,[8] and at civil affairs training programs at other locations (Bland 1991, 452-455).

When his entreaties to State produced no results, he reluctantly moved to organize within the War Department the machinery which would at least meet the initial need for civil governance that had been left to the Army by default. A new staff function was formed within the General Staff on March 1, 1943 and given the title Civil Affairs Section, or G-5. To lead it Marshall appointed an officer of great breadth of experience and judgment, General John Hilldring, who had served brilliantly as the director of personnel (G-2) of the General Staff until that time. Marshall made crystal clear to the new G-5 chief his perception of the critical role that the Army was to play in civil governance:

> He [Marshall] said, 'I'm turning over to you a sacred trust and I want you to bear that in mind every day and every hour you preside over this military government and civil affairs venture.' He said, 'Our people sometimes say that soldiers are stupid . . . I must admit that at times we are. . . . We have a great asset and that is that our people, our countrymen, do not distrust us and do not fear us. . . . They don't harbor any ideas that we intend to alter the government of the country, or the nature of this government in any way. This is a sacred trust that I turn over to you today. . . . And I don't want you to do anything, and I don't want to permit the enormous corps of military governors that you are in the process of training and that you are going to dispatch all over the world, to damage this high regard in which the professional soldiers in the Army are held by our people, and it could happen, it could happen, Hilldring, if you don't understand what you are about, and how important it is that this reputation we have is of enormous importance, not only to the Army but to the country. This is my principal charge to you, this is the thing I never want you to forget in the dust of battle and when the pressures will be on you, and the pressures *will* be on you" (Hilldring 1959, 59-60, his emphasis).

Hilldring's new office set to work establishing policies to guide military decisions concerning civil governance operations in both liberated and occupied territories. The work was coordinated with a similar Navy office through a new

Joint Civil Affairs Committee. Policies were further developed and coordinated with the British through a Combined Civil Affairs function of the CCOS. Civil governance thus took on the same organizational form as the overall conduct of the allied decision machinery. Also, a multi-agency committee arose composed of diplomatic and political chiefs of staff at the level of assistant secretary in the Departments of State, War, and Navy (1959, 42-43). All of this was done at the behest of General Marshall.

Next, using the output of the new School of Military Government at the University of Virginia, Hilldring oversaw the assignment of civilian governance officers to places that followed the path of successful US and British assaults in Sicily, Italy, France, and finally into Germany. These officials took over the direction of public safety and health, food and clothing supply, housing, and agricultural functions. Respecting public safety, the policy generally followed was that control should be exercised through the already-existing police organization of the occupied state, such as the Italian *carabinieri* (US Army Chief of Staff 1945, 90-91).

Of greatest urgency and enduring significance were the occupations of Germany and Japan.[9] State Department professionals gave only piecemeal and sporadic assistance, and in Hilldring's view State was simply unable to act promptly enough in a fast-moving military situation. Unhappy with having responsibility for making politically charged policy in lieu of State Department leadership, Marshall charged Hilldring's office and Assistant Secretary of War McCloy with the task. The resulting policy, known simply as JCS 1067, was an admittedly inadequate document that was not fully written until the allied troops were poised to enter Germany in January, 1945 (1959, 39-41).

When JCS 1067 finally reached the many professional civil affairs officers who had been standing idly by awaiting policy guidance before commencing their jobs in Germany, it was at considerable variance with their thoughts about what American policy in Germany ought to be (Hilldring 1959, 44-46). The officers also received technical advice on the preservation and restoration of art and archives from the newly established American Commission for the Protection and Salvage of Artistic and Historic Monuments in War Areas.

The nature of the transition of governing powers differed widely depending upon local conditions. While rather rapid transference of governance functions to Italian citizens occurred in Italy, full-blown military governance by allied forces was the rule in Germany. In France negotiations took place between the War Department and the French Committee of National Liberation, with development occurring largely under French law.

The smoothest transition in the Pacific theater occurred in the Philippines. Control was immediately ceded, in Marshall's words, to "Commonwealth Government and local officials of inflexible loyalty" who had "shown from the very first landings immediate competence to reorganize administration and reestablish orderly government" (US Army Chief of Staff 1945, 94).

The most difficult case was Japan. As MacArthur accepted the surrender of Japan aboard the USS. Missouri on September 2, 1945 there was no civil governance program in place for that country. Marshall favored MacArthur for the job of leading the effort to effect civil governance in Japan. MacArthur did so, imposed rule, created policy, and gained effective implementation through the device of using the emperor as the channel of implementation to the Japanese people (US Army Chief of Staff 1945, 91-92).

While some progress was being made by the military, as Hilldring saw it the overall situation of civil governance in occupied and liberated countries had been badly handicapped by political failure:

> In Europe we had the political fortunes and economic fortunes of three hundred million people in our keeping and we were never equipped, from the time military government started until the end of the war, with any mechanism for giving political guidance to the war. In other words, we didn't know what we were fighting the war for, really. We were fighting it to win battles. That's about all you can say as to the national policy enunciated in World War II (1959, 49-50).

Such a policy void was made worse by the failure of President Roosevelt to bring Vice President Truman into his confidence and the peace-planning process. The neglect of civil governance was to some extent replicated among the allies, who were further distracted by the dismal state of their own postwar prospects. At the Teheran and Yalta conferences, where these issues could and should have surfaced, uncertainty was the norm. The four allied parties—the UK, US, USSR and the free French—approached civil governance and occupation matters more as a matter of playing out a set of assumptions than as an exercise in strategic and tactical planning.

The assumptions reflected Roosevelt's thinking that the United Nations would fill the vacuum by setting the organizational framework for the re-emergence of democratic institutions, backed by the US, and that postwar peace treaties would resolve most of the other problems. Allowing these assumptions to replace hard policy choices reflected naivete about Soviet intentions as well as a profound weariness of war.

Demobilization

War weariness also drove much of demobilization policy, despite the fact that Marshall had begun at an early date to call the nation's attention to the urgency of retaining military readiness after the war ended. He established a demobilization task force, a team of well-respected military planners, in late 1942 under the leadership of John McAuley Palmer, to develop a basis for policy. In the back of Marshall's and Palmer's minds was the need to avoid the type of sloppy and overly rapid demobilization that occurred at the end of WW I that had so weakened the Army in the long term. Moreover, if the European war were to end first, as contemplated by the war planners, there would be a great need to redeploy troops and arms to the Pacific to bring final victory against Japan. To neglect policymaking and the implementing steps required would translate to huge inefficiencies in concluding the war against Japan. Rational demobilization, they reasoned, was a sensitive issue economically and politically as well as militarily, and so it should be approached cautiously and systematically.

Demobilization policy was created and executed with considerable secrecy. If demobilization planning became too obvious as the tide of battle was shifting in the allies' favor, the public would be encouraged to believe that the end of the war was imminent, which it was not. If this occurred, a loss of public support for continuation of the war could result in the resurgence of Axis efforts and an extension of the war. This kind of false public optimism would be especially harmful to plans to redeploy forces to the Pacific in the event invasion of the Japanese homeland became necessary.

The demobilization task force decided that since enlistment and conscription had depended heavily on individual factors of fitness and economic role of the individual, the discharge process should also be governed by focusing on individuals rather than military units. The democratic device of an Army-wide survey to discover what the troops themselves considered to be the fairest criteria to use for determining the timing of discharge and shipment home was undertaken. Survey results dictated that those who had served the longest, faced the most combat, and had children at home would be given priority. A point system was established implementing the criteria and the policy's application was made the responsibility of overseas commanders. Specifically, the system gave "credit for length of Army service, overseas service, certain decorations, battle stars" and the number of dependent children (up to three) under the age of eighteen (US Army Chief of Staff 1945, 116).

Care was taken in the policy's formulation to make separation from service both painless and helpful. Soldiers were to return to bases near their homes and undergo a final administrative screening procedure which would determine the amount of mustering-out pay and the issuance of uniforms, discharge certificates, lapel buttons, a separation record summarizing military service and qualifications, and the fare needed to get home. Each individual was to be given a pamphlet on veteran rights and benefits and advice on which government and private agencies could assist in locating employment. Those with impaired health would be retained in the service "until everything possible to modern medical science has been done for their rehabilitation."[10]

In the spirit of giving fair notice to the public of continuing military manpower needs in the post-war era, Marshall wrote the following words into his Biennial Report to the Secretary of War on September 1, 1945, intended for delivery to Congress and the general public:

> Our present national policies require us to: maintain occupation forces in Europe and the Pacific; prepare for a possible contribution of forces to a world security organization (the UN); maintain national security while the world remains unstable and later on a more permanent or stable basis (US Army Chief of Staff 1945, 116).

Born of a sense of his responsibility to present publicly his concept of what would be "required to prevent another international catastrophe," he included as a coda in the same report a message underlining the need for a continuing, strong military core:

> We finish each bloody war with a feeling of acute revulsion against this savage form of human behavior, and yet on each occasion we confuse military preparedness with the causes of war and then drift almost deliberately into another catastrophe. This error of judgment was defined long ago by Washington. He proposed to endow this Nation at the outset with a policy which should have been a reasonable guarantee of our security for centuries. The cost of refusing his guidance is recorded in the sacrifice of life and in the accumulation of mountainous debts. We have continued impractical. We have ignored the hard realities of world affairs. We have been purely idealistic (US Army Chief of Staff 1945, 117).

Summary: The Marshall Record in WW II

Marshall achieved nearly everything he set out to achieve in WW II for the Army and his nation, as well as for himself. As an ambitious young lieutenant he had set as his goal moving as high in the US Army command structure as he could go and to make as large a contribution to the nation and to the military profession as he was capable of making. The results were that he rose to the top of the military structure, built a magnificent army, and guided the allies in the path to victory, earning Churchill's description as "the organizer of victory."

His achievements were many. It is convenient to begin to summarize them by referring to the list compiled by the editors of *Time Magazine* in conferring its 1943 "Man of the Year" award upon the general. While not complete, it does manage to catch many of the highlights. According to the editors, his basic job and greatest achievement "was to transform a second-rate army into the world's most effective military power" in a relatively short time. Between September 1, 1939, the day that he was sworn in as US Army Chief of Staff, and the end of 1943, he was responsible for the following:

- strengthening a sadly depleted army in the face of widespread public opinion that supported non-involvement
- holding off on "hastily planned or ill-advised military operations"
- designing and bringing about a unified and integrated Allied command in every theater of war
- resisting, under extreme pressure, "nervous demands of theater commanders" for green and half-equipped troops
- recognizing "the importance of air power and push[ing] his airmen into bigger and ever bigger programs"
- breaking down "the traditionally supercilious War Department enmity toward innovations of equipment" (*Time Magazine* 1944).

In point of fact, his greatest achievements were less obvious. Although he could not sell the Congress or the Navy on consolidation and elimination of traditional service distinctions, he did provide a basis for continuing cooperation and joint efforts throughout the war, sometimes overcoming powerful political and personal forces to do so. His selection and reorganization decisions built a core of excellent general officers, assembled an expert General Staff, and developed a citizen-based army. He was in large measure responsible for bringing about the professionalism and morale in an army that became celebrated as the most powerful ever assembled. His ability to calm the nation in dire times and instill confidence and trust in a politically divided Congress was an important source of national strength. Subordinating his own ambition to the president's will in the matter of who would lead the invasion of Europe served the transcending need for stability and coordinated direction of the allied military effort.

Dating back to before the attack on Pearl Harbor in his embrace of air power, he had done more than push the air wing into bigger programs and had in fact given that wing of the army an independence and status that allowed it to grow and maximize its strategic as well as tactical potential. To do this he had to take on the united opposition of much of the Regular Army as well as the pre-Stimson war department hierarchy (Pogue 1966, 84-86).

Building the Army into a gigantic, effective force involved far more than bringing on new conscripts and overseeing military training, production, and infrastructure, as difficult as these tasks were. It also involved striving for a balanced buildup that would minimize the loss of effective fighting units that were compromised to furnish veteran trainers of new troops. As with the air arm, he had to overcome the inherent resistance of the Regular Army in order to effectively train, supply, and maintain the National Guard, ROTC, and the Army Reserve. On one hand, he convinced the nation and Congress that a huge build-up was necessary. On the other, he had to control the rate of the build-up so as to retain quality while building the Army's new citizen-based infrastructure.

New Lessons for an Old Soldier

Viewed on a larger canvass, WW II was a massive test of human will and the use of coercive power played out within the context of democratic government. With the authority of the office of US Army Chief of Staff, and possessed of extraordinary leadership qualities, Marshall was placed within and further, placed himself, in the vortex of wartime decision-making, and as a result was himself altered by its forces. The somewhat dogmatic view he had held at the beginning of the war, to the effect that military leaders and public administrators should refrain from making policy, underwent significant change. He had come to realize that elected politicians were required to act under constraints that in effect called for public administrators to exercise initiatives that fit a close observer's definition of policy making. He accepted these broader responsibilities so long as professional military objectives and lives were not sacrificed in the process.

Marshall clarified his revised view on the role of top military leadership in a 1949 interview. While he maintained the view that partisan politics should be avoided, "in a democracy in wartime the conduct of the war cannot be carried on independent of political considerations" (Marshall 1949, 22). His political sophistication had grown steadily as the war had progressed.[11] He would explain to his military subordinates that politicians are sensitive to demands of their constituencies, to powerful lobbies that supported them financially, and to leaders in their own parties, and that they constantly think in terms of reelection and gaining and holding influential committee positions. He had sympathy for politicians and approved, for the most part, of the political system which often made their self-serving behavior necessary.

Notes

1.   Brooke wrote in his diary: "I liked what I saw of Marshall, a pleasant and easy man to get on with, rather overfilled with his own importance. But I should not put him down as a great man" (Pogue 1966, 308). While Brooke's opinion of Marshall's personal qualities steadily improved during the course of the war, his disparagement of Marshall's judgment on strategy matters continued.

2.   On the other hand, it is at least arguable that if Marshall had convinced Roosevelt to back the cross-channel invasion before going into Italy, an earlier victory over Germany could have been achieved and the war ended before the Soviets had moved so far westward as to be in a position to gain dominance in Eastern and Central Europe (Black 2003, 799).

3.   In a rare interview in 1949, Marshall admitted that he was open to criticism on his position because, as secretary of state in 1947, he had supported intervention in Greece.

4.   Nowhere does it appear that MacArthur credited Marshall's role in this pivotal event in his life.

5.   Dean Acheson recalled a conversation between MacArthur and Marshall in his presence. MacArthur began "my staff tells me . . ." when Marshall interrupted: "You don't have a staff but a court" (Gesell and Acheson 1964, 3).

6.   Stimson wrote in his diary: "Under the impact of the setbacks and defeats and losses in the southwestern Pacific of the Navy, criticism of the Navy is growing to an extent which is unfair and dangerous. While they have brought it on themselves, it cannot be allowed to go on without damaging the united war effort. Now it seems that the Patterson newspapers which are the Fifth Column of this war are stirring up a beautiful story of how MacArthur has been kept out of the supreme command of these operations down in the southwestern Pacific in order to squash his presidential aspirations and the President has joined in this by dividing the jurisdiction so that the Navy would have the command in regard to the Solomon action" (GCMRL: Stimson Diaries XL: 182).

7.   Admiral of the Fleet Lord Cunningham (1961) gave his recollection of the thinking of the British chiefs on the Overlord command decision in an interview with Pogue well after the war. Cunningham: "The original idea was that Alanbrooke was to take command, but when it became so obvious that the American forces were going to be much larger than the British, Alanbrooke stepped down, and then the choice was left between Eisenhower and Marshall. Fortunately, it was Eisenhower. I am sure that none of our chiefs of staff could see how Marshall could be spared down from the job he was doing so well at the time." Pogue: "And you feel now, looking back, that it was better for him to stay where

he was?" Cunningham: "Infinitely better. We knew him and we knew all about him, and we knew how sincere and honest he was. Oh, it would never have done."

8.   Brigadier General Cornelius W. Wickersham, a reserve officer much respected by Marshall, was made commandant. Officers being offloaded under the pressure of demobilization by theater commanders and seeking new jobs were to be avoided.

9.   The other member of the axis powers, Italy, presented quite another situation. Churchill and Stimson sought to install Victor Emmanuel of the House of Savoy as the Italian monarch after American and British forces prevailed. Marshall was opposed, and with Roosevelt's support prevailed in preventing an Italian monarchical state (Hilldring 1959, 67-68).

10.   Comparison is invited to the controversy over treatment of veterans of the current war in Iraq (Priest and Hull 2007).

11.   Two books, both authored by Douglas Southall Freeman and concerning General Robert E. Lee, commander of confederate forces in the Civil War, were cited by Marshall as the most helpful books he read during WW II: *R. E. Lee: A Biography*, and *Lee's Lieutenants: A Study in Command*. He found much to be learned in Lee's political problem with Jefferson Davis, the President of the Confederate States, "and to realize that other people had that same problem was a great consolation to him" (Pratt 1962, 7). Understanding this made it somewhat easier to tolerate the fact that political issues often could not be separated from issues of national defense and thus eased his frustrations.

CHAPTER SEVEN
STATESMAN

It is unworthy of a great nation to stand idly by while small countries of great culture are being destroyed with a cynical contempt for justice.
—Albert Einstein
(Nathan and Norden 1960, 279)

If this Nation is to remain great, it must bear in mind now and in the future that war is not the choice of those who wish passionately for peace. It is the choice of those who are willing to resort to violence for political advantage.
—George C. Marshall
(US Army Chief of Staff 1945, 123)

Old Habits, New Role: From Waging War to Seeking Peace

Marshall retired three times. Immediately after the first retirement on November 19, 1945 the Marshalls left for a visit to their planned retirement home of Pinehurst, North Carolina. They returned to Dodona Manor in Leesburg, Virginia eight days later. General Marshall was intent on gardening, reading, and passing leisurely evenings with his wife. The telephone rang as they were unpacking. It was President Truman calling to ask him to go to China. Despite being a jarring prospect to him and a visceral blow to Katherine,[1] he unhesitatingly accepted the president's invitation. A new page in his career was turned.

As Truman's special ambassador to China the sixty-five-year old general, still erect, trim, and vigorous, was plunged into a seemingly hopeless and strenuous effort to work out an accord between the Chinese communist party (CCP) led by Mao Zedong and Chiang Kai-shek's nationalist government ruled by the party of the Kuomintang (KMT). Military engagement was now the furthest thing from Marshall's mind. He saw his duty as the president gave it to him: mediate the end of an ongoing civil war and achieve stability and political democratic reform within the existing government of China. True to his ethic that basic policy direction must be set by America's elected leaders and control his own actions, he played but a small role in shaping the directives that were to set his course of action in China. The guidelines he was given consisted of a memorandum from Secretary of State James Byrnes, a policy statement written by President Truman, and a personal letter from the president (Pogue 1967, 64-70).

Marshall had developed a growing abhorrence of war in the later part of WW II and in the months that followed. A lifelong interest in institution-building and the elements of civil governance had taken center stage in his life. These desires now coexisted in his mind with the knowledge and skills for planning, organizing, and waging war. The penchant for organizing for peace and harmony had shown itself many times in his career: at Tientsin in the pacifying of warlords; at Fort Benning in the designing of a social, family-friendly environment related to the training of army officers; at Forts Screven and Moultrie and Vancouver Barracks in organizing the elements of useful pursuits and personal renewal for the dispossessed youth of the CCC; and by empathy expressed for the suffering peoples of Europe after both world wars.

Instincts of this type had been overwhelmed during 1938-1945 by the nation's need to prepare for and wage war. Now, within the shadow of destruction resulting from successfully pursuing that goal and fueled by the challenge of undoing its social and economic effects, the self-confident Marshall rededicated himself to the tasks of bringing peace and stimulating democratic growth. He would begin by attempting to get China's warring factions to set aside their arms and work together to create a stable, democratic regime, objectives he shared with the president.

Qualifications for the Job of Mediator

Mediating an ongoing civil war in another country was not a common task historically. The KMT had reestablished the Republic of China (ROC) in 1928 and had consistently attempted to suppress and eliminate communist elements within it, people they regarded as no more than "bandits" (Myers 1998, 150). Despite the KMT's efforts the CCP had persevered and grown. It became an effective fighting force against the Japanese in WW II, despite the fact that the US concentrated its military aid on the Chiang-led government. US policymakers and envoys were frustrated by the KMT's preference for positioning itself for a post-war effort to crush the CCP rather than expending its resources against the Japanese, assuming that Americans would carry the burden expelling the Japanese from the Chinese mainland. Stilwell, in his dual position as assistant theater commander and chief of staff to the generalissimo (Chiang), despaired in his efforts to get Chiang's army to fight the Japanese. Lord Mountbatten, after being named the India-Burma-China supreme theater commander, did no better. The ROC army grew in strength and trained proficiency but did not fight.

The Marshall Mission had been preceded by the China Mission led by Roosevelt's envoy Patrick J. Hurley, aided by General Albert C. Wedemeyer, another "Marshall man." Hurley and Wedemeyer had sided strongly with Chiang's nationalist government and were unsympathetic to Stilwell and to pressuring for democratic reforms in the autocratic and corrupt KMT-led government. Strong anti-Communists, they favored Chiang's desire to use military assistance to eliminate the CCP.

A new China policy was worked out by the Truman administration in concert with the USSR at the Moscow conference in December 1945. An agreement, negotiated by Byrnes, Undersecretary Dean Acheson, and diplomat Averell Harriman with the Soviets, led directly to Hurley's angry resignation. The agreement recognized the nationalist regime of Chiang and the legitimacy of returning Soviet and Japanese lands and possessions in north China and Manchuria to that regime. It also adopted the principle that the US would bring pressure through a diplomatic mission to bring the CCP into a broadened, democratic nationalist government with the KMT.

While it is likely that the CCP hoped to use such a coalition government as a stepping stone to gain greater power and eventual domination in China's governance, it is also likely that in the short and medium term a broadened government would end the civil war and permit democratic reform and economic recovery. Truman's selection of Marshall to lead the diplomatic mission to achieve a combined, reformed government was welcomed by both major communist leaders, Mao Zedong and Zhou Enlai, who both respected Marshall as a world leader and agreed with the goals of the mission (He Di 1998).

Many foreign policy observers of the time were surprised by Marshall's appointment and wondered whether he was a proper choice for the role of mediator. He was, after all, a military man and not a career diplomat, and there were other persons of stature about (for example, Harriman) who had substantial experience with negotiation. Clearly, Truman had high regard for many of the general's qualities, but what did he find in Marshall that led him to call on the general to fill this particular role?

The choice of Marshall is often explained as a well calculated administration strategy meant to contain the political damage resulting from the resignation of Hurley, who combined leaving with harsh criticism of the administration's policy turn toward coexistence with the communists (Stoler 1998, 4-5). Appointment of a man respected by both major parties would blunt criticism of administration policy on China in the Congress and the nation at large. Still, there are more compelling reasons for his appointment found in the character, views and attitudes, skills, values, and experiences of the man.

Marshall had a track record for dealing successfully with contending interests, beginning with his much-admired ability to work with both the French and the British military commands in WW I.[2] He had worked on the transition from war to peace in the wake of the armistice of November, 1918 that ended the war. He had deplored the effects of the breakdown of local authority that he observed within the former fighting zones of northeast France and southwest Germany, noting, for example, the negative effect of wireless communication in the German sector. By making simultaneous and multiple communications possible, the wireless had the unexpected result of lessening the hold of centralized German authority within its own territory, bringing chaos and complicating the task of returning the state to normalcy (Marshall 1976, 200-205).

Most auspiciously, he had practical success in keeping the peace among Chinese warlords in his tour at Tientsin, China from 1924-1927, and had gained some knowledge of Chinese language and customs in the process. Thus his facility for dealing with Chinese culture had been demonstrated. He had scored a diplomatic triumph in his treatment of Soviet polar flight explorers at Vancouver Barracks in 1937 and his visit to Brazil in early 1939 had charmed Brazilians and helped to blunt the efforts of Germany to gain a foothold in the western hemisphere in WW II.

In the context of WW II, he had built positive relations with members of both parties and with several congressional committees, had worked with the British to create an effective military alliance, and had forged joint planning and operational linkages to the US Navy. Keeping a multi-fronted war effort together among strong military factions, domestic and foreign, burnished his image as an effective negotiator (see, generally, Stoler 1998, 6-13).

His international standing was high. Churchill often looked to Marshall on policy matters. Marshall accompanied Roosevelt and Truman to all major summit meetings and had prepared briefing books for the principals at these meetings. He had drafted high-level diplomatic messages for both. By 1944, he had become "Roosevelt's closest wartime adviser and in many ways the country's foreign secretary as well as the head of its army" (Stoler 1998, 13). He was open-minded in working with the Soviets, believed that he could work with them, and was respected and valued by Stalin and Soviet military leaders.

Of particular value in the China context was his facility with the Mandarin language and Chinese culture. He knew much about China's international relations and was closely associated with many experts working in China, including Generals Stilwell and Wedemeyer (Pogue 1987, 31-53).

Indeed, the reasons for appointing Marshall to spearhead the China negotiations were so compelling that Beetle Smith argued shortly after Marshall's time in China that "his (Marshall's) whole service had been a preparatory course for high-level negotiations" (1950, 216).

Context of the Dispute and Prospects for Success

Understanding the Marshall Mission and its prospects for success requires understanding the larger context of Soviet-American relations. The accord reached with Stalin at the December, 1945 Moscow Conference had temporarily brightened prospects for a return to the spirit of wartime cooperation between the former allies. The major features of the understanding were these: (1) the USSR was given a veto power on any major changes in the government of Japan; (2) the USSR agreed to turn over sovereignty in Manchuria to the nationalist Chinese government; (3) American marines would be accepted in China on a temporary basis to help secure the orderly transfer of sovereignty back to the Chinese nationalist government; and (4) there would be an attempt to create a coalition government in China, led by a representative empowered to give and withhold loans, determine the disposition of funds and equipment intended for military support of the Chinese military, and direct the activities of some fifty thousand US marines (this became the Marshall Mission). Overall agreement was also reached on bringing the CCP into the new government on three levels: cabinet, central bureaucracy, and provincial and local governments (Wehrle 1998, 65-90).

The Moscow agreement thus created an apparent Soviet-American consensus on China policy and a hopeful climate in which three-party negotiations could proceed (US, CCP, and KMT).

Other positive factors were present. Marshall's prestige as a military leader of victorious forces was high among the Chinese as well as the Soviets. Congress stood ready to authorize additional loan funds and military assistance, which Truman could and did place at Marshall's discretion to use as he may see fit. Both types of assistance were potentially very significant. Chiang's army had few resources other than troops and officers whose loyalty was shaky because they had been underpaid. Economic hardship dominated the land in the wake of Japanese occupation. Lastly, the nationalist government was dependent on US marines and technology for transporting its troops to northern China and Manchuria to take over control in key cities to be vacated by the Japanese and Soviets.

At this point in time CCP policy opposed large-scale civil war. The communists needed time to consolidate control in the areas it tended to dominate and feared American intervention on the KMT side. Mao and Zhou hoped to neutralize the US; they would take what Truman and the State Department were prepared to give them (a broadened role for the CCP in a democratic national government) and try to convert this advantage into long-term influence.

Despite these positive elements, negative prospects pervaded the climate. Marshall could not count on maintaining, let alone expanding, a US military presence in a period of rapid US demobilization. Intransigence and corruption characterized nationalist behavior. Territorial gains already made by the CCP, particularly in northeastern China, had frightened the KMT. There was underlying uncertainty about long-range Soviet interests in the area, particularly its designs on Manchuria. Finally, there was a lack of any significant historic tradition of democratic institutions within China, which added to mistrust of the kind of democratic reforms the Marshall Mission hoped to achieve.

The planning and policy analysis of the China situation given to Marshall by the State Department as part of his overall policy directive was not a realistic guide. Prepared by John Vincent Carter, the chief of the Division of Chinese Affairs in the State Department, it overvalued the influence of a number of non-communist, third-party political opponents of the regime. The Vincent plan favored giving this "third force" a large voice in any final coalition government that might eventually be worked out.

Perhaps most importantly, a crippling contradiction lay at the heart of the policy instructions Marshall had been given. He had been charged by the president with seeking a coalition government with expanded democratic elements. At the same time he was instructed to use American facilities and troops to transport and install nationalist troops in the northern regions in order to put the ROC in position to accept turnover of control from both Japanese and Soviet troops, in conformity with the Moscow accord. The sticking point was that the latter role was bound to undermine CCP security interests in the region and therefore likely to touch off disputes and even armed clashes. The good faith of nationalist leaders, never extended in the past to the CCP, could scarcely be assumed. These contradictory US roles foreshadowed serious and perhaps unbridgeable differences.

Those most familiar with the situation in China believed that successful negotiation was not possible. Wedemeyer and Walter Robertson, who was to serve as Marshall's assistant in China, shared their opinions with Marshall on his arrival that any hope of achieving a workable coalition between the KMT and CCP based on a shared vision of China's future was illusory on both military and political grounds. Marshall listened carefully but his response to Wedemeyer was characteristically direct and perhaps offensive to his former protege: "Well, it can be done, and you are going to help me" (Eiler 1998, 92; Wedemeyer 1958, 363).

The KMT and CCP had been fighting each other for twenty years over differing visions of China's future. Robertson later recalled:

> He [Marshall] asked questions, we discussed it, I had the very distinct opinion that he had been given a directive ... which at least the policy makers in Washington thought was possible of achievement. Neither Wedemeyer nor I thought it was possible of achievement (1962, 3-4).

Reflecting the division among the Chinese themselves, there were two American schools of thought on China policy. One, to which Wedemeyer subscribed, believed that communists could only be destructive to the nation. Although the nationalist government was rife with anti-democratic tendencies and corruption, the best and only course of action was to bolster Chiang. According to this view the major priority was for Chiang to first defeat the Communists and stabilize nationalist rule; only then could democratic reforms be pursued. This, they reasoned, the KMT could only do if America provided large-scale military and economic aid.

The second group, which included Truman and State Department officials, believed that there was little realistic prospect for that level of support (Eiler 1998). The best course of action was to seek accommodation among the warring forces in favor of a stable, democratic regime *before* pouring in economic and military support. Marshall accepted this point of view based in part on loyalty to the president and his advisors who had adopted it as official policy. He accepted on its face Truman's letter to him dated December 15, 1945 which read: "a strong, united and democratic China is of the utmost importance to the success of this United Nations' organization and for world peace" (Bland 1998, 550).

Chinese nationalist leaders, inexplicably neither consulted nor informed of the Moscow talks, had a much different view. They did not believe that Mao and other CCP leaders would agree to put down their arms and join a nationalist-led government or participate in the process of creating a constitutional and democratic government. They further believed the US, their wartime ally, should suppress the rebels, trust the KMT to democratize, and not restructure China's military establishment according to American concepts. In their view Truman and state diplomats were demanding changes that reflected ignorance of conditions in China and showed disrespect for the nationalist government (Myers 1998, 152). In this climate, the nationalists saw Marshall as a well-intentioned but naive agent of an unacceptable and disastrous policy. While personally admired, he was seen as someone likely to be duped by CCP and Soviet representations. Chiang himself believed that the CCP and USSR were working in tandem. Both he and the influential Madame Chiang took the view that Marshall had to be educated.

The Course of Negotiations

Characteristically, Marshall began his new role by gathering intelligence, consulting with representatives of all factions, and selecting a talented corps of young, seasoned, and intelligent officers. Working in the cold, unheated environment of the Chongqing winter, he systematically laid out his plans and began in an orderly way to pursue them.

The early stages of the negotiation were far more successful than Wedemeyer had foreseen. An incapacitated Mao left negotiations in the capable hands of Zhou Enlai, his right-hand man. Zhou and Marshall got on splendidly. Zhou explained CCP policies and goals candidly and intelligently, thereby gaining Marshall's confidence. Marshall in turn won Zhou's trust by taking concrete steps to set up tripartite consultative teams in a new executive headquarters composed of one representative each from the CCP, KMT, and US. In addition, they agreed that some work of the Hurley mission on new governmental structure would be retained. All decisions, most of which related to military matters, were to require the consensus of all three negotiation partners.

Consensus on a nationwide cease-fire and political restructuring was reached by the end of January, a scant one month into the negotiations. Zhou conveyed his opinion to Mao that all of these decisions were fair and that Marshall was not following the old, pro-KMT China policy of the Hurley-Wedemeyer era but rather the new China policy arrived at in the Moscow conference (Zhang Baijia 1998, 214-216). Zhou also reported to the CCP politburo:

> Marshall is plain, does not exaggerate things, considers issues calmly, doesn't jump to conclusions, and has the bearing of a chief of staff. The marshal [i.e., Marshall] came to China with just one civilian and one army man. He is a rather plain capitalist (Zhang Baijia 1998, 219).

In addition to the positive personal relationship developing between the two men, one representing Mao and the other Truman, two other factors were helping substantially to bring about accommodation: personal control by Marshall over economic and military assistance granted to him by Truman, and the favorable Soviet-US diplomatic climate created at Moscow.

The integration of CCP and KMT military command structures, a goal regarded by Marshall as especially important, was proving to be far more difficult. Some cautious steps were approved by early March, but both Mao and Chiang harbored deep reservations. Marshall's faith that a professional and non-political military could be built was at odds with how the Chinese nationalists viewed the source of their power. Nonetheless, by early March much had been accomplished and guarded optimism was being expressed.

In a period of less than three months Marshall had in hand a formal agreement on a cease-fire, preliminary agreement on major government restructuring, and some halting progress toward integration of the armies. Perhaps most surprisingly, there was progress in the orderly transfer of sovereignty from the USSR to Chiang's government in Manchuria. In early March Marshall conducted a grand tour of North China in which he found his three-member truce teams working effectively. At communist headquarters in Yan'an he secured Mao's avowed full support for his policy goals. So successful had these early efforts been that Wedemeyer began to sense the possibility of a miracle in the making (Eiler 1998, 97-98). The following comment, intended as propaganda by the leadership, appeared in the CCP press in Yan'an:

> This [the products of the first phase of Marshall's mission] is the result of the prolonged struggle of the Chinese people, as well as Marshall's. His effort has achieved glorious success. The Chinese people will cooperate with him, because his endeavor is in accordance with the fundamental interests of the Chinese people and world peace (Yu Shen 1998, 256).

Up to this point in time the communists had been easier to deal with than the nationalists. Zhou was candid and clear about CCP goals and tactics, especially the sincere desire to bring about a dawning of democratic government in China (whatever might be the CCP's long-term intentions). Conversely, Chiang and other key members of the KMT were difficult to pin down. In point of fact, most of them wanted the mission to fail in such a way that blame for failure could be placed on the communists. At one point, Chiang's assurance of the KMT's acceptance of the cease-fire was directly contradicted by reports from American field staff that nationalists were engaged in attacking communist positions.

What Marshall called the "CC clique" was undermining negotiations. The clique included reactionaries among Chiang's generals and advisors, in particular Chen Li-fu and his brother Chen Kou-fu, men with strong anti-labor views who had encouraged Chiang's earlier break with the CCP. These men feared the loss of personal power and position that would likely come if negotiations succeeded. The Chens used their control of financial agencies, key newspapers, and patronage to select party and government leaders and furnish a power base for Chiang. Also, they positioned themselves to prevent any move of the Generalissimo toward accommodating dissident elements. They came to "view the Marshall Mission as unfriendly and dangerous, a source of weakness, with proposals of compromise and conciliation that must be resisted" (Pogue 1987, 83).[3]

Negotiations went off the track in March. The first misfortune was Marshall's timing in his returning for a short time to Washington to shore up congressional support for a sizable economic aid package he believed necessary to the next steps in building a coalition government. Negotiations continued in his absence, but without Marshall's personal presence the agreements that had been verbally reached and assumed to be in hand were now disavowed by both sides (Eiler 1998, 101). The CC Clique openly subverted arrangements assumed to be settled. Chiang's troops experienced a run of military successes in the field (owing in part to American transporting of nationalist troops to the north), encouraging Chiang to hope for military victory and an end to negotiations.

Chiang's perfidy also had the added effect of convincing the communists that Marshall had been acting in bad faith all along and was working with the KMT to implement the old China policy. In truth, Marshall and his staff had been committed by their policy directives and according to the Moscow accords to perform the transport. But to Mao and Zhou, who had been counting on a cease-fire in the northeast as a respite to build up CCP forces and supplies, it appeared that Marshall had betrayed them by helping the KMT on the ground. Both Marshall and Chiang were blamed for the breakdown, and the CCP turned to favoring military strategy itself and using negotiations only when it was to their advantage. The fighting began to spread to other parts of China.

Perhaps worst of all, the understanding that had existed between the US and USSR dissolved over a new issue—Soviet claims to industrial materiel and economic concessions in Manchuria. These demands were regarded as unfair in the US, particularly in Congress, and strengthened the position of anti-communist groups in the US. Marshall was barraged by these political forces while in Washington, and returned to China with a firm resolve (and something like a mandate) to forcefully establish Chiang's control in Manchuria. In doing so, he underestimated its effect on CCP cooperation.

With Marshall now more or less in tandem with official Washington views on the invalidity of Soviet claims on Manchuria, Chiang became more strident in opposing economic concessions (Yu Shen 1998, 267-268). He declared he had no intention of making any concessions until the Soviets had withdrawn their troops from Manchuria and turned over control to nationalist forces (which they had already started to do). This posture led directly to a change in Stalin's tactics—no longer would he deliver strategic cities and railroad junctions directly into nationalist hands when his troops withdrew. Rather, he ordered withdrawal in such a manner as to allow the CCP to gain tactical advantage. Chiang thus lost leverage in regaining territory in his quest to avoid making economic concessions (Wehrle 1998).

With the cease-fire, integration of professional armies, and political reform all now in shambles, Marshall would not have been faulted had he abandoned negotiations, yet he persevered. Any prospect for success in the negotiations now rested on a few bargaining chips: his personal prestige; his control of economic aid so desperately needed by Chiang and the Chinese people; the likely continuance for the time being of the US Marine force; and the personal relationship he had formed with Zhou Enlai. One additional plus was bringing on board, as ambassador to China, Dr. John Leighton Stuart, a distinguished elderly educator and one-time missionary known and respected by the Chinese, including many communists (Eiler 1998, 104).

Seen from a global perspective, growing Cold War fever had replaced the atmosphere based on the Moscow talks and turned US public opinion against the USSR. Marshall was thus forced to shift his focus and reflect Washington's desire to place Chiang in firm control in Manchuria. Entirely gone was the credibility he had earlier enjoyed with the CCP based on his being seen as impartial and more in sympathy with the Moscow accords than with the old China policy. In summary:

> Soviet-American confrontation over Manchuria shattered the impressive, but fragile, expectation of big-power cooperation in reforming China. The expectation of Soviet support, or noninterference, in American China policy, which had been one of Marshall's most positive weapons, was turned against him. Chiang's dire warnings of a combined Soviet-Chinese Communist threat to China, at least in Washington, became doctrine (Wehrle 1998, 89).

The crumbling of the original accords not only doomed the negotiations, it also soured the Zhou-Marshall relationship. The CCP turned away from negotiations in favor of waging the all-out war that Chiang, with superior military force, had imposed on it. The demise of this relationship doomed any prospect for getting the talks back on a constructive track, although they formally continued at Marshall's urging. Marshall's leverage on Chiang was now countered by pro-Chiang pressures coming from America. The KMT and the CCP resisted all efforts to put down their arms—for both, the fighting was to continue alongside negotiations, and only military events on the ground moved the talks. The talks continued only because neither side, for propagandistic purposes, wished to be blamed for killing them (He Di 1998, 184-185). Chiang, especially, sought to bolster his image in America as a man of peace and reform.

When circumstances were such that one side or the other felt superior in military terms, the party in the better position on the ground felt free to ignore or sabotage any Marshall move to get an old understanding reestablished or reach a new agreement. As the fighting intensified both sides willed the negotiations to fail and for Marshall to withdraw. Mao lost all faith that Marshall's mediation could restrain Chiang. Increasingly, he used the talks as a tactic to secure delays to help him prepare militarily for Chiang's expected attacks. Communist propaganda characterizing America and Marshall as colonizers supporting the puppet regime of Chiang became a powerful tool for winning popular support and mobilizing troops for the CCP (He Di 1998, 195-96).

As the negotiations continued to deteriorate, and as the fighting mounted, Marshall realized his usefulness was at an end and eventually returned to the states in early January, 1947 to assume the new role of secretary of state. In the long run, the American public tired of supporting Chiang; Congress gave only token military aid to Chiang and no US military forces. The sympathies of the Chinese people swung strongly to the CCP, bringing about an unexpectedly rapid collapse of the KMT and its withdrawal from the Asian mainland. In recent, admittedly biased, Chinese scholarship on the civil war and the Marshall Mission, Mao is portrayed as the advocate of peace, Chiang and the KMT as saboteurs of the peace process, and Marshall as helpless in a situation that he could neither influence nor control (Yu Shen 1998, 269).

Negotiating Tactics

By turns, Marshall had used orderly analysis, argument and persuasion, economic sanctions and incentives, and the threat of his own withdrawal as mediator to move the parties in the direction of cooperation. Most difficult for him was dealing with the ideological intolerance of the nationalists for the survival of the communist party in any form, and the barrage of anti-American and anti-Marshall propaganda issuing from the CCP once it had decided appeals to the masses and military action were its best options. Although Chiang appeared at first to be amenable to negotiations and to broadening the government to include the communists,[4] he later clearly displayed reluctance to move against the more reactionary elements of his party. He was able to avoid making concessions and still gain economic and military assistance by making an end run around Marshall to court anti-communist support in the US Congress and public.

Preparation in developing the factual bases for negotiation sessions was a feature of Marshall's technique as a negotiator. Despite the acid environment that developed in March of 1946, he worked tirelessly to pursue progress, following every lead and considering every possibility. During his entire time in China he did not spare himself, working long hours under difficult conditions in mountain cold and sweltering city heat and enduring frequent and arduous journeys. At times, he appeared to be overwhelmed with the enormity and difficulty of his task (Barrett 1959, 24). His perseverance and hard labor took a toll on his health, and the work certainly kept him from other tasks at home in which he could have been more usefully employed, and from the retirement he so richly deserved (Caughey and Hutchin 1957, 1).

One of the strengths he demonstrated as a negotiator was the respect he showed for those with whom he dealt, not always returned in kind. Some of the general's detractors charged that he had been taken in by the sophisticated Zhou; others on the scene recalled Marshall being "impressed but not influenced." He would listen patiently to Zhou and then go out and get the facts and confront Zhou with them at their next meeting (Caughey and Hutchin 1957, 1).

There is no evidence that he ever threatened or considered the prospect of military force. He thought that such a move would be counter-productive to the negotiations and, in any case, would not be supported by American public opinion.

Was the Marshall Mission a "Failure"?

Throughout his time as special ambassador in China Marshall followed the political leadership of the president and the guidance he had been given by the president and his advisors. He had refused to be drawn into the civil war on the side of Chiang. His own views were in accord with the president's. He believed a civil war could not be won by the KMT because the Chinese people were exhausted, poverty-stricken, and alienated by corruption and incompetence in the nationalist government. The nationalist army was controlled by self-interested warlords, poorly equipped, and exhausted from long fighting. He reasoned that any new energy that might arise from the general population would favor the CCP, not the KMT.

Chinese scholars have themselves recently come to the conclusion that the inability of the Marshall Mission to resolve the conflict is traceable to America's flawed China policy and not to Marshall personally. According to them, policy was not only divided in trying to please two opposed camps but also its assumptions demonstrated "ignorance and arrogance of America's attitude towards China." Marshall and his bosses followed western models of European parliamentary democracy and the American two-party system and ignored the difficulty of transplanting these into hostile Chinese soil (Yu Shen 1998, 269-270). Yet there was praise for Marshall's efforts, and a hint of his influence on Zhou Enlai:

> Obviously, Marshall left a positive impression on the leaders of the CCP and they were grateful for what he did, though they wished that he could have done more (Yu Shen 1998, 271).

Stateside critics accused Truman, Acheson, Byrne, and Marshall of having "lost" China. The sharpest barbs were reserved for Marshall who was on the ground in China and could have used his leverage to increase support going to Chiang. Henry C. Luce, publisher of *Time, Life,* and *Fortune* magazines and a major influence on American public opinion, was especially personal and vitriolic:

> By prolonging negotiations, Luce believed, the prestigious General Marshall had blocked a public debate on the American role in China. This, of course, is precisely why Truman sent Marshall to China, but to Henry Luce, Marshall's mission had become a prelude to Chiang's doom (Herzstein 1998, 145).

The more rational among the critics of Truman's new China policy (like Wedemeyer) believed that China was never ours to lose. The American public would never have tolerated participating in a potentially exhausting and hugely expensive war through committing troops or expending vast amounts of aid in what was likely to be a losing cause. Few in power with knowledge of Chinese affairs expected Marshall to succeed. Once it was clear that the peace effort was dead, it was probably not a viable option to throw American support to Chiang in an attempt to destroy the CCP militarily. Despite superiority in men and equipment, the dissension-riddled Chiang government lacked popular support. His army was underfed, poorly led, and lacked the will to fight (Timberman 1959, 41-42).

Under such circumstances, using the word "failure" to describe the Marshall Mission misses the mark. "Futile" may be a more accurate descriptor. In fact, had diplomacy with the Soviets taken a different tack, there is a possibility that some type of accommodation could have been worked out. Certainly, in the realm of political debate it is at least arguable that Truman and his diplomatic advisors chose a reasonable policy course. Marshall likely performed as well as anyone under the circumstances in giving that policy a fair chance to succeed, but the odds were clearly against success (Pawley 1962, 19; Robertson 1962, 6).

In very real human terms, how did Marshall react to the popular perception that for the first time in his long and distinguished career he had failed? Clues may be sought in his letters and actions as he left China and returned home to assume his new duties as secretary of state, and in his interviews with Pogue (Bland 1991, 575). Regarding the actions of others, he always held that fault-finding was a waste of time and energy. Did he apply another standard to himself? Evidence that he reflected on the matter are not found—he seems to have put the matter behind him quickly and redirected his whole attention to his new and more comprehensive role as secretary of state.

The more pragmatic and less value-laden question to ask is: what lessons did Marshall learn from the China experience which he could take with him into his next role? A safe assumption is that he gained ability to operate in the larger context of world affairs. With his characteristic capacity to learn and to grow Marshall would have advanced his knowledge about the processes and dynamics of conflict and its resolution, knowledge that was to serve him well in the policy and administrative tasks he was to face as secretary of state.

Marshall did confide in a letter written while still in China to Bernard Baruch that he was experiencing new insights relative to statesmanship. Regarding the effort to find a middle way:

> It grows more clearly evident to me every day out here that suspicion of the other fellow's motives, lack of understanding of his conception of your motives are the greatest stumbling blocks to peaceful adjustments. . . . I have sat in the middle for many months and listened to an outpouring of suspicions and beliefs of the representatives of each side regarding the other. I find that in most instances neither side properly, or even casually, evaluates the fears or suspicions of the other and their effect on the action taken or the attitude in negotiations. When I emphasize this state of affairs neither side treats it as of much importance, but as a matter of fact from my middle position it has appeared to me of the most vital importance because misunderstandings are a fruitful cause of unhappy situations or events (Bland and Stevens 1996, 5).

Would this profound insight, properly includable in a textbook on negotiation, have entered Marshall's thinking and behavior had he not gone to China? The likely answer is that Marshall at the age of retirement was still developing the empathy and skills needed to mediate conflict and seek peace among contending forces in the world. If this be true, his achievements yet to come and their contributions to world peace and prosperity may have owed much to his time in China, and the Marshall Mission must therefore be counted as a positive contribution.

Marshall Takes Over As Secretary of State

In 1946 President Truman was having both personal and policy problems with his secretary of state, former Senator James Byrnes, and decided to replace him with Marshall, the man he referred to as "the greatest living American." He disliked having to ask him to take the job because he knew Marshall would accept unselfishly and that it was unfair to ask yet more of him. Still, he felt he needed him because of his ability, unquestionable loyalty and, not least, his reputation and credibility in both houses of Congress.

The invitation was extended through Eisenhower, now Army chief of staff, who visited China in the spring of 1946. Contingent on the yet-to-be-made decision to ask Byrnes to step down, Marshall would have eight months to contemplate the prospect (Steelman 1958, 1-4). Predictably, he indicated his willingness to accept the job if the president needed him. To sweeten the offer, the president promised to vest in him unusually expansive powers for a secretary of state. Marshall would be free to develop policy initiatives on his own and he, Truman, promised to back him (Pogue 1987, 153). Having labored mightily in the cause of peace in China, Marshall now turned his attention to international statecraft, especially to finding common ground with the Soviet Union.

One political obstacle to his confirmation existed—the fear of some, particularly Senate Republicans, that he could use the new post to position himself to seek the presidency. The fear was soon dispelled. He left China on January 7, 1947, and after relaxing in Hawaii with Katherine, arrived tanned and rested in the nation's capital on January 21. As he alighted from the train he was surrounded by reporters who pressed him about rumors that he harbored presidential ambitions for 1948. He disavowed any interest in elective office in unequivocal language (Carter 1959, 1-5; Pogue 1987, 144-45).

Marshall approached his new tasks with characteristic self-confidence. Dean Acheson, held over from the Byrnes administration and Marshall's choice for the position of undersecretary of state, wrote to Stimson: "General Marshall has taken hold of this baffling institution with the calmness, orderliness and vigor with which you are familiar. We are all very happy and very lucky to have him here" (McLellan and Acheson 1980, 64).

Prompt action was taken to set the approach and management style to be taken, through several organizing decisions (Carter 1959, 24; Lovett 1973, 52-53; Acheson 1957, 4; Pogue 1987, 144-150). To begin, he retained on the payroll all of the current staff at the department. A systematic reorganization much like he had carried out in the War Department in 1941-1942 followed. This was done quietly so as not to arouse fear of change among department veterans. Marshall enlisted the help of Marshall Carter and Acheson to put together both the new organizational structure and a decision process very similar to the system used within the wartime Office of the Chief of Staff. All matters to be decided by the secretary of state were to come through Acheson, who would first ensure that all important factors had been analyzed and the decision options clearly outlined. Carter was to be responsible for coordinating information and communication, much as the secretary of the General Staff had done. This was a sharp departure from the prior practice at State in which individual officers heading the various units of the department had worked out individualized relations with the secretary of state according to private understandings, thus bypassing the undersecretary (Carter 1959, 24; Lovett 1973, 52-53; Acheson 1957, 4).

Marshall also created a strong office for planning and policy development, the Policy Planning Office (PPO). Its establishment set a precedent for civilian agencies of government. It would function much like the old WPD within the Department of War to ensure a place where creative people could be allowed to concentrate on the future and the development of policies to get there (Pogue 1987, 151). On the advice of Acheson and others, he hired George Kennan, a brilliant thinker and expert on Soviet affairs.

Marshall did not become vested in the nature of diplomatic professionalism as he had with military professionalism in the Army. The background, strengths, and weaknesses of foreign service professionals did not attract his attention. He did, however, take an important step to improve the foreign and diplomatic services by establishing a precedent by appointing career professionals to ambassadorial posts instead of political friends (Kennan 1959).

Management Style

Many were surprised, given his background in military administration, to discover Marshall's management style. Here was a leader who was collaborative, sensitive to change, a good listener, and attuned to the needs of his people. He was not, in the military tradition, an authoritative figure giving orders and applying stern discipline (Steelman 1958). He was found to be truly solicitous of the opinions of others (E. Roosevelt 1958, 1-2, 12). He made explicit to his staff that they should not be focused on pleasing him but rather to do the best job they were capable of doing, and demonstrated a penchant for "organization and responsible action" (Acheson 1957, 4). Dean Rusk gave this description:

> Marshall was no tub-thumping militarist. At a morning staff meeting he once told us, 'Gentlemen, let's not discuss this problem as if it were a military problem; that might turn it into a military problem. Military action must always be the last resort.' Politically sophisticated, Marshall was a great soldier and a great civilian. He firmly believed in civilian control of the military and had enormous respect for our constitutional system (1990, 134).

These same observers may well have been surprised by Marshall's support of the Baruch Plan that was the basis for the Acheson-Lilienthal report to President Truman. Baruch called for international control of fissionable materials through the UN, an idea condemned as ultra-liberal by the Republican majority that was at that time in control of Congress. The idea followed from the assumption that knowledge and capacity about producing nuclear weapons would eventually become universal, and that UN control would be the best and perhaps last opportunity to direct nuclear energy production solely toward peaceful purposes.

> As a military man he understood what nuclear weapons did to the concept of war as a means for settling disputes. Had Marshall opposed international controls, the Baruch Plan would never have gotten off the ground (Rusk 1990, 139).

Confronting the USSR

Marshall's first major external act as secretary of state was to go to Moscow in March, 1947 to meet with Soviet, British, and French foreign ministers— Vyacheslav Molotov, Ernest Bevin, and George Bidault, respectively. Multiple objectives were on the table: negotiating end-of-war treaties respecting Germany and Austria; determining the scope and nature of German reparations; and settling questions regarding the administration of occupied Germany, then divided into four zones.

Unlike most policymakers in Washington, Marshall had not lost hope that the Soviets could be reached by reason and good faith (Harriman 1975, 5; Bohlen 1967, 1-2). He had perhaps been influenced by the forward-looking joint China policy that had been worked out among the old allies in Moscow in December of 1945 that had strengthened his hand in China. Perhaps he had been encouraged by personal relationships developed over time with Soviet leaders, including Marshal Georgy Zhukov and Stalin. He approached the Moscow meetings in a spirit of cooperation "in the hope that Stalin would come along and would join whole-heartedly in a common effort to bring about the reconstruction of the war-torn countries including Russia" (Hoffman 1960, 4).

As he left for Moscow he instructed Acheson to work on an aid package to Greece and Turkey designed to reject Soviet influence in those countries (the policy initiative was to become "the Truman Doctrine"), and to do so without considering its effect upon his deliberations in Moscow. Acheson thought this a courageous act, as if a commander had called down fire on his forward position in order to hold off the enemy (Acheson 1969, 221).

No cold warrior, he was reluctant to be confrontational with the Soviets. His discussions with Kennan and Bohlen had reinforced an inclination to use a nuanced approach emphasizing firmness along with patience. He much preferred building Europe's economic strength to arms-building and military alliances as a way to react to Soviet political aggressiveness. He sensed that the latter would trigger Soviet paranoia and hostility and make an arms race and military confrontation more likely.

Once in Moscow dissension developed in the American delegation team. It was sparked by John Foster Dulles, a Republican pushed onto the team by Senator Vandenberg, the Republican chair of the Senate Committee on Foreign Relations. Dulles alienated team members through his imperious manner and his support for internationalizing the Ruhr Valley (lying between Germany and France) in order to block Germany taking a strong role in European recovery. Dulles insisted that the delegation take this stance early in the talks. Marshall handled the crisis by simply declining to raise the issue until late in the talks and then defined the issue so broadly that the internal debate evaporated (Pogue 1987, 174).

A major gain made at the conference sessions was the warm and intimate association established with British foreign minister Bevin. The heavy-set, clumsy, mercurial, rough-spoken and working-class Bevin, so unlike the erect and proper Marshall, charmed the general with a surprising eloquence and mental quickness (Pogue 1987, 174-76). Their newfound partnership was to pay big dividends.

All of the careful preparation, patience, and hard work invested in the Moscow talks achieved little. Molotov played out his role as Stalin's pawn in a strategy designed to keep Western Europe weak and Germany destitute and defenseless. He frustrated every initiative put forth by Bevin and Marshall; in this he was supported by the French foreign minister, Bidault, whose government dreaded a reinvigorated Germany. Marshall had learned in Paris en route to the conference how little discretion Bidault was being allowed in the negotiations, and so extended to the Frenchman his moral support in order to "stiffen his spine." The US, he told Bidault, would not abandon France, and that in the long run it would be best for France not to divide the western allies (Pogue 1987, 178). Bidault appreciated the space and understanding given to him by Marshall, but clashed frequently with Bevin.

Despite Molotov's intransigence, US Ambassador to the USSR Beetle Smith had hopes that Marshall would ultimately prevail:

> I had no misgivings whatever. I had seen General Marshall under all conditions of stress and strain, and I had never seen him fail eventually to dominate every gathering by the sheer force of his integrity, honesty and dignified simplicity. . . . I knew that he would say little until he had all the facts well in hand and that he would make no mistakes. When necessary, he is patience personified, and no one ever takes liberties with him (Smith 1950, 216).

Smith was correct in not expecting much civility on the part of Molotov. Marshall and Bevin pushed for human and civil rights for the European nations and for suppressing reparation demands but were opposed on all counts by Molotov except those that he (Molotov) found ideologically comfortable, in particular union rights and land-reform. Marshall's pleas for the adoption of democratic principles fell on deaf ears. He saw Mototov as doctrinaire and obstinate. The Russian insisted on reading aloud, followed by translation, his policy arguments in great detail and continued to insist on the rightness of his arguments, even in the face of statements to the contrary that he had already agreed to and had signed off on.

Finally giving up on the exasperating Molotov, Marshall made his plea directly to Stalin, to no avail. Stalin waved him off with vague assurances that ultimately all would be resolved. This bland rejection marked a critical historical moment, for it stirred in Marshall the resolve to organize a unilateral American initiative to achieve economic recovery for the Europeans independent of Soviet participation (Bohlen 1967, 1-2).

Birth of the Marshall Plan

Agitated and resolved, Marshall returned in April to America and reported by radio to the nation:

> . . . [W]e cannot ignore the factor of the time involved. Disintegrating forces are becoming evident. The patient [Europe] is sinking while the doctors deliberate. So I believe that action can not await compromise through exhaustion . . . (Pogue 1987, 200).

This hint of major policy to come was prelude to his famous speech at Harvard University's commencement ceremonies on June 5, 1947, usually cited as the birth of the Marshall Plan.

Working closely with Acheson, Kennan, Will Clayton, Bohlen, and Averell Harriman, Marshall had led the initiative that led to the Harvard speech. His basic idea was to generate economic recovery in Europe through American assistance in a way that did not exclude or challenge the Soviet Union. The process would require the donee nations to take the lead in formulating specific economic projects and cooperate with each other in determining how aid was to be used. In short, it would benefit European nations individually and Europe collectively but not threaten the USSR.

The decision to invite the Soviet Union to join as a donee nation was not an easy one since it was acknowledged that working with the Soviets would be difficult (Harriman 1975, 20). On the other hand, it was reassuring for the planners to hear from Kennan and others that the USSR was likely to decline the invitation given its reluctance to join an interactive and cooperative European organization, which would require an acceptance of some loss of sovereignty. Almost certainly, it was felt that Stalin would not allow the USSR or nations under its control to participate.

The extent of Marshall's role in the Marshall Plan (formally, the European Recovery Program, or ERP) has been debated. Its evolution involved many within the Truman administration and Marshall never claimed major credit. To be sure, others played important roles. Will Clayton, as assistant secretary of state for economic affairs, conducted a tour of Europe and his report on the dire state of Europe's economy helped to lay a factual basis for the necessity of such an initiative. Acheson, acting for Marshall, made a key speech backing the general idea of support to Europe before Marshall's return from Moscow. Kennan crafted some of the major features of the plan, including the critical concept that the Europeans should collectively agree on the projects to be funded. Bohlen was assigned by Marshall the task of writing the speech that Marshall would deliver at Harvard (which Marshall freely edited). Bevin was the major actor in organizing the quick and favorable European response coming immediately after Marshall's Harvard address.

Those closest to the origins of the Marshall Plan are nearly unanimous in assigning the greatest credit to Marshall himself. Bohlen said the Plan was clearly inspired and organized by Marshall and owes its successful birth to him (1967, 1-2). According to Paul Hoffman, the main actor in the implementation of the ERP, it was Marshall, Truman, and Vandenberg who played the major roles (1960, 10). Marshall's prestige was responsible for the quick buy-in by the Europeans, and his eloquence and passion for the efficacy of its concepts got the bill through Congress (Hoffman 1960, 3-4). Finally, Lovett, who replaced Acheson as undersecretary of state soon after the Harvard speech and was at Marshall's right hand throughout the legislative battle for enactment, put the matter this way:

> Nobody did it all except the old man (i.e., Marshall), who did it all by personal image and the convincing picture which we presented to Congress (1973, 7).

President Truman endorsed and enthusiastically supported the initiative and was the one who insisted on calling the ERP the "Marshall Plan." Truman reasoned that the legislation's clear association with the highly respected Marshall would enhance its progress through the Republican Congress.[5] Vandenberg supplied energy and skill to help win public support for its passage, blunted the opposition of fellow Republicans in Congress, and provided the arrangements for its effective organizational implementation.

In discussions at State about "selling" the ERP, Marshall at first resisted Lovett's suggestion that he lobby Vandenberg and other key political leaders in Congress. Bohlen explained Marshall's resistance:

> Politicians were a race that Marshall got along with but did not understand. Their motivation mystified him (Isaacson and Thomas 1986, 424).

Marshall preferred to believe that Vandenberg would be guided by the national interest and was in no need of being persuaded. Finally succumbing to Lovett's urging, he approached and then grew very close to Vandenberg, whose support in securing passage of the European Recovery Program indeed turned out to be essential (Isaacson and Thomas 1986, 424).[6]

It was Vandenberg who insisted that Hoffman, president of the Studebaker corporation and wartime munitions producer (and a great admirer of Marshall's), be made the head of the Plan's key implementing agency, the Economic Cooperation Agency (ECA), both because of Hoffman's abilities and the fact that Senate Republicans had little confidence in the professional staff of the State Department who were regarded as overly liberal (Isaacson and Thomas 1986, 404-410; Pogue 1987, 202-205; Donovan 1987).

Marshall, Lovett, and Vandenberg labored valiantly through the balance of 1947 and into the summer of 1948 to get the ERP enacted in essentially the form in which it had been proposed. The level of monetary support was initially unacceptable to a congress that was in the mood to stop funding foreign causes and to economize. The USSR inadvertently helped to move the ERP legislation forward by virtue of its hostile acts toward Czechoslovakia. Also assisting were the growth of communist parties in western European nations and especially the severe weather that wreaked havoc on Europe in the winter of 1947-1948, which heightened public awareness of Europe's plight.

Effects of the Marshall Plan

The Marshall Plan has been universally hailed as the most noble and successful economic venture in American foreign policy history. Although other economic factors emerged at about the same time to spur Europe's economy, it is fair to say that without the Marshall Plan a far more difficult road would have resulted in the attempt to both effect economic recovery and avoid falling further under Soviet political influence (Harriman 1975, 8). Perhaps most significantly, the United States set a new standard for international generosity and established in Europe and beyond a respect and attachment to the US that was to anchor international relations in the West for at least half a century.

Soviet Reaction: The Berlin Blockade

Stalin reacted angrily and impulsively to the Marshall Plan by blocking western access to zones of occupation in Berlin, Germany's major city (West Berlin was occupied by the allies, but was totally enclosed within the Soviet zone.) All goods, including foodstuffs, medicines, and supplies, and visitors from the West were denied entry into Berlin and its environs through the armed checkpoints manned by Soviet troops.

The military governor of the American zone, General Lucius Clay, recommended the use of an armed train convoy to force access to the west Berlin zones held by the US, UK, and France. The train would have to traverse a distance of about one hundred kilometers over ground held by the USSR. Marshall here reverted to his military expertise in opposing Clay's proposal, voicing the belief that the forcing tactic would expose American troops to attack from the hills along the path through which any railroad convoy must pass and invite heavy casualties and a general escalation of conflict with the USSR. He saw the tactic as putting the Soviets in a position from which they could control events. He nonetheless noted that, as secretary of state, it was not his decision.

Lovett supplied the solution. A former assistant secretary of war on air matters in WW II, he believed that enough airborne capacity could be generated to keep West Berlin supplied without resorting to methods likely to produce a major conflict. Marshall agreed with Lovett and supported him in passing on this strategy recommendation to the White House. Truman agreed. The result was the Berlin Airlift, a fully successful operation that ultimately forced the Soviets to lift the blockade.

Other unanticipated benefits flowed from the Lovett-Marshall strategy. In answer to Clay's appeal, thirty-one thousand German citizens came out to remove rubble from runways at an airport in the French sector to make it usable for blockade-running aircraft. First with their bare hands, with women cradling rubble in their aprons, and then with bulldozers flown in by air cargo, the airport was readied in one week to serve as an additional reception area for supplies. The achievement was a tremendous morale boost for the West Berliners, proof to them that the West and particularly the US would not let them fall under the influence of the Soviet Union (Lovett 1973, 77-80).

Other Actions at the Dawn of the Cold War

The Marshall Plan and the Berlin Airlift were peaceful policies designed by the State Department under Marshall's leadership to counter aggressive Soviet actions that were intended to undermine European recovery and cooperation. Together, along with the implementation of the militaristic Truman Doctrine in Greece and Turkey, the US successfully prevented the extension of Soviet power into part of central Europe and all of western Europe. The Cold War had begun.

From his actions and words during this period, Marshall made clear his belief that military action against the USSR must only be taken as a last resort (Rusk 1990, 134). As late as May, 1948 he approved sending a message composed by Kennan and Bohlen to the Kremlin that stated: "the door is always open for full discussion and the composing of our difficulties" (Isaacson and Thomas 1986, 448-449).

Although his health deteriorated through the summer of 1948 and his energy ebbed, Marshall did not relinquish decision-making influence to Lovett (Shames 2005). He handed off many of the daily duties to his undersecretary, but he kept informed on a daily basis with his undersecretary by telephone, often from his hospital bed, and continued to take the lead role in major decisions. It was probable, however, that his reduced presence reduced chances that the USSR would seek accommodation with the West (Lovett 1973, 62-63).

Truman, pressed by a strongly anti-Soviet and Republican congress and facing a presidential election, increased his support for military measures. Lovett and Vandenberg took the lead in crafting trans-Atlantic military defense alliances in an increasingly hostile east versus west climate. Building on the Brussels Treaty (a mutual defense pact among Great Britain, France, the Netherlands, Belgium, and Luxembourg directed against Germany), the Vandenberg Resolution created a trans-Atlantic military alliance aimed at protecting West Europe against the communist East, a step that led to the creation of the North Atlantic Treaty Organization (NATO) in 1949. This turn to military alliances constituted an important turn in American foreign policy (Isaacson and Thomas 1986, 450-451).

Believing that Spain could be an important asset to the defense of West Europe, Marshall quietly dispatched William Pawley, a former ambassador to Brazil, to Spain to quietly seek the dictator Franco's agreement to permit American bases to be established in that country. Franco consented with the proviso that roads and railways in connection with the bases be built by the Americans. He pledged three million troops for the defense of West Europe within the boundaries of Spain and one-half million outside of Spain so long as they were led by either Spanish or American officers. As part of the bargain Marshall pledged to give support to Spain in its effort, which proved successful over Truman's opposition, to cancel a 1946

UN resolution which had declared Spain an enemy to world peace (Pawley 1962, 7-10). These arrangements between Marshall and Franco came about quietly and outside of the NATO framework that was building simultaneously.

Weighing in on Military Reorganization

The Truman administration and the Congress undertook to reorganize military administration in 1947 with the objective of bringing all forces together under the umbrella of a single department. James Forrestal, then serving as secretary of the Navy, opposed creating a strong secretary position within the new Department of Defense in order to preserve the Navy's autonomy (an action he came to regret when he was appointed to the position). Marshall, staying carefully within his role as secretary of state, did not take a lead role in the legislation, but his testimony and views were eagerly sought. He expressed the opinion that the traditional separate military services should be abandoned in favor of a functional division into air, ground, naval, and service units. His views carried some weight, but in the end the separate, traditional services remained in the legislation.

The Question of Israeli Statehood

Marshall approached the related issues of the partition of Palestine and Israeli statehood in his usual manner of processing major decisions. He sought factual data and recommendations from State Department staff within their areas of expertise. Great Britain was relinquishing its role of peacekeeper in Palestine as of May 15, 1948, and had turned the problem of how to govern Palestine over to the UN. Controversy raged within the General Assembly of the UN between those nations favoring the partitioning of Palestine into autonomous Jewish and Arab sectors, and those nations opposing autonomous Jewish areas.

State's diplomatic staff stood solidly against partitioning. Partitioning would entail recognition and sponsorship of autonomous Jewish sectors within Palestine, and inserting the US into Britain's role of peace-keeper. Forrestal and Acheson joined opponents of partition (Isaacson and Thomas 1986, 451). Opposition was based on three arguments: (1) partition would create two separate states (one Jewish, one Arab) with opposed interests and a high prospect of multiple wars that would necessitate entry of US forces to defend its client Jewish state; (2) unilateral recognition of a Jewish state would sour relationships with the Arab world and thus strategically threaten access to oil needed for national development and defense; and (3) withdrawal of the British under these conditions would make warfare imminent. State therefore proposed that Palestine be handled within a special UN "trusteeship" that would shift the onus of decision-making to the international body. Such an arrangement had the advantage of buying time in which some accord among Jews, Palestinians, and Arab nations might be worked out (Rusk 1990, 146-147).

Partition was favored by the American delegation to the UN, which included Adlai Stevenson, Eleanor Roosevelt, and Dean Rusk (State's representative on the

UN delegation). Marshall received the group's unanimous opinion expressing support for partition on a personal visit to New York. Stevenson had found Marshall supportive:

> He [Marshall] said very simply and very quietly that that being the view of the delegation, it was his view too, and accordingly we were instructed to go out to the headquarters and support the partition on that basis (Stevenson 1958, 2).

It is not clear how or why Marshall's view was altered after this meeting, but he went into a pivotal meeting at the White House on May 12 strongly allied with the anti-partition sentiment which ruled at State. So far as Marshall knew, the president was undecided, irritated with the aggressive tactics of the American Zionist lobby, and willing to at least hear out the argument for trusteeship. It was a fact that Truman sympathized with the displaced Holocaust survivors, and also a fact that he badly needed the support of American Jews in his bid for reelection as president. For his part, Marshall respected the right of the president to make this key foreign policy decision and understood his own role to be the major foreign policy advisor to the president, not the decision-maker. He saw his role as conveying to the president the professional advice of his department.

As policy discussion went on under the increasing urgency of Britain's planned withdrawal date, Marshall engaged in an angry exchange with the president's young legal counsel, Clark Clifford, who strongly advocated partition and Jewish statehood. Marshall objected most strenuously to Clifford's assuming a leadership role at the White House policy session. In his view, Clifford was presumptuous in speaking for the president (whose position had not yet been made clear to the general) and insultingly dismissive of State Department views despite his own comparative lack of experience and expertise.

A decision was not immediately forthcoming, as Truman was not inclined to make one until Marshall was on board. In the void, State was left with its UN trusteeship preference. At this point Lovett intervened, and with his excellent negotiating skills shuttled back and forth between Clifford and Marshall until he achieved an understanding which avoided an open breach between the president and Marshall. While Marshall recognized that it was the president's constitutional choice and duty to decide the question, it was clear that he was unhappy with both the process (especially Clifford's role) and the final decision (Isaacson and Thomas 1986, 452-53).

Independent statehood for Israel, the growth of Israeli democracy, Israel's permanent and vital alliance with the US, a series of Middle Eastern wars, and growing Arab resentment of America's support for Israel were the long-term results of the final UN vote in favor of partition. The decision represents an important watershed in the history of the region and strongly influences current relations of the US with the Arab and Muslim worlds. Marshall's role in the decision remains controversial, but the key point is that in the end he recognized his role as subordinate to the president's and acted accordingly.

Marshall as a Cabinet Member

As secretary of state, Marshall faithfully attended all cabinet meetings and stood out as the most conscientious and best prepared cabinet member. He was also prized for his calmness in the face of conflict and for his consistently reasonable and cooperative behavior. As the head of the oldest department in the government he had seniority on the cabinet and was cognizant of his right to speak first. He asked many questions in order to better grasp the issues being discussed. Frequently, he brought two or three staff people with him to get all the facts out on the table. Truman's chief of staff, John Steelman, said of Marshall's role during this period: "He was a great humanitarian in wanting to solve the problems of the world on a real fair and honest basis so we all had great respect for him" (Steelman 1958, 7-9).

     Without intending to do so, Marshall took the major leadership role in the cabinet. An illustration of his integrity is the fact that when military matters arose at the table, as they often did, he took no part in the discussion unless asked to do so. Steelman commented: "unless you already knew it, if you sat in those conferences I don't think you could ever tell he had ever been connected with the military" (Steelman 1958, 9).

Resuscitating the American Red Cross

Intestinal illness led to Marshall's second retirement in January of 1949, this time from the post of secretary of state. After a period of convalescence, President Truman offered him the post of president of the American Red Cross (ARC). Truman regarded the position to be low in pressure but high in visibility, from which his favorite public servant could draw satisfaction without exerting great effort. The president underestimated both the job and the man. To Marshall, who saw the ARC within the broad sweep of history, the assignment appeared to be anything but a pleasurable ride. He accepted the job and vowed to reporters that he would not be a figurehead.

     One of the magnets that drew him to the position was his knowledge that no less than fifteen million new veterans had been added to the four million pre-WW II veterans as potential clients of the ARC. Many of them suffered from war-related trauma, particularly psychoneurotic afflictions, as well as physical disabilities, and he saw as an important mission of the ARC serving this population.

     Marshall was well enough to commence his service to the ARC in October, 1949. He came with a built-in sympathy for the organization based on his wartime experiences. He was aware that the ARC, like the Young Mens Christian Association (YMCA) in the previous war, had suffered in reputation from its failure to perform certain promised services. He was also aware that it had some of its resources taken away from it by competing Army needs and budget cuts and that members of the armed forces were not aware of these cutbacks. The inability of these and similar organizations to deliver on wartime promises (especially at the fronts) had resulted in their losing face and had drastically cut post-war donations (much of which were expected to come from veterans). In Marshall's view, veterans and their military friends had blamed these agencies unfairly:

> I was interested to find, when I came into the presidency of the Red Cross, exactly the same reaction against the Red Cross that there had been against the YMCA and for exactly the same reason, because they had undertaken all the obligations and, of course, they had [imposed on them] all kinds of difficulties in carrying them out (Bland 1991, 200).

Marshall threw himself into his new role with characteristic energy. Within a month of being hired he began a cross-country tour in which he covered seventy-five hundred miles and talked to two hundred-and-fifty-four chapter chairs. His purpose was to discover both strengths and weaknesses in ARC operations. Soliciting their views on ARC operations and policies, he learned among other things that many of the chapter chairs complained that far more money was raised in their local communities than they got back from the national organization in the form of services (GCMRL: 10/24/1949, Box 167, Folder 21).

This arduous trip was followed three months later by a series of trips that lasted two months in which he visited thirty cities, including Honolulu, and "saw about twenty-five to thirty thousand of the most active Red Cross workers." He came away with one outstanding impression which he shared with the national convention in June, 1950 that "many of the most active workers in the organization had a very limited knowledge of the whole organization" which led to public confusion about what the organization was doing. The solution, he said, was to begin a concerted effort to orient active ARC employees about the organization's general program. He felt every member should know why the ARC was founded, its relationship to the International Red Cross Committee and the League of Red Cross Societies, and its responsibilities to the armed forces and the victims of disaster (GCMRL: 6/26/1950, Box 168, Folder 44).

He also invested great effort in the national blood program, a key ARC program. In answer to fears expressed that the program signaled a turn toward socialized medicine, he countered:

> Actually, nothing could be very much further from socialization than the Red Cross approach. Socialization implies an activity required of the people by legislation or government decree. Asking the strong and the healthy to donate their blood voluntarily for the relief of the sick and injured is the exact opposite of the socialized approach (GCML: 6/26/1950, Box 168, Folder 44).

Neither, he added, did the ARC stifle competition among blood banks. Regional centers for procurement and distribution of blood were opened only where commercial facilities were non-existent or inadequate.

A budget shortfall was the ARC's most pressing problem. Reserves built up during the war years had run out. Reaching fiscal equilibrium depended on increasing donations and cutting expenses. Gaining donations depended heavily on correcting misconceptions that servicemen had formed about the Red Cross during both wars. Marshall counseled the ARC board of governance to take several actions, to include: (1) raising money by ARC auspices only and not in concert with other charities (to highlight the ARC's special status and appeal); (2) stressing the central importance of the volunteer to the organization; and (3) undertaking vigorous education of ARC personnel respecting the national mission and history of the organization and exact nature of its vital programs. To stimulate volunteering he stressed the motivational value of giving volunteers important work to do, so as to vest in them real responsibility and heighten appreciation for them by their local communities (GCMRL: 6/26/1950, Box 168, Folder 44).

It is intriguing to think of what would have been the result of his final initiative had he stayed with the ARC. Noting that the Junior Red Cross had an enrolled membership of about nineteen million young people, mostly women and girls, he offered a powerful vision recalling CCC service in an earlier era:

I think it is important that young women—girls, as a matter of fact, should be encouraged to take advantage of certain excellent training opportunities that the Red Cross offers, the better to prepare themselves as citizens. I am thinking of the extensive health programs in home nursing, first aid, and food and nutrition. The position of women in the country is such that they are destined to take a large part in public affairs. Some preparation for the duty of citizenship is therefore an obligation for the young women of the nation (GCMRL: Box 168, Folder 44, 13).

Working the press, he stressed the unfortunate experience of the YMCA in WW I and the best efforts of the ARC to meet its objectives under the unfair burdens imposed on it in WW II (Bland 1991, 362-363). He traveled to many ARC work sites around the country to stir enthusiasm and invited the press to come along, and because it was Marshall who invited them, they came. On these visits he gave newspaper interviews and welcomed publicity, a marked departure from prior behavior.

Finally, he stressed to the public and to the organization itself the relationship of the ARC to world affairs. Agreements to do good works around the globe could be effective only if people of good will did the work they had agreed to do. He insisted that the ARC was peopled by persons uninterested in power or self-advancement who labored only for humankind. The ARC could count on finding fellow Red Cross workers in the operations of sixty-seven other countries and thus extend its good works globally (GCMRL: 6/26/1950, Box 168, Folder 44).

It was important to get the relationship of the local chapter to the national organization right. He saw "a tendency of the chapter to over-emphasize the community aspects of the Red Cross at the expense of the great national and international functions of the organization which give the Red Cross symbol its greatest significance" (GCMRL: 6/26/1950, Box 168, Folder 44, 6). Giving the ARC a local emphasis only confuses the public. Neither the public nor the active ARC member knew or appreciated the fact that seventy percent of the money raised in fund campaigns and sent to the national organization was being returned to the local community or was spent on its behalf.

He framed the core of ARC's mission in this remark to the national convention:

It is true that chapters in certain areas relatively immune to disaster do not always receive a dollar for dollar return on the funds allocated to national from local campaigns. But one never knows when disaster may strike nor its nature, and it is the basic *philosophy of the Red Cross to accept responsibility for the other fellow's welfare* whether he be across the street or in the next county or in a distant state. *If we begin now to question the soundness of that philosophy, then we are no longer the Red Cross, but some other organization* (GCMRL: 6/26/1950, Box 168, Folder 44, emphasis added).

Through such communication he pointed out the "localism" implicit in the attitudes of many Red Cross chapters and chapter chairs who had complained about the "selfishness" of the national organization. He did this in an inoffensive manner by calling forth their best instincts for service. He also asked the chapter leaders to take the initiative to spread the national and international philosophy of the organization in their communities.

In the judgment of Forrest Pogue, Marshall restored to the ARC its original position of dignity and prominence that had been partially lost through internal conflict and bad public relations left over from the war (Pogue 1987, 415-419). He did so within a single year. He gave every indication he wished to stay and follow through on the initiatives he had started, but once again a national emergency intervened, prompting yet another telephone call from the president.

The Last Assignment: Secretary of Defense

When North Korea invaded South Korea on June 25, 1950, threatening to push the pro-western and semi-democratic regime off the Asian continent, President Truman responded in two ways. First, he internationalized the conflict through securing armed action by the United Nations. Second, he asked General Marshall to return to the cabinet to help cure divisions in the president's camp by taking the post of secretary of defense. He needed a replacement for Louis Johnson, whom he had just fired (Isaacson and Thomas 1986, 445).

Probably already known to the president, Marshall had been involved in planning action in Korea. On or about June 26, a number of civilian officials (Bohlen, Acheson, Carter, and perhaps Kennan) initiated a meeting with the general that occurred in the garden patio at Dodona Manor, the Marshall home in Leesburg. The group had bypassed Secretary of Defense Johnson in seeking his counsel. At the meeting, Marshall inquired into the availability of trained troops that could be moved into the region (Carter 1959, 32-33).

The president's telephone call reached Marshall while the general was on a fishing vacation. He drove fifteen miles to take the call in a remote country store. Truman said, "General, I want you to be Secretary of Defense. Will you do it?" "Yes, Mr. President," he answered simply, and hung up. When they next spoke, Marshall explained: "I want to tell you why I had to hang up in such a hurry . . . it was a general store, and all the cracker-barrel experts were sitting around there waiting to see what I was going to get from the president" (Miller 1974, 226).

As he had done when appointing Marshall secretary of state, Truman vested full policy authority in the man he most respected. Marshall, distrustful of power that he felt was not constitutionally his to exercise, was determined on his part to impose a type of self-restraint on his decision-making (Pace 1959, 10). As with his earlier cabinet post, he asked not to be politically identified with the Democratic party through mail listings, invitations to party functions, and the like. He did not wish to feel a greater commitment to political leaders of one party so as to preclude his ability to serve in an administration of the other party (Carter 1959, 1-3).

Marshall exerted a steadying effect on policy and nerves as American held territory shrank to a small perimeter around the city of Pusan at the southern base of the Korean peninsula. As calls for withdrawal from the peninsula mounted, Marshall called attention to the need to preserve intact the security of the command and indicated that the fluctuation of opinion in Congress was not a new thing and that the defeatist mood would not last (Kennan 1959, 7-8). His calm confidence helped to pluck up the courage of other members of the Truman team, and the line of defense held. According to Kennan, Marshall's insertion at Defense kept the US in Korea.

The Defense Department was quickly reorganized by Marshall to reflect the same organizational integration achieved in his posts as Army chief of staff and secretary of state. He had made Lovett's appointment as undersecretary of defense a precondition for his own acceptance and brought him on immediately. General Omar Bradley, a Marshall protégé, was already in place as chairman of the Joint Chiefs of Staff (JCS). The State Department, which had distanced itself from the Defense Department while Johnson was secretary of defense, was invited into joint discussions and decision sessions. Its representative in these sessions was normally Secretary of State Acheson, Marshall's former undersecretary at State. With Humelsine and Carter, two men who had served Marshall both in the Army and at State, serving respectively as executive secretaries at State and Defense, there was an almost immediate blending of the efforts of the two departments. Inter-departmental and team collaboration and harmony now prevailed (Pace 1959, 8-9; Carter 1959, 33).

Marshall's confidence in his new subordinates, coupled with his professionalism, had an infectious quality on agency morale. Consistent with his concept of separating civilian and military roles, he did not interfere in any way with the operations or decisions of the JCS or with internal army matters. This self-imposed distance, however, did not keep him from playing a role as a mentor. For instance, he instructed Secretary of the Army Frank Pace on how to identify men who could become future leaders of the Army and to make sure that their performance became known throughout the country. From their long discussions, Pace was able to say of his teacher:

His vast background in the Army was a tremendous guide to me in accessing and meeting the problems. Some of the things I was able to do, he quietly suggested to me and I put them into effect (Pace 1959, 8).

The Removal of General MacArthur

Douglas MacArthur had always been a political gadfly and a frequent irritant to Presidents Roosevelt and Truman and to Marshall. Marshall had nonetheless protected and promoted him, first in rescuing him from Corregidor and securing his appointment as a theater commander, and then as the supreme commander in Japan at the war's end. New problems arose when the Korean war erupted. MacArthur violated military ethics by communicating without clearance directly with Republican Speaker of the House Martin, expressing his views on far eastern strategy which differed from those of the administration. Despite this transgression, MacArthur's administrative triumph in managing the occupation of Japan as well as his military brilliance in the early stages of the fighting in Korea had won for him the support of the secretary of defense. Any transgressions were up to Bradley and Truman to assess and take action on, not him, since he was not in a position of military command.

General Ridgway (serving as the commander of the Eighth Army in Korea) had laid out maps showing the military situation in sharp relief: American and UN forces were moving north in eight or nine locations on either side of a mountain ridge running north and south within North Korea. This separation caused the two major forces to be vulnerable both because of their disconnection and because their rapid movement northward had dangerously extended their lines of supply. Moreover, troops had moved north of the latitude of the positions that Bradley and Truman had communicated to MacArthur were defensible, an action which both thought could induce the armed intervention of China or the USSR. Bradley, Ridgway, Marshall, and Acheson reacted with alarm. Still, Marshall refused to give a military judgment, holding only to his view that the field commander must either be trusted or relieved (Acheson 1957, notes, 1-2).

In cabinet meetings Marshall spoke out often and favorably of the job MacArthur was doing with the occupation, recovery, and democratization in Japan. He asked that no immediate action be taken respecting MacArthur inasmuch as important appropriations bills vital to national defense were pending in the Congress should not be jeopardized (Truman 1960, 6).

Truman flew to Wake Island in order to make clear to his Far East commander he could not agitate for a war strategy, MacArthur, at odds with that adopted by the administration. When MacArthur gave evidence on his return to Japan of continuing on his separate policy track, Truman's patience ran out. He and his advisors, save Marshall, determined that the Far East commander must be relieved, but looked to Marshall for approval before acting (Steelman 1958, 11-12). Finally, Truman asked Marshall to review the correspondence of the preceding two years that had passed between the president and MacArthur; he told Marshall that he would not remove MacArthur if Marshall continued to oppose such action. According to Truman:

> General Marshall did that and the next morning he came in to see me and told me that he had gone over all those telegrams and communications . . . and had come to the conclusion that the General should have been relieved two years before.
> . . . I told General Marshall to write the order relieving him, and he was relieved and brought home, and you know the results (Truman 1960, 7).

Lovett saw the situation in this way:

> I think what actually happened was he stood it as long as he could hold the others together and then finally when they said, 'This is it, we've had it,' he said, "Fine.". . . I'm absolutely sure the President would have delayed it if Marshall had fought but I think Marshall said 'Let's think it over, let's take our time about this, there is no urgency about it.' . . . But here had been week after week after week of these most exasperating purple phrases coming in over the cables, you know. . . . Finally it just got too much to stand (Lovett 1973, 76-77).

Marshall thus played a decisive but reluctant role in the decision to relieve General MacArthur as Far East commander and to replace him with General Ridgway (Pogue 1987, 481-490). In the final analysis, it was a combination of MacArthur's political trespasses and tactical blunders that finally set Marshall against his historic foil.

There clearly was sympathy and even a touch of remorse within Marshall when MacArthur finally returned by plane to Langley Field, Virginia, from Japan. Marshall was the only representative of the administration on hand to greet him.[7] The following day MacArthur delivered an emotional address to a joint session of the Congress that had gathered to hear him, leading to a national outpouring of affection for him coupled with vilification of Truman for his decision to fire one of the "old soldiers" (as MacArthur had described himself in his speech to Congress).

Following MacArthur's triumphal departure from the city amid calls for him to run for the presidency in 1952, General Marshall was called hastily to the hill to testify and to explain the president's decision. He testified for a full week, patiently laying out the facts in the record that had shaped the situation which had prompted the president's decision. The reaction to Marshall's matter-of-fact presentation was back-pedaling by many MacArthur supporters and silence from the nation's opinion makers that appeared to doom a serious MacArthur bid for the presidency.

Coda: Marshall's Post-Retirement Influence

General Marshall retired for the third and last time in September of 1951, but he continued to influence American and world government and their administration in subtle ways.

Soon after leaving Defense, he joined the board of Pan-American Airlines. As a board member, he occasionally called the White House at the behest of Pan-

American with gentle inquiries, never pressuring and fearful lest his prestige might unduly influence White House officials to take action or consume valuable time. One contact led to the prevention of an airline strike (Steelman 1958, 15-17).

President Eisenhower asked General Marshall to head the American diplomatic mission to attend the coronation of Queen Elizabeth II in June, 1953. He was received warmly by the British public. The general used the occasion to note that the UK had failed to grasp the extent of American sacrifices in Korea and erroneously thought of the United States as "thirsting for war." He added that "Anglo-American unity was the main hope and support of peace" (*International Herald Tribune*, June 6, 1953).

Also in 1953, the Nobel committee selected General Marshall to receive the Nobel Peace Prize. In introducing him to the assemblage in Oslo, Norway on December 10, Carl Joachim Hambro, a member of the Nobel Committee, referred to Marshall's devotion to the morale of the common soldier and to his love of peace,[8] reading Marshall's words that are quoted at the beginning of this chapter.

Marshall used the occasion of his own death to make a point about how he believed the passing of a major public servant should be celebrated. The pageantry of the funeral he had planned and carried out for General Pershing in 1948 had been distasteful to him because of the pomp, the expense to the government, and his belief that Pershing had already been sufficiently honored and rewarded by his country. Although entitled to a special military funeral at Arlington National Cemetery, in keeping with Marshall's wishes the rites to be observed were "among the simplest ever conducted for a man of his rank and prestige."[9]

His body was borne to Bethlehem Chapel at the Washington National Cathedral in a small motorized cortege, where it remained for twenty-four hours for visitation by the public. It was then taken to the post chapel at Fort Myer for the funeral service that was attended by the family and a limited number of invited guests. A private burial service in Arlington National Cemetery followed. The grave site, a little to the east of the Memorial Amphitheater, had been selected by General Marshall some years earlier. It contained the grave of the general's first wife, Lily Coles Marshall, and her mother.

The six body bearers included one enlisted man from each service including the Army, Marine Corps, Navy, Air Force, and Coast Guard, and a single cadet from VMI. In addition to family, guests included President Eisenhower and former President Truman, Secretary of State Christian A. Herter, former Secretary of State Acheson, Ambassador Harriman, and Generals Bradley, Gruenther, and Ridgway. Canon Luther Miller of the National Cathedral conducted a simple funeral service from the Episcopal Order for the Burial of the Dead. There was no eulogy.

Marshall and Change

This and the preceding two chapters, along with chapter two, tell the story of Marshall's career, his actions and attitudes displayed in many different roles, both military and civilian. They give evidence of the qualities of his mind and spirit, his achievements, and his influence upon others. Perhaps the attribute that best explains the combination of extraordinary longevity in public service and the uniformly high level of performance detailed in these chapters was his ability to accept the need for change and devote his whole being to bringing it about.

Frank Pace reflected on how Marshall always took the long view, seeing contemporary history in relation to both the past and the future: "He was moved less by the current events, and felt less impressed by them than practically any other man I was associated with in my entire time in government" (Pace 1959, 1). This observation lends support to Neustadt and May's thesis that great leadership requires thinking in time streams (1986, 253-254). When Pace returned from the Wake Island meeting of MacArthur and Truman, he reported to Marshall that MacArthur said the war would be over by Christmas. Marshall told Pace he was troubled by such a report. "Troubled?" asked the surprised Pace. "The American people," answered Marshall, "have not learned the meaning of a cold war. They are not aware of the fact that we're going to be engaged in this kind of struggle in one way or another over a long period of time and that our old determinations of what war means have got to be revised in the light of the world in which we live" (Pace 1959, 16).

Notes

1.   Mrs. Marshall was left with a bitter feeling toward the president. In a letter to aide Frank McCarthy, she complained: "This sounds bitter. Well, I am bitter. The President should never have asked this of him and in such a way that he could not refuse" (Pogue 1987, 29-30).

2.   Fox Conner, head of operations for the AEF, later advised his young protégé, Dwight Eisenhower, to get an assignment with Marshall because future warfare would require cooperation among allies and Marshall was the most skilled officer in arranging allied commands (Eisenhower 1967, 192).

3.   Marshall blamed the CC Clique, rather than Chiang himself, for bringing down the negotiations. Chen Li-fu admitted in Taipei years later that he may have erred in keeping Chiang's offers of cooperation in check, that he and Marshall could have worked out a better arrangement (Pogue 1987, 84).

4.   What he was telling Marshall in face-to-face meetings was often at odds with what he was writing in his diary (Myers 1998).

5.   Truman told Marshall: "General, I want the plan to go down in history with your name on it. And don't give me any argument. I've made up my mind, and, remember, I'm your Commander in Chief" (Miller 1974, 5).

6.   Lovett recalled Marshall saying modestly that his greatest contribution to the enactment process was persuading Senator Vandenberg that the initiative was nonpartisan (Lovett 1973, 13).

7.   "I remember when I came back from Korea after my release. George Marshall . . . met me at the plane and shook hands with me and said, 'Douglas, I had nothing to do with your release.' And I believe it" (MacArthur 1961, 2).

8.   Retrieved from http://nobelprize.org/nobel_prizes/peace/ laureates.

9.   Obtained from www.arlingtoncemetery.net/gcm.htm, the website for Arlington National Cemetery.

CHAPTER EIGHT
ORGANIZATIONAL PHILOSOPHY AND MANAGEMENT STYLE

I feel that we have made tremendous progress. And even in the turbulent days which come with the declaration of war . . . we were able to straighten our house out and get down to smooth business within twenty-four hours. That has been a great reassurance and encouragement to me. Not that there isn't plenty of business, not that there isn't far too much business, but we have been able to keep our heads well above the floor, and it is regularizing and systematizing smoothly and more smoothly each day.
—George C. Marshall,
Address at the National Council Dinner of the Reserve Officers'
Association of the US, Washington, D.C. January 9, 1942

Some Background on Organization Theory and Management Style

There is no bright line between leadership and management. Although it is frequently said that the essence of leadership is change and movement over time and that the core of management is bringing order, stability, and consistency to the organization, leaders must see to it that management functions are properly performed in order for their organizations to be successful.

In Luther Gulick's famous work (1937), the functions of management are listed as *planning, organizing, staffing, directing, coordinating, reporting* and *budgeting*. (Gulick 1937). Coordinating, which encompasses the other functions with the purpose of working toward the achievement of organizational goals, is the management function that most overlaps with the function of leadership. It is preeminently the task of leadership to oversee that all management functions are being performed, and to personally take a hand in coordinating them. Leaders play a major role in detecting when management functions misfire and in precipitating action to get them back on track. They also internalize within the organization the learning gained from the experience of misfiring, discovery, and correction.

The process of acquiring leadership skills does not mean that the management portion of leadership is lessened or neglected. Management continues to be important to leadership, but the leader must be freed from the performance of most of the management functions themselves—like budgeting, staffing, or day-to-day directing. For example, a leader doesn't have to be farsighted if he or she understands that planning is a prerequisite for the learning organization. It is sufficient if he or she values the planning function and ensures that it is respected

167

and made an integral part of the organization's decision-making. Again, it is the ability to *coordinate* the other management functions within the organization that is itself most closely related to the steering and guiding function that is one of the hallmarks of leadership.

Many factors affect organizational effectiveness: the size of the organization; its sources of support and opposition; the fit between its culture and the culture of the wider society in which it is implanted; the geography of the area to be served or affected; the degree of hierarchy; whom and how many it serves; the skills and behavior and motivation of its members; and the technologies it employs. In the public realm, the list of factors grows: the organization's public reputation, its relations with the three political branches and other levels of government; and its relations with the media, interest groups, and various constituencies in the public at large.

Typical public organizations take the objectives and resources they are given by the lawmakers and seek additional resources, knowledge, particularly that will help them accomplish their objectives. Truly successful organizations must do more. They must be able to determine (1) how well they are doing in meeting their goals; (2) how to better use the human, financial, and knowledge resources they already have; (3) what new skills they will have to find and incorporate; and (4) how to scope out change in their environment and respond to it.

Marshall rarely thought about organizations in theory terms. Given to action instead of words, he put his beliefs to work in the form of concrete decisions and processes. He was an observer who asked many questions and then stated his thinking in the form of a carefully written letter or memorandum to a staff member in an appropriate office to do something: make a study, gather data, take an implementing action, or combine with others to perform a task (Pasco 1997, 50). Divining Marshall's thinking about organizational philosophy and management style thus requires making inferences from actions and the observations of those who worked with him.

These observations are very consistent regarding his performance as Army chief of staff, secretary of state, and secretary of defense. In each of these roles he acted in ways consistent with certain views about how organizations should be designed and how people should be managed. Organizational design features included unity of command, teamwork, an orderly process for making decisions, close coordination of management functions through a centralized office, delegation of decision-making along with the authority to enforce the decisions, the need for planning, maintaining focus on goal achievement, and open communication. These elements are the substance of this and the next chapter. Chapter Ten will concern itself primarily with managing people.

Unity of Command

Unity of command is an organizing principle for which Marshall is well remembered. He regarded the concept as exceedingly important and "basic to the whole control of the war" (Bland 1991, 358). The essence of the idea is that responsibility for making and carrying out fundamental decisions must be lodged in a single authority and cannot be split among different authorities (whether these be nations, commanders, or governmental actors). The principle was clearly evident in the reorganization of the War Department in 1941-1942, the shaping of the combined allied command structure in 1942, and the post-war reorganizations of the State and Defense Departments (Bland and Stevens 1996, 41, 63-65; Acheson 1957, 2; Carter 1959, 13-17; Lovett 1973, 52).

Marshall articulated and defended the concept at the Arcadia conference in December, 1941. His ideas, recorded in the minutes of the conference, were of the utmost importance in achieving a unified allied approach in the face of Churchill's objections:

> I express these as my personal views and not those as a result of consultation with the Navy or with my own War Plans Division. As a result of what I saw in [WW I] and from following our own experience, I feel very strongly that the most important consideration is the question of unity of command. The matters being settled here are mere details which will continuously reoccur unless settled in a broader way. With differences between groups and between services, the situation is impossible unless we operate on a frank and direct basis. I am convinced that there must be one man in command of the entire theater—air, ground, and ships. We can not manage but by cooperation. Human frailties are such that there would be emphatic unwillingness to place portions of troops under another service. If we make a plan for unified command now, it will solve nine-tenths of our troubles (Sherwood 1948, 455-457).

The major guiding decisions for military strategy and the allocation of resources were to be made at the top by an authority representing the combination of allies, and tactical and allocation decisions in each region of warfare (called "theaters") were to be made by a single commander with direct authority over ground, air, and naval forces of all allied nations operating within the region.

Decision-Making: Delegating, Trusting, and Deciding

Another principle of organizational design was that authority should be delegated from the top of the organization downward, within the framework of organizational objectives and subject to evaluation of the results of the implementation by those delegating the authority. This design feature requires great care in choosing the officers who are to be delegated authority to ensure a level of knowledge, judgment, and dedication necessary to performance. It also requires that the authority delegated be sufficiently broad to cover likely and even unforeseen contingencies; trusting those delegated the authority enough discretion, space, and resources to do the job; and getting out of the way in order to allow them to act (Bland and Stevens 1996, 383; Clifford 1991, 16; Brett 1962, 13; Bryden 1958, 9).

The delegation-discretion-trust pattern held for all of the management environments in which Marshall operated—the military hierarchy within the Pentagon, military field offices, the infantry officer school environment, and cabinet level departments. He delegated responsibilities that were officially his to subordinates, gradually working up from minor to more significant responsibilities. He carefully analyzed the qualifications and personal suitability of potential delagatees. He wanted persons who would make sound decisions, given general policy guidance, and then act on their own initiative within these prescribed zones. The ideal here was to gain speed and efficiency in reaching objectives, both of which were lost when decisions were deferred to the higher authority.

When Eisenhower reported to the General Staff in 1941 Marshall told him bluntly that "the Department is filled with able men who analyze their problems well but feel compelled always to bring them to me for final solution. I must have assistants who will solve their own problems and tell me later what they have done." He was very tolerant of honest mistakes resulting from taking initiative and typically supported and encouraged subordinates as they gained experience, although fewer errors were expected over time (Cray 1990, 265-266).

Paul Hoffman, chief administrator of the Marshall Plan's implementation, could not recall receiving a single suggestion from Marshall concerning operations or appointments despite Marshall's huge stake in the efficient operation of ERP programs (Hoffman 1960, 15).

Marshall operated on the assumption that heads of governmental agencies, such as cabinet secretaries, should do only those things demanded of their role and leave the rest to properly qualified subordinates who had been properly briefed (Rusk 1990, 131). He believed, further, that parceling out responsibility and placing confidence in people was necessary to develop needed managers and leaders and to build organizational competence. If the delegated assignment was carried out well, the reward was the delegation of another task or function somewhat higher on the scale of responsibility, and the result was an escalation in the quality of internal management and leadership.

One example well illustrates his belief that the subordinate's growth had to be fitted to the larger importance of serving public goals. Marshall was critical of his chief of personnel on the General Staff, General Hansell, for proposing an action which Hansell intended using to improve the position of the Air Forces as distinct from the Army as a whole. Marshall told Hansell that "unless I [Hansell] could divorce myself from selfish ambitions . . . and think only in terms of what was best for the national effort, he could dispense with my services." Thereafter, Hansell made only one selfish proposal—when asked to recommend a supreme allied commander for OVERLORD, he recommended Marshall. His boss again admonished him (Hansell 1959, 4).

As Army chief of staff and as a cabinet secretary, Marshall took pains to keep his centralized staff people (and himself) from giving advice or demanding routine reports from field commanders, ambassadors, or other officials in decentralized locations where the real action was occurring. Field personnel, he reasoned, were generally in a better position to assess facts and make judgments on localized, intangible factors that headquarters people were unable to understand (Bland 1988, 36). As a consequence it was better and easier to allow field commanders to make changes in their organizations without interference from headquarters (Taylor 1972,

97). It is probable that some of this perspective had been gained by Marshall when, as chief of operations of the First Infantry Division in 1917-1918, he had felt harassed by irrelevant suggestions made by visiting officials and "experts" unfamiliar with actual conditions at the front (Marshall 1976, 65-66).

Following Up

In delegating responsibility, Marshall wanted officers to both make and execute their own decisions and not to come back to him over the matter. In this regard he faulted General Gerow, WPD chief, for protesting that the decisions were too important for him not to keep checking on whether he was acting properly. Eisenhower also complained that when he was a WPD staff officer and sent Gerow his findings and decisions, Gerow would convert these into "recommendations" and feel free to deviate. This was a major reason for Marshall replacing Gerow with Eisenhower (Ambrose 1983, 136).

What protection is there in the inevitable case of a subordinate who does not measure up to the task? Marshall's practice was to check back on what the officer had accomplished after he had handed him a task (usually with few instructions). If, in Mashall's judgment, the subordinate had performed acceptably, he or she would be given a larger job with more responsibility. If performance was unacceptable, he or she was moved into another position or assigned another set of responsibilities without admonishment or loss of face. If the poorly performing officer was a staff officer, Marshall would let the person know of the shortcoming in a respectful way so as not to cause embarrassment (Gerow 1958, 34-35).

This pattern characterized the Marshall-Eisenhower relationship. In their first work-based interview after Eisenhower took over as WPD chief, Marshall assigned him the task of developing a two-front war strategy. Eisenhower returned with an impressive basic blueprint for a cross-channel invasion. Satisfied, Marshall then sent Eisenhower to London with the task of designing a European headquarters and a theater organization, as well as detailing the types and identity of officers that would be needed in that headquarters to lay the basis for the cross-channel invasion.

Once Eisenhower was in England, Marshall asked Churchill for a report on his performance in London; the prime minister was highly pleased (Pogue 1966, 337-339). Marshall followed up by recommending to the CCOS Eisenhower's appointment as commander of the European theater command. Successful work in that command led to Eisenhower's elevation to commander of the TORCH campaign and ultimately to his leadership of OVERLORD.

Another example of Marshall's handling of promising new officers involves Maxwell Taylor, a future chair of the JCS. Assigned in mid-1941 as a junior staff officer to the office of the Secretary of the General Staff (SGS), Taylor appeared in Marshall's office with a sheaf of papers in response to Marshall's request to inquire into whether the National Guard units in Alaska should be augmented, a question then disputed between two assistant chiefs of staff. Taylor had prepared well and proceeded to present the facts surrounding the various positions taken by the deputy chiefs and the issues involved. Then, Marshall "looked across the desk

at me with cold appraising eyes and asked, 'What do you think about it, Taylor?'"
Abashed that he should be asked his opinion after summarizing the recommendations of his superiors, he had difficulty summarizing his own view. He recalled
many years later:

> ... the embarrassment taught me a lesson which I never forgot; thereafter, I never
> took another paper on any subject to George Marshall or to any other superior in
> later years without having made up my mind in advance as to the decision I would
> take if the matter were my responsibility (Taylor 1972, 38-40).

Managing Field Operations

Field commanders were often surprised by just how much discretion they were
given. General Mark Clark said of his experience as a lead field commander in
Italy:

> I knew that there were times when things sort of bogged down in Italy. . . . It
> wasn't a terrain you could charge with cavalry or charge with tanks. I could never
> get my tanks to roll. My goodness, they were bogged down right away, mountains
> and defiles and things of that kind. . . . I knew there were times that they must
> have been terribly frustrated in Washington with the progress in Italy as I was . .
> . but never once, never did I get the feeling that Marshall wasn't supporting me
> one hundred percent and I know he must have had misgivings (Clark 1959, 58).

While Clark struggled in Italy, Marshall busied himself shoring up support for
Eisenhower, the theater commander, at home. Marshall doubted that Eisenhower
knew all the things he was doing in Congress "building up his (Eisenhower's)
position so that he could resist any attacks that would come with any misfortune"
(Bland 1991, 346). And the attacks were coming frequently, from both sides of the
Atlantic, first over Eisenhower's perceived over-cautiousness in tactical choices in
North Africa and Sicily, then over political fumbling of the issue of who to assign
to lead the Free French forces, and finally with the American troop reversals
associated with the German counter-offensive in the Battle of the Bulge. Churchill
proposed to replace Eisenhower with British Field Marshal Harold Anderson, but
Marshall warded off the challenge (Bland 1991, 345; Ambrose 1983, 217-218).
    Marshall made it his business to stay well informed about what his command-
ers were doing (Brereton 1962, 13; Bryden 1958, 9, 33). General Brereton, Pacific
air commander, noted Marshall's presence despite the distance between them:

> He was all around me and I had occasional communications from him. I think he
> made a practice of writing to his commanders, particularly commanders on
> independent command, occasionally just to tell them he knew they were there. He
> wasn't exactly breathing down their necks, but he knew what they were doing
> (1962, 13).

On occasion commanders were removed, something Marshall found difficult "because he had to remove men that he thought a lot of but he had the courage to do it and it takes courage" (Devers 1958, 157). On other occasions he allowed veiled criticism to creep into his communication. In a radiogram sent in September 1943 to Eisenhower regarding the Sicilian campaign, he related that he had discussed battle tactics with Field Marshal Dill and agreed that "you give the enemy too much time to prepare and eventually find yourself up against a very stiff resistance" (Bland and Stevens 1996, 136). Eisenhower responded indignantly the following day: "I do not see how any individual could possibly be devoting more thought and energy to speeding up operations or to attacking boldly and with admitted risk than I do," and he further noted that Churchill had thanked him for taking risks (Bland and Stevens 1996, 136-137).

Just one month later, Eisenhower accepted more readily another Marshall suggestion on tactics. To keep the Germans from noticing that combat units were being shifted from Italy to Great Britain in anticipation of the cross-channel invasion, Marshall suggested planting information likely to cause the enemy to counterattack in Italy. The idea was for Patton and his staff to visit Corsica to make it appear that an invasion of north Italy or southern France was imminent. Eisenhower replied more graciously to this idea:

> As it is I am quite sure that we must do everything possible to keep him (the enemy) confused and the point you have suggested concerning Patton's movements appeals to me as having a great deal of merit. This possibility had not previously occurred to me (Bland and Stevens 1996, 163).

Marshall was also disappointed with Eisenhower's failure to seize Rome with the 82nd Airborne Division. He asked Eisenhower "if he had considered the possibility of halting . . . efforts toward Naples . . . and making a dash for Rome, perhaps by amphibious means" (Ambrose 1983, 264).

Both examples of second-guessing are intended to highlight how rarely they occurred and how gently they were handled with the focus remaining on the objective sought to be achieved. More typical was Marshall's action in the aftermath of one of Patton's indiscretions. Patton had said to a British audience, "It is the evident destiny of the British and Americans to rule the world." Marshall wrote to Eisenhower:

> You carry the burden of responsibility as to the success of Overlord. . . . The decision (how to punish Patton) is exclusively yours. Consider only Overlord and your heavy burden of responsibility for its success. Everything else is of minor importance (Ambrose 1983, 297-298).

When a clash occurred between a field commander and headquarters staff over whether some centralized procedure should be applied, the field commander's position based on his field objective usually carried the day. Marshall insisted that headquarters staff efforts be focused on providing service—both to the field and to himself as chief of staff. Staff discretion could not be allowed to stand in the way of meeting legitimate needs of field commands. Procedures were at times sacrificed in order to support legitimate aims of field commanders. General Devers, commander of US Army Forces in Europe, came to plead for an administrative officer he badly needed. On meeting resistance from the personnel division (G-1) of the General Staff, he went directly to Marshall, explained what he needed and why, and got it. He attributed Marshall's success as "a great and successful administrator as well as a general" to:

> . . . the fact that he operated that way. He had a staff, yes. He listened to them, but he cut across their lines when it was necessary to get something done (Devers 1958, 15).

Marshall was firm but flexible; if given a good reason, he would shift and act in a supportive way, and quickly (Devers 1958, 24).

Structuring the Staff Decision Process

When Major Charles Bolte of the Army War College faculty took over the WPD of the General Staff in 1938, he approached General Marshall, his boss and the man he was replacing as WPD chief. Charged with supervising the creation of an operations section (G-3) of an army headquarters staff, and knowing that Marshall had headed such a function in WW I, he asked the general what he thought the officer structure of a G-3 staff should be. Marshall answered immediately: make the head of the section a major so that he can speak with the authority of rank, give him no advice from above lest it conflict with the man's judgment, and give him a staff of young, smart officers to do his bidding. Then, trust him to make a decision (Bolte 1958, 6-7).

During WW II there was a constant concern with wasting valuable time and energy. Assembling the information that was needed to make a sound decision within the chief of staff's office had to be done promptly and reasonably completely (to insist that information be *absolutely* complete would greatly compromise speed, essential in wartime). Decisions had to be made by those in the best position to make them, in a timely fashion without excessive argument or protracted discussion, and with the implementation planned in advance so that the decision could be immediately carried out. Asking for an implementation plan to accompany the recommendations required staff to think in advance about the solution to the problem.

At Marshall's direction the SGS was to control the decision process and see that it operated with precise regularity. All staff studies and recommendations, whether requested from above or originating with the staff, had to come through this office, whose job it was to ensure that the record was factually complete when it came to the chief of staff. The deputy chief of staff might refer routine decisions for implementation by other offices, but prioritized the remainder and gave them to Marshall in summarized form for a decision, typically in one page with conflicting opinions and arguments laid out.[1]

Marshall might send an item back so that additional material might be added; he might ask the staff officer who generated the report to recommend a decision, which he would then follow. In the rare case of a disagreement on an important matter Marshall would call a meeting, ask for the reasoning of each participant, and then make the decision himself (Pasco 1997, 2-3, 14-15, 18).

With the SGS, he was a stickler for following a detailed, thorough procedure. Papers brought to him for decision had to be in proper sequence, precisely tabbed, and the reasoning reduced to the fewest words possible while retaining clarity. The summary was accompanied by a recommendation and a plan of implementation and, anticipating his assent, accompanied by all the orders, memoranda, and telegrams needed to instantly begin to implement the decision, requiring only his signature (Hansell 1959, 3). Any written material had to be in a form which he or any other senior official could easily read and understand, devoid of legalese, overly subtle analysis, or stilted language. Recalling his experiences in WW I, Marshall wanted orders, directives, and accompanying factual matter in such a form as to allow them to be read easily and acted upon, even under the most difficult conditions.

In summary, while the *substance* of the decision was delegated broadly to staff officers, the decision *process* was tightly prescribed—it had to be done Marshall's way (Bolte 1958, 32-33). The procedure especially stressed the efficient and clear use of language. His extensive editing and kicking back of reports reached almost legendary status; he seemed never to read but with pencil in hand. To write something for him to read which did not evoke a torrent of editing from the chief was considered a coup (Bolte 1958, 33). Perfection was demanded and carelessness was not tolerated. Time was almost always of the essence. If a recommendation was of sufficient merit to be approved, it deserved to be put into effect as quickly as possible.

Given the severe regimen imposed, it was of the utmost importance to have a strong man at the chief's side to force matters to the decision stage and then to implementation.[2] The position required reviewing all relevant facts and arguments related to the decision, setting out the foreseeable implementation steps, and immediately seeing that the matter was referred to a staff office having the proper scope and authority and exercise to implement it.

Although infrequent, internal staff meetings were run in a prescribed way. Marshall would announce the topic (typically those present had advance notice) and go down the line according to seniority, soliciting each person's input. Questions were put, usually by Marshall, in an effort to open up new angles of thought and get clarification of views and issues. When he finished listening to everybody he ended the meeting without tipping anyone off to how he might be leaning on the decision, and then made the decision privately and promptly. Afterwards he would be perfectly comfortable in not revisiting it (Clark 1959, 21).

Marshall was satisfied enough with the decision-making system nurtured with his help at the War Department that he later transplanted it to the Departments of

State and Defense. There, under-secretaries of State and Defense functioned much as did his deputy chiefs of staff and the executive officers function at the SGS. Similar care was taken to ensure that staff work was complete prior to decision by Secretary Marshall—including complete factual review and analysis, policy recommendations, and measures for carrying out policy in the event of adoption (Rusk 1990, 133). High standards continued to be set and enforced for completeness, accuracy, and analysis (Isaacson and Thomas 1986, 404-405). Similar to Taylor's experience, Marshall told Dean Rusk, the head of the State Department's UN liaison: "Never bring me a question unless you include your proposed answer. Because without an answer, you haven't thought enough about the question" (Rusk 1990, 133).

Although the nation had moved to peacetime, the time taken to process a decision continued to be of the greatest importance. George Kennan, in his initial meeting with Marshall after having been appointed to head the policy planning office (PPO), was told by Marshall to get together a European economic development and recovery strategy within one week:

> I want you to get moving on this immediately, I want you to get the people together, and to look at this whole question of Europe and to tell me, give me an opinion as to what you think I ought to do (Kennan 1959, 6).[3]

When Kennan reported back, Marshall called a meeting among the major participants working on the initiative to consider the planning staff's recommendations. They set forth a general scheme for dealing with European recovery and made a specific recommendation relating to the problem of German coal production. These actions became the basis for the European Recovery Program (ERP). Kennan recalled being much impressed with the way Marshall conducted the meeting:

> He went around the table in his very courteous and orderly way and asked each person in turn his opinion of this memorandum and listened patiently and attentively but without comment to what each person said . . . , he nodded and didn't comment, he went all around the table. . . . When this meeting was over General Marshall thanked everyone and made no comment (Kennan 1959, 8-9).

Marshall's decision followed shortly thereafter. It included recommendations from several of those at the meeting. Kennan sized up Marshall's ability to understand the role of planners in the decision process: "he was the only man who ever understood this orderly and deliberate procedure and use of the staff" (Kennan 1959, 10-11).[4] Following the decision Kennan and the PPO continued to work on ERP problems that the planners collectively believed most required clarification without being asked to do so by Marshall. He simply assumed that the task was important to the nation and that Marshall wanted him to do it.

Delegating and Trusting—Effects Upon Staff

The effects of this stringent and exacting work environment upon staff are worth examining. The major effect was the growth of professional pride and an emotional attachment to the leader (Hansell 1959, 3; Kennan 1959). Also, it increased strain due to fear of falling short of the leader's expectations. There were clear rewards: for those in the Army who performed well it meant rotation to a field command position or higher staff positions and promotion eagerly sought by almost all military officers.

Most noteworthy is the fact that the trust and confidence and high expectations engendered by the broad delegation of both responsibility and authority bred a passion to do the job well, not so much to win their leader's praise (after all, there was little of this) as to achieve the organizational objective he was teaching them to serve. Kennan demonstrated he had learned this important leadership lesson. In giving the policy planning staff's judgments to the Harriman committee (an ERP implementation group), he recalled the staff's working motivation:

> . . . we endeavored to be self-effacing, we felt that was what General Marshall wanted of us, that our job was not to get credit for things but to see that things got done (Kennan 1959, 14).

Kennan also recalled a Marshall request of the PPO to make a recommendation on the question of whether Yugoslavian gold confiscated during WW II should be returned to Yugoslavia. He knew Marshall was not in favor of doing so, but he, Kennan, was getting conflicting opinions from different offices of the department. The PPO finally recommended returning the gold. Although Marshall did not like this course of action, he agreed (Kennan 1959, 18-19), further demonstrating his willingness to back up his trust with action supporting the judgment of the person or persons delegated the task.

Living With Decisions

Once having made a decision, Marshall owned and accepted responsibility for it, rarely if ever agonized over it, and turned his attention elsewhere. He understood that any decision, however successful it may turn out, inevitably is exposed to ridicule and second-guessing, a lesson he had learned through observing General Pershing in WW I. In a rare and early revery on decision-making, Marshall wrote about Pershing's thoughts as the hour of the most decisive battle of WW I approached:

> He had created a distinctive American combat army, despite almost overwhelming difficulties, and in opposition to the pressing desires of all the great Allied leaders and most of their statesmen. . . . [H]is reputation was decidedly in jeopardy. Any degree of failure or difficulty, even if approximately normal to the average successful engagement, was bound to be seized upon by all those who wished themselves to employ his fresh divisions of magnificent young men. . . . There

would come the chorus of 'I told you so's' from all those who in the previous three years of the war had not done it in just that way (Marshall 1976, 143).

"Don't worry about what you can't fix" seems to sum up the lesson. When Kennan and Bohlen, observing the Soviets' humiliation in the affair of the Berlin airlift and the turn toward militaristic US policy in Europe, showed Marshall a conciliatory note they had drafted to be sent to Molotov holding open the possibility of future negotiation, Marshall approved sending it. When the note was misconstrued by the press and interpreted by Molotov as meaning the US was proposing a two-party conference with the Soviets, the Europeans were upset and the press attacked Marshall. Kennan felt terrible about his role in stirring up the fuss. He apologized to Marshall and expressed shock that the press could have misunderstood him. Marshall told him, "Kennan, . . . that recommendation you made me was duly considered by the President and the Cabinet and it was our decision to go ahead with it. The only trouble with you is that you don't have the foresight and the perspicacity of a columnist, now get out of here" (Kennan 1959, 30-31). Kennan's reaction was gratitude and awe that Marshall could so calmly and with such good nature take the full burden of the decision on himself.

By way of comparison, Kennan complained that Acheson, Marshall's successor at State, would not defend his people against allegations from Senate ultraconservatives that they were communist sympathizers. The record was clear that their decisions were consistent with department policy and procedure. He argued that the failure to back up agency professionals working in good faith was both a serious leadership flaw and a lapse of ethics. He insisted that General Marshall, in similar circumstances, would not have abandoned public servants working under his aegis (Kennan 1959, 12-14). Lovett, without this particular case in mind, agreed:

He had this extraordinary ability to give you his complete confidence once he tested you and if he gave you his complete confidence he never let you down, never (1973, 20).

Planning and Change

Planning and change are naturally related. The essence of planning is thinking intelligently about the implications of change. The certainty that change will occur is the primary reason to plan. To be done well, planning must be built into the organizational structure and particularly the decision process, and at the same time be protected from the operational side of organizational activity. To be an integral part of decision-making, the organization's leadership must value the planning function. Proper planning necessitates regular examination of the changing environment and therefore should be a continuing rather than an episodic function.

Marshall's understanding of the need for regular planning in organizations began early in his career. His role prior to WW I in organizing National Guard simulated war maneuvers had led him into planning future scenarios. Writing the actual battle plans during WW I was essentially a form of planning in the short term. After WW I he turned to planning for a peacetime army over the long term, this in the context of a congressional debate over permanent levels of manpower and funding. His time at Fort Benning was dominated by how to project and then react to conditions likely to exist in a future war through the training of infantry officers.

The WPD and Pre-War Planning

The WPD was established in 1921 as the strategic planning unit for warfare, within the General Staff of the War Department. It was charged with formulating strategic plans for military operations, including inter-service strategic plans. The scope of this duty gave it primacy over the other divisions of the General Staff and encompassed the work of those divisions, although its recommendations required concurrence of the others (Cline 1951, 29-30, 40). Because the Army had been stymied since WW I by official neutrality, war planning (harnessed as it was to international and inter-service deliberations) had become the most comprehensive and useful kind of Army staff work (Cline 1951, 50). WPD thus attracted the most qualified and disciplined thinkers in the officer corps, Marshall included.

The very close relationship existing between the chief of staff and WPD virtually assured that the latter would act as an alter ego for the former. There was hardly an important matter handled by the chief of staff that was not referred to WPD for study or placed on the chief of staff's agenda by the head of WPD (Watson 1950, 74-75).

Although Marshall led the WPD for only a few months, his continuance within the COS insured an integral relationship with it. Global information led to new alternative planning scenarios focusing on both Germany and Japan. When Marshall became acting chief of staff on July 1, 1939 he strengthened the capability of WPD by expanding its budget, recruiting the best officers he could find, and making the division more sensitive to the potential role of air power, in which he had recently been schooled. Also, he strengthened WPD's joint planning efforts with the Navy through developing a joint staff under the Joint Army and Navy Board and the Standing Liaison Committee, which included the Departments of State, War, and Navy (Cline 1951, 40-47).

Marshall and Gerow, who had been brought in as the new WPD chief, secured for the WPD the best military minds they could find (Cline 1951, 54).[5] Using their own extensive knowledge of army officer personnel, they personally chose or had referred to them people with an instinct for organization, collaboration, and thinking ahead—people like Colonel Joseph McNarney, Colonel Dwight Eisenhower, and Major Albert Wedemeyer. Eisenhower became especially active and his style and judgment were greatly valued by both Gerow and Marshall.

Under Marshall the WPD, in conjunction with navy planners, produced its most important product in 1939-1941. Five "Rainbow" plans were developed for consideration by war planners, including the President, in the Fall of 1939. All assumed the probability of war against more than one nation and in more than one theater of operation: Rainbow 1 stipulated the waging of a defensive war limited to protecting the Americas; Rainbow 2 added the element of maintaining the sovereignty of democratic powers in the Pacific; Rainbow 3 added the element of securing control of the western Pacific; Rainbow 4 focused on protecting the western hemisphere and permitted sending US task forces to South America and to the eastern Atlantic; and Rainbow 5 sought to protect the western hemisphere, to include Africa and Europe, in order to bring about the defeat of Germany and Italy in cooperation with the UK and France.

Rainbow 5 was adopted by the planners, who then determined the specific activities needed to implement the plan and continued to study and modify it as conditions changed. This was the plan in place when the Japanese struck in December, 1941. The most important point, and the one that demonstrates the importance Marshall placed on the planning function, is that this plan became the basic strategy adopted in WW II.

In 1941, under Gerow's leadership, WPD led the way in responding to President Roosevelt's call to undertake studies leading to the formulation of an integrated national industrial plan. Gerow's view was that decisions on industrial production goals should follow directly from military planning. First, there should be decision on a strategic concept of how to defeat potential enemies. Second, a decision on the specific roles of the ground, naval, and air forces was needed. The US should not simply outproduce its enemies. Gerow's process was adopted by Marshall and Stimson and put the WPD in the lead position in determining industrial production.

The strategic concept adopted by the Army in Rainbow 5 was related to the "Victory Program" of September, 1941, which became the starting point for all wartime calculations of munitions production (Cline 1951, 60-61). Marshall gave WPD the discretion and support necessary for it to play the lead role in industrial production planning. When the national mood turned to intervening in Europe in the spring of 1940, planning could be stepped up with relatively more (but still far from complete) assurance that the argument for preparedness and its attendant costs would eventually be accepted.

Despite the Neutrality Act, Marshall established lines of communication with the British Joint Staff Mission, a group set up by the British in Washington. This arrangement helped to bring about the meeting between political and military leaders off Newfoundland in August 1941 (the famous Argentia meeting), that led to the principles enunciated in the Atlantic Charter (Cline 1951, 47-49). He also resolved to give planning broader scope and central attention in the reorganization of the War Department that had begun to form in his mind and within the COS in 1941.

Both Marshall and Roosevelt had a splendid capacity for accepting the need for change and the capacity to convince others of this need. With the appointment of the principled Stimson as war secretary in mid-1940, a leadership team devoted to military preparedness was fully in place. As events increasingly sucked America into the war's vortex, Roosevelt took the lead in moving the country toward a war footing. As he did so "the views of the Army more and more corresponded with, *and in turn influenced*, national policy" (Cline 1951, 44).

There was less evidence of planning in the international realm during this period. Planning among the allies was largely hypothetical, poorly supported in the budget, and greatly handicapped by lack of any type of foreign policy consensus in American government as a whole. Also, it was unclear how much authority WPD had in taking steps beyond the planning stage—that is, to act on its own to begin to execute a policy that had been adopted with COS concurrence. Marshall yearned for an expanded WPD, an office that could take executive action beyond the planning and approval stage.

Taking a balanced approach to planning and growth of the Army is the key to understanding the nature of Marshall's approach in the pre-war era. An excellent example of this posture is the discussion that took place in May, 1940 when he appeared before the Senate Appropriations committee to urge support for new weaponry, materiel, and airplane construction to go along with the Army's planned increase in personnel. There was concern at this time in Congress over Marshall's unwillingness to put a high priority on local anti-aircraft batteries to protect American cities, a concern heightened by the bombing of London and the example set by the British in making huge outlays for anti-aircraft. After conceding that in the event of an attack on America there would follow a flood of demands from US cities for anti-aircraft installations, this colloquy before the Senate Appropriations Committee followed:

> Senator Lodge: I should like to do something to quiet the alarm about our ... vulnerability to aircraft attack ... is [it] not much better, if we are threatened by an attack from the air, to go directly and try to root out the land base from which the attack comes and be equipped to do that, rather than to sit back and wait for them to be on top of us and then shoot at them?
>
> General Marshall: You have given the answer.
>
> Senator Lodge: I think that ought to be made clear. People will say that this bill carries only one hundred and thirty-eight ninety millimeter guns, while they have five thousand around London, and the War Department will be accused of being negligent.
>
> General Marshall: In the first place, facilities for the manufacture of antiaircraft equipment are ... limited. ... What is necessary for the defense of London is not necessary for the defense of New York, Boston, or Washington. Those cities could be raided ... but ... continuous attack ... would not be practicable unless we permitted the establishment of air bases in close proximity to the United States. ...
>
> Senator Adams: What we need is anti-air-base forces rather than antiaircraft forces.
>
> General Marshall: You might put it that way, sir.
>
> Senator Chavez: Do they not go together, General?
>
> General Marshall: The whole thing is interwoven. ... I have referred to the matter of the practicability of placing larger orders at the moment ... [and] to the necessity of having a trained, seasoned enlisted personnel. ... All these matters have to be given proper weight to get a well integrated and balanced whole. ...

Frankly, I should be embarrassed at the moment by more money for materiel alone. . . . It is much wiser to advance step by step, provided these steps are balanced and are not influenced by enthusiasm rather than by reason (Watson 1950, 150-151).

Wartime Planning

Wartime military planning is made all the more difficult because of the speed at which conditions change and new factors intervene. Not the least of these intrusions are caused by the actions of the enemy whose motivation is often specifically intended to disrupt planning. Also, centralized headquarters planning differs markedly from field planning. Centralized planning is occupied by such matters as alliances, funding, training needs, shipping capacity for moving troops and equipment, and securing sea and air ports, docking and storage facilities. Field planning is dominated by such things as enemy movements, casualty rates, damage to facilities and ammunition stores, re-supply and maintenance needs, mobility needs, and tactical coordination of air, ground and sea forces. Working with both headquarters and field levels in WW I, Marshall appreciated the needs and frustrations of both sets of planners (Marshall 1976).

In essence, the creation of the CCOS, the JCS, and their combined planning staffs became the core of wartime planning. Indeed, planning became the primary activity of the defense chiefs of the allies and their general staffs.

End-of-War and Post-War Planning

The need for other types of planning increased as the fighting waned: specifically, planning for demobilization and for occupation and civil governance in conquered areas. Marshall addressed the downside of unplanned demobilization in an interview with Pogue:

> This denuding of the army always occurs. I have suffered from it myself. I walked into it in the First World War with the First Division when they had nothing. I walked into it in the Second World War when I came as chief of staff. And I walked into the same effect exactly when I came into the Korean affair. I'm an expert on what a dire situation it is. It seems to be the democratic way of doing it. They will spend billions as a result of the war and they won't spend a million or two to prevent the war. That's just about what it amounts to (Bland 1991, 253).

It is astonishing (especially from the perspective of the Twenty-First Century)[6] that as early as November, 1942 secret demobilization studies had begun in the War Department at Marshall's behest (Bland and Stevens 1996, 23-24). An advisory board was formed to look ahead to demobilization and other post-war problems that could be anticipated through intelligent forethought. Marshall was motivated by his fear that the Army could disintegrate after the war in much the way it did after WW I. Expecting that there would be political demands for rapid demobilization, he wanted to get out in front of Congress and the public and take the lead in planning the form, pace, and funding of the demobilization process so as to leave in place an effective force for occupation, civil governance, and response to possible German resurgence or Soviet aggression.

To the advisory group were appointed older, broadly educated men no longer fit for field commands, including Marshall's friend and historian John McAuley Palmer, General Stanley Embick, and General Wedemeyer who had served as chief planner in COS. These men were charged with the task of systematically looking ahead to define and plan for post-war problems. 'Building down' intelligently was the guiding concept.

In the aftermath of the war Marshall's thought processes adjusted quickly to global change. Europe lay in ruins, its people hungry and its economic engines decimated. Soviet leaders saw in this situation the promise of the extension of communism and Soviet influence to the West. In a retirement ceremony in November, 1945, after Japan's surrender, he spoke of the need "to avoid another world catastrophe. . . . Along with the great problem of maintaining the peace we must solve the problem of the pittance of food, of clothing and coal and homes" (Pogue 1987, 2-3).

One of his first moves as secretary of state was to create the PPO and install Kennan to head it. Kennan was informed that Marshall demanded "adequate organization for review and planning of policy . . . with the view to coordinating it with the overall policy and with a view to seeing that any proposals coming up to the Secretary really represent the considered opinion of all interested sections of the department" (Kennan 1959, 2). This type of planning, closely coordinated with the regular decision process, was closely identified with the role of planning that Marshall had developed as Army chief of staff. It was also a first-time innovation in a civilian government department.

Marshall had been involved in planning processes so deeply and for so long that he had formed a clear philosophy of how they should be structured and carried out:

> You can't plan and operate at the same [time]. They are two states of mind. . . . One or the other is going to suffer from it. Well, as the operation is the forcing procedure—it's on your back every day—you naturally do that, and the result is the other [i.e., planning] suffers. . . . It wasn't understood at all by the other [State Department] people. And then my problem was to prevent them from overloading [PPO] with a lot of things which were excrescences, and to get rid of them they wanted to refer it to that section. Well, I wanted [PPO] to handle the most important things we had. . . . Finally, we got the thing going. But you can't imagine what it was when you had no definite planning agency of any kind. You just had a hit or miss affair going on around there (Bland 1991, 562-563).

A Focus on Goals

Marshall's ability to stay focused on goals was perhaps the defining characteristic of his organizational philosophy. As early as 1907 this trait became obvious to his friends and associates. On horseback on a remote outpost of Fort Leavenworth, far from the main encampment, he would take the lead:

> We never bothered to find the shortest way—all we did was to watch George Marshall and he would go off as straight as a bee to a bee feed and we would follow him. Except once we were stopped beyond one of those western streams that run way down in the ground. . . . The banks perhaps were fifteen feet high and there were no bridges there except a railroad bridge. . . . It had a couple of simple planks laid across it for people to walk across on foot. And when we got there Marshall rode his horse across that bridge. Nobody followed him but he wanted to get home to Lily and . . . to work. That's always been a peculiarity of his—as soon as formation was over he went off like a bat out of hell. He never fooled around, and he knew exactly the way home as he did on all his problems (Herron 1958, 2).

In concert with Naval Chief of Operations Harold Stark, Marshall adopted the Europe-first strategy of Rainbow 5 to guide military decision-making. In early 1941 joint Army and Navy planners modified Rainbow 5 to include tactics appropriate to the small American force then in being—primarily actions in support of the British fleet in the Atlantic, knocking Italy out of the war, a major air offensive and minor amphibious operations against German-held territory, and encouraging resistance groups throughout Europe. A defensive, holding action was adopted for the Pacific (Pogue 1966, 127).[7]

Marshall would doggedly pursue the Rainbow 5 strategy throughout the war and pushed for a cross-channel assault in 1943 and attacking Germany frontally through France. He advanced the plan in April 1942 in a proposal that came to be known as the Marshall Memorandum. It called for an early assault across the English channel from a base of American forces to be built up in Great Britain (Pogue 1966, 34-36).

The British resisted and advanced alternatives favoring action in Asia and the Mediterranean. Despite the wavering of some American war planners, including Eisenhower, Marshall remained convinced of the need for pursuing the original, central plan. He urged it on Roosevelt, who approved it. Then, after persistent advocacy and some British military backsliding, he finally brought Churchill and the British imperial staff along with him (Cline 1951). Thus the guiding concept which ultimately ripened into Operation Overlord and the D-Day invasion of Normandy and the triumphant march through western Europe into Germany was largely the result of Marshall's single-minded focus on the major plan.

The correlate to being focused on ends is being impatient with unrelated means. Here the record is clear that Marshall never hesitated to undermine or ignore obtuse rules and procedures. For example, in November, 1940 he searched for and found ways to get rifles and ammunition to the Belgians, although doing so violated the spirit of the Neutrality Act.[8]

Consistent with his fixation on goal, he could not abide imposing technical requirements on field commanders that might interfere with their mission, and warned his general staff officers against raising technical objections in formal Army regulations. To do so was virtually a ground for relieving the officer insisting upon the rule and could invoke a display of anger that would frighten staff members out of their senses (Bull 1959, 33A-33B). For example, he asked his chief of Support Services, General Somervell, to check up on a camp commander who relied on a regulation forbidding the use of paint on target frames (which would have made them easier to see). "I am quite certain," Marshall fumed, "this was not the intent of the regulation, for training of troops is the purpose of the camp" (Bland and Stevens 1996, 697-698). Where purpose and rule clashed, the rule must go.

A famous example concerns the birth of the jeep. Secretary of the General Staff Beetle Smith interrupted a high-level meeting in the chief of staff's office to tell General Marshall that a man was in his outer office who had invented a small, highly mobile vehicle that Smith judged to be excellent for many field uses. The Quartermaster Corps and Field Artillery had blocked consideration. "Well, what do you think of it?" asked Marshall. "I think it's good," replied Smith. "Well," said Marshall, "do it. Do you think you can find the money?" Smith thought he could, and did, and the jeep was born (Bland 1991, 267).

Bypassing rules and established procedure was not to be undertaken frivolously, however. Marshall understood the need for rigorous testing of weapons and equipment. Under pressure from Congress the British were sent machine gun ammunition for use in high altitude aircraft which the Ordnance Department had not thoroughly tested as required by regulation. The weapons froze in combat and the Army had to sacrifice its standard ammunition allotments for American planes in order to meet British needs (Bland 1991, 265, 268). He believed that rules having as their purpose safety, if not overdone, should not be ignored. He struggled to find the balance between rules for the sake of rules and rules with legitimate purpose. He articulated this difficulty in a 1948 hearing on the ERP:

> I have struggled with red tape most of my life. I have been generally on the receiving end, but in later years sometimes on the cutting end. . . . It takes more knowledge and skill to cut red tape than any other particular endeavor I know in government, because you get into difficulty more quickly without realizing what the complications are going to be (US Congress 1948, 85).

Loyalty, Teamwork, and Coordination

Although his experience had taught him that decisions should come from a single, centralized command post having ultimate final authority (i.e., the unity of command principle), Marshall believed that to be effective, the process of making and implementing decisions must be based on a foundation of teamwork and coordination. Concentrating the whole process in a single person or office undermines the organization's effectiveness.

Similarly, although compliance with the central authority's orders is necessary, it should not be automatic and blind. Obedience must be earned through demonstrating to other levels that decisions are sound with respect both to their consistency with goals and the welfare of constituent units. To this end, consultation before the decision and implementation is essential and consensus is to be achieved through coordinating plans vertically between levels of command and horizontally across constituent units. Dialogue has to proceed at lower levels in order to set the stage for decisions at higher levels. Ultimately, decisions are made at the top with as full a deck of facts and opinions as can be gotten from each of the units as well as from qualified individuals in staff offices. Once made, the decision maker has to take responsibility for both the decision and its consequences.

Marshall valued teamwork for its positive effects on both decision-making and implementation. The team must be woven vertically as well as horizontally; that is, individuals at all levels and in different command structures must be known to each other and sympathetic to the needs at other levels of the same organization and to other, distinct organizations. He reserved the disparaging term "localitis" for the problem of commanders who were blind to needs outside their immediate organizational units (Pogue 1987, 517) and he had little patience for those who could not work with others.[9] General Fox Conner advised Eisenhower to follow Marshall's example in approaching his new job as European theater commander: "in the new war we will have to fight beside allies, and George Marshall knows more about the technique of arranging allied commands than any man I know. He is nothing short of a genius" (Eisenhower 1967, 195).

Although Marshall fought tenaciously against adoption of some policies and specific actions within the War Department and the White House, he vigorously supported every decision after it was made despite any personal reservations about its wisdom. His loyalty was absolute. He understood, or rationalized, that the perspective of the leader, be he command officer, president, or congressman, is dictated by one's unique responsibilities and role. The leader sees things in the context of a bigger picture and must be obeyed. Thus he disagreed when Portal, the British air chief, sympathized with the commander of a fighter unit who was reluctant to send his planes as escorts on a deep bombing mission:

> It had always proved the case that a combat commander was loath to release any forces in his possession lest they should not be returned to him. As far as the air forces were concerned, there was required a commander for the strategic air both in Italy and in Europe who, *by reason of his position*, was not affected by this very human weakness (Parton 1986, 334; *emphasis added*).

Nonetheless, when he was in the lead position, he listened carefully to the views of his unit commanders. He welcomed dissent—indeed he demanded it among his people *before* decisions were made. He saw active disagreement on facts and arguments over cause and effect as essential to making good decisions. How, he would ask, could he know he was making the right decision unless the problems with it were brought to light before its making (Bradley 1951, 20; Acheson 1969, 3-8)?

Stimulating active disagreement should not be confined within the boundaries of the organization and officers should be encouraged to raise differences with their superiors. Marshall entered freely into consultative relationships with officials in

The Marshall
children: Marie,
Stuart, and
George/
Uniontown, PA
(circa 1885)
Courtesy of the
George C. Marshall
Research Library,
Lexington, Virginia

1st Lieutenant Marshall
in dress blues prior to
graduation from
Command and General
Staff School, Fort
Leavenworth (May or
June 1908)
Courtesy of the George C.
Marshall Research Library,
Lexington, Virginia

Marshall and Churchill reviewing the troops in Hyde Park, London (July 1919)
Courtesy of the George C. Marshall Research Library, Lexington, Virginia

Treasure hunt breakfast, Fort Benning (1927–1932); Norwegian officer top row, left; sister, Marie Marshall, is standing 3rd from left
Courtesy of the George C. Marshall Research Library, Lexington, Virginia

Supervising war games, Illinois National Guard (1936)
Courtesy of the George C. Marshall Research Library, Lexington, Virginia

The Marshalls on fishing vacation, Oregon countryside (1936–1938)
Courtesy of the George C. Marshall Research Library, Lexington, Virginia

Visit to Brazil as Deputy Chief of Staff (May 1939); Brig. Gen. Marshall is saluting on right front side of automobile.
Courtesy of the George C. Marshall Research Library, Lexington, Virginia

Chief of Staff Marshall at press conference explaining difficulty of conscripting war-related industry (August 7, 1940)
Courtesy of the George C. Marshall Research Library, Lexington, Virginia

*Conferring with Secretary
of War, Henry L. Stimson
(January 16, 1942)*
Courtesy of the George C.
  Marshall Research Library,
  Lexington, Virginia

*Leaders of War Department
reorganization (March
1942); from left to right: Lt.
Gen. Joseph T. McNarney
(standing), Lt. Gen. Henry
("Hap") Arnold, Gen.
Marshall, Lt. Gen. Leslie
McNair, Lt. Gen. Brehon
Somervill (standing)*
Courtesy of the George C.
  Marshall Research Library,
  Lexington, Virginia

Marshall and Chief of Naval Operations Admiral King testifying before Joint Military Affairs Committee (September 20, 1943)
Courtesy of the George C. Marshall Research Library, Lexington, Virginia

Patton and Marshall on deck of invasion craft watching landing maneuvers, I Armored Corps Headquarters inspection trip, North Africa (1943)
Courtesy of the George C. Marshall Research Library, Lexington, Virginia

With aide Colonel Frank McCarthy (circa 1943)
Courtesy of the George C. Marshall Research Library, Lexington, Virginia

Generals Patton, Marshall, and Bradley meeting in France (October 7, 1944)
Courtesy of the George C. Marshall Research Library, Lexington, Virginia

With Eisenhower and Arnold at Normandy beachhead (June 1944)
Courtesy of the George C. Marshall Research Library, Lexington, Virginia

*Chatting with Speaker
of the House Sam
Rayburn (D-Tex)
(January 19, 1945)*
Courtesy of the George
 C. Marshall Research
 Library, Lexington,
 Virginia

Taking oath before testifying to committee investigating Pearl Harbor attack (December 6, 1945)
Courtesy of the George C. Marshall Research Library, Lexington, Virginia

Marshall and Madame Chiang play Chinese checkers (March 1946)
Courtesy of the George C. Marshall Research Library, Lexington, Virginia

*Settling into spacious office at State Department (May 16, 1947); portrait
of Stimson on back wall*
Courtesy of the George C. Marshall Research Library, Lexington, Virginia

With chauffeur, Sgt. James W. Powder (undated)
Courtesy of the George C. Marshall Research Library, Lexington, Virginia

With Lewis Douglas, Ambassador to the UK, testifying in favor of ERP before the Senate Foreign Relations Committee (January 1948)
Courtesy of the George C. Marshall Research Library, Lexington, Virginia

With President Truman and Basil O'Connor, outgoing chairman of the American Red Cross (October 4, 1949)
Courtesy of the George C. Marshall Research Library, Lexington, Virginia

With staff members of telecommunications office of American Red Cross, Chicago (October 25, 1949)
Courtesy of the George C. Marshall Research Library, Lexington, Virginia

The Marshalls at home at Dodona Manor, Leesburg, VA
Courtesy of the George C. Marshall Research Library, Lexington, Virginia
Source: King-Features Syndicate, NY Journal-American, September 13, 1950

At the Pentagon with Anna Rosenberg, named by Marshall to serve as Assistant Secretary of Defense (October 19, 1950)
Courtesy of the George C. Marshall Research Library, Lexington, Virginia; Official Department of Defense photo

With Prime Minister David Ben-Gurion (L) and Ambassador to U.S. Abba Eban of Israel (May 4, 1951)
Courtesy of the George C. Marshall Research Library, Lexington, Virginia

MAULDIN

Photograph of original Bill Mauldin syndicated cartoon (October, 1959) on the death of General Marshall

Used by permission, State Historical Society of Missouri, Columbia

other agencies and with officials at higher levels of the same agency. His working relationship with Secretary of War Stimson in World War II was excellent because, as Harvey Bundy, an assistant secretary of war noted, neither man stood on the formality of law in working at common problems:

> ... where is the line between the civilian activities of the Secretary of War and the military activities of the Chief of Staff, ... you can't find it in the books, you know, practically can't find it in the statutes, what the rights of each of them are. If it hadn't been that the two men were intimately talking with each other, and neither of them had any ego so far as trying to build himself up. .... I don't think it would work. It didn't work in the Navy (Bundy 1959, 13).

It may have been a difficult line to walk, because Marshall followed strict protocol in respecting the status of superiors. When, as secretary of defense, he attended cabinet meetings with Secretary of State Acheson (who had previously served under him at the State Department), Marshall always waited for Acheson, the historically senior cabinet officer, to speak first. This unnerved Acheson, who revered the general and regarded him in the real, non-legal sense, as his superior. He would not disagree with Acheson on important issues in front of the president. Their discourse was nonetheless open and candid, because he would wait for a private moment to present to Acheson his contrary view of the matter. There was no hesitancy to speak with complete frankness in these private meetings and to seek a meeting of the minds (Acheson 1957, 4). In this procedure may be seen a blending of courtesy, respect, and an observance of loyalty based on position (for which Acheson was grateful), as well as an active dialogue permitting disagreement and eventually coordinated decision-making.

Marshall recognized very early on the importance of British and American military personnel to function as a team in meeting the German threat. He showed a willingness to do everything in his power to arm the British, even at the cost of delaying America's own military preparations. British Admiral of the Fleet Lord Cunningham observed gratefully after the war:

> It was his most generous action, I thought, of sending off the tanks that time, and the five ships (thereby decreasing American stores). That, I should say, was [an] unprecedented act on the part of any big soldier, and he was a big soldier" (Cunningham 1961, 15).

Communication

Plainspoken and impatient with purposeless formality, Marshall placed great store in clear and concise communication. Messages and information were to be stated simply and flow smoothly. The lack of clear organizational communication was one reason explaining Marshall's desire to reorganize the War Department in 1941-1942 and his advocacy of a unified allied command structure and close joint working staff structure at the Arcadia Conference. Fortunately, his influence in clarifying communication began to assert itself before America's entrance into the war (Sherwood 1948, 270).

As a chief operations staff officer in WW I he had written the orders dictating the operational plans for the major American offensives. Part of his time was used in acquiring and assessing intelligence; a great deal in actually writing the order of battle. The balance was consumed in meeting with outside military and political figures along the front. General George Van Horn Moseley described the operations function and Marshall's conduct of it:

> It is the Chief [of operations] who must work out all the details of the operations, putting them in a clear, practical, workable order which can be understood by the commanders of all subordinate units. The order must be comprehensive, yet not involved. It must appear clear when read in a poor light, in the mud and the rain. That was Marshall's job, and he performed it one hundred percent. The troops which maneuvered under his plan always won (Bland and Hadsel 1981, 164-165).

Battlefield communications in WW I were undermined by rigid field command structures and pressures discouraging experimentation with its form. These conditions did not prevent Marshall from innovating to improve their quality. In one unique experiment, he used carrier pigeons to get an accurate and current picture of advanced locations of five different army divisions in the Meuse-Argonne offensive. Five bright, young officers attached to Marshall's Operations unit were directed to travel with the leading assault battalion of each of the five divisions, and to release one pigeon at each of six prescribed times with maps and coordinates of the points at which they were released. The received pigeon-carried messages were then communicated by the ordinary means to the army groups and division headquarters. The result was that all divisions in the field were supplied with an accurate and timely picture of how the advance was proceeding and where the other divisions on their flanks were; all of this long before the ordinary telegraph methodology could supply similar and less accurate information (Marshall 1976, 182-184).

In a second experiment Marshall stationed smart young reserve officers at critical places where things were likely to occur, with instructions as to how to handle communication if various things did occur (Bowditch 1959, 3). He anticipated that intelligent officers would be innovative if circumstances demanded.

Illustrating Marshall's emphasis on effective peacetime communication was his bringing Colonel Wilton B. Persons onto his personal staff in 1940. Persons had acted as Secretary of War Woodring's congressional liaison and was known for loyal service to his superiors. Marshall's instructions to Persons were brief:

> I [Persons] was to keep in mind that he was somewhat closed in by the four walls of his office and that he depended on me to bring directly to him everything of importance that occurred on Capitol Hill which might affect the Army (Pogue 1973, 130).

Persons reacted to this vague directive by bringing Marshall a report each morning to keep him aware of the "temper" of Congress and preparing biographical sheets on key members as well as analysis of their attitudes toward the Army and specific projects (Pogue 1973, 130).

Communicating with the President

The one big gap in the communication network, in Marshall's opinion, lay between the JCS and the White House. Roosevelt was accustomed to hoarding information and not sharing it with those with a need to know it. This tendency, whatever its political explanation might have been, undermined military planning and preparation. Marshall chose Hopkins as his instrument of choice, not unlike a carrier pigeon, to improve communication with the president. Hopkins carried Marshall's words to Roosevelt and was able to repeat them, and to amplify them because of his respect for Marshall and his personal rapport with the president. In Marshall's words:

> He was always the strong advocate, it seemed to me, of almost everything I proposed, and it required quite a bit of explanation from time to time to have the president see that the set-up could not be handled in the ways he sometimes suggested. And there had to be a very firm position taken in these matters. So he [Hopkins] was quite invaluable to me and he was very courageous[10] (Bland 1991, 433).

Further complicating communication was the fact that Roosevelt solicited military advice from many people, some of whom lacked knowledge about the critical factors present in a particular decision situation. Those with primary responsibility for data production and implementation (Marshall, Stimson, and King) were often not present to fill in facts or question the logic of advice the president was getting (Pogue 1966, 131). This remained a problem, although it lessened with the growth of confidence between Marshall, Stimson, and Roosevelt.

To limit misunderstanding and to permit subsequent and accurate reference, Marshall and Stimson recommended that notes be taken by aides at meetings of Army and Navy personnel with the president. To their great frustration the suggestion was spurned by Roosevelt (Pogue 1973, 69-70).

For these reasons Marshall marveled at the quite different way in which the British defense establishment conducted its internal communications. All principals, civilian and military, were kept privy to all opinions and statements of the prime minister, including information received from Roosevelt and the JCS.[11] In contrast, Roosevelt's private and separate military discussions were likely to ignore formal military communication lines and thus risk failure to inform the military chiefs of their content. Marshall was not alone in this opinion.[12]

Marshall found a partial solution to the communication gap with the president through his association with British Field Marshal Dill. The trust relationship was so strong between the two men as to allow them to discuss anything (Ismay 1960,

6; Danchev 1986, 60).[13] According to their arrangement, Marshall kept Dill well informed on American intelligence he received from Army inspections and fact-gathering (Handy 1956, 3). Reciprocating, Dill showed Marshall almost all staff reports and memos he received from the British military chiefs, which not only included copies of Churchill's messages but also included many messages originating with Roosevelt of which Marshall had no prior knowledge (Danchev 1986, 56). In this way the British were given important insight into Marshall's thinking and Marshall obtained knowledge about what Roosevelt was thinking and saying.

Dill's tipping off Marshall to British military inside information and planning did not in the least compromise Britain's self-interest, or Marshall would probably not have permitted Dill to pass it. On the contrary, Dill's confidences inspired reciprocity from the Americans, whose thinking was in turn shared with the British chiefs. If the Americans were privy to British plans they would tend to support them; if not, they were likely (out of suspicion of British motives) to resist allocating resources or to be uncooperative (Danchev 1986, 59).

Churchill probably would have objected had he known that Dill was carrying his, Churchill's, requests of Dill to quietly plumb Marshall's mind on various matters directly to Marshall. Together, Dill and Marshall would read Churchill's messages and compose a reply that Churchill would think was Dill's sole conception of what Marshall thought. This gave Marshall another advantage:

> And very often, when I wouldn't agree with it at all, very decidedly wouldn't agree to it, I would comment very forcibly and very freely to Dill in a way I couldn't possibly comment to the prime minister. Then Dill would report that to Mr. Churchill. That's what I said to Dill, and that way my own feeling got across to Mr. Churchill (Bland 1991, 414).

This complex web of *sub rosa* communication, made necessary by Roosevelt's aversion to openness, was entirely to Marshall's satisfaction. The general said he was "kept *au courant* with what was going on, and I couldn't have got it any other way" (Bland 1991, 413-414). It is small wonder that Marshall went to extraordinary lengths later in the war to protect Dill from being downgraded or transferred by Churchill out of Washington.[14] It was true that Marshall was taking a calculated risk—if the president ever got wind that his confidences were being leaked to Marshall without his permission and by Marshall's design, Marshall could lose Roosevelt's trust and perhaps his position.

Fortunately, the personal relationship between Marshall and Roosevelt continued to improve. It had improved so dramatically by 1943 that Marshall was composing many of Roosevelt's messages. He wrote to Stalin over Roosevelt's signature in April, 1945, taking Stalin to task for impugning US motives when negotiating with the Germans in Italy was being considered. Marshall's demonstration of growing political judgment had gained the president's confidence. They now met privately, as Hopkins had earlier desired. Marshall could not judge the reason for Roosevelt's increased reliance upon him: a desire to lessen the burden of responsibility, the president's failing health, or the growing trust between them (Bland 1991, 417-419)? In retrospect, it seems likely that all three factors played a significant role.

Inter-Service Communication

Another gap, not as easy to bridge, existed between the two military services. Unable to bring Chief of Naval Operations King and the Navy into a full, information-sharing relationship with the Army, Marshall used several devices to at least cope with the problem. He began by asking King and Navy leaders to agree to open JCS meetings to civilian officials at the assistant secretary level of both War and Navy Departments so as to keep their departmental hierarchies fully informed. Assistant Secretary of War John McCloy was pressed successfully by Marshall to attend JCS meetings, but King would not consent to having an equivalent Navy Department official attend. The basic reason for King's reluctance is that he had not been taking Navy Secretary Forrestal into his confidence. Thus Marshall took it upon himself to ask McCloy to brief Forrestal on JCS deliberations.

Surprisingly, the naval military personnel had better communication with Marshall and his people than they had with their own civilian officials. The contrast between internal army and navy communication processes was striking. "There was an iron door between the uniform people in the Navy and Forrestal," as compared to the Army where "the contacts with Marshall seemed to be always very frank. . . . a very free talker, ready to talk to you about anything at any time . . ." (McCloy 1959, 12). An open door existed in a literal sense between Marshall and Stimson's adjoining offices and they used it constantly.

Another channel was Dill, who tipped off the British chiefs that the Army was more sympathetic to certain British positions than was the Navy and asked them to refrain from exploiting these differences by playing one side off against the other. The assurances and information that Dill got back from the British chiefs could then be worked into the internal, JCS decision-making without divulging to the Navy that Marshall was the source (Danchev 1986, 60-62).

Communicating with the Public

The normal demands for military secrecy and diplomacy create natural limitations on communications between the military and the State Department on one hand and the general public and the media on the other. Regardless of this reality, a remarkable openness and candor characterized Marshall's communications with both. Habits of openness and candor had been forged in the building of community relations at Forts Benning, Screven, and Moultrie, Chicago, and at Vancouver Barracks. The tools used were public and civic meetings and speaking events, news releases, and invitations to community members to visit the Army posts, much of it personally arranged by Marshall. Cultivating mutual trust had become a habit.

As pressures on his time and energy grew more intense in the period leading up to US entry into the war, some additional barriers were erected to public access to protect the chief of staff. Staff carefully winnowed incoming correspondence. The media were kept at a distance. In this climate, *Life Magazine* published a very critical article about large-scale military maneuvers in the south replete with photographs of carousing soldiers. Based on the piece, the *New York Times* asked both Stimson and Marshall for permission to send one of its reporters to camps in the area to further check out and develop the story.

Marshall surprised the *Times* by giving its reporter *carte blanche* to go anywhere and talk to anybody, including access to his commanding generals. The *Times* reporter visited Second Army camps under the command of General Van Leer and found much misconduct, mostly among National Guard units. The *Times* informed Marshall what it had in advance of publication. Marshall then visited a Third Army post in Louisiana commanded by General Walter Krueger and there found drunken officers and soldiers fraternizing in hotels and bars with prostitutes (Bolte 1958, 46).

It is remarkable, given today's journalistic practices, that the *Times* did not publish the story on the grounds that exposing troop misconduct would ill-serve the country when war was imminent. Marshall requested and got the unpublished article, had it purged of names, units, and places, and sent it out to military units so that they could reflect upon it and act to remedy the situation. The incident was handled as a learning experience and opportunity for reform. The net result was more recreational facilities and organized entertainment activities at training sites.[15]

Communication Within the Army

Marshall developed and used a variety of innovative methods to promote intra-Army communication at all levels. At the highest level of command, the practice of daily morning briefings was initiated by Marshall, using media-savvy presentations, a world-wide display format, and rapid-fire briefings. It was his intent to make internal Army top command communication efficient, comprehensive, and dramatic. Young men were chosen as presenters based on their acting ability, speaking voices, and general intelligence. Under the tutelage of General Handy and Colonel Truman Smith, props such as a large board map and movable symbols were employed to indicate the positions and movements of naval, air, and ground forces within all theaters of command. The sessions were prepared through the night and reviewed and rehearsed by Handy in the early morning. They were by all accounts attention-riveting models of information transfer (Handy 1959, 30-32). The sessions were routinely attended by top War Department staff, ranking military personnel, and other invited civilian officials. In Marshall's view:

> They became very expert at it and it was really a thrilling presentation. You saw the whole war up to the last minute, done in such a way it was easy, in a sense, to comprehend (Bland 1991, 352-353).

Colonel Smith was effusive in his praise of both Marshall and the process:

That's where he (Marshall) ran the war. . . . Before this assemblage, came the reports of the day. In other words, we of the War Department General Staff presented him with a view of what had happened since the preceding morning. . . . In three minutes I would present the situation of the enemy in Europe, following the Operations man giving the situation with his maps of what our troops had done. At the end of that period, Marshall with this group would make the decisions. For instance, Arnold would say he wanted to transfer a couple of flying groups from Southwest Pacific; or if a diplomatic thing were involved, I have heard him . . . call Roosevelt himself. Also, I have seen him go out in the middle after something had arisen and bring in from the next room Stimson. . . . Then we would go out and in would come the Mediterranean people. Then they would go out, then the Southwest Asia people and the Central Pacific people, then the Burma. The whole thing would take about an hour and three quarters but it was so boiled down by Marshall's skill that an immense amount was accomplished in that one hour and a half. That is where I formed my opinion that he was the greatest staff officer that America, or any nation, has ever had (T. Smith 1959, 12-13).

Another, less dramatic but effective method to promote headquarters interaction was the open door policy adopted by Marshall both as chief of staff and cabinet secretary. Any staff officer with an item felt to be important could approach him at any time. The officer would enter Marshall's office and take a seat before his desk, be recognized and asked to state his business. Since Marshall's demeanor, at least at COS, was often cool and impatient with inefficient presentation, this procedure did not always work well. Still, the opportunity was present for any staff officer to use.

Communication with ordinary soldiers concentrated on explaining the reasons for the war and the general strategy of its waging. Such effort appealed to Marshall because he believed informing them as citizens of a democratic nation gave them purpose as well as improved their morale. This approach complemented an intense effort to commit the officer corps to give the welfare of the troops the highest priority. Information and morale officers were chosen carefully according to whether they were articulate and capable, and not, as it was often claimed, that they were unsuited for any other kind of duty.

An independent press was funded by the Army as a service to non-commissioned officers and rank-and-file soldiers. Persons of these ranks monitored their own expression of views and current needs, with a minimum of censorship from above.

Language

Marshall believed that language used in organizational communication should be brief and concise, employ the plainest words capable of conveying intended meaning, and be appropriate to the audience. He was a compulsive editor in the service of these guidelines, a skill he had acquired at Fort Leavenworth in 1906-1907 where he spent his study time reading, simplifying, and clarifying. Editing, he said, teaches one to set down problems in concise form and cut out verbiage that gets in the way of thinking (Gallagher 1962, 48).

Even when writing to informed insiders, including the president, he followed the practice of presenting his case in non-technical terms and in as brief a form as possible. He developed the habit of presenting to the president his requests on a single piece of paper one-third the normal size, finding that "the technical General Staff document was seldom read beyond the first few paragraphs, and usually provoked [irritation]," especially from a chief executive reading it under pressure (GCMRL: Speech at National War College, 6/20/1947, Box 157, Folder 29).

No report or speech written over Marshall's name was accepted until he had worked it heavily to fit his thoughts and style. He revised his first biennial report to Congress eight to ten times, editing and adding new thoughts as he delved more deeply into his subject (Sexton 1958, 11-12). Nearly every letter that went out to a group on a serious matter, such as one to the wives of commanders captured in the Philippines, contained some individual comment that he inserted that related to his personal association with that officer (Sexton 1958, 20).

The general's writing habits were not admired by everyone. Some, like General Haislip, thought he was wasting valuable time. One officer partially agreed, but also thought his almost instinctive editing was an unconscious act of teaching another to think more clearly—"he always said the right things very, very simply." Marshall himself explained the practice simply as a part of his nature: "once an editor, always an editor," he said (Gallager 1962, 49).

Language had to be common and acceptable, not stuffy. With a training pamphlet intended for intelligence personnel relating to lessons to be learned from fighting in North Africa, he sent along an eight-page paper authored by a private, instructing Chief of Army Ground Forces General McNair: "The fact that it was written by [an enlisted man], that it was noted by his Division commander, by General Eisenhower and by me personally, if stated in the pamphlet, would fasten the attention of the enlisted man to a degree not possible by ordinary instructional methods" (Bland and Stevens 1996, 5).

Dean Rusk gave this example of Marshall's response to a letter of reply that Rusk had prepared for his chief's signature:

'Dear Dr. Brown,' I began, 'I have read with much appreciation your letter of March 18. I feel that—.' Here he stopped me right there. 'Now wait a minute, Rusk. I didn't read his letter. You did. And I didn't appreciate it one damn bit. So let's strike that out. Let's just say, "I received your letter." ' And then he said, 'I feel? I don't have feelings about matters of public policy. If I think it, let's say, "I think it." I don't feel it' (Rusk 1990, 132-133).

Recognizing his limitations and his quickness to anger, he instituted a policy of having the more difficult letters reread by a trusted staff member, usually Handy or McCarthy, in order to catch mistakes, add necessary information, or correct an undisciplined tone (Handy 1959, 34).

Communicating with Congress

Much of Marshall's success in gaining resources and public support for his organization flowed from his ability to communicate with the congress. His frequent testimony and periodic reports inspired confidence and even gratitude among congressmen. Noting its directness, lack of politically couched language, and emphasis on facts, most congressmen said they could rely on what he said and appreciated that it was said simply, understandably, and with honest conviction. It was clear to them that what he asked for he believed was in the nation's best interest.

The key to his success, according to Pasco, was his respect for the institution of Congress, which he viewed as one of his constitutional bosses. He took care to promptly and courteously answer every inquiry sent by a congressional member or legislative staff-person and signed (Sexton 1958, 7). Every legislator was to be respected and served. He prepared his testimony by digesting relevant staff studies in his office before going to the hill and then would leave them behind, choosing to rely upon his memory and forcing himself to focus on the fundamental facts and issues that were the focus of what he had read. He spoke logically, comprehensively, and tersely, with confidence and accuracy. "[H]is character just sold itself. . . . Congress never doubted his integrity, and anything that he said was right out of the book. There was no question about what he said was right. If Marshall said it, it was true" (Pasco 1997, 45-46).

He refused to begin his testimony with a prepared statement (Sexton 1958, 7). He preferred to work "without any notes, because I found that the minute you began to read you lost your audience. It was better to forget something" (Bland 1991, 355). He would arrive about two minutes late ("so there'd be a little suspense") and say "You gentlemen want to talk to me? What do you want to know?" He took questions, and then unloaded the gist of the staff studies on them, from memory. He normally had an aide or two with him who possessed special knowledge, and he not infrequently turned to ask the aide to respond to a question or point, just as Pershing had done with him (Bland and Hadsel 1981, 194).

It was through this process that his close association with Senator Harry Truman was formed, a relationship that laid the basis for the last phases of Marshall's career and helped to define Truman's. From 1941 to 1943, Truman chaired the Senate Special Committee to Investigate the National Defense Program, created out of congressional unhappiness with the Army's construction program, especially its costs and delays. In considering the approach to take with the Truman committee in advance of the hearings, Marshall informed his deputy chief of staff that a defensive posture would not do:

It seems to me that a free and easy and whole-souled manner of cooperation with these committees is more likely to create an impression that everything is all right in the War Department, than is a resentful attitude, and that it must be assumed that members of Congress are just as patriotic as we . . . (Pogue 1966, 108).

As a result of this attitude and approach to the committee, as well as the full cooperation of the COS in following up on matters that the committee wished investigated, Truman came to rely with total confidence on the general's honesty and directness.[16]

Marshall conceived of the biennial report of the Army Chief of Staff to the Secretary of War, with Congress as the true intended audience, as the best method of keeping Congress, and indirectly the public, informed about Army preparedness and, later, the progress of the war effort. The first biennial report was sent to Congress in 1941. It was grave in tone, a call to action in the face of national emergency, and requested a larger army and an extension of the twelve-month draft. It was not received well in a Congress still uncertain of America's role in the war and split on whether to allow the draft to expire (Bland and Stevens 1996, 100-103).

The second report in September of 1943 was more optimistic and was written as "a record of what was done and why it was done . . . to permit a better understanding of the great offensive operations now in progress." Marshall wrote the thirty-six page narrative portion himself, including within it a current assessment of prospects and needs and a review of international conflicts preceding Pearl Harbor including the Battle of Britain and the German invasion of the Soviet Union. He also included a history of the near-dismantling of the Army caused by Congress's razor-thin vote to extend the draft, as well as the War Department's reactions to Pearl Harbor and the loss of the Philippine Islands (Bland and Stevens 1996, 103-105).

In his adopted role of JCS spokesperson Marshall also included in the 1943 report: the story behind the Navy's dramatic successes in mid-1942; the growth of offensive capabilities including the air assault in Europe; the background of strategic decisions underlying the Pacific and North African campaigns; the role of shipping constraints in making strategic choices; dealings with the French resistance forces; the positive performance of the allies; and major US Army command changes. The report concluded that the war's progress had tilted in favor of the allies, that air power had played a dramatic role in the turnabout, and that the need for the Army's growth had been replaced by the need to concentrate on its efficiency (Bland and Stevens 1996, 105-107).

The *New York Times* observed that the 1943 biennial report was viewed by many in Congress as "one of the most comprehensive and remarkable public documents of the war" which gave insights into the future course of the war. Further, it lifted the curtain of military secrecy on past decisions and answered "many questions that a reporter would have been reprimanded for asking at the secretary of war's press conferences" (Bland and Stevens 1996, 106-107). The report was distributed widely by Marshall with the president's approval (Bland and Stevens 1996, 107).

During the conference of foreign ministers in Moscow in the spring of 1947 Secretary of State Marshall, urged on by Bohlen and Kennan and disturbed by the saber-rattling associated with the Truman Doctrine's military aid support to Greece and Turkey, sent word through Bohlen to Clark Clifford, the president's aide, that he wanted delivered to the Congress "a weak message, drop intemperate language . . . simple, businesslike, no 'ringing phrases'—nothing warlike or belligerent. Don't denounce, just state the facts." He warned President Truman that a hotheaded speech might "pull the trigger—start the war" (Isaacson and Thomas 1986, 441).

The most vital communication with the Congress in the postwar era came in the effort to enact the ERP. In his testimony to Congress he departed from his usual practice of grounding his remarks in the factual record to engage in passionate advocacy and hyperbole. He declared that Congress's upcoming action on the ERP would be "the greatest vote in our history," and that "if the United States (Congress) was unable or unwilling effectively to assist in the reconstruction of Western Europe we must accept the consequences of its collapse into the dictatorship of police states. . . . There is no doubt in my mind that the whole world hangs in the balance" (Isaacson and Thomas 1986, 432-433).

His past practices of being circumspect and avoiding grandiose claims made his argument all the more compelling, since he had always been known as a man who spoke comfortably within his zone of knowledge. This tactic speaks to the immense importance that he himself placed on the legislation, as well as his confidence that he could communicate the magnitude of its significance to the Congress (Isaacson and Thomas 1986, 439-440).

Balancing Open Communication and Secrecy

As a personal value, Marshall believed it was better to be open rather than secretive, to be candid about weaknesses as well as strengths, and to stand or fall on verifiable facts. But secrecy was regarded in the law as essential to war planning and operations, and thus it was vital to keep secret material of potential use to the enemy out of the hands of the public.

What should be kept secret was by no means always obvious. He had seen the tendency of random observers to be mistaken in their assessment of military facts and to draw erroneous conclusions from them. Included among the amateurs were news commentators like Walter Lippman who attempted to influence public opinion without full knowledge of military realities. Lippman had argued on the eve of Pearl Harbor that defense appropriations should be directed toward the Navy, British and Soviet military arms and the strategic bombing of Germany, and away from building larger ground forces.

Marshall accepted the fact that less than rational views are commonly voiced in a democratic society. But he could not allow unprofessional judgments to get in the way of pursuing and achieving public policy goals. Because he believed it was vital to protect the security of most information about weaponry and supplies, strategic and tactical decisions, logistics, location and movement of forces, and plans for specific military actions, he insisted on harsh punishment for officers and other personnel who were careless in handling classified material. He viewed the telephone as a particular evil, given what he thought was the typical American's tendency to overuse it and to be naive about eavesdroppers (Taylor 1972, 41-42).

To mitigate damage from breeches in security he took upon himself an educative role that could allow him to steer a path between openness and secrecy. He did this by bringing the media into his confidence and sharing with them the 'big picture' but keeping the details secret, requesting their cooperation in not drawing unwarranted inferences, and to delaying in some cases the release of information.

Negotiation

The ability to negotiate differences in order to contain or reduce conflict or to convert it to cooperation is a vital but underappreciated aspect of management. It is essential when the organization being led is loose-knit, as in an alliance of independent nations, a group of governmental departments, or a department of semi-autonomous bureaus. In some government settings, such as regulatory agencies, negotiation with clients or regulated groups is often necessary to gain the compliance that is ostensibly required by law.

Marshall's mission to China in 1946 very obviously depended on the ability to negotiate, but so did most of his other career roles benefit from the same skills, practiced in less noticeable ways. Building and maintaining the wartime alliance with the UK and USSR, mounting joint operations with the Navy, and carrying on joint campaigns with the British in Africa and Europe are clearly organizational tasks in which negotiation turned out to be critical to success.

Several elements in Marshall's character combined to make him a successful negotiator. The first was his ability to listen and to question in order to compile an accurate and comprehensive factual basis for action. The second, equally important, was the genuine respect he extended on a personal level to all principals involved in a dispute. A close observer of his performance in China in 1946 observed that Marshall constantly functioned during his career to "listen to advice from people and adjudicate between opposing views" (Barrett, 1959, 40). A third element was the virtue of persistence and hard work. The final elements were an ability to mount persuasive arguments based on logic and facts, and patience.

These abilities working together allowed him to move disputants toward agreement. He was able to not only show respect for the views, information, and intentions of Zhou Enlai and Chiang Kai-shek, but also do the hard work of developing an independent knowledge base and not be dependent on either of them. He fully expected disputants to try to influence him with half-truths and to withhold information not helpful to their cause; these acts are to be expected as manifestations of human behavior. Being in command of an additional and sizable knowledge base tended to keep the disputants honest, increase their respect for him, create more and better information that could be shared, and augment his persuasiveness.

Anti-communist politicians at home attacked Marshall for being even-handed. Their view assumed, first, that Soviet communists were ideological and irrational and, second, that Chinese communists were no different in their mind-sets or tactics than Soviet communists. Marshall believed that making assumptions about people's beliefs based on their political labels made moving toward agreement more difficult. Other observers charged that, while the communists were certainly not blameless, most of the underhandedness was displayed on the nationalist side. Marshall similarly dismissed these charges. Against the odds and predictions of China experts that negotiation could not be effective, he temporarily resolved some major differences and had reached partial accommodation on others, although final success eluded him.

Scanning the Political and Policy Environment

To be an effective governmental manager at the head-of-agency level, an administrator must be able to judge clearly other actors and forces in the political system. Marshall came to understand, over time, the importance to leadership of scanning the organization's external environment to gain knowledge and the tools to get general system decisions that would increase the effectiveness of his own organization. He did not overreach; he understood his own role as a subordinate actor in the constitutional-political environment in which he operated.

As Army chief of staff it was important to learn how the US Navy, the British defense establishment, the Congress, and the White House approached and made their decisions. He learned that it was important in order to gain the confidence of the Congress to be specific about funding needs and future plans so as to underscore respect for that body's special constitutional responsibility. Careful planning was far superior, he reasoned, to operating by alternating between large budgetary windfalls and having to make drastic cuts under pressure. It was necessary as well to learn the interlacing network of decision systems between and among the branches and levels of government and the political calculus undergirding how resources are acquired; for example, the means by which the President could gain leverage with Congress.

Perhaps the hardest lesson to learn for an agency or department head is the critical need to build a support network drawn broadly from the society at large in order to influence the official decision makers. It is not enough for Congress and the general public to see the organization is operating in good faith and in compliance with law and being frugal with its budget. In order to be effective it must also build its image so as to be trusted with new programs and given latitude to pursue its vision of future needs. A particular ethical virtue of Marshall that helped build this type of broad, supportive constituency was his insistence on a high level of professionalism. He and his organization were widely viewed as patriotic, reasonable, well trained, and committed, and this image in turn enabled the agency to gain greater resources and pursue its vision.

Finally, Marshall was sensitive to the fact that many legitimate demands for resources coexist in the political system, and the administrator should not reach beyond that which analysis demonstrates is reasonable. Teaming with Senator Truman's military spending watchdog committee did more than increase the efficiency of appropriated resources; it demonstrated good faith both to Congress and the public that in turn enhanced the Army's reputation and therefore its effectiveness.

Both Presidents Roosevelt and Truman were keen enough to spot Marshall's innate talent as a spokesman for worthwhile public goals that appealed to the public and to both major parties. They accordingly used him to take the lead in informing, persuading, cajoling, and calming a divided Congress into attitudes of support (Parrish 1989).

The type of frequent and straightforward communication with the Congress, the executive branch, administrative peers, interest group representatives, and the media that were discussed in this chapter allowed Marshall to build credibility and political capital and to fend off political opposition from isolationists, budget hawks, and detractors of ground forces. Ultimately, the weight of his evidence and the soundness of his judgment gave him the tools he needed to allow his organization to succeed. He worked tirelessly at these tasks, never asked for special treatment or arranged political tradeoffs, and suffered setbacks secure in the knowledge that his goals were worth the price. Sherwood summarizes well:

> Faced with stupidity and shortsightedness [of many within the Congress] which would have driven a weaker man to despair, Marshall maintained at least the semblance of calmness and patience; but it can never be doubted that he endured intense inward suffering, not from frustration for himself but for the integrity and security of the Republic (1948, 165-165).

Being a team player with a well developed and articulated view of his constitutional role, Marshall was able to harness his passions when political decisions went against him. Aware of the constraints under which politicians and especially presidents acted, he saw the necessity of providing his superiors and allies with face-saving alternatives and symbolic victories falling short of optimum results but allowing them to fight on. Here was an administrator who was uniquely designed to excel and to lead in a democracy.

Notes

1.   Marshall believed that if the matter could not be summarized in a single page it had not been thought through.

2.   Among those holding this position were Walter Bedell Smith, Joseph T. McNarney, and Thomas T. Handy (Devers 1958, 16; Eisenhower 1962, 4).

3.   Kennan's work during this week, and that of his staff, were to become major ingredients in the ERP.

4.   Kennan regretted the fact that "the staff was never used in the same way again" at the Department of State by Marshall's successors (Kennan 1959, 13).

5.   Marshall and Gerow relied heavily on recommendations of WPD officers, service records, and military education, in that order.

6.   This foresight may be contrasted to the inability of the Bush administration to plan even the immediate aftermath of what it expected to be an easily achieved military victory in Iraq.

7.   Marshall ordered his Pacific commanders to put Rainbow 5 into effect hours after the bombing of Pearl Harbor (Pogue 1966, 233).

8.   Marshall told Stimson he would "see if some devious method might be found" to get the rifles to the Belgians, perhaps by asking the British if they would allot some of their ammunition for the purpose (GCMRL: 11/29/1940, Box 84, Folder 2).

9.   MacArthur, he often observed, was so afflicted. Eisenhower, on the other hand, was chosen as supreme commander in Europe because of his ability to think broadly and work well with others across both vertical and horizontal lines.

10.   The descriptor is a reference to Hopkins' poor health.

11.   It helped that Churchill was Minister of Defence as well as prime minister.

12.   Secretary of State Cordell Hull complained that he had to learn from Lord Halifax and from the British ministries what was going on between the president and Churchill. Marshall went so far as to prepare a draft letter to Hopkins asking him to use his influence to overcome the president's "pathological aversion to a record being kept" at his meetings and in his correspondence. The draft was never sent, although it is possible he made such a request of Hopkins verbally (Danchev 1986, 57-58).

13.   Dill shared with Marshall his discomfort with what he considered Roosevelt's superficiality and selfishness, and Marshall complained to Dill how difficult it was to explain things to the president (Danchev 1986, 57-58).

14.   Marshall orchestrated an effort to have Dill honored in multiple ways to impress Churchill. He asked War Department official Harvey Bundy to arrange an honorary Harvard University degree for Dill. Harvard couldn't do it, but Yale, which Bundy had attended, arranged a special award recognizing Dill's contribution to international relations in a lavish ceremony receiving abundant publicity (Bundy 1959, 23-24). Based on this and other arranged tributes, Churchill reconsidered and kept Dill in Washington.

15.   The effort led to creation of the United Service Organizations (USO), among other improvements (Bolte 1958, 47).

16.   The committee's solid achievements catapulted Truman into prominence and positioned him for selection by Roosevelt as vice-presidential running mate in 1944 and, ultimately, the presidency. Truman in turn enabled the post-war phase of Marshall's career.

CHAPTER NINE
MARSHALL AND REORGANIZATION

All effective performance depends on the refinement of methods for reaching whatever goals are sought. But when new realities call for new methods, it turns out that the old ways of doing things have hardened into inviolable routines. Innovation is blocked by a thicket of fixed attitudes, habits, perceptions, assumptions, and unwritten rules. . . . Organizational arrangements and strategies designed to deal with old realities must be redesigned to cope with new challenges. Individuals who are performing far below their potential must be awakened.

—John W. Gardner, former Secretary of Health,
Education, and Welfare, 1965-1969 (Gardner 1986)

Marshall's constant concern with the effectiveness of management tools was demonstrated by recurring renewals and designs of organizations, events that reflected Marshall's organizational philosophy as well as his management style. These events also inform about how he viewed leadership because they reach the question of what kind of adaptation is required by different forms of change. Organizing and reorganizing are important aspects of the Marshall legacy and hold important lessons for both practitioners and students.

Six reorganizations will be dealt with in this chapter.[1] The term "reorganization" is defined broadly to include the design of a new organizational identity that is needed to augment an existing set of organizations with the aim of achieving a related mission. Three of them happened during the same time period: the 1941-1942 reorganization of the Department of War, the conjoining of British and American military establishments into a grand alliance with a unified military command, and the building of the American inter-service relationship. All had their roots in WW II, both in preparing for it and waging it. The fourth and fifth reorganizations came in the post-war era with Marshall as secretary of state: the reorganization of the State Department, and the creation of a set of new organizations for implementing the Marshall Plan. The sixth, the reorganizing effort within the Department of Defense, mimicked the State Department reorganization and will be touched on only lightly.

History of the War Department

Some American military history must be given before telling the story of the 1941-1942 reorganization. Covered briefly will be the sweeping reforms accomplished in the first decade of the Twentieth Century under Secretary of War Elihu Root, the battle for control of the Army during and immediately after WW I, and the organizational difficulties encountered in the pre-WW II period after Marshall's appointment as chief of staff.

Until the Spanish-American war of 1898 made the inadequacy of military organization obvious, the authority of the Department of War, the administrative center of the US Army, had been split between the secretary of war (a civilian and a cabinet member), a commanding general of the Army, and independent bureau chiefs. The latter included the Quartermaster, Adjutant General, Judge Advocate, and Cavalry and Artillery chiefs, among others. They competed with and sometimes dominated the commanding general. This structure carried through the Spanish-American War into the twentieth century.

Elihu Root, appointed secretary of war by President Theodore Roosevelt, proposed and carried legislation through Congress in 1903 that produced two new organs within the War Department: a forty-five member General Staff designed to exercise centralized control of such functions as personnel and supply; and the Office of Chief of Staff (COS), led by a presidentially appointed chief of staff designated as the Army's principal officer. The chief of staff was to be the principal advisor to the president on military matters and was to derive his powers from the president, yet he lacked power to direct activities within the War Department except with the approval of the secretary of war, ensuring that his powers remained purely advisory (Watson 1950, 57-58).

As the system worked itself out in practice, the bureau chiefs were able to block reforms or changes by exercising their leverage on the Congress. Through the same channels they were able to restrict the powers of the General Staff right up to the eve of WW I. The result was a woeful fragmentation that cost the Army dearly in its conduct of the war in France (Watson 1950, 58-59). Disaster may have been avoided solely because three outstanding men, Secretary of War Newton D. Baker, AEF Commander General Pershing, and Army Chief of Staff General Peyton G. March were in place as the war broke, permitting the Army to function well enough to get the nation through it. Their ability and wisdom helped to counteract hostility toward the Army emanating from Washington and the bureau chiefs.

With Pershing set to take over command of forces in France, General March was sent back from France to Washington to serve as chief of staff. For the duration of the war Pershing made all military decisions and March furnished support from Washington. Although the war was waged more or less successfully on this basis, serious problems erupted. When March arrived back in Washington his impulse was to take more and more control. Pershing, in frustration, wrote to Baker that "our organization here is so bound up with operations and training and supply and transportation of troops that it would be impossible to make it function if the control . . . were placed in Washington." Baker wisely intervened to bridge the differences between the two men (Bland 1991, 269).[2] Still, it was clear that the army succeeded due to the qualities of these three people and in spite of the organizational arrangement.[3]

March vs. Pershing and the National Defense Act of 1920

The near debacle of 1917 set the stage for the enactment of the National Defense Act (NDA) of 1920. The success of the AEF organization, as it was organized internally within France, was the model used for the legislation and Pershing was the model's major advocate. Under the terms of the NDA the General Staff was placed under the COS and made responsive to him, and organized into Operations, Intelligence, War Plans, and Supply divisions (or "sections"). However, the crucial procurement of supplies function was placed in the hands of an assistant secretary of war. In this latter official, acting with the guidance of General Staff planners and with the support of the president and Congress, was vested the authority for obtaining the ordnance and materiel necessary for conducting the war. The chief of staff was charged with the planning, development, and execution of the military program during wartime. He was also designated the commanding general of peacetime field forces.

The COS was to consist of the chief of staff, the General Staff, the Secretary of the General Staff (SGS), and the various deputy chiefs of staff. The General Staff, SGS, and deputies were seen as an extension of the chief of staff himself. The General Staff was primarily limited to planning and policy development duties and was to perform only the administrative duties implied by the section names, but it could be enlarged as time went on and in fact was enlarged (for example, the personnel division was added).

The SGS was in a particularly sensitive and crucial position. He was to perform as the major linchpin between the COS and most other army units that worked, at least within the law's intent, under the General Staff. These units were arrayed in various hierarchies underneath the General Staff and included the *special staff offices* (quartermaster corps, ordnance department, adjutant general, judge advocate general, and finance division); the *combat arms* (infantry, artillery, engineering, signal corps); *nine corps areas* within the US (concerned with supply and administration); the *field forces*; the *overseas establishments*; and the *air forces*.

The NDA had another crucial feature. In the event of war the General Staff was to establish a General Headquarters (GHQ) in the war theater and staff it from its own ranks. In this way the formula that was used in the war in France, providing a fully operating and self-directing army in the theater, was to be used again in future wars. This feature was to become a major issue as the nation prepared for another great war in 1941.

How effective was this organizational arrangement? It was heavily layered, complex almost beyond understanding, and had a weak chain-of-command. The looseness of the command structure was responsible for much wasted time in negotiating, communicating, and just plain hand-holding. Because the General Staff served under the chief of staff and could not take executive action on its own,

enormous responsibility was placed on the chief of staff himself to get action
(Watson 1950, 64-69):

> [T]he Chief of Staff was accountable in some degree for almost everything that
> was done or not done by the Army. His enormous responsibilities, however, were
> not balanced by the power to fulfill them, and could not be [since he was
> dependent on the secretary of war, the president, and the Congress for approval
> and funding of his decisions] (Watson 1950, 75).

Mounting Pressures to Reorganize

As the war in Europe raged from 1939 to 1941 and the Japanese threat in the Pacific
grew, a new reality was forced on military planners and administrators. For those
who saw the need to plan for the possibility of American entry into a world war, the
situation was this: US military forces would likely be fighting a far more dispersed
war than it had in the prior war with multiple theaters of operation, with a broad
network of formal and informal alliances, and with greatly altered technology
including revolutionary weaponry and worldwide systems of communication
(Watson 1950, 2). These factors were forcing new thinking about command
structures and decision processes in the minds of military thinkers and planners.

Preparing for a wider war demanded renewed attention to the way in which the
War Department was organized. Yet, to an ever greater degree than before the chief
of staff and his aides were being hounded by distractions, having little to do with
potential war, that were seriously draining Marshall's energies. Toward the end of
1941 it was estimated that sixty-one officers had direct access to the chief of staff
and that he had under his command thirty major and three hundred and fifty smaller
commands (Pogue 1966, 290). Much of the burden could be attributed to the
decentralized and semi-autonomous bureau system (Cline 1950, 65-66).

On top of these internal demands on the chief of staff came external demands
from congressional committees and individual congressmen, scientists, industrialists, and foreign military attaches. As war became imminent the demands of the
secretary of war and the president on the chief of staff increased greatly and drew
top priority.

It is true that Marshall had the War Plans Division (WPD) and the rest of the
General Staff at his beck and call, and that one of the WPD's functions was the
coordination of the work of the other General Staff sections. Yet it was in
Marshall's nature to involve himself in whatever decisions of importance were on
the table:

> [H]e personally acted on every policy or command decision, often intervening in
> the process of drafting studies to make extremely detailed changes both in
> substance and language. . . . His handwriting is in evidence on drafts of nearly
> every important paper and on many comparatively unimportant ones" (Cline 1950,
> 65-66).[4]

General Gerow, the chief of WPD, shared the load with Marshall. Neither man felt entitled by law to delegate the work to others. Every piece of correspondence or report that came into WPD or went out received Gerow's personal attention; he complained that the paperwork permitted him little time for any matters of importance, including basic policy formulation (Cline 1950, 66).[5] Meanwhile, the matters which Marshall and Gerow felt they should be involved in, but could not, grew in range and complexity. For example, conferring with the allies should have taken priority over such matters as arranging housing for expanded training camps, which should have been but could not legally be handed off to the General Staff.

Marshall's great strength was that when he sensed the need for change, he used his staff and his organizational powers, formal and informal, to gain more information, analyze the situation, and make logical decisions. He therefore asked Deputy Chief of Staff Handy and the executive officer of WPD, Walton Walker, to identify the processes that needed to change for the COS to be effective in wartime. They found:

> Many questions now presented to the Chief of Staff do not require a decision by him. They could and should be acted upon by a division of the General Staff after being properly coordinated with other divisions (Cline 1951, 39).

Marshall resisted reorganization for several reasons. First, as a product of WW I thinking who worked with Pershing to formulate the new approach that was adopted in the NDA, he could be expected to try to make a system work that he had played a role in creating. Second, he had always been accustomed to taking on large workloads in a hands-on fashion and found the pattern difficult to change. Third, he was perpetually reacting to multiple pressures and had scant time to think ahead. Finally, the COS lacked legal authority to command and direct the many units reporting to it, many of which were protected by Congress (Watson 1950, 81-82).

Resistance to change characterized attitudes of most older officers, including air officers, who agreed with the old Pershing view that the General Staff should be restricted to a service operation during peacetime. Although in theory the most progressive and dynamic part of the Army, the Air Corps had in fact a large contingent of older officers of generally higher rank who were lodged in comfortable offices and disinclined to leave them. Further, aviation functions were divided among the different air commands.

As an initial reorganizational move, Marshall and Stimson decided in March 1941 to place the entire air arm under a single commander. Arnold was raised to preeminence in all air matters. Through the Air Force Combat Command, he controlled "all aerial operations" save for units assigned or attached to task forces, overseas garrisons, or other commands. He was also responsible for planning the air defense of the United States (Bland, Ritenour and Wunderlin 1986, 682-685).

Marshall also recommended to Stimson that the position of Assistant Secretary of War for Air be revived. Stimson followed through and appointed Robert A. Lovett to the position. Lovett's charge involved two major tasks: promote aircraft production and streamline the organization of the air arm. The reestablishment of this position elevated even further the stature and priority linked with air matters within the War Department.

For decades key officers of the infantry, field artillery, coastal artillery, cavalry, judge advocate general, quartermaster corps, ordnance department, and other bureau units had exercised control in the training and equipping of troops assigned to them. Officers commanding these units were at the major general rank and they wielded substantial influence in Congress and had many friends throughout the War Department. Insistent on being consulted on every decision that concerned them, they could be counted on to stand against any reform that interfered with their status and influence. The net result is that they weakened the chain of command that would be essential in wartime (Pogue 1966, 293).

Marshall's reluctance to reorganize had been overcome by a combination of the enlarged scope of his job, an inability to take on any more responsibility, and the growing expectations of others. He needed allies in anticipation of a bitter fight over reorganization and he found many. National Guard commanders supported him because they knew he had supported their struggle for status and recognition in the Army. He could also count on a crop of younger air officers who were unhappy with traditional Regular Army prejudices, airmen like Frank Andrews, Hap Arnold, Joseph McNarney, Laurence Kuter, and Ira Eaker. And, of course, there were the "Marshall men" whom he had schooled and nurtured at Fort Benning who were now rapidly advancing up the ranks.

It was necessary to change both existing law and practice. An office to command and oversee the implementation of COS decisions was an absolute must. Although WPD had earlier functioned only as a policy and planning body and coordinator of other General Staff sections, it was now critical that it take on a more aggressive role. War Department decisions were being made that required the defensive deployment of the Army in the Pacific and Central America, and these led to detailed WPD plans for facilities and personnel and inter-service and international agreements. It was only natural for the WPD to undertake operational steps to follow up on these. Delegation was logical because WPD was already accustomed to coordinating the functions of other General Staff divisions as well as advising and coordinating the activities of the semi-autonomous bureaus.

Marshall therefore delegated the implementation of these decisions and plans to WPD, largely ignoring its lack of legal authority (Cline 1951, 55). This pattern of organizational functioning was consistent with Marshall's management style of delegating large amounts of discretion to his subordinates within generally agreed frameworks of principles which had been discussed and mutually understood to be necessary.

The question of the effectiveness of the WPD in wartime was opened to debate. Gerow and others supported the original idea that in the event of war all administrative functions should be furnished by the WPD within a GHQ set up in the war theater, to be commanded there by the chief of staff (Marshall), who would be designated as the war theater commander. General McNarney led a group opposing this concept, composed mostly of airmen. This latter group believed it was essential for the Army to have coordinated, central direction of its operations lodged in the

War Department in Washington. McNarney recommended against transferring any WPD planning and operation functions abroad.

Marshall was at first inclined to side with Gerow and try to make the GHQ concept work, and thus continued with the process of building it. But he was troubled by the prospect of splitting administrative staff functions between the field and Washington (Bradley 1951, 174). He thus directed the matter be studied by a committee composed of representatives drawn from all General Staff divisions and the Air Forces (Cline 1951, 66-67). The committee concluded that the GHQ question could not be resolved by administrative action alone and that a major reorganization by the president, Congress, and the War Department was needed (Cline 1951, 70). The committee's recommendations added momentum to Marshall's reorganization initiative.

In August 1941, Marshall set in motion three separate reorganization studies, referred to for simplicity as the Harrison study, the Spaatz report, and the Arnold initiative. The Harrison study was led by Lt. Col. William K. Harrison of the WPD staff. Its findings and recommendations supported the development of a new operations section within the General Staff to assist the COS in the exercise of direct command functions over all overseas departments and bases, defense commands, task forces, and theaters of operations. The GHQ office, which had already been created by WPD in anticipation of war, should be abandoned and its resources folded back into the WPD's Washington office. The Spaatz report, prepared by air officer Brigadier General Carl "Tooey" Spaatz, proposed to reorganize the War Department much along the same lines proposed by Harrison.

Then, in November 1941, General Arnold took the initiative (perhaps at Marshall's urging) to recommend that the chief of staff act as the commander of all military forces within the Department of War to include all continental commands (ground, service, and air) through a streamlined General Staff. Just how the General Staff would exercise its command function was not made clear by Arnold (Cline 1951, 70-72). Marshall indicated his favorable reaction to the Arnold report on November 25, a scant twelve days before Pearl Harbor (Cline 1951, 73). WPD was given the job, under Harrison's leadership, to develop the reorganization plan along the lines recommended by Arnold.

The Reorganization of 1941-1942

The stage was now set for reorganization to occur. To effect any of the major features in either the Harrison, Spaatz, or Arnold versions, redistribution of authority within the War Department would be necessary and thus require congressional action. It would take an unlikely political consensus to make it happen. Even with the threat of war, a great deal of courage would be necessary on the part of would-be reformers. Congress, subject to pressure from specialized Army units, could be expected to oppose meaningful reorganization and take the legislation in an unexpected direction or defeat it altogether. Action was thus risky and in any event a huge drain on time and energy that Marshall and Stimson could scarcely afford; they would have to sell the plan to Congress on top of their crushing agendas (Nelson 1946, 335).

Many of the details of the reorganization, along with planning for accompanying shifts in personnel and supporting evidence and reports, were in place by December 7. A fair measure of consensus had been achieved within the War Department concerning the direction of reform and the functioning of the War Department and the COS. The political resolve had not yet coalesced. Many obstacles, the most important of which were the presence of opposed power centers and the certainty that a large-scale shifting of duties and responsibilities would create harmful uncertainty at a critical historical juncture, stood in the way.

The shock of the attack on Pearl Harbor drastically changed the prospects for reorganization. First, the conversion of a potential war into a real and official war strengthened Marshall's argument for building the General Staff into an effective command post. Second, the war cleared away political resistance to whatever arrangement might be decided upon by Roosevelt, Marshall, and Stimson. Still, the thought of the wrenching effects that large-scale change inevitably brings worked against making the effort. Experiencing short-term organizational inconvenience in a war that was already going badly in order to get possible long-term efficiencies was not a welcome prospect. Viewed in the context of the dark days of January, 1942, the choice was not obvious. Taking the lead, Marshall decided the time was ripe and took the leap.

> The going was tough, not so much because of strong disapproval of the idea, but largely because of passive attitudes and the propensity to procrastinate and urge that action be deferred to a more opportune time (Nelson 1946, 345-346).

A painstaking analysis of the consequences of reorganization and a rational comparison of work processes under the old and new systems, normally a sensible way to proceed, was ruled out because of the time such an analysis would take away from other urgent tasks. At this juncture, faith and iron resolve were the essential elements were needed to sustain the reorganization initiative.

Marshall and Stimson took the first step by approaching the president to get his help in gaining the necessary political support. At the president's urging Congress passed the War Powers Act on December 18, 1941, giving the president or his agents (the secretary of war and the chief of staff), the necessary authority to reorganize the War Department and any related other agency to "expedite the prosecution of the war effort" (Cline 1951, 91-92). Marshall now had the authority to make the structural and process changes he desired, although he still might be subject to political counterattack. The political momentum now belonged to the chief of staff and was draining away from the opponents of reform.

What had to occur at this point, given the crush of other events, was entrusting the myriad details of the reorganization plan to an effective administrator. For this purpose Marshall selected General Joseph T. McNarney, recalling him from London where he had just been reassigned away from his WPD post in Washington, promoting him to major general, and placing him on the War Department's

Reorganization Board. In March, a scant two months later, he was named deputy chief of staff and given wide authority to carry out the reorganization. All the while Marshall acted with the knowledge that, if given time, opponents within and outside the Department of War could defeat any plan.

McNarney was an airman with a WPD background who wholly supported reorganization. While respected within the WPD, he was a no-nonsense and blunt person with little sympathy for the Army's old guard. He was given to prompt, direct action, and was single-minded in pursuit of a goal, a thick-skinned stalwart who often evoked the epithet of "hatchet man" (Pogue 1966, 292). To many, he "was just a pain in the neck" (Groves May 14, 1970), but to Marshall he was the essential linchpin for forcing the changes vital to realizing the reorganization's goals.

McNarney first met with his team on January 25, 1942. With him were Harrison, Major Laurence S. Kuter, a promising young Air Corps officer; and Lieutenant Colonel Otto Nelson, a Harvard-based scholar with expertise in army reorganization (Nelson 1946, 345). McNarney's demeanor and mood were evident as he instructed the committee that this was "not a voting committee . . . not a debating society . . . [but] a committee to draft the necessary directives" to put the organization into effect (Cline 1951, 92).

By selecting McNarney and giving him near carte-blanche authority, Marshall signaled his preference for forcing policy and shifting influence in ways that were contrary to his normal management style. Of course, the circumstances were special. The Army had been thrust into world war with an ineffective central command structure and processes.

> Only because he believed ruthless changes were vital to the effective waging of war did General Marshall demand the immediate adoption of a program that might otherwise have been debated for months (Pogue 1966, 295).

In less than a week McNarney's team had the plan completed and his team's recommendations in Marshall's hands (Pogue 1966, 294); they were all approved the same day. The plan was then carefully vetted to the General Staff, GHQ, Air Forces, and the deputy chiefs of staff. It was not shared with the chiefs of combat arms and special staff services—the officers of units most likely to be opposed. There would be a residue of unhappiness in certain army enclaves but the deed was done. According to Nelson, the junior member of McNarney's team:

> [T]he task of selling a particular reorganization at a particular time to all in the higher levels of the government required a delicate handling. If piecemeal criticism and grumbling over details were not avoided, delay would ensue, and the longer the delay the greater were the opportunities for those adversely affected or otherwise opposed to rally their forces to obtain a further delay. Had such tactics ever been permitted to develop, the reorganization project would probably never have been carried out (Nelson 1946, 348).

Had Nelson's fears been realized, the army's ability to wage war may well have been compromised. The recommendations, as they eventually appeared in Executive Order 9082, effective on March 9, 1942, were as follows:

(1) free the General Staff from all activities except strategic direction and control of operations, determination of over-all military requirements, and determination of basic policies affecting the zone of interior (i.e., commands within the US);
(2) create three new commands, including the Army Air Forces, Army Ground Forces, and Services of Supply (later renamed the "Army Service Forces"), to which the General Staff could delegate operating duties connected with administration, supply, organization, and training;
(3) eliminate GHQ, the Air Force Combat Command, and the offices of the Chiefs of Air Corps, Infantry, Field Artillery, Coast Artillery, and Cavalry as being "unnecessary or obsolete headquarters"; and
(4) create an "executive committee responsible only to the Chief of Staff" to put the reorganization into effect without giving the "interested parties" a chance to record non-concurrences and cause "interminable delay" (Cline 1951, 91).

Arnold's support had been crucial. He had worked closely with Marshall to enhance the influence of the air units within the new structure. At the same time, distrusting the competence of much of the old Air Corps staff, Marshall wanted to submerge the air staff within the General Staff and therefore opposed the creation of a separate air force service branch. Because Arnold had great confidence in Marshall he could better accept the reasons why Air Corps staff should not be given too much authority (Pogue 1966, 290-291).

Marshall took two other actions to nurture the growth of effective air forces. He kept a close eye on younger air officers of promise and made sure, with Arnold's help, that they were brought along rapidly so as to replace older, less competent officers. Also, soon after the reorganization became effective, he recommended to Roosevelt that Arnold be named to the new Joint Chiefs of Staff to assure equal status to the air forces in strategic decision-making.

In another move connected to reorganization, one clearly demonstrating Marshall's knack for combining structural reform and personnel changes, he selected Brigadier General Eisenhower to be Gerow's replacement (the latter was transferred to duty with troops) as head of the strengthened WPD. Thus Eisenhower became one of the two closest advisors to Marshall in the new Washington command post.[6] To recognize the altered status of WPD as a slimmed-down, more effective command and operation unit as well as the primary planning and policy making body, it was renamed the Operations Division (OPD). In effect, this move gave Marshall, in the form of Eisenhower:

... an additional deputy for planning and controlling military operations, and this deputy, the Assistant Chief of Staff, OPD, was given an adequate staff to carry out his broad responsibilities. OPD was WPD plus GHQ (without its training functions) plus the superior authority GHQ had lacked. Or, to put it another way, OPD was in itself a virtually complete general staff, tight-knit in a way the old

War Department General Staff had not achieved at the time it was necessary, and definitely oriented toward operations in the field (Cline 1951, 95).

Two other alterations resulting from the reorganization merit description. Marshall acquired the services of Wilton Persons and his staff in Legislative Relations to keep him informed about what was going on in Congress. Also, an Office of Morale was established at Marshall's urging. Later headed by Frederick Osborn, it coordinated a vast range of services, such as the United Service Organizations (USO), and extended its reach to supply these to army posts world-wide (Pasco 1997, 37-38).

Effects of Reorganization

As expected, making the transition to the reorganized system did not happen without difficulty. Confusion and overlap in function cost time and money and equipment in the spring and summer of 1942. In the opinion of at least one highly placed general staffer this translated into a tragic loss of life (Bolte 1958, 10). Others disagreed. Personnel Director (G-1) Hilldring said that the huge cut in officers in his unit (from about sixty down to ten) actually allowed that office to do its job for the first time. Until that time the large staff was intruding into functions properly belonging to other units such as the Adjutant General, the Surgeon General, the Inspector General, and Ordnance.

While the director of the president's Bureau of the Budget enthusiastically endorsed most of the provisions of the reorganization, his office was quick to caution that it was essential, in order to shield the chief of staff and OPD from having to review minor matters, "to work out the specific assignment of functions all the way down the line," and "to revise and simplify procedures to fit the new structure" (Nelson 1946, 352). Many more high level civilians with necessary technical and administrative skills would have to be hired to do these tasks (Nelson 1946, 353).

> And I think they got the general staff streamlined to the point where it was in shape to fight the war, and to give the detail, the execution of doctrine and policy over to the operating staffs where it belonged . . . we did a better job in my judgment, a much better job (Hilldring 1959, 17).

The appointment of General William Somervell to the position of Chief of Army Service Forces (G-4) was variously viewed as a blessing and a curse. Somervell was both ruthless and highly competent, an empire builder who loved to dominate and control. He attracted personal power and bred resentment among others. Marshall supported Somervell strongly because he could produce fighting units that were desperately needed at the beginning of the war:

> Actually, he was one of the most efficient officers I have ever seen. And he got things done in Calcutta just as fast as he did in the meadows there around the

Pentagon. Whenever I asked him for something, he did it and he got it. He was very forcible. He reformed, and I am using the word accurately, he reformed the Adjutant General's Department and others. He found conditions there were just intolerable and, naturally, they were all bitterly against him. . . . If I went into control in another war, I would start out looking for another General Somervell the very first thing I did, and so would anybody else who went through that struggle . . . (Bland 1991, 445).

Somervell got the supplies to where they needed to be gotten for troop training and the cadre reported on time and the training started on time (Hilldring 1959, 19). That he was disliked by General Staff people and that he was not on close personal terms with Marshall were secondary, at least in the short run.

Overall, the results of the reorganization were startling and not long in coming. The number of people with access to the chief of staff dropped from sixty-one to six. The three General Staff offices other than WPD went from a combined staff of three hundred-and-four to just thirty-six officers and their functions limited to planning and policy. Two of the three deputy chiefs of staff were eliminated. The myriad special units in the field were recombined within the three continental commands (Ground, Air, and Service Forces) and made directly responsive to the OPD acting on behalf of the chief of staff. The Army Ground Forces were given all administrative, organizational, and training responsibilities for ground troops. The Army Air Forces were given sole authority to develop and procure aviation equipment. The Army Service Forces (Somervell's command) acquired many administrative functions including the processing of personnel, communications, hospitals, training of service troops, directing recreation and morale services, military justice, mail delivery, and the chaplain corps (Pogue 1966, 295-297).

Reorganization was resented by some, praised by most. Following on the heels of the policy of eliminating older officers from command positions, it further wounded the egos of those who had been rejected for command assignments and who now had their administrative jobs downgraded. Many felt keenly that a great disservice had been done to the traditional army. On the other hand, air officers were delighted. Carl "Tooey" Spaatz, who later led the European arm of the air war, called the reorganization "an act of genius" that was to permit the air forces to function fully throughout the war (Spaatz 1959, 15).

In the broadest context, the value of any reorganization depends in large measure on whether new organizational structures and processes result in more effective pursuit of public policy goals. Much of this effect ultimately flows from putting capable people in roles that allow them to have greater impact on outcomes. Much also comes from breaking down what organizational theory labels *sub-optimization* and Marshall called "localitis." Sub-optimization is a major bureaucratic dysfunction that interferes with the pursuance of overall organization mission. It is the phenomenon of a distinct unit within the whole organization putting its own interests before those of the entire organization of which it is an integral part. The sub-optimizing unit's goal (which may or may not be intentional) is to gain greater influence and resources for its own defined mission and its leaders, yet its effect is to weaken the organization as a whole. The damage done by sub-optimization is to the building of unity of purpose throughout the entire organization.

A critical function of leadership is to suppress the natural tendency toward sub-optimization through the employment of strategies that maintain focus upon agreed-upon and central goals of the whole organization. In the case of the military establishment at war this means subordinating the interests of individual service branches, personalities, special offices, and even allied nations to the common goal of achieving ultimate victory over the enemy. Such a vision underlay the actions of Marshall in reorganizing the War Department.

Marshall harbored no doubts about the reorganization's positive consequences. "In his view the reorganization made possible the effective waging of war by leaving him free to concentrate on strategy and major operations abroad" (Pogue 1966, 298). If he was right, and he likely was, the effect of the reorganization was to increase the War Department's positive role in all of the nation's subsequent wartime activities.

Reorganization, despite its rationality, had been slow in developing and had to await the coming-together of a specific set of conditions. Timing was crucial. The Japanese attack brought about a state of total war and removed many obstacles to law change and implementation. Courage was also crucial. In the midst of a world war, with attention dominated by events, many characterized by disaster and sacrifice, it would have been understandable had the effort been put on hold.

Not content with reorganizing his home organization, Marshall was simultaneously scanning the external environment contemplating two other organization-building ventures: designing a system of combined command with the allies; and creating a structure to hopefully blend the decision-making and operations of the US Army and the US Navy.

Building the Allied Command Structure

Some type of organization was needed to harmonize the activities of allied military forces engaged in a multiple-theater war. The loose-knit relationships that had evolved in the two years before Pearl Harbor were not sufficient to produce an efficient cooperation of forces and will.

The term "boundary-spanning" means to reach out beyond one's organization to consider and utilize other factors, organizations, people, and systems in order to more effectively pursue organizational objectives. Both formal and informal means are involved. Formal means include the definition of common goals and the creation of multi-national bodies with the authority to pursue effective means to reach these goals. Informal means include expanding information sharing, harmonizing cultural interaction, and building personal relationships.

Marshall's informal boundary-spanning skills and instincts were sketched in earlier chapters. From his early career assignments working with native councils in the Philippines, organizing National Guard maneuvers, coordinating war front activities with the French and British, gaining knowledge about Japanese battle methods from Japanese commanders, learning Chinese culture and language, to his community building and citizen groups at Benning, Screven, Moultrie, Chicago, and Vancouver, Marshall had made building bridges to other nations, cultures, and peoples a comfortable habit.

At the Department of War after Germany's invasion of Poland, he was made keenly aware that America could be drawn into a general war on the side of the British, French, Dutch, and other western democracies. The Soviets were added after the Stalin-Hitler pact fell apart and China when that nation was attacked by Japan. It had thus become necessary to work across national lines to find a role for the US in the effort to build a cooperative defense to German arms and aggression. As Japan continued to expand its empire the scope of concern grew so as to include British, Dutch, Chinese, and Filipino interests. Even Central and South America came within the scope of his radar. Cross-national relationships thus became critical to War Department functioning well before Pearl Harbor.

His organization's effectiveness thus came partially to depend upon understanding, communicating with, negotiating, and operating in concert with other organizations, domestic and international, whose purposes, methods, cultures, and political bases differed in significant and sometimes profound ways. It meant interacting with people at all levels, heads of state and foreign ministers, local officials and military leaders in other nations, all of whom possessed different kinds of backgrounds, allegiances, personalities, and points of view.

There are no known formulae for success in cataloguing and relating these extra-organizational complexities and phenomena to one's own organization. Interests of other organizations always differ, yet they overlap in important and sometimes unseen ways. Patience and effort are required to find common ground.

Organizing the Allies at Arcadia

At the Arcadia meetings, British and American political and military leaders sat down with the intention of establishing the formal arrangements that would be used to undergird the alliance. Marshall's major organizing contribution to the conference, as distinct from the leadership role he played, was the unified theater command concept. It was his idea to divide the war organizationally into geographical theaters of operation. In each of these theaters a single supreme military commander from one of the allied nations was to be designated. Under the supreme commander's authority would be the individual naval, air, and ground commands of the various nations led by officers of their respective nationalities. The supreme commander was to coordinate and to resolve all plans, logistics, issues, and conflicts relative to the employment of all allied forces in the theater. Some of the theater commanders would be British and some American, and some could even be Dutch, French, Chinese, or other nationalities included within the alliance. Supreme commanders could be either ground, naval, or air officers, depending on the character of the theater and their individual competencies.

Marshall drove home the unity of command principle through persuasive argument and promises that decisions could and would be made in such a way that the unity principle would not be unfair to any individual nation. He used analogies based on the ill effects of having lacked such unity in WW I. The first unified command established was the Southwest Pacific Theater, a vast region ranging from Hawaii to India (Pogue 1966, 276-281). To model the idea of fairness, Marshall proposed that British General Archibald Wavell command the theater, a move that helped to secure Churchill's agreement to the underlying principle.[7]

Marshall enthusiastically supported the British proposal to create a single guiding body, titled the Combined Chiefs of Staff (CCOS) and composed of the military ground, air, and naval chiefs of both nations, that would be empowered to decide basic matters of war strategy and resource allocation. Theater commanders would be subordinate to this body. However, he insisted that Washington should be the only permanent meeting place of the CCOS in order to centralize the operation of a joint UK-US staff mission and promote unity of command. The staff could pursue the agenda of the British chiefs of staff *in absentia* between the full meetings of the CCOS. This arrangement provided the opportunity not only to bolster CCOS staff effectiveness but also to secure Marshall's friend and confidant, Sir John Dill, a permanent station in Washington as its head (Pogue 1966, 282-284). In this way Marshall could achieve broad, joint war planning as well as a natural docking point for boundary-spanning activity.

An added benefit of the CCOS arrangement was that the inclusion of British Air Marshal Charles Portal gave Marshall the opening to argue that an American air chief should also sit on the body. He carried the argument and then chose to fill the position with his subordinate, General Hap Arnold. In this way, he gained leverage on the CCOS as well as a seat at the major strategy table for advocates of air power.

The third organizing principle established at Arcadia was related to how war goods production was to be allocated. The process proposed by Marshall was adopted. Production allocation committees were to be created in both Washington and London which would make recommendations to the CCOS for final decision. In this way, the CCOS would not find itself in the position of having its strategic decisions frustrated by an independent body of civilians or firms or politicians preferring a different allocation (Pogue 1966, 285-287).

Some negotiation was necessary to get the war production allocation system accepted. Both Roosevelt and Churchill resisted the arrangement sought by Marshall because they desired more personal control. Marshall, on the other hand, was opposed to the insertion of an unelected civilian body that could interfere with military planning. He went so far as to tell Roosevelt that "if control of supply matters by the Combined Chiefs of Staff in Washington was not accepted, he [Marshall] could not continue to accept the responsibilities of his office" (Pogue 1966, 286-287). Hopkins agreed with Marshall, and Roosevelt relented. Perhaps as a face-saving device, a civilian body was inserted that would have the limited power to appeal the allocation committees' decisions to the president and prime minister.

Personal Relationships Underlying the "Special Relationship"

More needs to be said about the importance of interpersonal relations in spanning boundaries. In an environment desperately calling for cooperation, Marshall played a major role in building and leading "the special relationship." Almost alone on the American side, he liked and respected the British, and they reciprocated.[8] The affinity between them came in part from his experiences in WW I fighting alongside and fraternizing with them as well as being a recipient of the outpouring of affection given to Pershing and his aides when they visited London soon after the war's end. Later, he deepened their trust through his generosity in responding to British requests for assistance against Hitler. Marshall's provision of aircraft and ammunition were made at the expense of US Army preparedness (Cunningham 1961; Deane 1960, 14).[9] Finally, he may have had special insight and sympathy for British positions and they for his by virtue of his personal relationship with Dill. Their association allowed the two sides "to iron out many little differences which might have become big differences if they had not been resolved early on" (Hollis 1961, 1-2).

Marshall and Brooke regarded as the first among equals in the CCOS, wisely did not over-assert their natural leadership within the CCOS. Brooke may have wished to do so because he held a low opinion of Marshall's strategic abilities.[10] Two factors mitigated against division. First, Brooke well understood the special relationship Dill had to both sides and therefore included him at all combined meetings of the British and American military chiefs (Danchev 1986, 133). Second, although Marshall had strong convictions about what should be done, he typically submerged his views if he was convinced that his British comrades had made a strong case (Hollis 1961, 2).

Another important support was the British Air Chief Portal, respected by all the Americans for his cool head, intelligence, and persuasiveness (Deane 1960, 15). Portal often worked in concert with Marshall to overcome or at least neutralize the sometimes extreme and antagonistic views of King and Brooke and to keep the dialogue going in the effort to find a middle road. With the strong Marshall-Dill-Portal interpersonal connection, the CCOS functioned effectively as the military linchpin in the alliance (Pogue 1966, 270-272), similar to that formed at the political level by Churchill and Roosevelt.

Yet another reason for Marshall's popularity with the British was that he had a deep respect for the British intelligence service over American intelligence "because," as he said:

> it had a long start on us; it was closer to the operations; it had its people engaged a longer period and had had all the while a steady development . . . because of its intimate relations with the Continent (Bland 1991, 441).

The British-American military alliance thus created was best summarized by Marshall himself in remarks made to the US Governors Conference in June, 1943:

And I think the greatest thing we've done, the greatest thing we've accomplished, the most potent factor in this war today is the fact that we have secured a method of arriving at unity of operations among the Allies. That is extraordinarily difficult as you know in your own affairs and in your own political organizations. . . . Because in a war of this nature which literally covers the globe the complications are beyond description. But we've developed an orderly precision, (an) orderly method for doing this thing. *We know each other* well, know each other *intimately.* One of the most surprising things of all, if you go out here to Africa and find this combined staff, you can hardly tell, unless you look at the uniform closely, which service, which nation, the officer represents. . . . All these people close together—this staff all combined—with just one single idea, with one purpose; the whole thing integrated and developed to the point where they can get by the vicissitudes which always occur in a campaign. . . . (Bland and Stevens 1996, 30, 32, emphasis added).

In sum, from the British perspective the CCOS arrangement worked spectacularly well, a conclusion eventually supported even by Brooke, who originally deplored the arrangement (Ehrman 1956, 338-351).

An important side-effect of Marshall's informal leadership within the allied command structure was that it helped him to further earn the admiration of Roosevelt and especially of Churchill (Pogue 1966, 287). There were several reasons for this. In advance of CCOS meetings and aided by Hopkins, Marshall was successful in gaining Roosevelt's support on major strategy decisions (Bland 1991, 433). Churchill, knowing that Marshall wielded this influence on Roosevelt, instructed the imperial staff to be very careful not to antagonize the general. Churchill also remembered with gratitude the support the British had received from Marshall in the dark period preceding Pearl Harbor.

Inter-Service Cooperation

Just two months after Arcadia and while he was overseeing the ongoing reorganization of the War Department, Marshall took on the problem of reorganizing the always difficult relationship between the two major American service branches. Historically and by law, the Army and the Navy had maintained a careful separation, enforced it with autonomous traditions, and drew upon divergent political bases of support. As war now approached, the persistence of their rivalry, although understandable in political, sociological, and historic terms, was impossible to defend on either policy or administrative grounds.

As early as 1921 Marshall, working with Assistant Secretary of the Navy Theodore Roosevelt, Jr., asked for an exchange of Army and Navy officers so each could see how the other worked, an initiative quite uncommon for the times (Bland and Hadsel 1981, 593-594). Then, at Fort Benning Infantry Officer School, Marshall impressed on his students the tactical possibilities of joint infantry-naval operations.

Historically, the major point of contact between the two services had been the Joint Army-Navy Board, created in 1903 by agreement of the secretaries of war and navy. The board met infrequently and did little beyond exchange information and reach agreement on very practical matters. As chief of staff, Marshall developed a close working relationship with his naval counterpart, Admiral Harold R. "Betty" Stark. The two were able to both surface disagreements and work together, bound together by their mutual beliefs that war was likely and the need for preparation urgent (Stark 1959, 26-27). Only then were the two services able to activate true planning within the board drawing upon the War Plans Divisions of both services (Watson 1950, 79).

As war approached, regular consultation, exchange of views and information, and coordinated operational planning strengthened. There was resistance. The two services gravitated toward different strategy preferences befitting their special fighting qualities: the Navy's priorities focused on the far, watery reaches of the Pacific; the Army's mission was keyed to the land struggle in Europe. The matter was complicated by the rise in influence of the Army Air Forces, subordinate organizationally but given practical autonomy by Marshall in areas of aircraft design and development and strategic employment. The need to harmonize the functions of ground, air, and sea forces became more obvious (Cline 1951, 96), but doing so would require tamping down both the egos and autonomy of all military chiefs. Internal war department reorganization had already begun to achieve a smooth coordination of land and air forces. Now, there was a need to bring about something of the same sort with the Navy.

To achieve this end, Marshall used the simple mechanism of sending an administrative memorandum to the president after Arcadia,[11] in which he recommended that the Joint Army-Navy Board be replaced by a four-member body to be titled the Joint Chiefs of Staff (JCS). The JCS was to include Chief of Naval Operations Admiral King, Army Chief of Staff General Marshall, Chief of Air Forces General Arnold, and an additional naval officer. With the air force an active part of the army, Arnold was subordinate to Marshall in the command structure although the two were of a similar mind on the uses of air power. Therefore Arnold could be expected to support Marshall in JCS deliberations and side with him in disputes. By adding a fourth, naval member, Marshall hoped that the decision process would be balanced (Deane 1960, 13). King went along with this thinking. Marshall had in mind Admiral William Leahy for the position but still had to convince the president. Leahy was then serving as Roosevelt's military advisor and assistant and FDR preferred he remain as such (Handy 1956, 3). A compromise was reached whereby Leahy would continue to serve Roosevelt as an aide but take the seat as the fourth member of the JCS.[12]

Within the JCS Marshall saw himself as but one member of a consultative all-force strategy and coordination team, whose thinking and decisions could then be fed into the CCOS process and then underlie joint US military operations.[13] As events turned out, Marshall often presided over JCS meetings because of Leahy's frequent absences. Even when Leahy was present, Marshall was looked upon as the senior member for purposes of guidance and judgment (Eaker 1959, 4). This may have been unfortunate in the sense that Marshall's original idea was to promote trans-service thinking and submerge service differences in a body dedicated to overarching national objectives. In point of fact, Leahy tended to side with Marshall and Arnold in many of the disagreements that arose between the services, and this dynamic probably served to put King in the position of defending the "naval" position.

The principle of unanimity in JCS decision-making, while it allowed the frequently dissenting King to block consensus, was probably wise because it forced strategic conflicts out into the open where they could be debated. The president could then be brought in to exert his powerful influence as the situation demanded. The difficulty was illustrated by the fight that broke out between the Navy and Army Air Corps over which branch would command the operations of torpedo aircraft in the Aleutian Islands against an expected invasion by half of the Japanese fleet (*US News & World Report* 1959, 52-53).

At least from the perspective of General Ira Eaker, who sat in frequently for Air Chief of Staff Arnold, the JCS was a harmonious body. It was this way because Marshall had an unusual ability to appreciate the Navy's requirements and was adroit at balancing the interests of all the services; a quality Eaker described as "judicial temperament." Also, Marshall could be counted on to solicit and voice air forces views in both JCS and CCOS deliberations (Eaker 1959, 4-6). Eaker no doubt accurately voiced the air force's perspective, but his assumption of Army-Navy harmony is generally disputed.

Continuing Military Reorganization Efforts

Marshall consciously drew on the example of the British military defense organization in his continuing efforts to improve and reform the Army's decision processes. While visiting England in April, 1942 in his effort to sell OPD's cross-channel invasion strategy, he attempted to learn as much as he could about the workings of the British military hierarchy. He observed that Lord Mountbatten, chief of the combined headquarters that reported to the British Chiefs of Staff committee, was able to get the representatives of the various services to work closely and cooperatively. He thus eagerly accepted Mountbatten's invitation to send American service representatives to work with the combined operations staff in London (Pogue 1966, 312).

The systematic way in which Churchill kept his Defence Ministry people informed drew special attention. Marshall had already learned much from Dill, who had supplied details of the procedure. From these, Marshall drew ideas that he was able to incorporate within the new Army structure.

Marshall did not always prevail in reorganization battles. His goal of making management more effective had to contend with considerations of politics, position, and power.[14] His efforts at defense reorganization beyond the 1941-1942 reorganization thus had only minor impact. At the height of the war he sought a thorough overhaul in the whole US military structure, advocating a unified War Department and abolishing a separate Department of the Navy. The proposal was never taken up seriously, probably due to the press of events and the lack of taste for the political fight that would have likely erupted. Further reform would have to wait until the war was over.

The substance of the doomed proposal nonetheless throws light on how he thought about military organization in general. The new War Department, he proposed, should be organized into four major groupings: ground forces, air forces, sea forces, and a general supply service. A military chief of staff to the president should be established who was not a member of the War Department but rather an officer directly responsible to the president. He should have under his command a general staff for strategic, operational, personnel, and equipment policy matters. The three then-existing service chiefs of staff (Marshall being but one) plus the newly created chief of the supply service would constitute the general staff and be served by the necessary subsidiary groups (Bland and Stevens 1996, 156-157). The president's chief of staff would prepare the entire military budget for the president and, after enactment by Congress, would divide appropriations among the ground, air, and naval forces (Bland and Stevens 1996, 160). The structure came close to duplicating the British model.

After the war, with Eisenhower as Army chief of staff and Marshall serving as secretary of state, General J. Lawton Collins headed a small group charged with planning for service unification. In this context, the reorganization of the military establishment came to be debated in the Congress. Marshall was called upon to present his views and was expected to play an important role in the decision-making. As things turned out, his contribution was minor. He supported two major reforms that were initially included but then dropped. He wanted both a single chief of staff directly serving the president and he sought the retention of the JCS to both advise the new secretary of defense and take a part in both war planning and budgetary matters. The Navy strongly objected to Marshall's insistence that JCS recommendations must reach the president even if opposed by the secretary of defense. Marshall's view that the president deserved to have the military's unfiltered professional advice in any decisions involving armed force did not prevail (J. Collins 1958, 13).

Reorganizing at State

Many of the same principles Marshall used in reorganizing the war machinery were repeated when he assumed leadership of the Department of State in 1947 (Acheson 1969, Lovett 1973), and, to a lesser extent, when he became Secretary of Defense in 1950 (Lovett 1973, 52-53). In 1946, before his return to the states from China but after being informed of his designation by the president as the next secretary of state, Marshall had his former aide at both the Pentagon and in China, Marshall Carter, sent into the department with instructions to look over the organizational situation and report back. Carter found more than a dozen persons who exercised near-autocratic power in their areas of responsibility with no real coordination among them (Carter 1959, 24; Pogue 1987, 144-150)

When he arrived at State Marshall hired Frank McCarthy as Assistant Secretary for Administration to analyze and regularize the staff decision process. McCarthy found that internal authority relations had been established with little attention given to communications and coordination; McCarthy became so frustrated over his futile efforts to change the dynamics that he left the agency after a few months. Carter stayed on to assist Marshall in the transition (Carter 1959, 13). Specifically, under Secretary Byrnes's patrician form of stewardship, a personal style of management had become the rule throughout the department. Byrnes operated by working out a set of individualized relations with the heads of various offices, regional desks, and special program areas. Each of these people had personal access to him and he negotiated with each in isolation. Policy and implementation decisions were made behind closed doors without any systematic effort to ensure that other interested parties had input. Assistant secretaries routinely screened ambassadorial reports intended for the secretary and if they happened to disagree with the ambassador on either their analysis or recommendations respecting a particular country, then the assistant secretary's report was all the secretary saw. The faithful communication of the ambassador's observations and recommendations often disappeared or was altered in the process of being transmitted to the secretary. The result was that a decision could be made or affirmed by the secretary that never had the benefit of the ambassador's perspective (Acheson 1957, 4; Acheson 1969).

Marshall kept all State Department administrators. By this intentional non-act he gained many advantages: (1) he demonstrated that he trusted and valued the officials that were already in harness (some of extraordinary quality), thereby ensuring their loyalty; (2) he allayed fears that he would pack the department with old military people and run it like the Army (Carter 1959, 18-19); and (3) he elevated the status of seasoned professional diplomatic hands with experience in international relations.

Next, Marshall undertook to radically change the organizational structure and functions along the lines that he had developed in the War Department. The goal was to create a decision process that would bring to bear on each decision all the major facts and analytical talents that the various units of the department could muster (Carter 1959, 16-19). All matters for decision were to come through the office of the undersecretary (the first man in this position was Acheson) who would make sure that all important factors had been analyzed and the decision options clearly outlined. Then Acheson was to prioritize the decisions to be made by Marshall and make the minor ones himself, thereby preserving Marshall's energies and focusing his attention on the more important ones. In effect, the undersecretary became Marshall's chief of staff, the conduit through which all must pass in order to get the secretary's attention. This was a sharp departure from the prior practice at State in which the secretary acted on private understandings without input from other offices that might have relevant material to contribute (Carter 1959, 24; Lovett 1973, 52-53).

Carter, followed by Carlisle Humelsine, was interposed in the new position of Executive Secretary between the department's various units and Acheson. Humelsine, one of only three men brought over from the Pentagon (Carter and Brig. Gen. Charles H. Bonesteel were the others), was to be responsible for coordinating information and communication that would come to the undersecretary. This operation was similar to the Secretary of the General Staff's function at the War Department. Hummelsine received information copies of all overseas communications. These were screened and the important ones reviewed by Marshall every morning in the form in which they arrived. He relied on the executive secretary and his office, the Secretariat, to "insure that all facets (of the issue) were in the advice given" by the assistant secretaries in economic and political areas (Carter 1959, 20). If the assistant secretaries had conflicting views, or if studies or reports on the subject of the report existed in the department, these were collected by Hummelsine and presented *in addition to* the ambassador's report to the undersecretary under a covering summary.

The third organizing move was the establishment of a strong planning office, setting a precedent for non-military departments. Seeing the need for a group of intelligent, progressive people to specialize in policy-scanning and planning for the long term, Marshall established the Planning and Policy staff (PPO) (Pogue 1987, 151) and sought a person with vision to lead it who could think ahead about trends and policy options in the field of international relations, especially Soviet affairs. His consultation with Acheson and others produced two persons who fit: George Kennan and Charles ("Chip") Bohlen. He hired both although he had not previously worked with either. Kennan came on to head the PPO, and Bohlen was picked to serve as special counsel for Soviet affairs. Kennan then selected the PPO officers.

One of the effects of the reorganization was to raise the status of ambassadors and the stature of their opinions, in much the same way as theater commanders were favored over headquarters staff in WW II. The assistant secretaries came to act as coordinative administrators for various geographical or functional areas of interest. Their views were taken into account but were not allowed to be substituted for those of the ambassadors. The coordinative function of both the executive secretary and the undersecretary guaranteed that these disagreements were recognized and the various views developed and supported, thus ensuring that more informed decisions would emerge. Marshall rarely made a decision affecting a particular nation without first contacting the ambassador directly and getting his or her thoughts on the matter being considered (Carter 1959, 16-17):

> General Marshall looked to two sources for political advice, in a particular area or in a particular country. He looked to the ambassador of that country as one source, and he expected that ambassador to give him the full, rounded picture, and he looked to the Assistant Secretary of State, who was charged with that primary responsibility in the State Department to advise him (Carter 1959, 21).

Marshall and the undersecretary met and talked every morning to ensure they were similarly informed; the undersecretary could then act for the secretary on most matters (Lovett 1973, 60). The door between their offices remained opened.

Marshall felt it was important to make reorganizational changes quietly and quickly, a lesson he had learned and followed in the reorganization of the War Department (Carter 1959, 19). Order and rationality in the decision process came rather easily as a result (Carter 1959, 14-16; Lovett 1973, 51-53). "It was just a question of making the damn thing work as simply and as easily as possible" Carter said, adding:

> We were operational before people had realized what we were trying to do, and then as soon as they realized the service that they were getting from the executive secretariat, then we had no trouble at all (Carter 1959, 19, 21).

As secretary of state, Marshall preferred to function as the chief implementer of the president's policies and not the independent policy maker Truman invited him to be. In this, he was extending his traditional view of just what his proper constitutional role consisted. He allowed decisions and policy recommendations to arise from below on the basis of institutional analysis, full factual development, and professional expertise. The resulting recommendations went to the president.

The new arrangement was almost entirely dependent on the professional staff people of the State Department. It earned for Marshall their deep respect and fierce loyalty. For the long term, Marshall appointed ambassadors from among the ranks of foreign service officers rather than basing appointments on political patronage, a practice which strengthened professionalism within the department as appointment could be used as a reward for professional excellence (Carter 1959, 24).[15]

Acheson was not wholly satisfied with the decision model that Marshall had worked out. He felt that since Marshall had the ear of the president and was his right arm for foreign policy, he should let his advisors and administrators know *in advance* what the president thought and said about different policy issues. In this way, these officers would be given some direction and would not waste their time developing initiatives having little chance of survival in the event they reached the president's office.

Acheson's view clashed with how Marshall liked to approach policy-making; the general persisted in using his own style. His preference was to assemble all the facts and collect all the opinions unprompted and uncolored by his own or the president's views, often using the device of a plenary meeting of the major participants. He would conclude the meeting by saying how it looked to him and what must be done, and then give his advisers one more chance to change his mind (Carter 1959, 23; Shames 2005). Soon thereafter the decision was made and the major implementing actions taken simultaneously.[16]

The reorganized decision system that Marshall engineered at State resulted in decisions that reflected rationality, completeness, and political sophistication, and they had monumental and positive effects. The major initiatives of the department during his tenure included the creation and implementation of the European Recovery Program (ERP or "Marshall Plan"), the Truman doctrine, and the creation of NATO.

Organizing the Marshall Plan

Marshall and Kennan and Bohlen, the PPO and the Senate Foreign Relations committee under Vandenberg built into the ERP a number of innovative features that were to drive the Plan's ultimate organization and processes. Europe, acting collectively, became an integral part of the Plan's design. The participation of the European states was assured through the device of making them an offer they could not refuse: "if you come up with an integrated economic plan for development in your countries, we will give you the money and provide technical assistance to make it happen." Both Kennan and Marshall believed that ultimate economic recovery depended principally on integrating economic and political efforts within Europe.

European donee nations were required to initiate the process by defining feasible projects that were within the capacity of America to fund or otherwise support through the exportation of goods, equipment, technical expertise, or financial credit. The meshing of American largesse and technology and European development needs would require careful coordination. Huge incentives for American industry and politicians lay in the fact that excess American economic and agricultural productive capacity hungered for new customers and expanded markets. If foreign governments were given the capital and used it for development, economic growth would be assured in both Europe and America. The goods that could fuel economic development in Europe would be defined broadly to include basic foods and raw materials needed for survival of European laborers, monies for reducing international debt balances, and machinery and building materials that could be used to produce power, operate utilities, produce machines and factories, and enable large-scale mining.

A tripartite organizational scheme was designed to implement the four year program. The first part of the structure to form was the collective of sixteen donee nations brought together by the Conference for European Economic Cooperation (CEEC), organized by Bevin and led by Sir Oliver Franks of Great Britain and Jean Monnet of France. This group set about analyzing the resources and capabilities of the sixteen nations that met in Paris immediately after Marshall's Harvard speech. The conference reached preliminary agreement on what each country should be expected to accomplish and what aid it would require (Price 1955, 36-37). The CEEC would eventually ripen into the more permanent Organisation for European Economic Co-operation (OEEC) in April, 1948.

The second piece of the organizational architecture was the Economic Cooperation Administration (ECA), which came into being at the insistence of the chairman of the Senate Foreign Relations Committee. Vandenberg wanted the steering operation to be in the hands of an organization politically independent and distinct from the State Department. Marshall, Lovett, and Harriman also favored this course of action, persuaded by arguments for "leadership skilled in practical economic operations" that was freed from "the conduct of continuing, long-term relationships" characteristic of a long-established government agency (Price 1955, 251). At the urging of both Vandenberg and Acheson, President Truman selected the Republican Paul Hoffman to lead the ECA (Price 1955, 71-72). Hoffman had experience as president of Studebaker Automobile and had worked on foreign assistance and in arms production during the war, where he had interacted productively with Marshall. ECA was to oversee the solicitation and approval of project requests, provide technical assistance, and ensure transparency and accountability for each project.

Hoffman was an excellent choice. He set to work immediately constructing the ECA[17] to last four years, its authorized duration. He insisted that all planning had to be done by the OEEC and conceived of the ECA as a type of investment banker. He and his people decided that the ECA staff should intensively study and coordinate individual country programs (Price 1955, 73-75).

The third piece of the organizational machinery grew out of the decision to individualize the program on a country to country basis. A set of "country missions" was created by the State Department and headed by Averell Harriman within the Office of the Special Representative (OSR). The OSR was a large force of experts, bipartisan in makeup, which was to serve as a regional headquarters of the ECA. The special quality of the country missions was that they were composed of exactly the kind of experts that fit the projects proposed in each country (Price 1955, 75-77) and were people of stature who could deal directly with the OEEC.

Once a country's project was approved by the ECA, purchasing was done only by the participating nation. This arrangement had the advantages of avoiding a large, costly procurement bureaucracy and making use of private trade channels within the US, while avoiding the guiding of business to suppliers for political reasons. Keeping corrupt practices to a minimum was accomplished by strict screening by the ECA under carefully crafted procurement procedures performed by expert staff (Price 1955, 78).

One Marshall contribution to the organizing brilliance of the ERP was his wise choice not to seek a dominating role in its implementation and to place his confidence in Hoffman and the Europeans. The whole, complex organization was put together rapidly and about four-hundred million dollars were allotted in the first four weeks following enactment of the program. Marshall remained in the background during this phase but consulted frequently with Hoffman and Harriman, sometimes directly and sometimes through Lovett.

The impact of the ERP is well documented both in its general and specific nation effects (Price 1955). The earliest, immediate actions centered on the supply of critical foods, fuel, and fertilizers and other raw materials. These assisted basic survival and delivered an immediate psychological relief to Europeans. Middle-range effects coming one to two years after the beginning of the ERP were the building of productive capacity through the delivery of machinery and factory parts and facilitating the acquisition of capital. The allocation of funds to donee nations and the way these nations chose to use what they got varied greatly.[18]

Considerable stress was placed on integrating West Germany's economy into the general European community on terms acceptable to France. By 1949 the European Coal and Steel Community (ECSC) was formed, a common pool for coal and steel production which had been agreed to by France and West Germany.

Creation of the ECSC was a huge achievement as it represented a breakthrough in regional governance and in the cooperation of traditional enemies, the practical equivalent of a peace treaty between France and Germany.

Through their collective actions in organizing Plan projects, donee nations were laying the foundations of long-term relations among themselves and between Europe and America. One long-term consequence was the reduction of trade barriers and tariffs among OEEC countries, which led successively to other inter-European bodies of cooperative economic and political decision making: the Organisation for Economic Co-operation and Development (OECD), the Common Market and, ultimately, the European Union. Another consequence was the North Atlantic Treaty Organization (NATO). Economic development flowing from the Marshall Plan was somewhat reduced because Congress changed the funding priorities in the last two years of the program from economic development to military assistance.[19]

Seen in broad perspective sixty years after its inception, the most important long-term effects of the Marshall Plan, besides its contribution to West Europe's economic recovery, were the political and economic integration of Europe, a certain degree of psychological bonding between the peoples of Western Europe and America, and the cementing of the cross-Atlantic alliance that has anchored American and European foreign policy up to the end of the Cold War and beyond. Not coincidentally, through its economic impact, it fostered democratic politics and helped to foil Soviet designs for weakening Western Europe democracies and laying them open to the spread of Communist and Soviet political influence. In sum, the Marshall Plan is properly regarded as perhaps the outstanding example of economic statesmanship in American history.

Marshall's Organizational Style and Impact: Conclusions

The organizing and reorganizing activities presented in this chapter demonstrate Marshall's keen understanding of how a studied manipulation of organizational structures, dynamics, and processes can lead to an increase in organizational effectiveness. They also give evidence of the organizational philosophy and management style of Marshall as discussed in the preceding chapter. Of central importance to Marshall's thinking and actions was building organizations capable not only of surviving, but also of growing, changing their missions and practices to serve changing needs, and learning from their successes and failures.

Building a Learning Organization

The "learning organization" contains within its core the ability to *teach itself to learn from its experience, including its mistakes and false assumptions as well as its successes, and from scanning its changing environment, in order to better adapt and succeed in its current and evolving missions.*

Several indicators of the learning organization are found in Marshall's philosophy and practices: (1) placing stress on developing sound factual bases for making decisions; (2) accurate recording of organizational memory and history so as to permit tracking progress and permitting planning over time; (3) placing a high priority on scanning the organization's environment and to stress the organization's planning and policy-making activities to allow the organization to respond to change in timely and rational ways; (4) cultivating communication and interaction between and among all units within the organization and with relevant external entities; (5) promoting thoughtful reflection and encouraging rather than simply permitting constructive criticism of organizational processes and actions; and (6) providing a climate that encourages members of the organization to accept orderly and rational change.

How did Marshall's leadership build the capacity in organizations to learn? First, he used a combination of authority, teaching ability, and the example of his personal virtues and practices to influence behaviors conducive to reflection, skepticism, and open questioning. He encouraged his subordinates and associates to be critical of him, to question current organizational methods, and to put forward and defend their own ideas for change and the actions to test them. Second, he systematically built into his organizations relatively autonomous planning and policy units, staffed them with bright, usually younger people, gave them mental space and respect which allowed them to work according to their own lights, and gave them direct access to the organization's top-level fact-finders and decision makers. Finally, he created a climate in which their outputs were taken seriously and likely applied by those decision makers.

Reorganizations in the offices of the Army Chief of Staff, the Department of State, and the Department of Defense were all designed in part to achieve these ends. Also, the efforts were often planned to go along with changes in external, parallel organizations. For example, the 1941-1942 War Department reorganization was accompanied by pushing forward coordinated planning activities with the Department of the Navy. Also, both the 1947 reorganization in State and the 1950 reorganization in Defense consciously stimulated the coordination of planning and joint operation activities between the two departments.

Another critical element in building a learning organization is the willingness to use experimentation and research to expose both ineffective and effective practices and premises for action. If outcomes, errors as well as achievements, can be linked to causes, procedures can be developed to improve performance. Marshall was not at all bothered by the potential embarrassment that could be associated with exposing error in his organization so long as the source of the error could be discovered and then either eliminated or at least mitigated. Blaming those associated with bad consequences was not regarded by Marshall as a remedy, particularly if the error was traceable to system failure rather than human failure. The best course of action was for organizational leaders to correct the organizational practice or mind-set that was responsible for creating the error and strengthen the practice or mind-set that led to a positive result.

An example involves the US Army discovery in 1940 that B-17 "Flying Fortress" bombers, which had been supplied to the British complete with bombsights, were not being used in battle though they were superior in mobility, speed, and in other technical ways to British bombers. American air officers, assuming that the British did not know enough about the equipment to use it properly, were doubly irked because the planes were badly needed for training American pilots. Marshall, on the other hand, began with the belief that encountering problems was an opportunity for learning and improvement.

Assuming that since the British were doing the fighting they must have special understanding of both advantages and disadvantages of the equipment performing under combat conditions, Marshall pressed the British Royal Air Force for an assessment of the plane's battle worthiness. They reported that although superior technologically to British craft, the lack of tail guns made it likely the planes would be shot down by enemy interceptor planes. With certain modifications the bombers could be made more effective without loss of their technical excellence (Bland 1991, 264-65), and this was done.

The same lesson was later applied when the British made known their disapproval of an American tank model despite its greater mobility (Pogue 1966, 65-67). According to Marshall:

> We just didn't understand them and they certainly didn't understand us. And they had information as to the battle efficiency of things that we just refused to accept. And yet we were without experience in the matter. We did have experience in the mobility of tanks because we could do that without a battle, but in the fighting of the tank we had that quite wrong (Pogue 1966, 67).

The Army internalized the practice of trading ideas on effectiveness with the British and trusting them. Both sides were found to be right and wrong. The practice of unilateral testing was abandoned and a new process involving cooperation and battle testing evolved to solve multiple weapons problems. The keys to the new procedure had been the development of an attitude of mutual respect and a practice of cooperative inquiry.

The last and current chapters have focused primarily on organizational philosophy and design and the management of tasks and processes. In the next chapter, ideas and practices relating to people, managing them and making them into leaders, are taken up. The mostly harmonious outcomes that have been described did not come about without conflict—personal, organizational, and societal—over the allocation of responsibility and power. Telling the story of how Marshall managed and inspired people in the organizations he led will lend additional insight into the nature of his ethical leadership.

Notes

1. A "reorganization" is defined to include a reforming (or original forming) of structures, processes, and positions relating to a specific organizational unit and its activities. The resulting organization system may alter former jurisdictional lines, authority patterns, and decision processes and redefine the missions of the parent and constituent organizations.

2. Marshall revered Baker as a wise and patient man.

3.   It is certainly ironic that when Pershing was made chief of staff in 1920 he found much merit in strengthening the hand of the COS, at least in peacetime (Watson 1950, 60-61).

4.   "He even asked for preliminary drafts to be sent up, so that his early review would act to blunt the need for later rejections or changes" (Cline 1951, 65-66).

5.   It lends some perspective to the load being borne by Marshall to note that the WPD staff at this point in time was less than ten percent of the size of the German general staff.

6.   The other close advisor, General McNair, was the single deputy chief of staff who left after the reorganization

7.   Like Marshall, Stimson believed that the single commander policy would avoid much of the tragic loss of life and territory that resulted from the haphazard assembling and cooperation of allied forces in WW I, in which he had participated as an artillery officer (Pogue 1966, 281).

8.   Marshall's comfortable relations with the British were such that, in anticipation of his being appointed supreme commander in Europe in 1944, he stated his preference for the British General Frederick Morgan to be his chief of staff. He brought Morgan to the US to familiarize him with the activities of Washington headquarter operations and to attend all critical briefings (Handy 1956, 6). He discovered, however, "that the principal British leader (presumably Churchill) was violently, almost vindictively, opposed to him" (Bland 1991, 322).

9.   Deane (1960) recalled to Pogue: "For instance, one of the things he did for the British that they will never forget was when he sent over three hundred guns to the Far East. They were anti-tank guns of some sort and they were capsized in the middle of the ocean. He immediately sent another three hundred without being asked to. He sent some ammunition that we could ill-afford to send at that time. The British were very grateful for that. I think in a great many instances he deferred to the Navy if he thought it was in the best interest [of the country]. He always kept sight of the big picture and never just his own particular interest."

10.   Brooke, a strong personality himself and a brilliant intellect, might have contended for leadership but hurt himself by being overly partisan to the British side and none too tactful; tendencies obvious to the other British chiefs as well as the US chiefs (Deane 1960, 14).

11.   The elements of the JCS were later sanctioned in a Roosevelt executive order.

12.   Marshall said in 1957: "Even though Leahy's time was more completely given to attending the president in his political meetings, nevertheless, it was quite essential to have the arrangement as it was, because it would never have done to have tried to have gone right straight through the struggle with Admiral King in a secondary position and me as the senior, where I was also the senior of the air. And it was quite essential that we have a neutral agency at the top, and Leahy, in effect, was that so far as the army and navy requirements and positions were concerned" (Bland 1991, 433).

13.   President Truman put the matter plainly, when he later said, "everyone knew exactly the qualities of General Marshall . . . he was not an overbearing man. . . . He had the ability to get along with people, and people wanted to work with him because they knew he was trying to do the right thing" (Truman 1960, 4).

14.   Harold Seidman's classic study of reorganization concluded that reorganizations were typically motivated by considerations of power, politics, or positional authority, and not by considerations of economy or efficiency (Seidman 1970).

15.   Political considerations sometimes interfered with this practice.

16. Action elements would be the obligation of the executive secretary and the undersecretary to prepare in order to fairly present and support each of the major decision options. According to both Lovett and Carter, he had acted in this way in the Army and was to repeat the method later as secretary of defense (Carter 1959, 24).

17. Donald C. Stone, an experienced government administrator and future dean of the Graduate School of Public and International Affairs at the University of Pittsburgh, was selected to head a special task force to work out the organizational pattern.

18. The United Kingdom received about twenty-five percent of the total funds and used it for debt retirement. France (twenty percent) used its share for capital investment, mostly in the coal and steel industries. Italy and West Germany (ten percent each) used theirs for capital investment. The Netherlands received 8.4%, Greece 5.5%, Austria 5.2%, Belgium 4.3%, and the other nine nations combined (including Sweden and Switzerland, non-combatants but to some degree affected by the war) the remaining 11.5%.

19. Truman referred to the Marshall Plan and NATO aid as "two halves of the walnut." Strobe Talbott has described the dual phenomena as a combination of hard and soft power.

CHAPTER TEN
LEADING OTHERS

It is the love of the people; it is their attachment to their government, from the sense of the deep stake they have in such a glorious institution, which gives you your army and your navy, and infuses into both that liberal obedience, without which your army would be a base rabble, and your navy nothing but rotten timber.
—Edmund Burke, *Speech on Conciliation with America*, March 22, 1775

The core of transformational leadership is the ability to change the organization by changing its people. In this chapter several aspects of Marshall's interpersonal skills and attributes are examined in detail—teacher, trainer, judge of talent, concern with morale, ability to separate the person from the problem, tolerance of error, and motivator. These skills and attributes complement those discussed in the previous two chapters to explain the nature of transformational and ethical leadership, and the legitimacy of the claim that Marshall is an ideal example of this type of leadership.

Teacher and Educator

The ability to teach is an underappreciated but important function of leadership, and for Marshall, a constant feature of his particular brand of ethical leadership. Much of his success is undoubtedly explained by the value he placed on the educational function.

Occupying the roles of educator and teacher may have laid the basis for his ability to judge talent and assess strengths and weaknesses of people. In fact, his activities and observations at Benning directly led to his identification of a lengthy list of excellent officers who became the backbone of Army command and administration in WW II. The cognitive content of what he taught and had others teach explains most of this outcome; communicating the process of organizational problem-solving explains the rest.

Mostly, the subjects which Marshall taught were the stuff of professional knowledge, but they represented his understanding of the things he had critically observed and that went on around him. He missed little and integrated all of what he remembered, and his memory was considerable, into teachable lessons. The observations came from a variety of staff assignments, including many in which he was left free to experiment and to learn from doing. His first intensive learning occurred well after attending VMI, while he was both a student and an instructor at Fort Leavenworth, Kansas from 1906 to 1908. There, he cultivated within himself a passion for self-discipline. Also, in that place, he was in the unique position of instructing and evaluating student-officers who were both older and of higher rank. The challenge in doing this and the respect he earned from his more senior students could only enhance his self-confidence in his ability to teach.

Curiosity about all manner of things drove Marshall to go beyond subjects of military organization and tactics. His inquiry into horses and horsemanship was one example. Foreign language and culture fascinated him, French and Mandarin Chinese in particular. He traveled widely when he was able and in his travels added to his store of knowledge about warfare, as he had done in Japan in 1915.[1] He studied the contemporary history of the Philippine Islands. He studied politics in the company of Pershing, making the rounds of political capitals and sampling the political climate in Washington. He became an avid reader, a fan of movies, a hunter and a fisherman, and enjoyed horticulture. To expand the amount of time available to indulge his love of learning he avoided social events, spectator sports, partisan politics, and dining out.

Much of what he learned he enjoyed passing on to others in the hope that they would make similar connections to their professional lives as he had. For example, he made sure that his officers at Tientsin were taught Chinese and encouraged them to use language and cultural knowledge in performing their duties:

> He was intensely observant and . . . having studied Chinese . . . conversed with them quite extensively . . . and it must have made a great impression on them (Barrett 1959, 4, 6).

Developing others often occurred in the pursuit of increasing officer and troop morale and extended to recreation and community life. Development often included the families of the men with the goal of enhancing the values of family life within the community. Wherever he commanded, libraries were expanded, programs of cultural enrichment (including plays, concerts, dances, and competitions) were organized, and facilities for religious instruction were made available. His intense curiosity and educational zeal astonished his peers:

> There was nothing that he didn't become interested in, and when he became interested in something he got to the bottom of it, and if he thought something should be changed or improved or that we should do something, he started in on the business, and he would see it through (Gallagher 1962, 43).

On joining the Chief of Staff's office in 1938 he took on the task of educating himself about air power, enlisting Arnold and Andrews in the quest. He toured the nation's air production and training centers with Andrews. Arnold later recalled that Marshall had been an eager student:

> The difference in George, who presently was to become one of the most potent forces behind the development of a real air power, was his ability to digest what

he saw and make it part of as strong a body of military genius as I have ever known (Arnold 1949, 163-164).

Training, Training, and More Training

The professional activity that ignited Marshall's passion more often than any other was training, especially infantry training. No branch of the army required as much training as the infantry because of the changing conditions and hardships under which it labored.

A major, recurring feature of Marshall's career was organizing, conducting, and evaluating large-scale military maneuvers. Beginning with the Pennsylvania State National Guard in 1907, and continuing with other state National Guard and Regular Army units up through 1915, these intense mutual learning experiences laid the foundation for the pivotal leadership role he would play as an educational innovator at Fort Benning from 1927 to 1932. Large scale training projects continued at Forts Screven and Moultrie and then intensified with the Illinois National Guard when he was assigned to the Illinois 33rd Division in Chicago.

These assignments usually involved designing, overseeing, and evaluating maneuvers and war games involving multiple units and thousands of troops. Experimentation with differing scenarios and varying the combinations of type and numbers of troops permitted new insights into tactical and logistical factors. It allowed him to observe the interaction of battlefield conditions with decisions and behaviors of field commanders under conditions of stress and shifting circumstances. The lessons learned were used to adapt training methods to differing conditions with an eye attuned to the war to come.

Training was the preeminent military function in both wars, as combat readiness of the military units far outranked the factor of mere numbers:

> He used to talk about the necessity of always having so many men in every division up against the enemy, and he used to complain about the talk of divisions, the numbers game. . . . Unless you could have a division fairly constantly at the front, constantly pressing its energies against the enemy, there wasn't that much sense in talking about the number of divisions . . . and he kept saying that a division is just a skeleton through which you move trained men, and to keep that flowing, to keep that speeded up was all that you needed, and that there should be no break in that continuity (McCloy 1959, 2).

His attention to training could appear to be obsessive. At Tientsin he gave intense personal attention to the detailed training of small groups of soldiers, including giving direct supervision to infantry squad firing and the critique of small squad performance in field exercises. Some felt this was beneath the dignity of a lieutenant colonel second in command of a regiment, to personally involve himself instead of delegating the responsibility, but others recognized in his actions the extraordinary importance he attached to training:

. . . that was really part of the essence of George Marshall, that basically when he thinks there is something that should be done that demands his personal attention, why he follows it right down . . . this is a strength and not a weakness that he's showing. . . . It's a place to do a job and do it very, very thoroughly and by golly he's doing it (Betts 1958, 2-3).

To the accusations of some that he was a military martinet and too much of a "spit and polish" man, he pled guilty to the spit and polish part but regarded attention to detail as evidence of a general state of discipline within a command. At the same time he believed that formality and procedure could be overdone, especially when it takes time away from large-scale field training. The latter demands absorption and imagination so as to intrigue the soldier and requires so much movement, territory, and expense that it is not easy to mount, particularly in peacetime. "I was intent on it and I made myself very unpopular" (Bland 1991, 251-252).

Marshall believed that corps and field army operational proficiency could only be attained through large-scale maneuvers. They were "a great college of leadership for the higher officers" and a "wonderful practical schooling" for younger leaders and their men (Bland, Ritenour, and Wunderlin 1986, 41-42, 56-57). As illustration, he discussed how hard it was to teach the need for air-ground teamwork and to have the airman, in particular, understand what his proper mission is until he is pressured by soldiers with life and death needs in the heat of battle (Bland 1991, 480). To approach the realism required for effectiveness, trainers with actual combat experience are needed. For this reason he opposed the efforts of Stimson to bring about an overly rapid expansion in the number of trainers early in WW II. Training markedly improved in the states once wounded men could be recovered from France and used as trainers. It was even better in England, "where they were pretty close to the conflict and saw the scars and strokes of some of the conflict" (Bland 1991, 481).

Military Officer Education is Multi-Phasic

The educative function in the preparation of military officers was seen by Marshall as multi-phasic. It begins with physical conditioning, obedience to command, and introduction to the fundamentals of military organization that are basic to the training of the common soldier. Next comes instruction in the realm of military tactics and especially logistics, critical in the preparation of the line officer. There follows the imparting to prospective higher-ranking officers, especially command officers, of an employee-centered philosophy of leadership. Training for leadership must focus on creating and maintaining general morale within the organization, motivating, promoting *self-discipline* to replace imposed discipline, delegating responsibility accompanied by the extension of trust, and throughout, inculcating a code of personal ethics. These phases are further described in the following paragraphs, along with the special problems of training national guard officers and inter-service cooperation.

(1) Basic military training

All recruits, including officers and troops, should be indoctrinated as to the reasons for the war effort. This was especially true because they would not be fighting to defend their homeland where the reason to fight is obvious and easily appreciated. When war is waged in strange places, the reasons for enduring hardship and the inevitable monotony of service duties must be convincingly explained. To help in this effort for the great mass of Army recruits he asked Frank Capra, the leading motion picture director of the era, to prepare films that would inform soldiers as to why they were being asked by their nation to break their normal routines, separate from their loved ones, and risk life and limb. The result was the film series, *Why We Fight*.

Training the infantry, troops and officers alike, was more difficult and required a more concentrated regimen than the training of any other military unit. Infantry operated under the most severe hardships of any military duty: fatigue, mud, filth, sweat, the stench of rotting flesh, long marches, battling mostly unseen forces, and enduring alternating periods of intense boredom, panic, and adrenalin flow (Pogue 1966, 87). Romanticism and hollow appeals to patriotism, Marshall felt, should play no role in training for war. To properly prepare the infantry soldier for what was to come, training had to be rigorous and acclimate the soldier to hardship, but without endangering his health. To this end, proper clothing, food, and medical care were mandatory. Yet, more was required:

> The greatest problem of wartime training . . . was to continue long enough with the basic training, of which they were all impatient. And it is dull, and it is long, and it is very strenuous, and unless it is well done, thoroughly done, the troops are going to be lacking in discipline and performance from that time on. And yet it is very hard to have them see the reason for it. . . . The men can never understand how intense this [training] must be in order to register in long drawn-out engagements and over the severities of a battlefield experience (Bland 1991, 468; Bland and Stevens 1996, 98-99).

He had honed his approach to training at Fort Benning's infantry officer school. There, he had abandoned the study of classical models that had been used in his own training and replaced them with simulated exercises employing battlefield conditions so far as they could be imagined in the context of the war to come: confusion, rapid movement, and the heavy use of the airplane as a tactical weapon. Recalling his WW I experience, he wanted his officers to think on their feet in the midst of confusion and fire and not to be handicapped by the detailed field orders that could be irrelevant by the time they reached the front (Bolte 1958, 49).

Infantry school instructors were asked to make a number of assumptions. Staff officers of the next war were today's civilian shoe clerks. Conditions in the field would reflect the inevitable fog and uncertainty of war (Bolte 1958, 41). There must be a willingness to experiment with and embrace methods that were theoretical and untried. The airplane would be essential not only as a tactical field force, but also as a long-range strategic weapon. The essence of field combat was to be the proper integration of infantry with air, tanks, artillery, communications, and even, at times, sea power. Emphasis must be on coordination and communication and not on the notion of autonomous units working in isolation (Hilldring 1959, 4-6).

This new educational philosophy was spread to the command general staff school at Fort Leavenworth, then to the General Staff of the War Department when he later came to Washington, and ultimately to the entire army training establishment.

Not content with trusting anecdotes as evidence of the effectiveness of training, Marshall ordered a study to be conducted by professional fact-gatherers in WW II. Infantry soldiers were interviewed during their initial stateside training and then queried again, after experiencing combat, about the adequacy of their training. The findings confirmed Marshall's thinking. During their initial training, the men complained bitterly about elements of the rigorous, unglamourous, and discomfiting training forced upon them in domestic training camps. The very same men concluded after actual battle experience that they should have received more of this training before arriving on the front line (Bland 1991, 468).

(2) Officer training and the teaching of logistics

As his own experience and personal education grew through working with Pershing's headquarters in WW I, appreciation for the role of logistics and mobility in overall military effectiveness grew apace. Perhaps no military staff officer in history better understood logistics from the dual perspective of the front-line staff officer and that of the headquarters staff officer. In the midst of WW II, he reflected at length in his unprepared remarks to a convocation of state governors on the crucial importance of logistics:

> My education was sadly neglected. I find now I am more—far more—deeply concerned over matters of ship-building, over matters of landing craft, over matters of engines for them, over matters of octane gas and the means of producing—over all those thousands and one details that are necessary in order that we may bring our great forces to bear. We have been in the past in a situation feeling very secure behind oceans. We are now in a position that we have to cross those oceans, to carry the war to the enemy lest he carry the war to us. That involves *all the great factors of logistics.* . . . So that each thing we do has to be calculated far in advance. The allocations have to be made with great exactitude. *. . . All of that has to be calculated.* It isn't inspirational, it isn't the spur of the moment. It's a carefully thought out thing months and months and months in advance. . . . All of that must be brought to a head in due course and due time having all of these various interests of various countries and sovereign powers we're dealing with, brought into accord and agreement. . . . (Bland and Stevens 1996, 30, emphasis added).

Vast, multi-state training maneuvers involving many units and commands were launched by Marshall in South Carolina and Louisiana soon after becoming chief of staff. He thought it essential that in the coming war field commanders become knowledgeable about how to move huge concentrations of troops over vast territories and to quickly relocate headquarters, established lines of supply, and store reserves. The lack of commanders with WW I experience was a problem. These were the men, now excluded from command because of their age, who could remember the essentials of logistics and importance of mobility (Baruch 1961, 23).

New commanders desperately needed this training that commenced with half a million men engaged. Because the maneuvers were expensive and widespread geographically, they aroused criticism on both budgetary grounds and because they inconvenienced or damaged the property of local communities and citizens due to the all-too-amateurish movement of men and equipment. Marshall responded in exasperation to one senator's complaint:

> My God, Senator, that's the reason I do it. I want the mistake down in Louisiana, not over in Europe, and the only way to do this thing is to try it out, and if it doesn't work, find out what we need to make it work (Pogue 1966, 89).

As he told the 1941 graduating officer class at Fort Benning:

> Warfare today is a thing of swift movement—of rapid concentrations. It requires the building up of enormous firepower against successive objectives with breathtaking speed. It is not a game for the unimaginative plodder (Pogue 1966, 103).

(3) Officer training and the nature of command leadership

To Marshall, genuine leadership depended on convincing those in positions of "followership" that their self-interest was best served by pursuing legitimate public policy goals, even if in doing so their methods diverged from those above them in the hierarchy. While the quality of leadership is to some extent teachable, it cannot be imposed and must be earned. Those who would be leaders must learn the lessons through example and self-discipline and develop leadership qualities within themselves. Leadership cannot be learned through drills or following orders.

He typically used the technique of assigning younger officers to perform duties common to the rank just above their current rank. He would make room for the performance of these accelerated opportunities by pushing older, more senior officers into less necessary jobs. If the junior officer, carefully observed, performed well, he would be given additional responsibility, and if he could succeed in that, be given yet more. The pattern would continue until it was observed that progress was not achieved (Gallagher 1962, 43-44). Eisenhower was a case in point.

The search for capable command officers on the eve of WW I had been frantic and Marshall determined that the process embodied in the Plattsburgh program should not be repeated in preparation for WW II. Primary emphasis in the selection process was now to be placed upon the criteria of ability to coordinate command functions, and physical condition:

> Leadership in the field depends to an important extent on one's legs, and stomach, and nervous system, and on one's ability to withstand hardships, and lack of sleep, and still be disposed energetically and aggressively to command men, to dominate men on the battlefield (Pogue 1966, 97).

He had witnessed the collapse of otherwise worthy men in WW I who had lost the ability to command through physical or mental exhaustion. In such a state they could fail to properly look after the needs of soldiers and junior officers:

> I was very careful to watch out for that in World War II. If I found I was running into an officer that was sort of harassing everybody, I either relieved him or tamed him down right away, because it was very important that the High Command be understanding . . . (Bland 1991, 241).

The type of leadership training that evolved after WW I at Fort Leavenworth and West Point was not to Marshall's liking. He reported to Pershing in 1924 that leadership training at West Point was overly rigid and harsh discipline practices at the military academy were likely to create lasting animosity in the cadets subjected to it (Bland and Hadscl 1981, 252). He moved to remedy the situation in the fall of 1939 through expanding the concept of leadership in Fort Leavenworth's training program (Pogue 1966, 90).

Field testing became the primary basis for determining who should be given command assignments. The training maneuvers of 1940 and 1941 permitted observation and evaluation under simulated battle conditions. Although Marshall was familiar with senior commanders who had led troops in the last war, they were found wanting and he relieved them in a no-nonsense manner and without opportunity to appeal (Pogue 1966, 91):

> We have tried in every conceivable way to produce leaders. We have been perfectly ruthless about it. Quite so far as we could, *but the man has to have it or he doesn't stay* [emphasis is Marshall's]. And we listen to no excuses of any kind. Because . . . a division being fifteen thousand men my vote is all for the fifteen thousand and not for the individual [officer]. We must have the very best leadership we can possibly give these men and we've stopped at nothing to produce that leadership (Bland and Stevens 1996, 33).

(4) Training the National Guard

Extensive background with state National Guard units had given Marshall greater respect for typical National Guard soldiers than was typically possessed by Regular Army people, who tended to be dismissive of the "week-end warriors." The respect was mutual. Still, he saw great obstacles that stood in the way of their effective training. His attempts to remove them met with only partial success since the authority to lead the state guard units was outside the reach of the Department of War during peacetime.

The peacetime training of national guardsmen suffered from several handicaps. The first was that the law did not provide enough time for meaningful basic training. New guardsmen were introduced to military procedure, weaponry and equipment, and army drills and physical training in short bursts characterized by a short introductory period followed by once-a-week meetings and two weeks of summer camp. Second, the officers assigned to do the training, also guardsmen, were so preoccupied with their civilian pursuits that they could not properly instruct their students in either knowledge or physical components. A third problem was the corrosive role of politics in the selection of National Guard officers (Bland 1991, 255-256).

Training would be geared to prepare for responding to a military emergency so as to heighten the Army's immediate effectiveness. The training could be intensive and designed in a manner similar to that of the career training offered a Regular Army member, but delivered in an easier-to-digest form suited to a person without prior interest in becoming a military professional. If Congress failed to adopt the policy, many features of the training format could still be incorporated into National Guard training.

(5) Inter-Service Leadership Training

Truly effective leadership, in Marshall's view, dilutes the jealousies and competition common between units of government, whether these be service branches, civilian agencies, or offices within a single department or agency. This belief followed his view that true leadership pursues planning goals and their accomplishment independent of who makes the decisions or gets the credit.

An example of working together was the very first joint service school, proposed by the Army Air Forces in 1942. The Navy endorsed the idea but opposed its creation unless the school could be established as an adjunct of the Naval War College at Newport, Rhode Island, with Navy control of the curriculum. The Army wanted a total sharing of functions in order to promote learning. If problems arose in what should be taught and how to teach it, or if the exercises went badly, so much the better, as this would provide an opportunity to learn about the problems of coordinating different modes of thought. Marshall wanted the school at a neutral location and objected to the lack of logistics in the Navy's proposed curriculum:

> It did not appeal to me because it was the old tactical stuff, whereas the most important factor in Army-Navy Joint Staff work lies in non-detailed consideration of tactical employment for air, ground and naval vessels, with emphasis on air and logistics. Probably the latter [logistics] is the most important consideration of all, and the issue least understood. [Although] [t]he air battle is debated back and forth continuously, . . . the logistical factors are rarely ever discussed and practically never understood (Bland and Stevens 1996, 7).

Learning for the purpose of improving the effectiveness of the military mission, he argued, is a process of discovering and correcting error and developing best practices. To do this, there must be a concentration on anticipating actual conditions as realistically as possible in order to surface error rather than avoid or hide it. This is the essence of the learning organization and distinguishes this approach to leadership from one that seeks to protect the organization from outside criticism and resist demands for change.

General Qualities as a Teacher

What qualities explain Marshall's superiority as an organizational teacher? Matthew Ridgway noted a discernment and penetrating logic, and the facility for the expression of logic in a manner which carried conviction (1959, 12). At Tientsin and again with the Illinois National Guard, Ridgway had been inspired by Marshall's critiques of his, Ridgway's, demonstrations and training exercises and touched by his superior's generosity in giving him his time and counsel (Ridgway 1959, 1a, 5).

Students were met at their own level. Cumbersome instruction and techniques were simplified to fit the type of citizen-soldier he expected would dominate the ranks in the coming war (Bradley and Blair 1983, 64). When war came millions of people, mostly men of common background and limited education, would have to be rapidly and efficiently trained. It would be the Regular Army's task to impart a bewildering array of specialized knowledge to people who were not inclined to become military professionals. This huge challenge called for a "studied simplicity" in instructional methods, which he called for in a speech at Princeton University in November, 1949:

> . . . a virile, above-board, convincing simplicity that makes the student realize his own unlimited capabilities, and instills in him the desire or enthusiasm necessary for full development of those capabilities.[2]

Dean Rusk quoted Marshall's teachings as he prepared himself to lead the State Department in the 1960s. Take initiative, do not "sit around waiting for me to tell you what to do. . . . Tell me what you think I ought to be doing!" Inspire confidence: "Take heart! . . . Don't despair!" Act: "Don't fight your problems, deal with them!" Calm your people. When, during the Berlin blockade, Soviets and Americans came dangerously close to shooting at each other, Marshall put the situation into perspective "by recalling worse times . . . the miserable unpreparedness of the military just before . . . the two wars . . . and inspire thereby by painting a picture of just how bad things could get" (Rusk 1990, 131).

Preparing Leaders

No set of activities is more important in building an effective organization than selecting, developing, and promoting effective leaders. The beginning point is to select persons of strong ethical attributes with a potential for task performance. These persons must then be trained and placed in positions for which they are well suited. Marshall's ability to recognize and place talent was in part based on his many years as a teacher, trainer, and staff officer, from which positions he observed people functioning in field and office, in official Washington and in distant outposts, in simulated and actual combat, and in interaction with people of different socio-economic class and varying cultures.

The approach he used to teaching leadership is best illustrated in his educational reforms at Fort Benning. Before his arrival, the learning model had been the group-based analysis of classic problems drawn from famous battles used as set pieces. The new model focused on new situations incorporating changing methods, new weaponry, actual terrain in which the training was set, and creativity in defining unscripted problems. Making mistakes and correcting them enriched and personalized the learning process (Deane 1960, 3).

The classroom was in main part the field and the focus was on what could be observed, moved, recombined, or innovated, rather than on textbook "principles." Students were urged to act on original ideas rather than on written guidelines and to apply practical thinking to tactical and administrative problems (Bull 1959, 2-5). If a student came up with a solution to a tactical problem which was not in accord with the "approved" solution but made sense and was workable, Marshall instructed that it was to be published and read by the class (J. Collins 1958, 2-3).

Efficiency was prized. Instructors were directed to budget class time strictly and to end sessions at the point discussion naturally ended regardless of the schedule. Bull remembers Marshall saying to his instructors:

> The way to save time is to budget tightly, but if you find you can do it in half the time, you get a gold star from me for that. . . . Talk half the time and then go home and note on your schedule for next year thirty minutes instead of fifty minutes, and that means time for something more valuable (1959, 3).

Map-reading was emphasized. Students were given road maps lacking detail of land features and were challenged to fill in the gaps. In this way, the uncertainty of the battlefield could be more accurately simulated. At times, students would be asked to stop whatever they were doing and write down what they had observed on the way from their lodging to where they sat at the moment—road junctions, bridges, odors, and the like. The familiar path must be made explicit, the unnoticed noted. They became better observers, developed the capacity for analyzing and remembering terrain, skills they would carry to their infantry, artillery, supply, and other units during WW II (Bull 1959, 16; Collins 1958, 11-12; Deane 1960, 4).

Emphasis was upon spontaneity instead of pedantry. Instructors were to speak without notes but allowed to refer to an outline for guidance. They were expected to exchange views frequently with each other and with Marshall, who would often be "popping in and out of classes" and accompany classes to the field to observe exercises. Students and trainers were brought in from other nations, including Japan and Germany, to add to the richness of exchange.

Marshall saw to it that infantry school instructors were interchanged with instructors of the artillery school. An artillery battalion was added to the infantry school and an infantry battalion was added to the artillery school. The technique helped to break down the traditional hostility between these two service units and bring about a blend that produced "the best darn team that you could ever ask for" (Bull 1959, 3-4, 10).

Overriding all was the concept that the Army's mission of preparing for the *next* war was the relevant and central impetus. The unlikelihood that another world war would come was not allowed to influence the mission.[3] Teachers and students were challenged to think about all the things that could happen to troops and their employment as terrain changed, as weaponry evolved, as enemy air strength increased, as presence or absence of supporting artillery contributed, and so forth.

Another innovation was teaching officers to write and speak clearly, concisely, and simply. A field order was to be reduced to its essentials, taking into account the possibility that an officer would have to orally deliver it to save time and avoid confusion under battlefield conditions (Ridgway 1959, 4). Each student was assigned an historical battle or campaign to research for four months with the prospect of communicating it in a twenty-minute oral presentation supported by visual aids, accompanied by a written presentation within a set limit of pages. A buzzer was used to terminate the session, sometimes in mid-sentence. The idea was to compel the student to complete the mission under many constraints with time being of the essence. To demonstrate, Marshall stood before the class without notes and gave a summary of the Civil War, "the most beautiful little picture of the Civil War and what it was all about, how it started and finished, in five minutes" (Bull 1959, 7).

Judging Talent

Marshall's ability to judge, choose, and place able officers in jobs that matched their abilities was one of his supreme administrative talents (Pace 1959, 2). The act of choosing was closely bound up with the same thought processes that drove his talents as an educator. Beginning with his assignment at Fort Benning a pattern developed that was to continue: he asked people how they would approach a particular problem, he then parceled out responsibility to them to work on the problem, evaluated their performance, and then assigned new responsibilities on the basis of the evaluation. In this way he constantly acted as a mentor, a delegator, and as an evaluator of performance. He avoided stereotypes and chose from a wide variety of types of people, people who might have very little in common but who could do particular things under differing circumstances (Pasco 1997, 22).

When, as chief of staff, he looked for men to fill military command roles, he acted upon a rather specific set of criteria. He gave to his staff as a standard for higher troop command "the physical vigor of the average man of forty-five." While this did not totally exclude older men with unusual vigor, like George Patton, he strongly believed a younger core of field generals would be more effective in the long, grueling campaigns that could be anticipated (Bland and Stevens 1991, 187-188).

While Marshall tended to be rigid on the age criterion for command field officers, he was not rigid on the question of physical condition. During the war it was suggested that Major General Troy Middleton, suffering from an arthritic knee, be sent home rather than be given the command of a field corps. Marshall wrote: "I would rather have a man with arthritis in the knee than one with arthritis in the head. Keep Middleton there." Middleton was made commander of Eighth Army Corps (Bradley 1951, 30).

In addition to using his stated criteria of integrity, competence, and offensive-mindedness, Marshall was sensitive to these qualities: alertness, initiative, lack of self-seeking behavior, and energy. "Passive inactivity" while waiting for specific orders is "a serious deficiency" (Pogue 1966, 104). Such qualities were systematically sought in the officer training schools of the Regular Army, the Army Reserve, and the National Guard. He expressed to General Keehn in mid-1942 that there was no option to a rigorous, nonpolitical selection process:

> The pace of modern war has increased greatly the burdens on leaders of all ranks.
> Highly efficient and energetic leadership is essential to success. No compromise
> is possible (Bland and Stevens 1991, 251).

In wartime, under the pressure of battle, the search for leaders is accelerated and will overlook men who are conservative, or are perfectionists, or do not instantly impress subordinates as leadership material, or have had little opportunity to demonstrate their ability. The opportunity passes before such a person is identified (Marshall 1976, 172). To avoid missing this pool of talent, it is crucial to have identified such people before the crisis arises through the orderly development of qualifications and organized training.

Still, systematic training and selection does not eliminate the need for officers to step into leadership ranks as the battlefield takes its toll. It becomes necessary to find men "of the dashing, optimistic and resourceful type, quick to estimate, with relentless determination, and who possessed in addition a fund of sound common sense, which operated to prevent gross errors due to rapidity of decision and action" (Marshall 1976, 172). This could be a very special type of man, one who may be out of place in more normal settings. Under urgent conditions, being honest with one's own shortcomings and needs is critical in a leader, along with the ability to learn from experience and observation. A defensive attitude calculated to avoid embarrassment is unacceptable; making excuses and blaming others clearly indicate a lack of leadership talent (Marshall 1976, 171-174).

Failure is an opportunity for correction and growth and not a premise for terminating trust and responsibility. Marshall instinctively favored for leadership positions those who were "[e]nthusiastic in anticipation of the opportunity before them, but a little fearful of following in the footsteps of their deposed predecessors," and he praised those who "pressed for tips or advice on how to succeed under the conditions of battle" (Marshall 1976, 173). Those who could seek and listen to advice, rather than "occupying the time in dogmatically outlining their own views and opinion," were far more likely to succeed (Marshall 1976, 173-174).

The search for leaders must be coupled with the delegation of command—discretion should be lodged in the men and women further down the organization's hierarchy to provide opportunities both to lead and to discover leaders.

Perhaps it was the demonstrating of independence of mind and self-confidence that caused Marshall to often favor people for leadership roles who spoke their minds freely and also refused to promote themselves. Such people would be able to act for themselves and not find their way back to him when trouble came. Eisenhower recalled being told by Marshall: "I am trying to find people who will solve their own problems and not bring them all to me" (Eisenhower 1962, 13).

Marshall studied Eisenhower closely before choosing him for a succession of assignments to increasingly responsible positions, culminating with his appointment as Supreme Commander for the European theater. Marshall had been pleased to find Eisenhower thinking in offensive terms, despite scarce resources, as he labored on the General Staff to help plan the Pacific defense:

> Marshall saw in his subordinate a man whose calm confidence in ultimate victory was derived from a remarkably accurate appraisal of the Allied military potential; from a clear conception of the proportionate emphasis to be placed on sea, air, and ground arms; and from a profound sense of global strategy (Davis 1952, 288).

From his position on the General Staff, Eisenhower was next sent to London to arrange new American headquarters for the European theater. In making this assignment, Marshall was looking for talents appropriate to the role of "a possible architect of unity" (Davis 1952, 326), and was pleased by Churchill's warm reports on how Eisenhower was being received in England.

Non-Command Selection: The Right Person for the Right Job

The Army was faced in 1942 with heavy casualties in jungle warfare because of the lack of heavy weaponry to support ground troops. Marshall asked weapons engineer Colonel William Borden what could be done with existing firepower until new weaponry in production could be delivered. Borden responded by shaving existing anti-aircraft shells down to fit existing trench mortars, greatly increasing heavy artillery power at the front. Building on this success, Marshall set Borden to work looking for other efficiencies.

> Then I would send him over, wherever it was—later it was to Italy, I remember—then it was to the Pacific, and he'd have all these things displayed. I had them bring in all the principal officers . . . and they could indicate what they

wanted right there. He'd take the order and that would be shipped the next day from San Francisco. . . . When I sent a man like Borden over to the Ordnance Proving Grounds, I gave him a priority procedure that they would have to accept (Bland 1991, 266).

Many Reserve officers could be used extensively in administrative jobs because their personal goals were not to command troops but to serve for the short-term and get back to their civilian occupations (Pasco 1997, 49-50).

Marshall's unorthodox methods of matching needs to novel talents finds no better example than the case of John Hilldring. On Marshall's advice, Hilldring had reluctantly accepted in the early 1930s an appointment as the first line officer in Army history to be assigned to duty with the Medical Department. He later looked back on this assignment as a critically valuable career decision (Hilldring 1959, 2-3). A second cross-roads was reached early in the war when he was assigned to troop command in the southwest Pacific theater. As he prepared to leave for duty he suffered a heart attack and was hospitalized and set up for retirement by a medical board. He telephoned Marshall and acquainted him with the medical facts.

[I told Gen. Marshall] I'm a professional soldier in the middle of a war and how long I live I don't think is particularly significant to the Army. If I don't care I don't see why the Army should care. 'Well,' [Marshall] said, 'I don't either.' I said, General I'd like a job. Alright, he said, I've got one for you (Hilldring 1959, 35-36).

Marshall made Hilldring the first director of the new Civil Affairs Division (G-5) of the General Staff. The job required making and carrying out policy for the occupation of conquered territories, a function he was to shoulder for three years (Hilldring 1959, 36). He was destined to play a critical role in the difficult and necessary task of bringing the Army into a reluctant leadership role in civil governance.

The Hilldring case illustrates an ability to match special tasks to an appropriate set of talents. Typically, officers perceived by their wartime theater superiors as unfit for field command positions were channeled into dead-end jobs and career oblivion because field command was conventionally defined as the core of an officer's worth. Yet Marshall retained an interest in seeing whether the officer had skills or an orientation that promised success in non-command, staff positions or in command positions outside the zone of combat (GCM ltr, 5/6/1942; Bland and Stevens 1991, 187-188). The interest flowed in part from the unexpected effect of the 1940 policy preventing older officers from taking field command positions. These men could be and were often transferred to non-command posts in which their talents promised effectiveness undiminished by reason of being less vigorous. So it was that Marshall appointed a retired Army general officer, historian John McAuley Palmer, to head the task force he created in November 1942 charged with formatting a demobilization strategy, plan for occupation, and attending to issues related to the future of the citizen-soldier (Bland and Stevens 1996, 23-24).

It was inevitable that the task of finding talented people in the number and variety necessary to build an army of over eight million persons soon outstripped Marshall's ability to choose leaders based on personal knowledge, and so he came to rely on the advice of others. When casting about for thoughtful people to work collaboratively in the WPD in 1939, he relied on the recommendations of Generals Gerow and Krueger in the selection of Eisenhower (Gerow 1958, 31; Pogue 1966, 162-163), whom at the time was not well known to Marshall.

When Marshall went to China in 1946 as President Truman's special ambassador, he asked Hilldring to give him the strongest man in G-5 to serve as his back-up man in Washington. Even though giving up James Davis was a blow to Hilldring's operation, Marshall could count on Hilldring's loyalty to get him the best man for the particular job he had in mind.[4] Davis performed superbly for Marshall (Hilldring 1959, Part 2, 7).

To fill diplomatic positions, Marshall looked for people who could move others to make decisions. The ability to compromise, to be personable, to understand diverse cultures, to work with a wide assortment of people and to be tolerant—these were all considered relevant and important traits. When he looked for someone who could act for him to promote a better working relationship with Roosevelt, he went to Hopkins, a man of action, and to Baruch, who was good at divining the climate around any decision situation and who could get rapid access to almost any public official. For working through thorny sensitivities to gain accord with the allies, he favored Eisenhower: "I always used Eisenhower when I wanted a compromise" (Gesell and Acheson 1964, 1). At State he turned to Acheson, Secretary of the Navy Forrestal, and others for advice on who to select, and got Kennan and Bohlen as a result. Ambassadors tended to be selected from among the career cadre of the Foreign Service.[5]

Complementing the function of discovering talent is stimulating talented people to seek employment. Many were induced to join Marshall's organizations because they saw that working under enlightened leadership is a path to legitimate and personally satisfying public service. Marshall's reputation for ethical leadership and for delegating meaningful responsibility was attractive. For example, Rusk turned down an attractive offer from the War Department in order to stay with the State Department. "I opted for State, to a great extent because of George Marshall. He was the most extraordinary man I ever knew" (Rusk 1990, 130). He stayed on at State to become a career diplomat and eventually secretary of state.

Criticism of Marshall's Methods for Choosing

General Wade Haislip, chief of G-1 (Personnel) of the General Staff just before the war, a man whose business was in part the selection and assignment of people in organizations, believed that Marshall had an insufficient understanding of the dynamics of personnel administration as a whole. Specifically, he felt Marshall was too free with promotions, often using them as compensation for men released from prisoner-of-war camps or as farewell gestures to officers terminating service. These appointments took up slots that could have been used for promoting high-performing, career-motivated officers. Also, he disapproved of the policy denying overseas command positions to officers on the basis of age. Experienced, educated men should be on hand to introduce younger officers into combat, give them what they could of their knowledge, and brought home when they were worn out (Haislip 1959, 9-11, 14).

Haislip's faulted Marshall particularly for trusting too much in his own judgment of people. He, Marshall, would often act impulsively on the basis of irrelevant factors, as when he withheld promotion on the basis of receiving a letter of support from someone outside the line of command. "He formed a lightning opinion of a man and it never changed" (Haislip 1959, 24-26). This criticism is most serious because it goes to the core of Marshall's reputation for fair-mindedness.

Eisenhower also found some of Marshall's methods of leader selection to be off the mark. He was especially put off by Marshall's preference of people able to speak their mind in his presence, because this worked unfairly on those intimidated by the general. Like Haislip, he disagreed with the unspoken rule that an officer orchestrating a campaign of self-promotion should be summarily dismissed (Eisenhower 1962, 5-7).

Talent, Purpose, and Organizational Barriers

Marshall firmly believed that an enterprise that is focused on giving talented people discretion to act in a coordinated way in the pursuit of important public goals builds motivation. The unselfish service implicit in this act improves performance and adds meaning to the lives of the contributors, and above all pays dividends in terms of organizational achievement. A reason to believe that net merit and achievement result from the harnessing of talent and discretion to public goals is that the people and teams so engaged, if their license is broadly defined, will freely cross lines of authority and other structural barriers to find the best solutions.

An anecdote that focuses on the team Marshall brought together when he came to the Defense Department in 1950 gives more shape to this idea. Marshall Carter, assistant secretary of the General Staff in WW II and executive secretary at the State Department under Marshall, was brought to Defense by Marshall. Carl Hummelsine, a WW II general staffer and administrator at State, was in place as executive secretary at State. Acheson, who had worked closely with Marshall at State, was secretary of state. Lovett had been brought on by Marshall as his number two man at Defense. With Marshall's blessing, a close working relationship blossomed between the Defense and State departments. Both were dominated by people who, by virtue of their earlier service with Marshall, were dedicated more to an ideal of public service than to a single organizational identity or a single person. A new interaction displaced the poor interdepartmental relations which had existed. State Department officials interacted frequently with the Joint Chiefs of Staff, and administrators of cabinet and sub-cabinet rank freely communicated with each other. The result was a great deal of work done on a set of common problems (Carter 1959, 33).

The Importance of Morale

The necessity of creating and maintaining high morale held a vital place in Marshall's notions of leadership and organizational effectiveness. He defined and described morale and its importance at a speech at Trinity College in June, 1941:

> It is morale that wins the victory. . . . It is more than a word—more than any one word, or several words, can measure. Morale is a state of mind. It is steadfastness and courage and hope. It is confidence and zeal and loyalty. It is *élan, esprit de corps* and determination.
>
> It is staying power, the spirit which endures to the end—the will to win. With it all things are possible, without it everything else, planning, preparation, production, count for naught (de Weerd 1945, 121-125).

Marshall's views on morale go to the heart of transformational leadership. They spring from a genuine compassion for human beings as well as a rational calculation of what makes an organization effective. Three examples taken from many in Marshall's career should suffice to indicate the depth of his commitment to the concept.

Left in command of tiny Fort Reno in 1905, he received a complaint from a soldier's wife about the drab colors of their quarters. If she would fix up her shabby, cluttered yard typical of other houses on "Soapsuds Row," he told her, he would have her house painted in the color of her choice. She accepted, he followed through with his promise, the idea spread, and the result was a spruced-up neighborhood, happier spouses, and an inexpensively achieved rise in morale for post families as a whole.

The second and third examples come from WW I and contributed to creating future national policy. Stationed at Pershing's staff headquarters, Marshall witnessed bored soldiers languishing in drab surroundings for weeks and sometimes months awaiting transport home, becoming increasingly bitter toward the Army for seemingly abandoning them after their heroic service. Marshall railed against this treatment with whomever he could talk to in the chain of command, without much effect except that his advocacy earned a whole lot of enmity toward him from the staff to whom he had carried the grievance, so much so in fact that it caused him to miss out on a field promotion to brigadier general (Marshall 1976; Bland 1991, 536-537). Later, he came to believe that the bitterness left among the rank and file by the experience damaged efforts to obtain higher levels of support for the postwar army.

At the heart of the matter, he concluded, was the need the troops had to keep busy and to feel involved in an activity significant to the war effort. Pershing belatedly acted to Marshall's satisfaction by prescribing a strenuous training regimen for men awaiting transport, which proved beneficial to discipline and efficiency (Bland and Stevens 1996, 175), and of great potential military importance had the armistice broken down.

The third example involved the morale of staff officers during WW I. In his roles as a chief of operations at division, army corps, and headquarters levels, he was daily presented with daunting problems: carrying through on plans that did not meet with the approval of unit officers; contending with frequent changes in orders; excessive formality of orders that made them tedious to read and difficult to use; and insufficient time to prepare and distribute orders to the units that needed them. All of this had led, in Marshall's opinion, to "half-hearted and pessimistic feelings of the general staff officer . . . reflected throughout the command" and to increased casualties among the troops, loss of faith in command officers, and irritable mental states among the staff officers themselves to the point that "[m]any officers broke under the strain of these conditions" (Bland and Hadsel 1981, 215). These impressions stayed with him, steeling his resolve to avoid their repetition in the war to follow.

The Dignity of the Doughboy

Marshall's attention was always focused on the morale of those at the bottom of the hierarchy—specifically enlistees and draftees, CCC recruits, and non-commissioned officers. So strong had his empathy for the "doughboy" (the WW II term for the ordinary soldier) become that he could say with unbridled passion in his 1943 biennial report:

> There is no way the American people can recompense the American soldier for the pain and suffering and hardships he goes through (US Army Chief of Staff, 1943).

Doughboys not only endured great misery and hardship but also carried the freight of prejudice heaped on them by outsiders, such that they were considered to be of a lower class not talented enough to be airmen or seamen. Marshall was much irritated by Winston Churchill's reference to British common soldiers as "the dull mass," believing that this attitude reflected poorly on the prime minister (Bland 1991, 15).

Troop morale depended heavily on enjoying the ordinary comforts of life, he had observed first-hand while moving about in the front line trenches of WW I and soldier life. Receiving constant artillery fire while stuck in a fixed position had a disorienting and terrifying power:

> It was not the ordeal of personal combat that seemed to prove the greatest strain in the last war. It was the endurance for days at a time of severe artillery bombardment by shells of heavy caliber, that proved the fortitude of the troops. To be struck by these hideous impersonal agents without the power personally to strike back was the lot of the American soldier at Cantigny. On other fields later on, he overran the enemy, advanced deep into his positions, and suffered far heavier casualties. But the conditions were utterly different and the strain on the individual less severe (Marshall 1976, 99).

Seeing and feeling and sometimes sharing the misery, he wrote to a former first sergeant in late 1917:

> War and training here is mud and rain and cold. The officer, platoon chief, who can keep his men's socks and shoes greased and dry and his horses groomed and picket lines above the flood of water and mud—he is the greatest contributor to our success in this war (Bland and Hadsel 1981, 127).

As chief of staff he required his subordinates to give special attention to troop morale. Receiving information that the same troops had long been stationed in the Aleutian Islands without seeing combat or periodic relief, and sensing the monotony, he directed the men be rotated home before the winter, and extended this policy to other remote posts in the Persian Gulf and Greenland (Bland and Stevens 1996, 95-96, 185-186). He took many other actions in a similar vein: directed the painting of drab training camps; championed comfortable clothing that was also fashionable; organized recreational camps and activities to counteract boredom and inactivity; and fought in Congress for the upgrading in rank and pay for army chaplains. The spiritual, recreational, cultural, and educational welfare of the troops provided constant motivation for much of his activity.

His earlier efforts to increase the morale of those he commanded tended to be random and personal rather than systematic. When he learned at Fort Benning that an issue of blankets had bogged down, he barked at the responsible officer:

> Get those blankets and stoves and every other damn thing that's needed here tonight . . . not tomorrow—tonight! We are going to take care of the troops first, last, and all the time (Carter 1972, 4; Buchanan 1958, 42).

In 1940, responding to reports of low morale in a small southern town near a military base, he checked into a local hotel in civilian dress, unsuccessfully searched for recreation and a decent meal, and witnessed soldiers chasing prostitutes. Returning to Washington, he ordered improvements in on-base facilities and community relations arrangements (Pogue 1966, 113).

Later, as his duties multiplied, his concern for morale continued but became more institutionalized. He began to keep notes of the men's complaints ("ordinary gripes" excluded) on his inspection trips and passed these on to an accompanying aide for action (Carter 1972; P. Smith 2004). He spoke with junior officers and enlisted men to discover the base's problems and how these affected the men, and to look into their diet, clothing, and treatment (Powder 1959, 16). He routinely checked on whether needs for entertainment and cultural enrichment were being met by movies, live traveling shows, local special services offices, Thanksgiving and Christmas dinners, library materials, game equipment, and newspaper printing facilities.

Staff was ordered to follow up on all the discrepancies he noted. Field commanders were held accountable for getting these corrected promptly. Failure to follow through served as fuel for negative comments in an officer's evaluation report and weighed adversely in future promotion and assignment decisions. "Morale is primarily a function of command," he told his generals, putting them on notice that they themselves would be held strictly accountable for the morale of their troops.

When he asked Oveta Culp Hobby, commander of the new Women's Auxilliary Army Corps (WAAC), to make a post inspection, she protested that she would not be able to discern the state of morale. "He looked at me and said, 'You will get to the point where you can walk on a post, camp or base station and know whether the morale is good or bad' " (Hobby 1963, 12). She recalled that she later reported to Marshall that she had observed women without warm overcoats on a cold-weather post in Des Moines, Iowa, that post authorities claimed this was because of a shortage of material, and that the men were wearing their coats. Marshall saw to it that the women were given the overcoats that had been made for the men even though they came down below their ankles (Hobby 1963, 13).

Accentuate the Positive

Coming down hard on commanders who did not take morale seriously was the hard approach. The soft approach was to write personally to the commanders of small, isolated posts, asking what might be done to make Army life more livable, and respond positively and quickly to the responses. This included getting information to hospitalized and wounded soldiers about the activities of their units to keep them feeling connected. He began a practice soon upon becoming chief of staff of having the Secretary of the General Staff prepare a summary list of messages received from servicemen and their families presenting both positive and negative points raised. Marshall would answer six of these each day, sending notes of congratulations for positive messages and notices of "meritorious claims" to field commanders on the negative messages directing investigation, action, and reporting (Pogue 1966, 116).

Stimson was asked by Marshall to appoint a Department of War community service committee to plan recreational activities. The initiative bore fruit in late 1940 with the birth of the United Services Organization (USO). The USO began immediately to create social and recreational activities on or near all Army posts, including "providing halls where servicemen on leave could buy light refreshments at reasonable prices, find a congenial spot to write letters, listen to records, or dance with partners selected by local committees" (Pogue 1966, 113). The organization gained fame during the war for mounting traveling shows in every theater of war and stateside bases, bringing the likes of Bob Hope, Betty Hutton, Donald O'Connor and Betty Grable to the troops (Pogue 1966, 113-114).

Of great urgency to Marshall was the need to find ways to explain to young people why they were fighting and making sacrifices. The Capra six-film effort advanced basic military training and acted as a morale booster (Pasco 1997, 7-8).

Special awards were created for the traditionally under-recognized infantry-man. Separate medals were developed for training personnel (thus recognizing a type of expertise), for individual combat excellence, and for small units recognizing all unit members participating in especially meritorious activities (Bland and Stevens 1996, 143-144, 170-171).

Controversy erupted over a Marshall policy that encouraged field commanders to make one immediate award in the field for every four recommendations made through hierarchical command channels (Bland 1991, 492-93). Opposition to field awards grew among headquarters staff because of the many mistakes that were made, but Marshall persevered:

> But it was a great deal better to have a man rewarded right then in the presence of the soldiers, than to have to wait maybe six months when it was done without any immediate relation to what his performance had been of that day and hour (Bland 1991, 490).

To charges that he was coddling the men serving in combat zones, he pled guilty and explained: "[We] had to do everything we could to make the men feel we had highest solicitude for their condition. . . . I was for supplying everything we could and then requiring him to fight to the death when the time came." Since scarce shipping space made it impossible to send the men home to rest, he deemed it urgent to do what could be done for them on or near the front (Bland 1991, 482).[6]

Officer Morale

Marshall was less concerned about morale at higher organizational ranks. When it was suggested at a State Department staff meeting that a morale problem existed among the agency's leadership corps, he leveled his gaze on those at the table:

> Gentlemen, it has been my experience that an enlisted man may be entitled to a morale problem, but an officer is not. I expect the officers of this department to take care of their own morale. No one is taking care of my morale.

Word of this circulated and morale throughout the department rose "to the highest point it has ever been before or since" (Rusk 1990, 633).

It wasn't that Marshall lacked interest in his officers' morale, but he believed that participation in matters that affected them was a better route to effect it than paternalism. When a group of Pacific theater pilots complained that their own planes were inferior to the Japanese Zero, he ordered an investigation that traced the perceived superiority of the Zero to its greater maneuverability. Removal of much protective armor would increase the agility of American fighter planes. The decision was left to the pilots:

> I wanted the pilots to feel that they could have any kind of plane they wanted and that they had a direct part in the whole matter. They wouldn't buy the stripping of the plane. It was very important to make these men feel that they were not just put out there and then forgotten (Bland 1991, 592).

Officers could best maintain their morale through self-discipline, which in turn depended upon putting them in roles where they fit and giving them the training and resources needed to do what they had to do. A case in point was Marshall's action to beautify Fort Benning in the late 1920s. He appointed an officer who loved horticulture to be in charge of post landscaping and planting and encouraged post residents to speak to people in his unit before attempting their own planting. The officer recommended plants that were consistent with the post environment and survived well, and he gave instruction in how to grow them. Marshall reinforced the goal by informing his officers that the appearance of an officer's home was one indicator of the officer's character, without making it a specific criterion in an officer's performance evaluation (Bull 1959, 23-24).

Officer morale also was pursued through steps to promote officer careers. Higher ranking officers were routinely rotated out of Washington staff offices to the field because Marshall recognized that Army career advancement turned on successful duty performance with troops. Being trapped in staff jobs had impeded his own career progress and he determined not to allow this to happen to others, at some cost to himself (Beetle Smith was of the opinion that moving capable people out of Washington worked to the general's disadvantage) (W. Smith 1958, 10-11).

Morale and Separation

Marshall's personal and frustrating end-of-war experience with Pershing's bored and disgruntled forces awaiting shipment home from France lingered in his memory. Convinced that long-term resentment and postwar weakness of the Army had been heightened by War Department mishandling of demobilization, he determined to arrange the process of demobilization in WW II so as to positively affect veteran welfare and their feelings about the army.

Palmer and other planners on the demobilization board lit upon a formula he approved. The idea was to send home first those who gave conspicuous service at the front, followed by those with somewhat less combat service, leaving for the last those in rear positions and those with the least time in combat zones. He urged Eisenhower to provide those at the front with a jeep and K-rations for two or three day vacation outings in Europe before being shipped home. Unfortunately, the plan was upset by virtue of the late developing, top-level policy decision to redeploy seasoned troops to the Pacific theater (Bland 1991, 537). Those who were sent home first because of their greater service contribution now found themselves plucked out of their home environments to new duty in the Pacific.[7]

At the Congressional level, Marshall's efforts at institutionalizing morale curried some disfavor. His directions to commanders in early 1941 to indoctrinate troops as to the heritage they were defending, supply special textbooks on American foreign affairs and international relations, and create and use a specialized set of morale officers to lecture citizen-soldiers smelled of a propaganda campaign to some. Greater success was achieved with the Capra film series (Pogue 1966, 117).

"Direct Your Anger at the Problem, Not the Person"

Marshall came at an early point in his career to appreciate the pointlessness of placing blame on *people* for organizational problems, at any level. Don't get angry at your people when things go wrong, he would instruct; instead, direct your anger at the problem. When occasional anger with individuals did surface, it was usually directed at superiors rather than at subordinates or peers. It was true that he could terrify young officers with an icy stare or a dismissive gesture, yet this behavior was without malice and his general demeanor was not personal and devoid of anger.

As a young first lieutenant commanding the Plattsburgh training center for officers in General Bell's absence in 1916, he became angry with a senior quartermaster who outranked him. The trainees were in need of blankets and other cold weather items and the senior quartermaster was dragging his feet on ordering these supplies because he was unconvinced by Lieutenant Marshall's claims that shortages existed. Marshall had an independent audit conducted which confirmed the shortages and then ordered the goods via an expensive express service before confronting the quartermaster:

> Well, I pulled him out this list . . . he had never seen such a thing and, of course, it was a gold mine of information, and he asked me if he could (have a copy). . . . Well, that made quite a change in him right away, because he saw that we really had something he didn't have. He was very much reassured and went ahead from that time on filling the orders . . . (Bland 1991, 186).

The incident illustrates how Marshall preferred to handle a situation that might easily have become a personal conflict. Although he himself would deny that he always operated in such a rational manner by focusing on the problem and not the person, as a general matter he stressed the importance of maintaining self-control and assuming that other people were essentially reasonable and committed to common goals and could thus be reached by reason.

Tolerance of Error and Second Chances

There is conflicting testimony as to whether Marshall was tolerant of mistakes. According to General E. F. Harding, Marshall was more inclined to be forgiving of someone who made a mistake than of someone who failed to do something he should be doing (Harding 1958, 16). Calling attention to errors in judgment of junior officers was distasteful to him, particularly if the actor was well intentioned and the mistake resulted from lack of training or inexperience or was within the realm of discretionary action reasonably undertaken. In WW I Marshall was assigned the role of faultfinder in the aftermath of a rash and possibly foolhardy raid led by a young infantry captain which had led to several deaths. He asked that a telegram be sent to the division commander "congratulating him on the offensive spirit displayed" by the officer and "expressing the hope that the unfortunate result would not deter the division from undertaking further offensive operations" (Marshall 1976, 121-123, quote at 123).

Sensitivity to the motives of the transgressor went hand-in-hand with directness and a reluctance for letting someone in high authority get away with misconduct. Marshall recalled:

> I would write to the fellow in the frankest possible way and tell him exactly what was wrong with him, and I would tell him that this letter was only seen by my stenographer, who could be trusted, and it would not be put in the files. But I wanted him to understand exactly how I felt and if it occurred again, I would relieve him. . . . What they couldn't tolerate was the thing being discussed around (Bland 1991, 241).

As an alternative he would call on responsible commanders to quietly call out the wrongdoer; serious errors and misbehavior should not be allowed to go unremarked. A practice was followed of not tolerating any repetition of error. Officers who acknowledged their errors and took steps not to repeat them drew Marshall's admiration. Those who pouted or complained could expect no further advancement in their careers.

Despite tolerating error resulting from inexperience or lack of training, Marshall was intolerant of certain types of mistakes. Low morale of troops dependent upon an officer was taken as direct evidence of a failure of leadership of that officer, and little or no sympathy was extended. Intolerance of voluntary or willful slip-ups grew as the end of war loomed and as wartime hardships compounded (Bolte 1958, 1-2).

When it was his judgment that an officer's continued weakness or demonstrated pattern of mistakes was having an adverse effect upon the troops under him, he could be ruthless. When General Harding showed an inclination to keep a man in command who had exhibited a character weakness, Marshall exploded:

> Harding, you're in trouble, you're too kind-hearted. You think too much of a man's feelings and not of the men he's got under him (Harding 1958, 22).

This stance brought two Marshall principles into conflict: the removal of commanders whose actions adversely affect troops, and trusting the field commander to make staffing and other decisions relating to his command.[8] The dilemma became painfully evident in the summer of 1943 when Marshall questioned Eisenhower's request that a Colonel Ratay be promoted to brigadier general, noting that Ratay once had been relieved from regimental command for "maltreatment of his soldiers." Eisenhower had found the officer had been doing a praiseworthy job in his current position. Marshall's intervention caused Ratay to be removed from the promotion list (Bland and Stevens 1996, 83-84).[9]

A consistent practice was moving officers to inactive status when they reached retirement age. He reasoned that men of such age and experience who had achieved rank by virtue of their longevity would dominate leadership roles in the units to which they might move. The net result was to block the progress of younger and perhaps more able men and women and risk their loss to the public service. Thus, overaged officers would be retained only if there was convincing evidence of both ability and necessity of their service (Bland and Stevens 1996, 122-124).

As Motivator

Motivating people in an organization is an imprecise talent. Any administrator who manages people has a bag of incentives from which to draw. Some are a consequence of the authority to make certain kinds of decisions: promotions, awards, job and training assignments, punishments, and the granting of leave. The skillful use of these tools has the potential to increase employee satisfaction and positively affect motivation. Some more intangible influences are at least as potent. Marshall used the latter to infuse his subordinates with enthusiasm and the desire to achieve the tasks he set out for them.

A key method he used, fundamental to ethical leadership, was redirecting loyalty and affection directed toward him personally into devotion to serving the organizational mission. His people understood that their leader was not interested in being an object of their admiration but rather someone to lead them toward accomplishing the public's goals. Thus, the primary motivation for the person delegated the task lay in achieving organizational objectives rather than in pleasing the boss. The best way to curry the boss's favor was to help accomplish the organizational goals the boss was in turn devoted to serving.

Still, striving for mission success did not eliminate their sense of obligation to Marshall, the man. Kennan worked hard and faithfully for Marshall but expressed regret that he had not been more aggressive so as to have helped him more (Kennan 1959, 26-28). Gerow, head of WPD in the very tough pre-war era, was "sorry that we couldn't relieve him of more of those problems" (Gerow 1958, 41). Others who were asked by Marshall to do a job typically worked very hard but often came away from the experience with the feeling that they could have done "a little better . . . for the old man" and with a resolve "to try and do better next time."

To get such loyalty from others requires reciprocity. The leader owes an extraordinary burden of care to those under his command. This fiduciary obligation extends to the very bottom of the organizational ladder (Truscott 1959, 19). The combination of their sense of obligation to both man and mission led to a redoubling of effort and a willingness to labor under great pressures. Even when they felt they were failing, Marshall would speak to them with a calm voice lacking any trace of personal animosity. With those who were reasonably competent and tried, "he has this wonderful gift of simply making them eager to do a helluva lot more for him than they have done up to this moment" (Betts, 1958, 34-35).

Hilldring gives further evidence of how admiration of Marshall was converted into goal-achieving performance. When Marshall informed him that he was being jumped two ranks in order to fill the post of chief of personnel (G-1) on the General Staff, Hilldring started to thank him. He recalled that Marshall stopped him:

'I don't want to be thanked.' He said, 'I'm not doing this because I like you, this is no favor to you. I've decided to make you G-1 because I think you will be a good G-1. I hope I'm right. I'll give you a little fatherly advice now,' he said. 'I don't think that everybody gets in this life everything he deserves, but it's been my observation he rarely gets anything he doesn't deserve. If you have any feeling of gratitude toward me for this, which you shouldn't have, you can display it by being tolerant of me when I am unreasonable with you in the months ahead. Got any questions?' (Hilldring 1959, 33).

The fact that Marshall was known to be knowledgeable and considerate, although sometimes intimidating, also induced people to want to perform for him. Each knew that he had "thought out what he wanted, . . . he would tell you what he wanted, and then you would do it" and if it wasn't done in the way he wanted "you didn't have to worry much about that; he would tell you in a nice way if he knew you were . . . making the effort" (Harding 1958, 31).

Part of his ability to motivate lay in the combination of having high expectations of others, trusting them by giving them increasing levels of responsibility as they fulfilled their initial one, leaving them alone to do the job, treating them with respect, and not accepting sloppiness or performance below their ability. Placing such confidence in people inspired dedication and efforts beyond those that people may believe they are capable of, and an acceptance of personal responsibility for actions (W. Smith 1958, Kennan 1959, Rusk 1990, Acheson 1969, and Lovett 1973).

Demands placed on officers and staff were enormous, but were not made worse by the feeling that the boss was dissatisfied with or riding herd over them. When he was dissatisfied over performance that he needed or expected, he was able to convince the officer that he was dissatisfied with the situation rather than the person.

Giving verbal praise was decidedly *not* one of his methods of motivation. Work done well brought an assignment of enlarged responsibility, which was taken by the subordinate as proof that the "old man" appreciated what had been done. Colleagues and subordinates learned that mere acceptance of the work was sufficient evidence of achievement. Eisenhower recalled:

The nearest that he ever came to saying [anything] complimentary directly to my face . . . was 'You are not doing so badly so far' (Pogue 1966, 338).

Inasmuch as trusting others with important responsibilities was central to his method of motivation, it was essential to choose capable, well-meaning people. Eisenhower, Beetle Smith, McNair, Pasco, Hilldring, and Handy in the administration of the US Army; Acheson and Carter and Lovett at State; Lovett and Carter and Rosenberg at Defense—these are but a few examples of thoroughly capable people directly subordinate to him whom he trusted without hesitation.

Helping others to see clearly where they fit into the existing organization and the overall plan for change is another important yet frequently overlooked factor in motivation, which Marshall observed. Hilldring is used again to illustrate the point.

When Marshall was making him the first chief of civil affairs in military history, he gave him a stern warning as well as an overview of the challenge and the milieu he was entering. Hilldring recalled Marshall's instructions:

> [He said] it was a very treacherous job that I was taking, that there wasn't much chance that the reputation of the Army would be in any way enhanced by anything that I might do, but . . . [the fact that the Army] might be . . . damaged was enormous and that I must . . . watch for the formation of clouds in the sky and unjust accusations, that the civilian agencies of the government were very unhappy about the fact that the Army, and not they, were going to have this problem . . . to put in order the areas that we had liberated and conquered.
>
> The description of the tenor of the job did not stop there. Eisenhower was disgusted with the seventeen civilian agencies roaming about in North Africa; he needed help so that he could do the rest of his job. The president was convinced that the original concept of civilian control by civilian agencies would have to be abandoned and given over to the Army. He, General Marshall, hadn't wanted the responsibility at all, and there were those in the cabinet and in the administration . . . who had very great doubts about the wisdom of giving to soldiers the amount of political power and influence to be exerted by G-5 in the years ahead. And that certainly was a prophecy that bore fruit (1959, 37).

It was an orientation lecture that Hilldring was to return to again and again for guidance in his most difficult assignment.

Dealing With People in a Democracy

There is yet another facet of Marshall's leadership that relates to people, yet to be touched upon. It has to do with the effect of dealing with others, internal and external to the organization, in the context of a democratic system of government. This is a vital facet of ethical leadership since democratic values inform both the form and conduct of American public administration. This is the topic that forms the basis of the next chapter.

Notes

1.   Japanese commanders were pleased to share with Lt. Marshall the battle techniques they prized, especially hand-to-hand bayonet combat and night fighting. When he returned to duty in the Philippines he presented these techniques to US officers and had them incorporated into training programs for American troops (Pogue 1963, 125).

2.   As policy to guide instruction of postwar reservists, Marshall exhorted his staff to stress the importance of "more expeditious methods . . . which facilitate the preparation of an Army for war in an emergency and also which permit the adequate instruction of the citizen soldier without too great a loss of time from his civil pursuits" (memo to Handy, 6/4/1945, Bland and Stevens 2003).

3.   "I think it was his job—to train people for battle whether it occurred or it didn't and he was one of these super-conscientious men who was convinced that if he was going

to train, it would be done right whether (or not) he thought there would never be a war" (Deane 1960, 4).

4.   Davis had put together a four billion dollar military relief program without a hitch.

5.   Marshall recognized the legitimate role of the president to override his choice for political reasons.

6.   Years later, organizational theory came to accept the value of making rewards soon after the performance that warranted them in order to increase the likelihood that the reward itself would help to motivate enhanced future performance.

7.   Although the atomic bomb made much of their Pacific duty unnecessary, this fact was unknown at the time it was determined that the redeployment was necessary.

8.   Inconsistency was noted by Gen. Harding, who served as assistant executive officer for the General Staff: "If he (Marshall) had already developed a strong feeling of admiration for an officer, he was more inclined to protect him, at least the first time he got into trouble" (Harding 1958, 17).

9.   Ratay's name reappeared on Eisenhower's next proffered promotion list and he was approved for promotion.

CHAPTER ELEVEN
DEMOCRACY AND BUREAUCRACY

God bless democracy! I approve of it highly but suffer from it extremely. This incidently is not for quotation.
—George C. Marshall
(Letter to Spencer L. Carter, Virginia-Carolina Chemical Corporation, June 14, 1948)

Democracy vs. Bureaucracy: Conflict at the Core of Administration

A key to George C. Marshall's success as an ethical leader was his commitment to democratic beliefs and citizen values (Bland 1988, 32-33). This was true despite the fact that the excess political processes made necessary by the democratic form of government made his job more difficult. His commitment to democracy was all the more remarkable because, as a military careerist, he had been trained to reflect the hierarchical and autocratic values characterizing army service.

Theoretically, there is every reason for a democratic nation to insist on efficiency and professionalism in the workings of its large bureaucracies. The people deserve to have the resources that its government has appropriated to serve its legitimate public purposes allocated and administered wisely in the pursuit of those purposes. If bureaucracies are the most effective and efficient way for governments to deliver services, as Max Weber theorized, then bureaucracy should be compatible with all forms of government (Gerth and Mills 1947). On the other hand, the inequalities that are built into the hierarchies and authority levels of bureaucratic organizations are implicitly inconsistent with democratic ideals.

Marshall was better grounded in American history and in the social and constitutional life of the nation than the typical career officer. He saw the armed forces as instruments of the will of the political branches of government as well as a professional pursuit. Such a world-view carries with it a restricted view of the Army's responsibilities and actions. It also includes a sensitivity to serving other, legitimate purposes of government besides defense. His belief in the rightness of democracy and the military's subordination to the civilian authority "was ingrained in his every thought" (Pasco 1997, 40). He himself preferred civilian dress when testifying before the Congress or appearing at military parades or ceremonies (Bland 1991, 443-444).

Marshall understood well the political reality that the executive and legislative branches would look with disfavor upon proposals coming from the defense agencies "which swell the budget, win no votes and threaten the continuation of the dominant political party in power," as he said in a 1947 speech. To be effective, an administrator must accept this truth as a condition of operating within a democratic government. He continued: "Democracy has its difficulties. But democracy is what we fight for" (GCMRL: Box 157, Folder 29).

Merit and Exclusion

The merit principle, the ethic which teaches that persons should hold positions of employment based on their ability to do the job, is a well established tenet of democratic public administration as well as a revered American social value. Confusion arises when the merit *system*, the laws and rules and practices that have grown up around attempts to implement the merit *principle*, are criticized as working against the merit principle. The basis of the criticism is that the system too often pursues arcane, rule-bound procedures which elevate compliance with the rules over performance of job duties.

At its core, the merit principle requires hiring, advancement, reward, and retention of employees doing the government's work to be based solely on qualifications and performance as these are related to the duties of the positions they occupy. The merit principle therefore lines up closely with values of individualism, efficiency, accountability, and equal opportunity under law.

In the military services as well as in all other government fields, merit implies the selfless pursuit of publicly legitimated goals and a refusal to allow factors other than the ability to perform the job to be conditions for hiring, advancement, reward, assignment, or retention. This means that race, sex, religion, age, family and friendship, ethnicity, physical and mental disability unrelated to job performance, and political affiliation should not be considered.[1]

The best and most faithful applications of the merit principle entail making hiring, promotion, reward, and retention decisions solely on the basis of a good-faith prediction of an employee's capacity to competently perform the duties required by a position. Since military and foreign service members traditionally follow careers that mix various job types (combat command, administration, training, diplomacy, et al.), the estimate of the member's potential for service should cover more general abilities over the long term rather than an assessment of the specific skills, knowledge, and abilities connected to a present assignment.[2]

Comparative Treatment of the Races in Military Service

In order to correct the situation in which African-Americans were traditionally under-represented within the military services, the Army adopted a policy in 1937 requiring mobilization of whites and blacks in numbers proportional to their percentages in the population at large (Lee 1966, 37-38). This policy did not extend to the elimination of segregated units within the Army, which had also existed traditionally.

To implement the promise of proportionality, the Army was faced with the choice of either creating more units dominated by African-American soldiers or integrating existing and newly created units. The latter option entailed equally distributing African-American soldiers and officers geographically as well as within the various types of Army services (infantry, artillery, air, signal corps, and so on).

In 1937 and for many years after that, segregation practices existed throughout all the military services and discriminatory segregation laws were in place throughout the southern states where the bulk of military training was likely to occur. The Army's burden was especially great because the Navy Department did not follow suit and develop or pursue a policy of proportionality. Neither the Navy nor the marines had brought more than a handful of blacks into their ranks, and had instead devised means to preclude taking any more (Lee 1966, 51, 89).

Implementation of the Army's new policy to absorb and distribute more black soldiers was handicapped from the beginning. For one thing, few Negro units existed. The bigger obstacle lay in the insistence of the War Department and Army that all military units be segregated by race, thus necessitating that, if proportionality were to be achieved, extra and parallel units and additional service facilities (health, recreation, mess halls, and so forth), and even exclusive training locations would have to be provided for black troops. All of this additional organization added great expense and administration that was, in the strictest sense, both unnecessary and ran counter to the ethics represented by the merit principle. It was also antithetical to an army in need of resources in its struggle against many challenges. Moreover, some Army units, most notably the Air Corps and the Signal Corps, were taking their own measures, contrary to the War Department's policy, to avoid taking blacks altogether (Lee 1966, 88-89).

Under Marshall's tenure as chief of staff, voluntary enlistment was initially encouraged and then the draft was used to build the Army's size. As the selective service system took hold in late 1940, the numbers of both white and black troops grew explosively. The number of black troops grew from 3,640 on August 31, 1939 to 97,725 on November 31, 1941 (a twenty-five fold increase), and then to 467,883 by the end of 1942. The number of blacks volunteering for army service exceeded, on a proportional basis, the number of whites volunteering, due in large measure to the greater lack of job opportunity for blacks in the civilian economy.

Despite these numbers, after selective service conscription began in the fall of 1940, many eligible blacks volunteered but were not inducted because of the insufficient number of Negro units that had been formed to receive them, while white recruits could be accommodated in existing units (Lee 1966, 88). War Department officials, Marshall included, argued that orderly growth and functioning of the Army required an emphasis on merit in selection and assignment. They asserted that blacks were generally of lower skill levels and the goal of equal (i.e., proportionate) employment of the races must be subordinated to the goal of military competence, especially under the conditions of a threatening war.

The War Department and the office of the Chief of Staff (COS) took the position that Negro units would be constructed and black troops would be absorbed within them, but that the timing of these developments would be delayed. The argument accepted and expressed the logic that segregation was a powerful social force in American society and had to be taken into account; now was not the time to experiment with social change of great magnitude and divisiveness. As events later showed, the situation was that the Army was uniformly opposed to the mixing of black and white soldiers in the same permanent units, but split on the issue of whether segregated black and white units could be trained in the same camps.

True segregationists preferred that black and white units be trained in separate camps, and that the black training camps not be located near southern communities. The biggest flashpoint of conflict grew out of Marshall's decision to form a new, mixed race division, the Second Cavalry Division, out of separate black and white regiments at Fort Riley, Kansas in early 1941. The chief of cavalry strenuously objected in a memo to COS on September 20, 1940:

> It appears to me to be obvious that such a unit, nonhomogeneous—half white and half black, cannot be as effective as a homogeneous or all black or all white unit. There is not only a difference in color but there is a difference in emotional reactions. The concentration of a large body of troops in one place, approximately half white and half black, involves the risk of bitter rivalries and racial clashes. I consider this to be an unwise improvisation (Lee 1966, 124).[3]

Housing was a particular concern. Acreage used for the vast amount of land needed for the housing had to be purchased or leased and then graded and plotted before construction could begin. In the South, construction teams were segregated and blacks and whites were not permitted by law to live in the same housing areas (Lee 1966, 97), and certainly not in the same buildings.

The COS ran into constant and stiff resistance from post and higher command-ers. Marshall ordered a resurvey by the General Staff of the allocation of Negro units with an eye to picking "locations adjacent to communities with a large colored population" in all parts of the country. Few commanders in northern, western, or southern states responded that blacks could be accommodated without causing protests and resentment within nearby communities (Lee 1966, 102). Commanders and communities in southern states wanted "no black Yankees," as black northerners were sarcastically described in a *Dallas Morning News* editorial:

> The federal government apparently has never learned that it can not without unfortunate consequences billet northern-trained Negro troops in the south. Until it does learn that axiomatic fact, there will continue to be trouble (Lee 1966, 103).

At Marshall's direction, commander of Ground Forces General McNair resisted segregationist pressure and put the burden of integration on local commanders by appealing to their patriotism and citing the dire wartime urgency. Although discontent continued to surface, the policy was held to. The net result, however, was to concentrate black soldiers in small black units and to locate them near communities in which they were more likely to be welcomed (Lee 1966, 104-106).

The hierarchy of the War Department, most of the General Staff, and the bulk of the Regular Army generally reflected the racial prejudice that was present in the larger society and particularly in the South. White southerners enjoyed disproportionate representation in the Regular Army of the day, and as a group they were staunch segregationists. Marshall recounted that the General Staff:

> insisted on putting some of these colored units (those that came from the north) in the north . . . they practically couldn't train at all, it was so cold. . . . I completely overlooked the fact that the tragic part would have these northern Negroes in a southern community . . . they found themselves very much circumscribed—to them outrageously so—because they were in there to train to fight for their country and put their lives ostensibly on the line, and they were being denied (Bland 1991, 458-459).

Secretary Stimson was clearly among those who opposed a mixing of the races. Upon being told in 1940 by Marshall that he, Marshall, had decided to organize a cavalry division of which two regiments were to be black ("this ought to be a very good recognition of our intentions toward the Negroes," Marshall briefed him), Stimson admitted in his diary to having "doubts as to their efficiency" and feared they would demonstrate a lack of initiative (Stimson 1940, XXX: 183).

Marshall was often unable to stand against the constant drumbeat of segregationist pressure. Even after an October 1940 War Department policy worked out by Marshall announced that Negro units were to be in all arms and services of the Army, the chiefs of certain branches and services were able to successfully resist. For example, the Air Corps managed to consign all black air units to the Tuskegee, Alabama site; it publicly expressed doubt that a black combat air unit could be formed in time to be of value to national defense. To compensate, certain kinds of units were created and most black soldiers were assigned to these: the Corps of Engineers, the Quartermaster Corps, the Chemical Warfare Service, and miscellaneous detachments such as sanitary units within the Medical Service. Unfortunately, all of these were low-skilled units performing menial and often undesirable work, further depressing the morale of black troops and angering black political groups (Lee 1966, 111-117).

On the face of it, the reasons to locate military training camps disproportionately in the south were compelling. Most army training had been done there historically. Most importantly, training would be more efficient because of the warmer climate and fewer days lost to bad weather. Unfortunately, the integration of races, even on land within the jurisdiction of the federal government, would be opposed. The conflict would be at its most intense level where northern blacks were being trained in mixed-race bases in the south. Dysfunctional conflicts, both violent and nonviolent, could be expected to disrupt training operations, increase discipline problems and crime, and strain military-civilian community relations. An added and perhaps even more significant effect was the undermining of political support and funding among southern politicians for large-scale training operations, which would certainly impair the war preparation effort at a critical time.[4]

Marshall persisted in his joint-race training strategy. He pushed for the accommodation of both northern and southern blacks and other minorities in southern camps, convinced that segregationists within the Army could be contained through policy, training, and discipline. At the same time, he made concessions to pro-segregation military commanders, similarly-minded troops, and nearby communities in order to moderate the disruption that could be expected to arise in the camps resulting from the outrage to the increased presence of African-Americans in the camps (Black 2003, 584-85; Cray 1990, 168).[5] Accordingly, he continued segregated dining hall practices and adopted a rule that when buses, integrated while they were on federal land, left US Army property and crossed into the southern state's jurisdiction, seating was to be rearranged to reflect local custom—that is, African-Americans were consigned to the back of the bus.

Unhappiness on both sides was the result. Marshall later concluded that forcing mixed-race training in the south had been "one of the greatest mistakes I made during the war" and that the prudent course would have been to train most African-American troops and officers in other regions of the country to prevent social unrest that was both socially disruptive and politically harmful to the cause of preparation (Bland 1991, 458).

Mounting Black Opposition

Black opposition to segregation practices and discrimination against blacks in all military services erupted, persisted and grew. The black press, led by the *Pittsburgh Courier*,[6] and the National Association for the Advancement of Colored People flooded the War Department and Congress with mail and editorials calling for greater military opportunities for blacks and ending segregated practices (Lee 1966, 51-54). However, given the pressure from segregationists and the need to train millions of troops in a short period of time and move them to the war theaters, the Army backed away from this politically and socially volatile course of action.

Judge William H. Hastie, African-American dean of the Howard University Law School who had been appointed by Stimson as Civilian Aide to the Secretary of War, charged on the basis of irrefutable evidence that the Army was dispropor-tionately assigning black soldiers to small service detachments "performing nonmilitary duties of unskilled and menial character." The basic problems, he asserted, flowed from "the fundamental scheme of separate units for colored soldiers" (Lee 1966, 136-138). Then, in his report to the secretary of war in September, 1941, he stated he found no willingness in the Army to experiment with a different plan, even on a limited basis:

> Insistence upon an inflexible policy of separating white and black soldiers is probably the most dramatic evidence of hypocrisy in our profession that we are girding ourselves for the preservation of democracy (Lee 1966, 138).

The Hastie report, with recommendations, went to Undersecretary of War Patterson, who sent them on to Marshall for his consideration. Three of four Hastie recommendations—(1) to create new Negro organizations to absorb the excess of black selectees; (2) to make Negro combat regiments part of larger units and eliminate isolated black detachments; and (3) to transfer small solely-Negro isolated units to other stations—were found to be workable in the long run. The fourth, calling for starting somewhere in the armed services the integrated employment of soldiers, was rejected. In a memo sent to the secretary of war just six days before the bombing of Pearl Harbor, Marshall said that he found this last recommendation:

> tantamount to solving a social problem which has perplexed the American people throughout the history of this nation. The Army cannot accomplish such a solution, and should not be charged with the undertaking. The settlement of vexing racial problems cannot be permitted to complicate the tremendous task of the War Department and thereby jeopardize discipline and morale (Lee 1966, 140).

The December 1 memo referred to factors the Army believed worked against integration: (1) social relations established through custom and habit; (2) lower intelligence (as demonstrated by Army General Classification Tests) and lower occupational skill levels of the black population; (3) a diminution in Army strength if some of the more extreme measures were forced; and (4) the danger that Army experiments to solve social problems would reduce efficiency, discipline, and morale (Lee 1966, 140-141).

Pressure from black and liberal organizations continued throughout the war to experiment with at least one large-scale, desegregated unit staffed by volunteers. The pleas came from black and white church and civil rights groups and intellectuals, including the wife of the president. The COS responded that volunteer integration was "an ineffective and dangerous" method that would interfere with "scientific and orderly selective processes" used by the Army (2/16/1942 letter to Dorothy Canfield Fisher, cited by Lee 1966, 126).

Clearly, General Marshall was conflicted. He appeared, surprisingly considering the timing, at a preplanned conference of African-American editors and publishers on December 8, 1941. At the conference, he expressed his personal dissatisfaction with progress that had so far been made in the Army's utilization of African-Americans. Attendees were generally reported to have been profoundly impressed with his sincerity (Lee 1966, 142) and of the opinion that he was out of step with his segregationist subordinates. P. L. Prattis of the Pittsburgh *Courier* said in his editorial of December 18 that the Army's chief "knows about our problem, is personally interested in it and personally desires that restrictions against the advancement of the Negro soldier be lifted," and that his attitude "is growing better and better." The Chicago *Defender* disagreed, finding the purpose of the conference was "an obvious attempt to appease belligerent Negro editors who have taken a critical view of the whole panorama of national defense" (Lee 1966, 143).

Despite Marshall's support for some of Hastie's recommendations, including the mixing of smaller, segregated black and white combat units within larger units, it seems clear that Marshall remained at some distance from the essence of black political, social, and organizational views. The same ambivalence may be detected in forming the Advisory Committee on Negro Troop Policies within the Department of War on August 27, 1942. Marshall recommended that the committee be kept small and that Assistant Secretary of War John J. McCloy, no friend of racial integration, head it. Further, the committee was formed and started its operations without the knowledge of either Judge Hastie or Undersecretary of War Patterson (Lee 1966, 157-158).

Black Officers

Black officers hardly existed in the United States Army before WW II. Only five served before the 1940 mobilization, and three of these were chaplains. It was expected that all Negro combat troops would be led in the war by white officers, and that only some specialized non-combat units would be led by black officers. The prevailing belief among whites (and some blacks) was that whites possessed better leadership qualities and that black troops preferred to be led by them. It was further assumed that these white officers should be southerners as southern whites were more familiar with African-Americans, having interacted with them in the south, a region having a much higher percentage of blacks. Notwithstanding this simplistic logic, relations between southern white officers and their black charges were often strained and many white officers were found to be unfit for the duty (Lee 1966, 181-182).

Bending to the pressure of civil rights and liberal organizations, President Roosevelt pushed for proportional representation of African-American officers in both the Navy and the Army as well as desegregation in service facilities. While the Navy scarcely bothered to explain its noncompliance, the Army was responsive. Black officers increased steadily in number toward the target of ten percent of the total number of officers (Black 2003, 584). They also succeeded in making inroads into the previously closed officer ranks of the armored, signal, and air corps.

Opposition to the influx of African-American officers came originally from the War and Navy Department chiefs, Stimson and Knox respectively. Stimson finally bowed to presidential pressure and moved to a position of accepting the proportionality principle (about ten percent), even if this had the result of bringing in some under-qualified officers. This brought Stimson into conflict with Marshall, who held the view that black officers should be appointed only on the basis of merit, that proportionality was irrelevant, and that the ultimate percentage of black officers could be below or above ten percent.

General Hilldring, then heading G-1 of the General Staff, was dispatched by Marshall to acquire the opinions of four respected black political leaders, including Judge Hastie, on the issue of proportionality versus merit as the guiding principle for commissioning black officers. Hilldring reported back their unanimous agreement with Marshall's merit-based position. Armed with these findings, Marshall and Hilldring confronted Stimson. Hilldring recalled:

> General Marshall's advocacy of this policy was eloquent and persuasive, magnificent, and he did persuade the Secretary that this was certainly the correct thing to do, not only in the interest of the Army, but of the colored man as well. We adopted the policy (1959, 66).

Once Marshall's preference had been accepted as policy, enforcement became the issue. More than a few training school and camp commanders were opposed to any commissioning of black officers under any circumstances. Appointing black officers and finding assignments for them in these places had to be imposed against their will (Pogue 1973, 538-539). Acting on Marshall's orders, Hilldring spread the message to every commanding general in the field that "regardless of their attitude about it the colored man would be given an equal opportunity." Thousands of black officers were thereupon commissioned and, according to Hilldring, did exceedingly well "because they were qualified before they were commissioned" (Hilldring 1959, 66-67).

The Continuing Struggle

Eleanor Roosevelt exerted a powerful influence in the continuing battle over racial equality in the military services. She persisted in her efforts to achieve integration and equal treatment not only on behalf of African-Americans but also of other racial, ethnic, liberal and radical groups. She urged the War and Navy Departments, and Marshall personally, to take action on allegations of specific abuses as well as general patterns of discrimination that came to her attention in overseas commands as well as domestic sites. Marshall instructed that these inquiries be flagged within the COS so that they could receive prompt investigation and special handling. The resulting reports were to include statements about actions and policy changes taken to resolve the matters she brought.[7] As the complaint caseload grew, two permanent staff members were assigned to examine all cases raised by Mrs. Roosevelt and her network of like-minded people (Black 2003, 824; Pogue 1966, 115-116).

As the war wore on, Marshall himself became increasingly sensitized to the issues of inequality that were raised. Several of his actions and decisions, some personal and some organizational, illustrate the point. At a personal level, he donated privately to the Tuskegee Institute, the Alabama site of the Army Air Force's training school for African-American fighter pilots. He received this reply from Frederick D. Patterson, President of the Institute:

> I am *almost* [emphasis is Patterson's] embarrassed by your generous contribution to Tuskegee Institute for I regard you as already one of our benefactors. I am constantly grateful for what you have done to make it possible for Tuskegee Institute to render a large measure of service to the war effort through its ROTC and its aviation programs which now include pre-flight training (Bland and Stevens 1996, 154).

Egalitarian instincts were also clear in his treatment of his Chinese-American cook, Sergeant Richard Wing.

> This is how he make me feel—being such a small man as I am, with a great man. He put me into a position. In other words, he know, being a Chinese and sometimes I was with him anyway, so what he gives me do whenever there's a meeting of the dignitaries, he would introduce me to them. This is Sgt. Wing, he say. . . . Very seldom, should I say, a man such as the caliber of a man like General Marshall, would introduce his personal assistant to other great people (Wing 1959, 7).[8]

At the organizational and societal levels, Marshall became particularly active. He advocated the formation of special fighting units of African-American, Japanese-American, and Native-American troops, although he kept generally to the practice of assigning white officers to lead them. General Charles Herron urged upon Marshall the use of Japanese-American troops he, Herron, had commanded in Hawaii. Sensing the strong feeling against the Japanese in the western US and not wanting Japanese-Americans to engage in conflict with people of their own race, Marshall turned to his commanders in Europe to take both Herron's battalion and another Japanese-American battalion being organized in California. Eisenhower's staff declined to have them, but General Mark Clark accepted them eagerly for service in Italy. Ultimately an entire infantry regiment (the 442nd Regimental Combat Team) was sent into battle and performed superbly, becoming the most decorated unit in the nation's history. Marshall's sensitivity to their merit and the importance of their inclusion in the war effort is seen in this reflection:

> I thought the organization of the additional battalions was very essential, because we felt unless we did something about the Japanese in this country, [the civilian population] would have a very hard time afterwards. . . . As a matter of fact, even with their brilliant performance abroad, some communities rather blackballed the men when they came home as veterans (Bland 1991, 470-471).

Following a sub-par performance of the white-led black 92nd Infantry Division in Italy, Clark wanted the 92nd taken out of the field. Marshall met with Clark in Italy and proposed that the division be reduced to regimental size and have selectively retained within it the top-rated personnel from the whole division. He further recommended that an outstanding black officer (a lieutenant colonel not then in a command position) be assigned to command the regiment as a brigadier general, replacing the white commander. Locate this streamlined, strengthened unit on the front, he advised, and place at its rear the crack Japanese-American 442nd Regiment. The Germans would attack the black regiment and be surprised and then overwhelmed when both the black and Japanese units counter-attacked (Marshall 1949, 17-18).[9]

Despite promoting a few non-white fighting units, including the 442nd Infantry Regiment, the 92nd Infantry Division, and the 99th Pursuit Squadron composed of Tuskegee airmen, Marshall's dominant concern was with achieving rapid victory in the war. Integration was a sidelight except insofar as it advanced the major goal. If a black fighting unit had performed in an inferior manner, as the 92nd Infantry Division was reported to have done in Italy, and the issue was whether to take at least part of the unit out of the line, Marshall came down on the side of effectiveness rather than inclusiveness (Pogue 1973, 539).

Race Equality and Military Efficiency

Any fair assessment of Marshall's interest in race equality must conclude that it took a subsidiary role to military efficiency, and that military efficiency was defined broadly to include not only merit but also political harmony (which in turn promoted military effectiveness through congressional support). He demonstrated these values not only through his luke-warm support in the build-up and deployment of black forces in the Army but also in the role he played (or chose not to play) during the internment of people of Japanese descent (mostly American citizens) in the western United States immediately after Japan's attack on Pearl Harbor.

The sighting of Japanese submarines off the west coast of the United States soon after the attack raised alarm among the citizenry, particularly in states bordering the Pacific Ocean. Of special concern to the military and the US government was the protection of defense industry plants and defense-related utilities in the region, particularly in southern California, the San Francisco bay area, and the Seattle region. Two-thirds of the population of Japanese descent living in the region were second-generation Japanese born in the US (the "Nisei"), most of them American citizens; the balance were generally older, first-generation Japanese (the "Issei"), most of them parents of Nisei.

Fear of sabotage from the Japanese population living in the region[10] was fanned by the press and prominent politicians (including Governor Earl Warren of California), and by Lieutenant General John L. Dewitt, head of the Army's Western Defense Command. Messages from the Japanese government had been intercepted which called on people of Japanese ancestry in the US to commit acts of sabotage. Primary responsibility for the perceived threat lay in the hands of the Justice Department and the Federal Bureau of Investigation.

Appeals for help to those fearing sabotage directed to the Army and other government officials resulted in the issuance of an executive order (E.O. 9066, Code of Federal Regulations) on February 19. The three officials involved in making the underlying decision and issuing the executive order were President Roosevelt, Secretary of War Stimson, and Assistant Secretary of War McCloy. Citing the need in wartime to ensure "every possible protection against espionage and against sabotage to national-defense material, national-defense premises, and national-defense utilities," President Roosevelt authorized and directed the secretary of war:

whenever he or any designated Commander deems such action necessary or desirable, to prescribe military areas in such places and of such extent as he or the appropriate Military Commander may determine, from which any or all persons may be excluded" and "to take such other steps as he or the appropriate Military Commander may deem advisable to enforce compliance . . . including the use of Federal troops" (Code of Federal Regulations 1942, 1092-1093).

Interpreting the order broadly, evacuation of about one hundred and ten thousand Japanese-Americans and those of Japanese descent was ordered in early March by "the appropriate military commander," General Dewitt, from the entirety of all three west coast states and part of Arizona, first to temporary assembly centers and then to ten guarded camps called "war relocation centers."[11] The evacuation and transfer to the camps was administered by the Army under the direction of General Dewitt. The Army's role in the affair ended about one month later when control was transferred to the new "War Relocation Authority" established by President Roosevelt in E.O. 9102 and headed by Milton Eisenhower, General Eisenhower's brother.

There is little evidence that General Marshall took any formal role or even an informal, advisory role in the series of events—including agitation, analysis, and decision-making—that led to the internment and its tragic consequences.[12] Still, there is some reason to suggest he was more than a simple bystander. The most bothersome detail is that General Dewitt, the major agitator for exclusion of Japanese-Americans from the west coast and their internment, was subordinate to and could have been contained by the chief of staff. Also, Stimson and McCloy, who did play a formal role in the decision-making, typically consulted closely with Marshall. Also, it seems likely that Marshall was in a position in which he could have advised the president not to sign the executive order.

This line of speculation, suggestive of possible complicity, is challenged by other factors. Marshall had to have been preoccupied by a shooting war that was going badly on all fronts, which may have led him to delegate the matter to General Dewitt or to an intermediate officer in the line of command between Dewitt and himself, such as General McNair, commander of domestic ground forces. Also, this had become a political as well as a security issue, and Marshall was disinclined to involve himself in a decision which he regarded as the president's to make. Further, it is possible that he did oppose the move. His later silence as to his own role in the decision would have been consistent with his usual practice of not pointing the finger at others and not going to any effort to defend himself after the fact.

The Inclusion of Women

Vigorous lobbying by women and women's organizations for establishment of the Women's Army Auxiliary Corps (the WAAC's) received General Marshall's complete support. He had been very much impressed by the industriousness and spirit of British women on one of his trips in which he witnessed them doing valuable work in a time of crisis. On his return from England he asked the General Staff for a study of how American women might be used in the Army. Resistance was stiff and immediate:

Everybody on the staff was unanimously against it—all. As I recall it, there wasn't a single concurrence for the whole concept. So when they came in he said, 'Well, thank you for the study—now we've got to organize it' (Taylor 1959, 24).

Marshall's motive in taking an active role in creating the WAACs was most likely the same one that had led him to undertake other innovations in military organization—promoting military efficiency. He was not carrying a banner for civil rights and equality (Stoler 1989, 122). His defense of the need for the organization and his facing down sexist claims in the Congress and in the media designed to prevent its creation were immediate. These attacks warned of harm to the Army's ranks coming from imagined promiscuity of the corpswomen and from "female emotionalism." The vigor and persistence of his defense was greatly appreciated by WAAC advocates and leaders (Treadwell 1954, 191-218).

Once created, the organization had to be defended in a continuing battle against its detractors, including some on his own staff and others within Congress (Bland and Stevens 1996, 15-16, 27-28; Hilldring 1959, 14). One tack taken by the opposition was to continue claiming that WAACs behaved immorally. Marshall found these charges "most atrocious, if not subversive," and a "vicious slander." He called upon the Conference of State Governors in June 1943 to counteract this "injustice done to one of the Army's finest organizations" (Bland and Stevens 1996, 25-28).[13]

In 1950, as he built his Defense Department staff, Marshall searched widely for a competent person to fill the new job of assistant secretary of defense for manpower and personnel. Several names were suggested to him, some by White House sources. Nearly all of these lacked an acceptable political background or adequate qualifications, and the position remained unfilled for some time. He finally settled on Anna Rosenberg, a Jewish woman, whom he identified as easily the best qualified and strongest candidate.

Opposition to the Rosenberg nomination came immediately from Senate conservatives. Criticism focused on her Jewishness and Hungarian roots. The fear was expressed that her last name, the same as the name of convicted nuclear weapon spies Julius and Ethel Rosenberg, somehow tainted her. Even Undersecretary Lovett had misgivings,[14] but Marshall gained President Truman's endorsement of Rosenberg before taking on the Senate confirmation battle. Racial and ethnic smears came as expected in the confirmation fight in the Senate. Marshall testified on behalf of Rosenberg and she was able to secure her appointment. Her performance vindicated his judgment. Carter later recalled of Rosenberg:

No other person that I know of, and certainly no male person, could have been as astute in pulling together these activities within the three and four services, which up to that time, had gone unilaterally off along their own ways" (Carter 1959, 6-7).

Freedom of Speech and of the Press

Marshall believed that the Army's mission frequently suffered from unfair reporting by the press. He noted its effects in both wars. In WW I journalists appeared in France, uneducated about the ways of war or the conditions to be found on French battlefields. In this state of ignorance they tended to concentrate on the inevitable confusion and illogic associated with any war front and spread the belief that Pershing's and the American military's handling of the war was inept.

In 1944 Marshall cited accounts in the press and in *Time* and *Life* to the effect that Italy had been forgotten by war planners after D-Day, as having "dealt a dreadful blow" to the morale of men in the twenty-seven divisions serving in Italy. Commanders had become desperate about how to handle discontent among their troops who "were obsessed with the idea that they were forgotten" (Bland 1991, 482-483, 592). It is revealing as to the value Marshall placed on freedom of speech that all army personnel in the Mediterranean war theater had been permitted to receive these press accounts owing directly to Army policy.

Marshall felt it important to morale that the words and ideas of the ordinary soldier be published even when their views expressed criticism of Army policy. This often occurred in the two service newspapers that the Army sponsored but whose editorial policy they did not control—*Stars and Stripes* and *Yank*. He believed that to strike a balance of views of the military hierarchy and the line soldier was essential. In his opinion:

> I think in a democratic Army a paper such as that is quite essential, as long as you don't . . . take cracks at the officer corps or a particular commander. It's very difficult to control that, because if you begin to restrain it, the paper loses its cast as the voice of the enlisted man (Bland 1991, 486).

Could troop morale in wartime, in his view so crucial to army effectiveness, be maintained while at the same time protecting freedom of speech? Were there not occasions, such as falsely reporting that Italy had been forgotten by Army leadership, where speech could damage morale? The answer was complicated. Morale was premised both on the sense of being involved in a mission important to the national interest and being recognized as a citizen having constitutional freedoms. Although vital to democracy, free speech could not be allowed to compromise national security. The Army was constantly pursuing policy and actions designed to pursue military mission success, and so the disclosure of hard information about such items as military planning, the training and use of service personnel, and the location of property essential to the war effort was clearly out of bounds. Allowing army personnel to talk to the press could and should be forbidden. On the other hand, analysis and speculation about the larger issues and flow of events was perfectly proper to keep the public informed about the big picture.

Although Marshall himself scanned several newspapers each day, he said that he and other officers could not afford to get too deeply enmeshed in responding to criticism they might find in the press, lest they lose perspective on the whole war and their roles in its waging. Fortunately, press negativity diminished as the war moved from the mobilization stage to the actual combat stage because combat engagement generates general support and common purpose.

Background information, as distinguished from specific details about plans, movements, and personnel, could and should be shared with the press so as to make them cognizant of the general direction and conduct of the war. A strict line was drawn between information that could compromise wartime security or undermine confidence in particular leaders, and facts of a general nature. The former was *verboten*, the latter consistent with the values of an open democracy.

It was Marshall's practice to meet with large groups of reporters immediately upon returning home from foreign travel. This exercise, he felt, cultivated a common sympathy for the problems of the Army and made allies of the press in the cause of national security. General Ted Brooks, chief of the Statistics Division at the War Department early in the war, had been puzzled about this practice, but "[a]fter you thought it over for a day or two, the fellow was exactly right. There was no reason why they shouldn't have it for background. I don't think any of those fellows ever violated his confidence" (Brooks 1964, 24).

A dramatic example of where the line was drawn between national security and free speech may be found in Marshall's reaction to President Roosevelt's directive that an article in an Army publication critical of the president be banned from overseas distribution to the troops. Marshall was opposed to banning the article, but because he felt ethically bound to carry out presidential directives, he made his support of critical speech known to the president by stating his intention to resign if the retraction appeared. Roosevelt relented, as Marshall expected him to, and the criticism was published (Southerland 1959, 55).[15]

Marshall and the Citizen-Soldier

The vision of creating an army dominated by citizen-soldiers and making it effective through intensive training and morale-building was at the heart of how Marshall thought a democracy should wage war and keep the peace. Although Edmund Burke probably had colonial Massachusetts patriots in mind when he addressed Parliament in 1775,[16] his description of the power that patriotic devotion lends to rule by democracy would have gladdened George Marshall's heart.

A career punctuated by working with the National Guard, Army reservists, and the young men of the CCC had carved the vision. In 1916 General Bell had sent Captain Marshall to a failing reserve officer training camp of urbane former officers at Monterey, California with instructions to identify the problems and bring them to General Bell's attention. Marshall had instead taken the course of befriending and assisting the officers and their commander in making training more rigorous and professional (Bland 1991, 178-181). He received further encouragement from his friend, future historian John McAuley Palmer, a powerful advocate of the citizen-soldier concept, during WW I. Marshall secured a position for Palmer on

Pershing's staff with the express idea of giving Palmer a better platform to advocate the idea.

These positive connections to civilian influence only strengthened after WW I. He assisted Pershing in fashioning policy recommendations regarding the number, training, leadership, equipping, and educating of army forces, including the management of the state National Guards and the design of a new Reserve Corps. In all of this, he was developing a personal philosophy about how the Regular Army should relate to a civilian corps which was being prepared to shoulder much or most of the Army's mission.

When he delivered an analysis of the Army's changing needs and prospects in 1924, his thinking began to have an impact. Although the Regular Army was being maintained at a high level approaching two hundred and fifty thousand men, many first world war combat command officers already had left the service. His analysis concluded that there were large numbers of Reserve, ROTC, and National Guard officers that needed to be brought in. Training them required the efforts of Regular Army officers with command experience; he did not consider officers without command experience qualified to instruct ROTC students in school settings or National Guard summer camps.

He believed the Regular Army had to accept a new reality—its dependency on a growing citizen army—in order to forge an effective army for the future. The dream of a small, highly trained and professional army of career soldiers that could be sent to this or that place in the world was a thing of the past. Regular Army officers were burdened by negative attitudes toward the new breed of civilian, part-time military officers, and it was necessary to adjust their ways. The new type had to be incorporated within the Army and learn its values and skills, not marginalized or put down (Hilldring 1959, 14). If this was not done, Marshall feared the Army would be helpless in the first year of a major war (Bland and Hadsel 1981, 240-243).

He showed little sympathy for Regular Army prejudices in a speech to the graduating class of the Army War College:

> It is hard for the man at a desk to see with the eye of a troop commander a business man struggling with self-imposed duties as an officer of the National Guard or Reserve Corps. Unintentionally a breach is created, which rapidly widens. It is the special duty of the Regular Army officer to close this breach. As a matter of truth, the establishment of a sympathetic understanding is more important than the performance of any routine duties (Bland and Hadsel 1981, 232-233).

Marshall's affection for and understanding of the civilian-soldier and his potential was greatly advanced through experience gained with the CCC, first in the southeast and then in the northwest district (by virtue of his command duties at Screven, Moultrie, and Vancouver Barracks from 1932 to 1938). Developing the disadvantaged and often troubled young men of the CCC challenged and intrigued him. Most of them he saw as enterprising and fundamentally intelligent. He worked hard, handing off many of his Regular Army duties to others, to give them opportunities for regular work, develop strong general educational programs as well as on-the-job skills training, and see to their basic care and recreation, with gratifying results for the young men and the seasoned general himself. The experience formed his faith that common folk could be molded into productive, valuable citizens.

The potential value of the CCC to the Army was firmly grasped by Marshall. Through the process of training CCC members, the Army would be gaining knowledge about how to train a civilian force into an effective fighting force. The experience of supervising thousands of adolescent boys and young men coming from all manner of backgrounds furnished insight into methods for training the millions of raw draftees and enlistees who were to pour into Army ranks in WW II. Marshall's passion was to get to know what these youth were thinking and how to reach and influence them in a positive direction (Pasco 1997, 7). Perhaps it was Chaplain Poch at Vancouver Barracks who best summed up what the CCC meant to George Marshall and what Marshall thought the CCC meant to America:

> I know he was always interested in the contrast . . . the boys from New York and Rhode Island . . . these boys from Kentucky and . . . Ohio . . . and some from southern California. We had Portuguese, Mexicans and mixtures and all that. Then to get the pattern of American life—it seemed so foreign to what you would call the military service. But the big lesson he taught us there was that *we were part of the community and also that the community was a part of us*—both ways, you see. He didn't lean over backwards to kowtow to the community. They too had responsibilities and it was a two-way street. But he grasped it. We weren't an entity over here strictly performing certain military functions. We were to add to the life and substance of the community and we were to profit by the contact with them. But *never lose sight that we were, in the final analysis, civilians in uniform.* Even then he caught it and that was much earlier, before we had the great draft and all these people coming in (Poch 1960, 30; emphasis added).

Marshall's good friend, John Lee Pratt, observed this about the relationship between the general and the CCC: "He once told me he would have rather been head of [the C.C.C.] than anything you could have given him because he thought that his full potentiality was never used" (Pratt and George 1962, 13).

He was thus vested with all of these insights gained from working with guardsmen, reservists, and corpsmen when he took charge of the Army in 1939. He came with an awareness of both their potential and the challenges they presented for military trainers, being young men of little educational and work background.

Experiences with citizen soldiers contributed greatly to his policy preference for compulsory, universal military training (UMT), which he regarded as highly democratic. The concept appealed to him on several grounds. As formulated in his proposals in 1939 and 1940, UMT would entail a six-month course of uninterrupted, intensive training, followed by short bursts of well designed sessions spent in refreshing or teaching new skills. All able-bodied men would be included regardless of income or civilian status or political clout. A back-up policy was to extend training periods for state National Guard units through federal law change. Both initiatives failed, leaving him with the much less effective option of trying to get training materials into the hands of the state units that would marginally improve training at the discretion of each state unit. Meanwhile, he would wait for a national emergency to create the conditions under which the national government would act to federalize these units.

Although the UMT initiative did indeed die a quick legislative death, Marshall never lost his enthusiasm for the concept. Long after the war he shared the thought with Pogue that:

> . . . the reason I was so—and am so—intensely in favor of universal military training is that you can create a respectable military force, in a sense, without having the fellows constantly in uniform. And that is the only way you can do it and have them ready to take the field instantly. There's no other way that I know of that's possible to have units at low strength and reserve units with an ability to quickly build up to fighting strength—the product of the universal training—the graduates, you might say, of six months' training. Without that you are lost (Bland 1991, 441-442).

The Importance of the Individual

The lowest ranking member of the armed services, whether of the civilian or regular career variety, was considered by Marshall as a person whose opinions mattered. That he or she mattered was essential to a democratic society. All complaints should be heard and favorable action taken on the meritorious claims. Every person must be treated fairly and accorded the same rights and the same treatment under the law.

Preservation of each person's dignity was the base. A policy was established which saw to it that a report of casualties—including a list of those killed, wounded, and lost in action—was each day sent to the president and secretary of war. He said he did want them to lose sight of the sacred trust that they, and he himself, owed to the troops.

Some Conclusions

Perhaps surprising for a military man, democratic values played an important role in George Marshall's brand of leadership. Just what the most important element in democracy is differs from person to person. Some stress the element of participation. Some concentrate on the element of equality, and even here opinion will vary as to whether equality of treatment or equality of opportunity is more important. Some stress freedom and basic individual liberties like freedom of speech or freedom of religion or the general concept of accepting the Constitution. Some will stress rule by the majority.

Marshall's style of leadership and management clearly included all of these except, arguably, equality. On the latter score, the record is clouded, as is the perspective from which a belief in equality may be defined. In this and the last generation the valuing, rewarding, and promoting of people regardless of their race, sex, physical disability (capable of being accommodated), age, or political affiliation in our public and private organizations have been looked upon as very important aspects of ethical leadership in America. This was not the case in the environment of a segregation-minded society and the segregationist army of WW II.

Although he was no visionary and far from a crusader on matters of racial inclusiveness, he was yet a pioneer in preparing new pathways. A basic humanity and innate sense of fairness worked within him to produce decisions and policy that in time came to be recognized as contributing to the advancement of race, gender, religious, and ethnic rights in an army and in a society.

On the issue of democracy in general, his role was much greater than generally appreciated by the layman. His vision and implementation of the concept of a citizen army, his respect for the Constitution and the political role of the military within our form of government, his support of women, are the leading but not the only evidence of this fact. Historian Kent Greenfield, chair of the Johns Hopkins History Department during WW II, sat in a Baltimore audience in 1941 and listened as Marshall addressed the state of progress and problems in the Army's building program. Impressed by his humanity and sincerity, Greenfield commented:

> If he represents our Army, the American Army is yet a part of the American people. . . . He pointed out the time consumed by working in a democracy, but with no impatience. He evidently thinks the advantages worth the waste of time (Pogue 1966, 118-119).

Notes

1.   The prohibition against considering disability as a disqualifying factor in employment applies only when a "reasonable accommodation" is available which permits the employee to perform the requirements of the job.

2.   In the military and foreign services, contrary to most other areas of the public service, rank resides in the *person* rather than in the *job*.

3.   Asked for comment, the Operations Division (G-3) stated in a memo to the COS on November 7 that it did not "look with favor on the mixing of colored and white troops in a unit if there is any way of avoiding it, especially where the preponderance of troops in the unit are colored" (cited in Lee 1966, 126).

4.   See, for example, the letter of US Senator Burnet R. Maybank to Marshall dated October 2, 1944: "I want you to know that again it is my humble judgment certain orders and regulations that have been issued by the army doing away with segregation and separation of the races in various camps, posts and air bases is not in the best interest of the war effort."

5.   Secretary of the Navy Knox threatened to resign if the Navy was forced to integrate.

6.   The *Courier* had taken the lead by organizing a campaign in 1938 to form the Committee for Negro Participation in the National Defense.

7.   The same files that yielded these letters do not disclose what actions Marshall took on these matters beyond promptly referring them to staff for investigation.

8.   Wing became a well-known restauranteur in California after WW II.

9.   Noting Clark's reluctance to award battle decorations to the 442nd, Marshall said to him: "If you don't decorate them, I will."

10.   The much larger population of Japanese-Americans in Hawaii was never interned. No acts of sabotage were ever reported in Hawaii (taken from http://en.wikipedia.org/wiki/isei).

11.   "Summary of the history of the Japanese-American internment," *Denver Post,* June 7, 1942, Section 3.

12.   The internment and related events were officially condemned by the US government itself through the Civil Liberties Act of 1988, featuring a public apology and paying compensation to those persons most directly affected (Marshall 1949).

13.   "I very much hope you gentlemen will take the lead in building up a public opinion which will suppress actions of individuals who abuse our liberties by propagating such outrages" (at p. 28). The rumors concerned immoral conduct of unspecified members of the corps.

14.   Marshall Carter recalled Lovett saying: "That is either a stroke of genius or the biggest blooper you've ever pulled," or words to that effect (1959).

15.   It may be asked whether Marshall was disingenuous in making this threat, since he clearly expected the president to back down.

16.   See quotation at top of Chapter Ten.

CHAPTER TWELVE
LEADERSHIP LESSONS, ENDURING ISSUES, AND RENEWABLE LEGACIES

The attitude of the taxpayer is human and inevitable. The differing reactions of the people in [different parts of the country] must be considered. The extreme distaste for things military . . . which always follows an exhausting war will have to be taken into account. Then with all of these reactions, how can we so establish ourselves that we will not be doomed to a repetition of the succession of tragedies of the past thirty years? We must take the nations of the world as they are, the human passions and prejudices of peoples as they exist, and find some way to secure for us a free America in a powerful world.
—Marshall, addressing the American Academy of Political Science, New York City, November 10, 1942

These words, uttered in a speech in the early, desperate days of WW II, demonstrate Marshall's ability to project his thinking into the future. They afford a rare view of his vision and his view of the nation and the world and foreshadow his leadership in the task of maintaining the peace through the dangerous postwar era and into the Cold War and beyond.

Stages of Leadership

Theorizing about leadership is an intensely personal endeavor. Given the differences in individual experience and situational contexts, multiple conceptions of just what constitutes good leadership arise naturally. It seems certain that Marshall's own perceptions and practices as they related to leadership did not remain static over the course of his long career. Rather, his thoughts on the subject evolved, were redefined, and were further catalyzed by new responsibilities and challenges and a changing environment as well as the adaptation of his attitudes and behaviors. Like a mountain climber, he was led or compelled to define for himself new approaches to leadership that were needed at each new plateau as he traversed an ascending arc of leadership.[1] An attempt to lay out the stages of his leadership development appears in the table.

Leadership Stage	Position(s) and Dates	Leadership Skills Acquired
I. Basic professional dimension	VMI cadet (1897-1901); platoon leader, junior post officer; Philippine Isl., Fort Reno (1902-1906)	Master general military tasks and skills
II. Advanced professional dimension	Student, instructor; Fort Leavenworth (1906-1910)	Analyze military tactics and logistics
III. Organizational dimension	State national guard maneuvers leader (1907-1916); *de facto* camp commander	Imàgine and test organization and situational scenarios; lead major organization
IV. Performance under stress	Chief of operations at division, corps, and HQ levels (WW I)	Making/implementing decisions under severe constraints
V. Inter-cultural dimension	Liaison duties with allies (WW I, 1924-1927)	Knowledge of cultural differences, languages
VI. Political dimension	Aide to Army Chief of Staff (1920-1924)	Learn dynamics of US political system
VII. Educational dimension	Dean of instruction, Ft. Benning (1927-1932)	Ability to pass on knowledge of miliary organization and leadership
VIII. Planning dimension	Ill. National Guard advisor; CCC leader (1933-1938)	Conceive plan for new basis of civilian army
IX. Global application of management and leadership skills	Army Chief of Staff (1939-1945)	Building/reorganizing army; forming Allied command structure; coordinating war effort; blending administrative and political dimensions
X. Statesmanship dimension	Special ambassador to China, Sec. of State, ARC president, Sec. of Defense (1946-1951)	Negotiation skills; relating to public; shaping law and policy

The early path of leadership included both the formal role of cadet leader at VMI and the more informal role of guiding small military units in the Philippine Islands. Leadership in these situations was straightforward. It centered on learning first-order military tasks and functions and methods of implementing commands, rules, and guidelines received from superiors. The most important ethical element in these roles was in accepting the commitment to master countless procedures and regulations, whether they related to taking roll, accounting for payroll or leave, or protecting against the spread of disease—that is, acquiring the practices and virtue of devoting oneself to accomplishing tasks and duties.

This concept of the leadership function was elevated through becoming engaged in the advanced and more abstract education offered at Fort Leavenworth. Greater knowledge about military tactics, organization, and history brought with it an enlarged view of decision-making and how to build military capability, especially in the waging of war. Marshall was challenged in two ways at Leavenworth: (1) he was charged with the daunting challenge of simultaneously learning, training, and leading men who were senior to him in both rank and age; and (2) he needed more than formal authority to get the job done—he had not only to transfer knowledge but also induce his students to reason rather than simply command them to learn.

Being given the opportunity to design, run, and evaluate state National Guard field training exercises allowed Marshall to take a giant stride in enlarging his leadership capacity. The objects that he was able to manipulate became large units of real men instead of individuals and textbook materials. Charged with creating and evaluating large group interactions, he was challenged to use his imagination to structure differing situations in which to study how organizational units and their members and leaders behaved. He introduced thousands of men, including himself, to the experience of confronting and responding to unique conditions and stresses in alternate environments of his own making. He could then alter the conditions and observe the consequences of varying such factors as unit strength, patterns of authority, and logistical factors.

During this same period, there was the more conventional duty of commanding large command posts while standing in for absent base and post commanders (often, General Bell). The nature of the role differed from normal post and troop command because he lacked the formal authority of command. He was thus challenged to find informal means to gain the cooperation of officers who outranked him in order to manage the routine affairs of the organization.

Through such experiences accumulated at a relatively young age, the growth rate of abilities to organize and plan were accelerated beyond that of a typical officer. His leadership arc was also atypical of most non-military organizational career paths in that the typical manager stays for several years in a role focused on mastering a narrow range of technical aspects of an organization's activity. Instead, he had the good fortune to observe and create for himself many roles and to exercise and experiment with their dynamics. He was given, and took, license to explore in a systematic way the interaction of organizational phenomena and human behavior to see how the interaction affected outcomes. The result was the early formation of certain practices he was to retain and deepen: reflective introspection, working in teams, seeing change as normal and manipulable, and judging the performance of people relative to goal aspirations.

WW I provided a cauldron-like setting in which skills and functions relative to leadership are practiced. Persons with leadership qualities that are appreciated in less stressful times are often unsuited to lead when conditions are altered by the uncertainties and hardships attending combat and wartime urgency which induce severe physical and mental stress. In one sense, his earlier discretion as a National Guard maneuvers designer was being displaced by variables defined by senior commanders, opposing forces, and situational factors (weather, supplies, training, et al.) and thus not of his making. In another sense, he was able to learn and test new skills of design and implementation of battle plans under conditions of uncertainty and stress. Doing this gave him insight into his own strengths and limitations under real rather than simulated conditions. Growing self-confidence in one's own leadership capacities could only come with the expenditure of effort, self-sacrifice, and exercise of judgment.

Another important element was placed in Marshall's leadership toolbox in WW I and added to in his assignment at Tientsin in 1924 through the experience of working across cultural lines with people of greatly divergent backgrounds, languages, and values. Working with the French and British (and with German civil authorities and Russian and Italian troops immediately after the Armistice), and with the Chinese at Tientsin, he gained emotional intelligence and facility working both trans-nationally and cross-culturally.

As Pershing's aide after WW I, Marshall entered the world of American politics at the highest level and was plunged into a new environment in which he came to understand in a way he never had before the importance of external political elements to the organization he directly served, the US Army. Lessons were learned, for example, about the dynamics of executive and congressional budget processes and military service reorganization politics, and how to effectively create, use, and maintain power in a pluralistic, democratic society.

The same role as Pershing's assistant allowed him to reflect upon how new weaponry, communications, the transport of goods, the training of soldiers, and a score of other military technologies were changing the nature of warfare and how this knowledge could become part of an existing organization (the Army) that tended to resist change. Tanks and armored vehicles made the cavalry obsolete, long-range airplanes and bombing systems created new uses for air forces. Fights over the allocation of appropriations between the military services exposed the wastefulness of non-cooperation.

In being given license to redesign teaching methods for the Army infantry officer school as academic head at Fort Benning, Marshall ascended to yet another plateau of ethical leadership. He took advantage of the opportunity to introduce a new paradigm of officer training, one based on innovation, observation, and coordination with other types of armed forces that had taken shape in his thinking. In this role, he conditioned the world-view and set patterns of thought about what it meant to be a professional military officer, the very essence of the transformational leader. His students and instructors would go on to form a new cadre of military leadership bearing his influence and perpetuating his teachings.

Leadership development continued. The next plateau was in large measure self-willed and not directed by the prescribed duties of a new position. Rather than simply operating through surrogates in running the CCC district in the southeast states, he set out to define how the Army should go about performing this newly legislated function. He linked this new role of helping young people develop the skills and character traits to help them survive the Great Depression to his long-time interest in citizen soldiery.

With all of these elements in place he entered a period in which his leadership would be extended to encompass the entirety of the US Army and would call upon him to meld all of his ethical leadership skills into a piece, order them within an effective and efficient organizational structure of his own making, and connect them to the people on the national stage whose power and personalities weighed so heavily in the success of the Army's mission. The earliest part of this period, lasting from September 1939 to December 1941, demanded rapid learning, enormous physical and mental stamina, and the optimism and courage to persevere against many in opposition. This dark passage prepared Marshall to function with great self-confidence at the head of the allied effort in WW II. Augmented by his *menschenkeit*, this preparation laid the groundwork for all of his subsequent achievements, both as a military leader and as a statesman.

Some historians assume that Marshall had by 1941 some kind of a detailed blueprint in mind regarding how the war should be waged. The reality is that he had a much more general concept, or vision, of what he wanted to accomplish, and that he shared his vision eagerly and widely with a growing multitude of talented others who together gave form and substance to the image over the course of the war. The vision was opened to many and flexible enough to support a wide range of actions. He participated vigorously with them in choosing among those courses of action based on a set of constantly changing conditions and projections about outcomes (Nelsen 1993).

The concept of a flexible, general, and changing vision generated by the leader in concert with others is a realistic and pragmatic theory of leadership. Within this paradigm, the leader sees the broad parameters, the outward shape of things, but the full effect flows from his outlining a coherent theme that begs fuller development:

> It is necessary to draw in others to fill in the picture, to use their perceptions and energy. Inevitably, this will take you beyond your original outline (Mertins 2005).

The original, general vision must make a distinction between change which is beyond the organization's capacity and change which it can help to bring about. Being focused on the latter encourages interchange between insiders that delineates and debates alternative courses of action which may influence change in different directions. No single person can act as the visionary because each person is necessarily limited in imagination. It is the collective imagination of a group of people brought to the table because of their talents by a visionary generalist which drives the process.

Some leadership qualities, self-confidence in particular, are in short supply during warfare. Communicating these to organizational insiders and the public and influential political players on the outside is necessary to acquire the unity so essential to success. Stress and burnout exact a heavy burden on self-confidence.

During the war Marshall had to teach himself to both conserve personal energy and maximize his outreach to an organization swelled to sixty times its prewar size and taking within its scope inter-service cooperation and a worldwide alliance. Other leadership qualities that grow more important in wartime are the ability to identify talent and use it to maximum efficiency, entrusting discretion and responsibility to these people, and to nurture in this cadre the qualities of ethical leadership.

Statesmanship requires yet another set of leadership skills. Principally, the scope of vision must enlarge to take in a wider set of variables which include national interests of other countries, differing cultural traditions, beliefs, and behavior, and the endless nuance of language. Such qualities of mind as patience and flexibility, the skills of negotiation and consultation, and an appreciation for the effects of time and timing are needed. In this context even failure can lead to success. Marshall's struggle in China to gain accord with nationalists and communists was invaluable to his development as a statesman-leader through sharpening his resolve and deepening his humility and patience.

In these latter stages in the arc of growing ethical public leadership, it is especially the abilities to grow, change, and encourage ethical leadership in others that are paramount. The ethical leader's vision, values, and virtues are multiplied when people of talent and ethical worth are recruited, developed, and advanced within the organization. When these persons move into positions of authority their behavior and decisions will be influenced by the leader's ethics and values, and the leadership they exhibit will amplify and extend the ethics and values of the leader. In such a way did Marshall's leadership continue to grow—in the hearts and minds of people like Eisenhower, Bradley, Hobby, Lovett, Acheson, Kennan, Collins, Bohlen, Smith, Ridgway, Rusk, Pace, Hilldring, Taylor, and Rosenberg. Ethical leadership begets more ethical leadership.

Applying Marshall's Virtues to Recurring Issues

On the face of things, George Marshall appears to be a leader beset with ethical contradictions. Although trained for the business of war he became a champion of peace, one of only two military commanders in history awarded the Nobel Peace Prize.[2] He presided over a classically hierarchical, command-control organization, the United States Army, but he favored leading through training, education, and delegation rather than by direct command. In an organization dominated by a professional military elite, he promoted a wider role for the citizen-soldier which directly challenged that dominance.

A closer look reveals an approach to decision-making and organization-building that consistently reflected his ethical attributes and democratic belief system as well as his professional knowledge. These manifested themselves on a range of major issues, some of which survive to the present day.

On War and Peace

Marshall was often on record abhorring the killing of citizens. As early as August, 1941, in the historic meeting of American and British political and military leaders aboard the H.M.S. Prince of Wales off Newfoundland, he courteously but firmly criticized the British war leaders for preferring to fight Germany through the device of long-range bombing. In his view, military aircraft were better used in coordination with army movements than in wasteful and "immoral" (Marshall's word) slaughter rained upon Germany's population centers (Black 2003, 654).

As WW II approached its end, Marshall gave repeated evidence that he was rejecting war as a justifiable means to maintain international stability. In a private letter addressed to an Iowa youngster in February 1944, he confided:

> . . . but I must confess to you that it makes me sad as well as very angry to think that these Japs and Nazis have brought us to such a pass that fine, clean young boys like you must be thinking of killing men, of machine guns, bombs and other deadly tools of war.

He expressed the wish that:

> . . . boys and girls like you may think more of kindness than of death and hatreds and may live useful lives in a peaceful world (Bland and Stevens 1996, 261).

In a nationally broadcast speech in September of the same year he said at an American Legion event: "War is the most terrible tragedy of the human race and it should not be prolonged an hour longer than is absolutely necessary" (Bland and Stevens 1996, 592).

Witnessing mass suffering and horror in both world wars weighed heavily upon him, and he was making a conscious turn toward peace and reconciliation in the aftermath of slaughter. Even the collapse of peace initiatives in China and the enmity of the Soviet Union from 1946 through 1948 leading to the Cold War failed to dissuade him from his new course of thought. While the nation must maintain a strong military arm lest its weakness tempt a ruthless aggressor, it must first and foremost pursue peace and prosperity for the world and its people. Speaking at Arlington National Cemetery on Memorial Day, 1950, he placed himself on the side of peaceful resolution of conflict:

> So long as there is a forum for open discussion of international disputes, the United States should be a participant. So long as there remains a conference table around which the nations can gather, the United States should be the first to attend and the last to retire. Only thus can we earn the right to stand here in the presence of these graves of the many men . . . almost Three Hundred Thousand of the nation's youth. . . . We have before us the greatest task ever faced by any generation of men in the fight to preserve peace. War, I say again, is no longer just an evil. In this age it seems intolerable (GCMRL: Box 168, File 38).

It was Marshall who led in extending America's hand, in the form of the European Recovery Program, to help all nations in the search for a permanent peace. The ERP included the Soviet Union as an intended beneficiary and thus offered a patently non-militaristic approach in contrast to the Truman Doctrine. While a goal of the ERP was to combat the spread of communism in central and western Europe, Marshall kept the flame of accommodation visible to the USSR. The Berlin Blockade reduced the flame to a flicker, but Marshall persisted in discouraging military action to deal with the blockade.

As the president's loyal foreign policy chief he had much to do with fashioning the policies and structures of the Cold War—in particular, the North Atlantic Treaty Organization—as the basic national policy designed to contain the Soviet threat. With a heavy heart but consistent with his views following both wars, Marshall continued to urge military preparedness as the *sine qua non* of American foreign policy.

Characteristically, the old general accepted the new realities that he could see developing and prepared to meet them with firmness. We see evidence of this when, as secretary of defense in 1951, he confessed to being troubled by General MacArthur's prediction that the war in Korea would be over by Thanksgiving and the troops home by Christmas. His reasoning was that the American people needed more time to adjust to a redefinition of what kind of struggle the Cold War had become (Pace 1959, 16).

Allowing himself to be guided by facts on the ground, he regarded as irrelevant his being labeled by the press or by the administration's critics as a cold warrior or a peace advocate—only the situation and the goal of avoiding war should dictate what policies and actions the nation should take. Ideology was a distraction.

On the Use of Nuclear Weapons

Any discussion of Marshall's approach to war and peace must include his view on the use of nuclear weapons. Here the irony is palpable: a humane and selfless man had overseen the effort to fund and build the atomic bomb and had kept the funding and operations for it in the strictest secrecy. Then, he was part of the team, along with Stimson and Truman, that decided to use it on Japan.

For Marshall, the decision had taken on the nature of a complex calculation. Would the bomb work? If it did would a second bomb be necessary? How many would the bomb kill? What was the likelihood that its use would cause the Japanese to surrender? How many people would its use save if it brought about a Japanese surrender which negated the need for a military invasion of Japan by American and Soviet forces?

Eleven years later, he told Pogue why he favored its use. First, he had reasoned that the Japanese would defend their homeland with great ferocity to the last man, woman, and child. He had drawn this conclusion from the evidence of the Japanese army's fanatic defense of Okinawa—one hundred and ten thousand dead with but a handful of voluntary surrenders—and then its deployment of suicide planes against US naval forces in the South China seas. The probable result of a concerted attack on the mainland was that American, Soviet, and especially Japanese lives, counted in the millions, as well as great treasure needed for reconstruction after the war, would be sacrificed in the assault. American losses, he had estimated, would amount to about one hundred and fifty thousand dead and Japanese losses at well over a million. His conclusion: an invasion of Japan would be one of the bloodiest chapters of the war and should be avoided if at all possible, even if to avoid it required dropping the atomic bomb on the mainland of Japan (Pogue 1973, 17-18).

His reasoning conformed to what has been conventional thinking about the logic of the decision to use the bomb. Less known but of great interest was Marshall's thinking and recommendations regarding the manner in which the bomb should be delivered. He argued that the method of delivery should be chosen with an eye to minimizing the loss of life to Japanese civilians. The bomb, he recommended, should be targeted on a military installation, preferably a large naval base. If its effect were insufficient to bring about surrender, then a second bomb should be used on an industrial center after warnings to evacuate were given to the civilian population through the dropping of leaflets well in advance of the actual strike. He also recommended, as an alternative to using the atomic bomb on the population of a city, the use of non-lethal gas to "sicken them so that the fight would be taken out of them" (Pogue 1973, 17-18).

Marshall's recommendations were rejected and in the final analysis, it must be noted, he supported the final decision to use the bomb on a civilian population and to do so without warning. He gave as his reason for doing so his belief that the decision was primarily a political one and thus properly the president's to make in his constitutional role as commander-in-chief. The decision was thus made to strike one city with one of the two bombs without warning, and then use the second bomb on a second city if unconditional surrender was not forthcoming. His reaction to the decision as a whole is unknown, but he later allowed as how it was "silly" after the fact to contend that the weapon should not have been used, given what he thought were reasonable projections of human and material losses that would have resulted from a prolongation of the war and an invasion of the Japanese homeland (Pogue 173, 17-18).

On Hierarchy and Democracy

While Marshall's reorganizing activities in the War, State, and Defense Departments reflect classic chain-of-command and centralized patterns typical of military organization, he chose a management style that was consultative in nature and decentralized much of the decision-making as a matter of practice. This is seen in his delegation of most of the responsibility for development, analysis, and recommendations that led to the making of the decisions themselves, although he alone made the final decisions and took responsibility for them. Moreover, he elevated the highest level of decision-making, that relating to major policy and military strategy, to the inter-organizational level, seeking joint action with the Navy, State and Defense Departments, and allied military command structure whenever it was feasible and logical to do so. He also sought to promote carrying out those decisions in concert with others. This was hierarchy with a decidedly consensual and shared governmental focus.

Broadening the decision base went even further than this picture suggests. In a military organization that had been dominated by a professional elite, he elevated the role of the non-elitist, non-professional citizen-soldier. He enlarged their numbers and enhanced their training. He recommended many National Guard officers for command and top administrative positions. His efforts simultaneously injected pride and greater commitment among millions of National Guard and Reserve troops and officers and offended many among the Regular Army elite.

Employing such strategies as delegating discretionary decision making, routinizing consultation, and promoting greater citizen participation raises a timeless issue in public administration: Is it possible to centralize control and promote unity of command while at the same time empowering a workforce characterized by broad decentralization of decision-making and encouraging cooperation among constituent units?

On the surface, to try to do both appears to contain an unworkable contradiction. By definition, a strongly hierarchical organization is anti-democratic because those who are positioned at higher levels with accompanying status and authority are free to dictate the actions of those with less status and less authority. This general situation, regarded by many as natural and traditional, is typically justified by the argument that decentralized administration and diffused decision making are inefficient in both military and civilian organizations because of a loss of clarity in the overall mission and the undermining of the professional core of the organization.

Marshall took the middle road. Within the allied command, he championed CCOS centralized decision making on matters of strategy and basic policy—these were not to be delegated under any condition. Yet, tactical and other implementing decisions were left largely to the theater commanders and their subordinates. Within each theater of war unity of command prevailed because a single commander was in control over naval, sea, and air forces of the several allied nations. The key to operating in this way was to sort out the strategic issues (those affecting the war as a whole or allocating forces and resources among the various theaters) from the tactical issues (those affected mainly by local conditions and contained within a single theater).

The same pattern was repeated in non-military leadership roles. Through organizational design and process important matters of general concern were allowed to drift to the top while minor and local matters were settled at levels where they could with more ease be analyzed and understood. For example, issues concerning the American Red Cross's budget and its reputation among veterans were identified as urgent and brought to the national board level for deliberation and decision while local chapters were encouraged to take on such tasks as the recruitment of volunteers and fund-raising.

The tug-of-war between democracy and hierarchy was very much affected by the importance Marshall laid upon the elements of morale and fairness. It was not enough to assume, as many did, that patriotism and devotion to victory kept lower-level personnel motivated and accepting of top-down control. In Marshall's view, not only the overall mission had to be recognized and shared by everyone in the enterprise, but also the people in the line must see that those who directed them and ordered their lives would give priority to: (1) their welfare; (2) sharing the burdens to at least an equal degree; and (3) ensuring that the best available in training and equipment was provided. Morale was seen to be dependent upon fair treatment and recognizing the values of respect and human dignity.

Preparing a Democracy to Fight a War: Professional Army vs. Citizens Army

How to construct a military force that is both effective and compatible with democratic values has been debated since the beginning of the republic. The points of view range from focusing on professionalism and delegating organizational matters to the traditional service branches to building a structure that rests on popular support with strong elements of volunteerism and citizen involvement. WW II veterans were of the general opinion that the US did well in the war because of the attention given to standards of fairness in who served and where, to the teaching of cognitive skills, to the provision of health care and rehabilitation services, and to motivating millions of men and women to accept the sacrifices involved.

Marshall believed that four elements were essential in the building of an effective army. First, a massive force must be gathered. With total manpower in 1939 of two hundred and fifty thousand, containing a mixture of Regular Army troops and officers, National Guardsmen, and reservists, it was obvious that both stimulating aggressive enlistment[3] and some form of conscription was necessary to amass the numbers that would be needed for all-out warfare. Second, the force must be well equipped, supplied, and housed. Third and most importantly, it had to be exhaustively trained. Finally, the burdens of service and sacrifice had to be distributed to as much of the American population as possible. On this last element Marshall and other war planners did not quite agree.

Supplies, equipment, housing, and training facilities were pursued aggressively with the Congress. The two manpower elements, those of total size of the force and the democratic composition of the force, were related. Marshall first sought the adoption of UMT, and then as an alternative a greatly strengthened National Guard, as means to accomplish these objectives. After Congress rejected both, a conscription system based on a national lottery system came into being in 1941. As war approached, the combination of an expanded draft, the federalization of the National Guard, and voluntary enlistments proved sufficient to meet total manpower requirements as well as move toward the goal of democratic compostion.

At the war's end Marshall turned his attention back to the kind of an army that would be needed under new post-war conditions. This depended on Soviet resistance to its own disarmament, Soviet-US mutual distrust, and the existence of nuclear weapons that, although they rested solely within US hands, could come quickly into the possession of other nations.

Marshall was outspoken in opposing a large professional army. In what he probably believed was to be his final message on military matters to the nation in late 1945, he announced his strong support for UMT, drawing support from reference to an American icon:

> What then must we do to remain strong and still not bankrupt ourselves on military expenditures to maintain a prohibitively expensive professional army even if one could be recruited? President Washington answered that question in recommendations to the first Congress. . . . He proposed a program for the peacetime training of a citizen army. At that time the conception of a large professional Regular Army was considered dangerous to the liberties of the Nation. It is still so today (US Army Chief of Staff 1945, 118).

The outgoing army chief of staff argued that the existence of a ready-to-deploy and thoroughly trained corps would deter the warlike intentions of other nations. The basis of such a force must be the citizen-soldier, he urged, and the purest and most democratic form of a citizen force would be UMT. In today's context of equal rights for women, he likely would have argued that women should undergo compulsory military training as well as men, given his support for a more active military role at that time in creating and supporting the WAAC's. The lack of such a force in America, his argument went, was one of the reasons that Hitler was encouraged to attack the West in the late 1930s. Both Truman and Eisenhower accepted Marshall's views and advocated for UMT (Ambrose 1983, 443).

In the same report he spoke passionately about the vulnerability of an undemocratic, professional army to being manipulated by a selfish political leadership:

> The enforcing power, however, must be maintained on a strictly democratic basis. There must not be a large standing army subject to the behest of a group of schemers. The citizen-soldier is the guarantee against such a misuse of power (US Army Chief of Staff 1945, 117).

This argument implies that the existence of a large, professionalized, and permanent military force could lead to "arrogance of power" among political leaders by inducing them to resort more readily to military means while ignoring diplomacy and economic means of resolution. A citizen-based military force, on the other hand, broadly representative of the American people, would work against taking an action based on a calculation of military superiority.[4]

The position that Marshall would have taken with contemporary challenges such as those present in the middle east is a matter for conjecture. However, there is enough consistency in his approach to international conflict over a long period of time to allow a general appraisal. What seems certain is that he would continue to insist on military preparedness at an appropriate level. What level is appropriate turns on an assessment of the phenomenon of non-national terrorism, the consequences of an increase in nuclear weapons production in certain countries, and relations among the great powers, particularly Russia, China, and the United States.

It is likely that a sophisticated, technologically elite, and highly mobile and flexible corps would be part of the mix. Such an organization would be needed to respond to situations that could be generated by super-empowered organizations and rogue nations, and also be less threatening to other nations. This force would necessarily have to be supported by effective intelligence as well as short-to-medium-term planning of high quality. Finally, it is probable that he would insist on some effective democratic institutional controls to oversee the use of these tools.

UMT would be favored as the major avenue for acquiring personnel in order to ensure that the burden of mandatory training and periodic retraining is shouldered by a representative cross-section of Americans. New learning techniques and teaching materials would be dictated by the larger environment. Language and instruction in cultural differences, including Chinese and Arabic, would augment general training regimens. Encrusted, traditional ways of doing and thinking would be challenged.

On the Military's Proper Role in Occupation and Civil Governance

Marshall had been reluctant to accept primary army authority in the area of governing the conquered territories. WW II experience in Europe and Africa had confirmed in him the view that governance, beyond establishing security in the area occupied by a land force, is more properly a civilian function controlled by State Department political experts acting in tandem with the president's foreign policy advisers, with the military playing a supporting role.

This was also Eisenhower's view. Made the Army's chief of staff on his return from Europe, he insisted that politically reasoned civil governance policy be worked out in the State Department to save military commanders the agony visited upon him and others in Europe and Africa. He sought a permanent office in the State Department to replicate some of the guidance Marshall had received from General Hilldring as chief of G-5.

Echoes of the difficult working relationship that had existed between the War and State Departments in 1944-1945 on matters of occupation and civil governance were heard again in Washington and Baghdad in 2003-2004. Secretary of State and former chairman of the Joint Chiefs of Staff General Colin Powell, perhaps drawing lessons from WW II, busied his department's planning staff with the occupation expected to follow the invasion of Iraq. In this he was frustrated by President George W. Bush's decision to hand the responsibility for civil governance over to the Defense Department. By the time responsibility was shifted to the State Department at the end of June, 2004, the security and political situations, overseen by the Coalition Provisional Authority reporting to Secretary of Defense Donald Rumsfeld, had reached a desperate state.

Legacy: Building a Learning Organization

An overlooked but major administrative accomplishment of Marshall was his partial success in building permanent learning organizations. This was done in several ways: stimulating the compiling of an accurate history of the US Army in WW II; the formation of strong policy planning offices in government departments;

and informally assembling a leadership cadre that was encouraged to think for itself and empower others to do the same.

At Marshall's urging an extraordinarily objective and exhaustive history of the War Department was undertaken during and after WW II so that the experiences and lessons of the global conflict could be captured.[5] The goal was to produce a multi-faceted and accurate history for use by future historians and policy planners. He explicitly sought to avoid the kind of individualized war histories that are intended to exculpate or implicate particular military commanders, put a different spin on a plan or campaign, or position primary actors in such a way as to give them future advantage.

Another important precedent in building learning government organizations was the locating of functions of policy analysis, planning, and program development in specialized organizational units whose only tasks consisted of these functions. Such an office, at least in name, already existed in the Army, but Marshall strengthened it through giving it more voice and adding special planning units to deal with the special problems of civil governance and demobilization. He then created this type of office in the Departments of State and Defense, giving them a large measure of autonomy and a significant role in departmental decision making in the process.

Legacy: European Cooperation and Unity

As great as were the economic effects of the Marshall Plan, they may well have been surpassed by the Plan's political and psychological impacts. ERP aid helped western and central European nations to resist the spread of communism and Soviet influence in the late 1940s, sow the seeds of European cooperation, and lay the basis of the cross-Atlantic alliance, which effects formed the basis of both American and western European foreign policy for the next half-century.

The shining light within this triple legacy was perhaps the role of the ERP in bringing about permanent cooperation in the region. Beginning with the Council of European Economic Cooperation (CEEC), cooperative interaction continued with the creation of the European Coal and Steel Community (ECSC), the Organization for Economic and Community Development (OECD), the North Atlantic Treaty Organization (NATO), the Common Market, and ultimately the European Union (EU). It is likely that some form of regional cooperation would have come about in any event, given the movement toward the formation of international compacts. But it is certain that the ERP served as a catalyst to jump-start the movement in Europe and markedly affect its strength and endurance. So powerful and consequential was this movement that it in fact made impossible the resurrection of those conditions of destructive conflict that had been the root cause of both world wars.[6] Marshall would be dumbfounded today to witness the realization of a hope he had uttered in his June 5, 1947 speech at Harvard University:

> There must be some agreement among the countries of Europe as to the requirements of the situation and the part those countries themselves will take.

. . . It would be neither fitting nor efficacious for this Government (the US) to undertake to draw up unilaterally a program designed to place Europe on its feet economically. This is the business of the Europeans.

The German Marshall Fund[7] and many other charitable organizations promoting exchange with America bear witness to the bond created between America and Europe as a result of the Marshall Plan. For several generations of Europeans, the Marshall Plan became the face of America that helped to shape the environment in which they lived and the prism through which they regarded their powerful ally.

Legacy: America as Nation-Builder

The United States has made many attempts to resurrect war-torn nations during the twentieth century, and continues to do so into the twenty-first century. In chronological order these efforts were mounted in the Philippines, Haiti, Western Europe, Japan, Somalia, Bosnia, Haiti (a second time), Kosovo, Afghanistan and Iraq. Nation-building typically follows military conquest and occupation and is accompanied by a desire to democratize the nation's political system, bring about social stabilization, and effect economic development and modernization (Dobbins 2003).

Prospects for success depend on a number of variables, all of which lined up favorably in western Europe at the time of the Marshall Plan: (1) technical know-how and an educated, skilled labor force that could put reconstruction monies to work; (2) the willingness to integrate a donee nation within a broader region; (3) virtual elimination of the old regime, its military support base, and its political structures; (4) an external threat; (5) absence of internal ethnic conflict; (6) a high level of commitment to stay and to provide financial support on the part of the occupier; (7) unity of the occupier's security arrangements; (8) unity of the occupier's governing arrangements; (9) some elements of a democratic tradition in the occupied nation; and (10) ability of the donor nation to manage the reconstruction process and assist technologically (Dobbins 2003).

Only the case of West Europe in the immediate post-WW II period met all of the conditions that favored success. Most of the factors operate in a negative direction for Afghanistan, while the situation is a very mixed affair for Iraq. Afghanistan's negatives include low resource commitment, US and NATO withdrawal tendencies, ethnic and tribal conflicts, uncooperative neighboring countries (Pakistan in particular), an uneducated and depressed population—especially women, and the lack of any kind of democratic tradition. Nation-building is therefore more likely to fail there.

Iraq is somewhat more promising, but still far from bright. On the positive side, a large commitment of $18.4 billion was made in 2003 in a Bush administration initiative termed "a Marshall Plan for Iraq and Afghanistan," with additional funds to be made available from Iraqi oil revenues. An Iraqi middle class and educated technological core exist, although much of it has either fled or been destroyed. An external threat to many in the form of Al Qaeda is present; an external threat to others may be present to part of the population in the form of Iran. Much of Iraqi society is secular in character, although religious fundamentalism is on the rise. American efforts to build native security and police forces capable of dealing with insurgency and protecting against foreign incursions have been ongoing and are beginning to have a positive effect. The American policy goal of achieving a productive, healthy, and more democratic society in Iraq, neither hostile to nor a threat to its neighbors, was initially clear but now seems more problematical.

Negative factors are very strong and appear as of this writing to overwhelm the positive. Clearly the most serious problem is the sectarian strife that threatens to undo any progress or stability that has been achieved. Add to this an insurgency movement that combines elements of the old regime and fundamentalist radical Islamists dedicated to undermining the government and killing Americans, and the result is a chaotic and dangerous environment that defies survival, let alone reconstruction. American will to remain for the time necessary to help achieve stability is undermined by a growing movement at home favoring withdrawal. Americans, not Iraqis, are choosing reconstruction projects and the work is primarily performed by US firms with American labor paid at far higher rates than Iraqis, thus aggravating unemployment and fomenting resentment. Poor transparency characterizes much of project management, and much of the responsibility for control and reporting is left to the contractors themselves, destroying accountability, and generating fraud, waste, and corruption. Neighboring Iran, Turkey, and Syria, each with a stake in the political outcomes of the conflict, have intervened in the new nation's affairs. Some of the reconstruction projects that have been put in place have been destroyed by violence. Others have been compromised through corruption, fraud, and incompetence.

A reasonable summary is that the prospect for reconstruction and nation-building in Iraq, while it fits some of the conditions that favored the success of the Marshall Plan, is problematic in Iraq. However, it is still useful to ask a question which bears on the strength of Marshall's legacy: What would an economic development plan in the middle east or Africa or elsewhere look like *if* the spirit of the Marshall Plan were to guide it?

The conditions for a fair test of the use of the Marshall Plan idea any place in the world are the following. An acceptable government must be in place, which means the elimination of large-scale resistance through a combination of the occupier's forces and the new regime's military power and civil police functions. The target for development should be a region within which several neighboring nations would be given incentives for success. In the Middle East, this might mean using an umbrella organization such as the Arab League to identify and help to implement projects. A major water project would be an example of enterprise that would engage the vital interests and stimulate the cooperation of nations within a region. Further, it is critical that whatever project is chosen must be chosen by the donee nations.

Any prospective plan worth comparing to the ERP would have to tap a large resource base and ideally involve multiple donors in the process. For example, the so-called developed world has an obvious stake in a stable, economically viable middle east. The European Union, the developed nations of East Asia, and Russia all seek a stable international climate with an associated reduction in terrorist disruption. Donors should also be enlisted from within the region who have abundant economic, technological, and human resources: in the Middle East this could include Saudi Arabia, Iran, Turkey, Israel, and the United Arab Emirates. A combination of funds from donor nations and oil-rich donee nations could be mixed into the development base. Recipient governments could be required to provide a match or commitment from their own budgets for such objectives as public education open to women and ethnic minorities, small business promotion, and human rights. NATO or regional organizations or non-governmental organizations (NGOs) could supplement or be substituted for American technical assistance or management to train necessary security and police forces.

Finally, some international administrative organization would have to oversee project administration, provide necessary technical assistance, and impose strict accountability and transparency on project management. Care should be taken to allow donee nations to participate in choosing the organizations, firms, and persons necessary to lead projects, and to utilize local labor. The emphasis must be on self-help to maximize long-term capability.

This type of approach would leverage the influence of progressive elements within donee societies and stimulate many small-scale projects that could have immediate and visible impacts, particularly those involving women and which reward entrepreneurial instincts and technological innovation. The strength of the Marshall Plan's vision in the context of the present international situation lies not only in its potential to advance free market economics, but perhaps more importantly to extend human rights and democracy through the promotion of free elections, public education, and civil rights.

There are clear advantages for donor nations as well, beginning with the reduction of tendencies among the disaffected in donee nations to want to sabotage donor nations through organized terrorism. There is advantage in strengthening the image of rich societies assisting poor societies, encouraging international and regional cooperation, and raising awareness of world-wide challenges such as global warming, water and air conservation, and declining food production. The broader appeal should hopefully be to serve multiple goals of modernization, an increased standard of living, and human freedom. Such a vision is truly in the spirit of the Marshall Plan.

Legacy: Inter-Departmental Collaboration

The desire of governmental departments and agencies for more and greater autonomy is probably the norm in American public administration (Kettl 2007, 40-41). To some degree the instinct is explained by the practical goal of increasing *esprit de corps* within these units in order to improve their effectiveness. It is also necessary to gather a healthy base of political and economic resources to pursue large tasks. But this drive also impairs the ability of different agencies of government to work together to pursue public purposes that are necessarily complex and beyond the reach of single agencies to achieve.

Marshall furthered cross-departmental cooperation in each of his three major governmental roles. As chief of staff he promoted cooperative working relationships in planning and policy-making with the Navy. As secretary of state he worked effortlessly across department lines with Secretary of Defense James Forrestal and chairman of the Joint Chiefs of Staff Omar Bradley. As secretary of defense he opened the doors to cooperation with Secretary of State Acheson and his deputies and staff at State.

In retrospect, it was unfortunate that Marshall did not feel it was his place as secretary of state to play a larger role in the design of the new Department of Defense in 1947. He held the strong view that inter-service rivalries should be submerged by stressing a purely functional arrangement of military forces into ground, air, sea, and supply and weapons commands, irrespective of their traditional service associations, and testified to Congress to this effect. However, he did not bring pressure on the president or the Congress beyond this personal expression of views, in keeping with his concept of his proper constitutional role. He thus had limited influence in the debate within the Republican-dominated legislature in the shaping of the new Defense Department.

Legacy: Epitomizing an Ideal of Public Service

A public servant searching for a formula on how to conduct a career so as to best serve could hardly do better than to model the virtues, organizational philosophy, practices, and management style of George Catlett Marshall. For Marshall, public service went well beyond simply being efficient, honest, and professional on the job, a prescription for performance that would satisfy almost any person's definition of an admirable career. It extended to doing everything within one's power to advance public policy.

With this view of obligation Marshall looked to expand his role as a military commander-administrator to encompass objectives that were not, strictly speaking, within his job. For example, he set out to make his regional leadership of the CCC a model of success. He took aim at improving the quality of reserve officer training in universities and colleges. He created organizations to afford women and minorities opportunities to serve. He labored to rationalize civil governance in conquered nations.

This broader concept of public service served not only to give greater meaning to the various roles he held. It further led him, with surprising ease, to move outside the military profession after retirement to take on much different but highly important roles: negotiating peace in China, orchestrating international diplomacy, harmonizing the civilian defense establishment, and coordinating disaster relief and veterans services for the American Red Cross.

Exercising this flexibility and taking an expansive view of government service sprang from his ethical core. In each role his goal was to serve the whole nation instead of just the organization that employed him. This ethical posture elevated his stature and inspired those who worked with him to redefine their own service ideals. Up to WW II his influence was based mostly on military professionalism. After the war began, it increasingly came to depend upon his character and vision.

Marshall personified the idea of service to country. Acheson, attempting to describe Marshall's greatness, referred to his "transfiguration through duty" that put him beyond other great personages of the century (McClellan and D. Acheson 1980, 182). Collins pointed to a unique selflessness demonstrated through a willing sacrifice of personal interest, as in deferring the retirement he had so much anticipated (J. Collins 1958, 14). The same quality was remarked upon by Marshall's doctor, Colonel Evan Lewis, who noted that his patient put his very life on the line by attending a meeting of foreign ministers in Paris in the summer of 1948. He had received a preliminary diagnosis of an advanced malignancy, but had put off further examination and treatment until his return from this important meeting (Mosley 1982); only then was it determined that the source of his extreme pain was not cancer.

Marshall not only inspired many who worked with him to extend themselves unselfishly. His example also served to reduce the influence of some people who were unethical in advancing their careers. Senator Joseph McCarthy of Wisconsin built a reputation in the US Senate by accusing government officials of being communists or "fellow travelers," including Marshall within the latter group. As the 1952 presidential election neared, McCarthy, Senator William Jenner of Indiana, and other rabid right-wing anti-communists felt they needed to discredit Marshall to lend justification for their assault on the Truman presidency. In speeches delivered on the senate floor, Marshall was vilified as an unwitting dupe who had conspired with Truman, Acheson and State Department leftists to "lose China" and thereby assist in the spread of communism. He was also impugned for disloyalty to America through his participation in removing MacArthur from command, thereby preventing the Far East commander from blocking communist aggression in Asia. This type of rhetoric succeeded mainly in rousing the ire of many Marshall admirers in the senate. McCarthy's downward spiral and eventual censure by the senate may well have begun with these attacks (Steelman 1958, 13).

"Ideal-Type" Public Leadership Is Based on Respect for the Individual

Marshall never did accept the conventional image of military leadership—stern, unquestioned, top-down command imposed by iron-willed men. Rather, he believed that ethical leadership depends upon the development of followers who are self-disciplined and capable of independent thought. The leader's task is to give the organizational member the incentive to perform well and to afford a view of what the organization might achieve, and not to force performance. Although there is a clear need for rigorous training and obedience to organizational mandates, organizational members must find within themselves the necessary purpose and motivation. The leader supplies the guiding vision of the ends sought as well as the general path that needs to be taken in their pursuit.

Inspiring others to act independently in pursuit of the organizational goals that are shaped by leadership is the universal rule, and it applies to all organizational members. Yet, the leader must be sensitive to the needs and the novelty of the situation as it strikes the newcomer. This obligation of respect was Marshall's constant message to the army officers who were entrusted with training the eight million raw recruits that were poured into the varied Army units being simultaneously designed and formed during WW II. Ultimately, the ability to extend this respect determines the quality of the organization.

Ethical leadership is dynamic. The common thread in Marshall's practice of ethical leadership, in so many roles and over such a long period of time, was not only his knowledge of military technology in its constant state of change, but also the ability to fit the person to the organizational need as well as the human situation. He opened himself to change and accepted the fact that it would make many demands on him on many levels: technological, social, psychological, political, and economic. By valuing the people that were making the adjustments along with him, and by seeking to understand and facilitate the variables in the change that was occurring, rather than resisting it, he learned how to change himself and those he led.

"Ideal-Type" Public Leadership Includes Passing on Key Ethical Values to the Next Generation

Foremost among the values that Marshall communicated to a new generation of leaders was the ethic of placing national policy goals far above the interests of one's own organization or one's own career. He was almost unique in his unselfishness, perfectly willing to allow another person, another unit, the Navy, another agency, or even another nation to take credit for a proposal or a success, so long as doing this promoted reaching a worthwhile public goal. To his people he passed on the belief that it was important to respect government office-holders as trustees in a legitimate political system who had acquired their positions through constitutional process and democratic election.

These were not the only important lessons he communicated. It was right and proper to insist on fairness in organizational dealings. It was urgent to recognize the forces of change inherent in any situation and to respond to it through conscious planning and making decisions consistent with the planning. The morale of the organization's rank and file was critical to its effective functioning. Meting out responsibility and rewards should be based on the demonstration of merit. The inculcation of all these values goes a long way in conserving the organization's resources, promoting a strong work ethic, maintaining direction and purpose, and staying focused on achieving legitimate public goals.

Personal ethics, when consistently practiced, become solid virtues. Recognizing the virtues and practices of the leader allow organizational members, as well as persons outside the organization, to make accurate predictions about how the leader will behave in key situations. Predictability leads to confidence. With Marshall, the virtues were of such strength and the practices associated with them were so consistent that behavior could be easily predicted, as though it resulted as much from an acquired reflex as from a volitional choice. Thus it was predictable that Secretary of Defense Marshall's first response to complaints about MacArthur's conduct of his Korean command would be to trust and defend his long-time military field commander, as well as his chief of staff, Bradley, and withhold substituting his judgment for theirs. It could also have been predicted that when asked to give his independent judgment by his constitutional superior, President Truman, he would comply and report with perfect honesty, properly relegating protection of his field commander to a lower priority.

Ethical virtues will be successfully transmitted to the next generation of leaders if the practices and virtues of the ethical leader are modeled and followed. Marshall, in his related roles of teacher, organizational leader, and mentor, continues to act as a beacon to both scholars and practitioners of the administrative arts to model and communicate the lessons of ethical public leadership.

Marshall profoundly influenced the quality of future leaders in many fields: military, diplomacy, statecraft, and administration. His effect on Eisenhower furnishes one example:

> Marshall came to have the dominant role not only in Eisenhower's career, but also in his thinking and in his leadership techniques. He was the model Eisenhower tried to emulate; he set the standards Eisenhower tried to meet (Ambrose 1983).

A typical expression of how this influence was imposed came from General Mark Clark, a major field commander in WW II, the commander of United Nations forces in Korea, and president of The Citadel military college:

> I had read about him, but I found him to be really everything that I admired in a senior officer and I was a relatively junior one . . . then, as I got to know him in Washington and to do business with him I found that he was absolutely dedicated. He wanted to do exactly what he thought was best in the interest of the Army or the country, whichever the case may be. . . . If it was right, then he would do it. If it was wrong, then we wouldn't do it and I developed . . . through the years my admiration for him (Clark 1959, 51).

General Collins expressed in a letter to Mrs. Marshall shortly after the general's death his "sense of obligation to General Marshall for the great example he set for me, and in fact for all American military men, in his long life of selfless devotion to country." The exceptionally talented group of officers assembled and led by Marshall at Fort Benning's infantry officer school "provided exactly the right type of leadership to stimulate, guide and encourage these relatively young men." The innovative training and instructional methods formulated there "contributed immeasurably to [the Army's] success in World War II in defeating the highly professional forces of Germany." Moreover, General Marshall's constant acts of "warm-hearted thoughtfulness" effectively reminded commanders of the concern each of them should have for the welfare of the people in their organizations (GCMRL: K.T. Marshall, Box 5, Folder 11).

Merrill Pasco, who served as Marshall's aide, learned brevity and directness of speech, the value of making things simple and being direct, plain, and honest, of being considerate to and saving the time of others, and making certain that people in need of information got it. All these lessons advanced his legal career and influenced his future public contributions (Pasco 1997, 52).

Maxwell Taylor gave credit to Marshall for both his career and the modern army. He regarded Marshall as "the first really global strategist developed in our history or in any country's history," "the father of global military strategy," and "the father of the modern American Army" (Taylor 1959, 23). Further, Taylor allowed as how there probably would not have been an independent air force without Marshall's influence.

The list of people who benefitted from Marshall's example goes far beyond the people that directly served with him. General Colin Powell, whose career so strongly parallels Marshall's,[8] eloquently stated the meaning of Marshall's leadership in his own life:

> What is it about George Marshall that stirs me? What is it about him that reaches across the years to touch so many Americans? . . . He was a man driven more than anything else by a sense of duty, by the powerful, overpowering obligation of service. To him it was never George C. Marshall who was important; it was the task at hand, it was the mission, it was the call of his army, it was the call of his country. Service, service, always service (Barber 1997, 25).

Legacy: Marshall's Advice to the Young

If Marshall himself were to attempt to frame his major legacy, it would very likely settle about his devotion to young people and his contributions to their self-discipline and judgment[9] and reflect the simplicity and common sense inherent in his character. Edward R. Murrow, doing a television interview with Marshall in 1953, asked the general if he had a message to leave to the children of the world. Marshall's response was typically direct, plain in meaning, kindly, and wise. They should, he said, practice searching for the facts in any situation that is important to their lives and not be overwhelmed by the deluge of political opinion and appeals to emotion captured in headlines or promoted through a prejudiced newspaper, columnist, legislator or interest group spokesperson. He concluded: "if they have the facts, they have a great advantage over their elders, particularly at the dinner table" (Murrow 1953).

Notes

1.   This analysis draws on the work of two scholars, father and son, Gilbert Fairholm (1998) and Matthew Fairholm (2004) respectively. The senior Fairholm's theory of leadership perspectives was used by the junior Fairholm in his later, empirical study using the perceptions of local government middle managers.

2. President and General Yitzhak Rabin of Israel was the other, awarded the prize in 1994.

3. It was hoped that enlistments would double the number within the Regular Army, as well as enlarge the Navy and the National Guard.

4. Would reliance upon a citizen army in which the children and grandchildren of elected leaders and the privileged were required to serve have altered the decision to go to war in Iraq in 2003? Or affected the way the war was waged after it began?

5. About one hundred volumes covering, in detail, army decisions and activities relative to WW II were produced within the army's Office of the Chief of Military History. These decisions and activities of the Department of War relating to WW II were documented and analyzed by reputable scholars contracted by the Office of the Chief of Staff. Marshall was explicit in directing that research and writing were to proceed in a manner that was objective, scholarly, comprehensive, and well supported financially (memorandum from Charles H. Franklin, Adjutant General Dept., to Col. Witsell, August 21, 1942).

6. Christopher F. Patten, the last governor of Hong Kong, speaking at the Thirteenth Annual Marshall Day Lecture in Vancouver, Washington in October, 2002.

7. The German Marshall Fund of the United States is a nonpartisan American public policy and grant-making institution dedicated to promoting greater cooperation and understanding between the United States and Europe. It was established in Washington through a gift in 1972 from the government of West Germany and maintains offices throughout Europe.

8. General Powell also served as chairman of the Joint Chiefs of Staff and as secretary of state.

9. His special devotion to the Civilian Conservation Corps has been noted.

APPENDIX A
CHRONOLOGY OF SIGNIFICANT DATES

December 31, 1880: born in Uniontown, Pennsylvania

September, 1897–June, 1901: attended Virginia Military Institute, Lexington, Virginia

September–December, 1901: commandant, Danville Military Institute, Danville, Virginia

January 4, 1902: commissioned as second lieutenant, US Army

February 2, 1902: married Elizabeth Carter Coles of Lexington, Virginia

March, 1902–November, 1903: service with the 30th Infantry, Philippine Islands (Manila and Mangarin, Mindoro), platoon officer

December, 1903–August, 1906: assistant to post commander, Fort Reno, Oklahoma Territory (detached for mapping work in Texas, summer 1905)

August 1906–June 1907: student, Infantry and Cavalry School, Fort Leavenworth, Kansas

Promoted to permanent rank of first lieutenant, March 7, 1907

Summers, 1907–1910: detached service at Pennsylvania National Guard camps

August 1907–June 1908: student, Command and General Staff School, Fort Leavenworth, Kansas

August 1908–June 1910: instructor, Army Service Schools, Fort Leavenworth, Kansas

1909: Father, George Marshall, dies

September, 1910–February, 1911: extended leave; traveled with Lily in New York, Europe

March, 1911–April, 1911: headed maneuver division, Texas

June, 1911–September, 1912: inspector-instructor, Massachusetts Volunteer Militia

September, 1912–June, 1913: duty with 4th Infantry in Arkansas, Minnesota, and Texas

August 1913–May 1916: aide-de-camp to Maj. Gen. Hunter Liggett, Philippine Islands

July 1, 1916: promoted to permanent rank of captain

July 1916–July 1917: aide-de-camp to Maj. Gen. J. Franklin Bell, Presidio, San Francisco, and Governors Island, NY

June, 1917–April, 1919: American Expeditionary Forces, France
    June 1917–July 1918: assistant chief of staff (operations), 1st Division,
    Duty with operations section, AEF General Headquarters, July–August 1918
    Assistant to chief of staff, 1st Army, August–October 1918
    Assistant chief of staff (operations), 1st Army, October–November 1918
    Chief of staff, 8th Corps, November 1918–January 1919
    Temporary promotions to major, lt. colonel, and colonel in 1917–1918

May, 1919–July, 1924: aide-de-camp to General Pershing, France and Washington, DC

July 1, 1920: promoted to permanent rank of major

August 21, 1923: promoted to permanent rank of lieutenant colonel

September 1924–May, 1927: duty with 15th Infantry Regiment, Tientsin, China

July–October, 1927: instructor, Army War College, Washington, DC

September, 1927: Lily Coles Marshall, wife, dies

October, 1927–June, 1932: assistant commandant (*de facto* dean), Infantry Officer School, Fort Benning, Georgia

June, 1932–June, 1933: commander, Fort Screven, Georgia and CCC District "F"

June–October, 1933: commander, Fort Moultrie, South Carolina, and CCC District "I"

Promoted to permanent rank of colonel, September 1, 1933

October, 1933–October, 1936: senior instructor, 33rd Illinois National Guard Division, Chicago

October 1, 1936: promoted to permanent rank of brigadier general

October, 1936–June, 1938: commander, 5th Brigade, 3rd Division, Vancouver Barracks, Washington, and CCC Northwest District

July–October, 1938: assistant chief of staff, War Plans Division, War Department, Washington, DC

October–June, 1939: deputy chief of staff, War Department, Washington, DC

July 1–September 1, 1939: acting chief of staff, War Department, Washington, DC

September 1, 1939: promoted to permanent rank of major general and temporary rank of general

September 1, 1939–November 18, 1945: chief of staff, US Army, War Department, Washington, DC

December 16, 1944: promoted to temporary rank of General of the Army

November 27, 1945–January 20, 1947: appointed special representative of President Truman to China with the rank of ambassador

April 11, 1946: promoted to permanent rank of General of the Army

January 21, 1947–January 20, 1949: served as secretary of state

February 28, 1947: retired from active military service (restored to the active list, March 1, 1949)

January, 1949–October, 1959: chairman, American Battle Monuments Commission

1946–1954: Board of Visitors, Virginia Military Institute

October 1, 1949–November 30, 1950: president of the American Red Cross

September 21, 1950–September 12, 1951: served as secretary of defense

May–June, 1953: chairman of US delegation to coronation of Queen Elizabeth II

December, 1953: awarded Nobel Peace Prize, Oslo, Norway

October 16, 1959: General Marshall dies, is buried in Arlington Cemetery

BIBLIOGRAPHY AND SOURCES

GCMRL = George C. Marshall Collection, George C. Marshall Research Library. Lexington, VA

Acheson, Dean. October 2, 1957. Interview with Forrest C. Pogue, transcript no. 72, GCMRL.
————. 1969. *Present at the Creation: My Years in the State Department.* New York: W. W. Norton & Company.
Ambrose, Stephen E. 1983. *Eisenhower, Volume I: 1890-1952.* Norwalk, CT: Easton Press.
Arnold, Henry H. 1949. *Global Mission.* New York: Harper and Brothers.
Bailey, Stephen K. 1964. "The Relationship Between Ethics and Public Service." In R. C. Martin (ed.), *Public Administration and Democracy: Essays in Honor of Paul Appleby.* Syracuse, NY: Syracuse University Press.
Barber, James G. 1997. *George C. Marshall: Soldier of Peace.* Washington, DC: Smithsonian Institution.
Barrett, David D. December 17, 1959. Interview with Forrest C. Pogue, transcript no. 96, GCMRL.
Baruch, Bernard. March 14, 1961. Interview with Forrest C. Pogue, transcript no. 93, GCMRL.
Bass, Bernard M. 1985. *Leadership and Performance Beyond Expectations.* New York: Free Press.
Betts, T. J. December 12, 1958. Interview with Forrest C. Pogue, transcript no. 5, GCMRL.
Black, Conrad. 2003. *Franklin Delano Roosevelt: Champion of Freedom.* New York: Public Affairs.
Bland, Larry I. (ed.), 1991. *George C. Marshall Interviews and Reminiscences for Forrest C. Pogue.* Lexington, VA: George C. Marshall Research Foundation.
———— and Fred L. Hadsel (eds.). 1981. *Papers of George Catlett Marshall: "The Soldierly Spirit," December 1880–June 1939, Vol. 1.* Baltimore: The Johns Hopkins University Press.
Bland, Larry I., Sharon Ritenour, and Clarence E. Wunderlin, Jr. (eds.). 1986. *Papers of George Catlett Marshall: "We Cannot Delay," July 1, 1939–December 6, 1941, Vol. 2.* Baltimore: The Johns Hopkins University Press.
Bland, Larry I., and Sharon R. Stevens (eds.). 1991. *The Papers of George Catlett Marshall: "The Right Man for the Job," December 7, 1941–May 31, 1943, Vol. 3.* Baltimore: The Johns Hopkins University Press.
———— (eds.). 1996. *The Papers of George Catlett Marshall: "Aggressive and Determined Leadership," June 1, 1943–December 31, 1944, Vol. 4.* Baltimore: The Johns Hopkins University Press.
———— (eds.). 2003. *The Papers of George Catlett Marshall: "The Finest Soldier," January 1, 1945–January 7, 1947, Vol. 5.* Baltimore: The Johns Hopkins University Press.

Bland, Larry I. 1988. "George C. Marshall and the Education of Army Leaders." *Military Review*, October, 27-37.

Bohlen, Charles E. May 31, 1967. Interview with Forrest C. Pogue, transcript/notes no. 12N, GCMRL.

Bolte, Charles L. May 28, 1958. Interview with Forrest C. Pogue, transcript no. 15, GCMRL.

Bowditch, Edward. January 19, 1959. Interview with Forrest C. Pogue, transcript no. 12, GCMRL.

Bradley, Omar N. 1951. *A Soldier's Story*. New York: Henry Holt & Co.

Bradley, Omar N. and Clay Blair. 1983. *A General's Life*. New York: Simon and Schuster.

Brereton, Lewis H. November 8, 1962. Interview with Forrest C. Pogue, transcript no. 39, GCMRL.

Brett, George H. November 8, 1962. Interview with Forrest C. Pogue, transcript no. 39, GCMRL.

Brooks, E. H. December 3, 1964. Interview with Forrest C. Pogue, 3, transcript no. 77, GCMRL.

Bryden, William. December 1, 1958. Interview with Forrest C. Pogue, transcript no. 28, GCMRL.

Buchanan, Kenneth. October 3, 1958. Interview with Forrest C. Pogue, transcript no. 51, GCMRL.

Bull, Harold. May 27, 1959. Interview with Forrest C. Pogue, transcript no. 18, GCMRL.

Bundy, Harvey. October 7, 1959. Interview with Forrest C. Pogue, transcript no. 57, GCMRL.

Butler, Frederick. November 3, 1960. Interview with Forrest C. Pogue, transcript no. 73, GCMRL.

Byrnes, James F. November 16, 1959. Interview with Forrest C. Pogue, transcript no. 97, GCMRL.

Carter, Marshall S. January 15-16, 1959. Interview with Forrest C. Pogue, transcript no. 98, GCMRL.

———. 1972. "Unforgettable George C. Marshall." *Reader's Digest*. July, 1-6.

Caughey, J. H. and C.E. Hutchin, Jr. August 6, 1957. Interview with Forrest C. Pogue, transcript/notes no. 32N, GCMRL.

Clark, Mark. November 17, 1959. Interview with Forrest C. Pogue, transcript no. 37, GCMRL.

Clifford, Clark M. with Richard Holbrooke. 1991. *Counsel to the President: A Memoir*. New York: Random House.

Cline, Ray S. 1951. *United States Army in World War II: The War Department: Washington Command Post: The Operations Divisions*. Washington, DC: US Government Printing Office.

Code of Federal Regulations, 1938-1943 Compilation.

Collins, J. Lawton. January 23, 1958. Interview with Forrest C. Pogue, transcript no. 35, GCMRL.

Coulter, Charles S. November 30, 1960. Interview with Forrest C. Pogue, transcript no. 24, GCMRL.

Cray, Ed. 1990. *General of the Army: George C. Marshall, Soldier and Statesman*. New York: W.W. Norton & Company.

Cunningham, Andrew Browne. May 2, 1961. Interview with Forrest C. Pogue, transcript no. 81, GCMRL.

Curtin, Ralph A. December 2, 1958. Interview with Forrest C. Pogue, transcript no. 11 and notes 30N (November 10, 1960), GCMRL.

Dahlquist, John. October 29, 1958. Interview with Forrest C. Pogue, transcript no. 29, GCMRL.

Danchev, Alex. 1986. *Very Special Relationship: Field Marshal Sir John Dill and the Anglo-American Alliance, 1941-44.* London: Brassey's Defence Publishers.

Davis, Kenneth S. 1952. *Soldier of Democracy: A Biography of Dwight Eisenhower.* Garden City, NY: Doubleday & Co.

de Weerd, H. A. 1945. *Selected Speeches and Statements of General of the Army George C. Marshall.* Washington, DC: The Infantry Journal.

Deane, John R. October 31, 1960. Interview with Forrest C. Pogue, transcript no. 58, GCMRL.

Denhardt, Robert B. 1993. *The Pursuit of Significance: Strategies for Managerial Success in Public Organizations.* Prospect Heights, IL: Waveland Press.

Devers, Jacob. August 12, 1958. Interview with Forrest C. Pogue, transcript no. 68, GCMRL.

Dobbins, James, John G. McGinn, Keith Crane, Seth G. Jones, Rollie Lal, Andrew Rathmell, Rachel M. Swanger, and Anga Timilsina. 2003. *America's Role in Nation-Building: From Germany to Iraq.* Santa Monica, CA: Rand Corporation.

Donovan, Robert J. 1987. *The Second Victory: The Marshall Plan and the Postwar Revival of Europe.* Lanham, MD: Madison Books.

Douglas, Lewis W. December 19, 1962. Interview with Forrest C. Pogue, transcript no. 44, GCMRL.

Eaker, Ira. July 10, 1959. Interview with Forrest C. Pogue, transcript no. 63, GCMRL.

Eden, Anthony. April 26, 1961. Interview with Forrest C. Pogue, transcript no. 80, GCMRL.

Ehrman, John. 1956. *Grand Strategy, VI.* London: HMSO.

Eiler, Keith E. 1998. "Devotion and Dissent: Albert Wedemeyer, George Marshall, and China." In Larry I. Bland (ed.), George C. Marshall's Mediation Mission to China. Lexington, VA: George C. Marshall Foundation.

Eisenhower, Dwight D. 1967. *At Ease: Stories I Tell to Friends.* New York: Doubleday.

Eisenhower, Dwight D. June 28, 1962. Interview with Forrest C. Pogue, transcript no. 55, GCMRL.

Fairholm, Gilbert W. 1991. *Values Leadership: Toward a New Philosophy of Leadership.* Santa Barbara, CA: Santa Barbara, CA: Praeger.

Fairholm, Matthew R. 2007. "Trans-Leadership: Linking Influential Theory and Contemporary Research." In Morse, Rick and Terry Buss, eds., *Transforming Public Leadership for the 21st Century.* M. E. Sharpe Publishers: Armonk, New York.

Fitton, Robert A. 1991. *Leadership: Quotations from the Military Tradition.* Boulder, CO: Westview Press.

Frankena, William K. K. 1973. *Ethics.* Englewood Cliffs, NJ: Prentice Hall.

Frye, William. 1947. *Marshall: Citizen Soldier.* New York: Bobbs Merrill.

Fussell, Paul. 1983. Class. New York: Touchstone.

Gallagher, Philip E. June 5, 1962. Interview with Forrest C. Pogue, transcript no. 95, GCMRL.

Gardner, John W. March, 1986. *The Tasks of Leadership: Leadership Papers #2.* Independent Sector.

Geier, Frederick V. April 23, 1959. Interview with Forrest C. Pogue, transcript no. 90, GCMRL.

Gerth, Hans H. and C. Wright Mills (trans. and eds.). 1946. From Max Weber: Essays in Sociology. New York: Oxford University Press.

Gesell, Gerhard and Dean Acheson. January 10, 1964. Interview with Forrest C. Pogue, transcript/notes no. 60N, GCMRL.

Gerow, Leonard T. February 24, 1958. Interview with Forrest C. Pogue, transcript no. 30, GCMRL.

Gibbon, Peter H. 2002. *A Call to Heroism*. New York: Atlantic Monthly Press.

Groves, Leslie R. May 7, 1970 and May 14, 1970. Interviews with Forrest C. Pogue, transcripts nos. 101-102.

Gulick, Luther. 1937. "Notes on the Theory of Organization." In Gulick, Luther and L. Urwick, *Papers on the Science of Administration*. New York: Institute of Public Administration, Columbia University.

Haislip, Wade. January 19, 1959. Interview with Forrest C. Pogue, transcript no. 31, GCMRL.

Handy, Thomas T. August 21, 1956. Interview with Forrest C. Pogue, transcript note 85N, GCMRL.

———. March 23, 1959. Interview with Forrest C. Pogue, transcript no. 43, GCMRL.

Hansell, H. S. July 9, 1959. Interview with Forrest C. Pogue, transcript no. 33, GCMRL.

Harding, E. F. October 23, 1958. Interview with Forrest C. Pogue, transcript no. 13, GCMRL.

Harriman, W. Averell. June 18, 1975. Interview with Forrest C. Pogue, transcript no. 121, GCMRL.

Hart, David K. and David W. Hart. 1992. "George C. Marshall and J. Edgar Hoover: Noblesse Oblige and Self-Serving Power." In Cooper, Terry L. and N. Dale Wright (eds.), 1992. *Exemplary Public Administrators: Character and Leadership in Government*. San Francisco: Jossey-Bass.

He Di. 1998. "Mao Zedong and the Marshall Mission." In Larry I. Bland, (ed.), *George C. Marshall's Mediation Mission to China*. Lexington, VA: George C. Marshall Foundation.

Heffner, William. June 30, 1995. Interview with Larry I. Bland and Joellen Bland, transcript no. 1, GCMRL.

Herron, C. D. May 28, 1958. Interview with Forrest C. Pogue, transcript no. 2, GCMRL.

Herzstein, Robert E. 1998. "Henry Luce, George Marshall, and China: The Parting of the Ways in 1946." In Larry I. Bland (ed.), *George C. Marshall's Mediation Mission to China*. Lexington, VA: George C. Marshall Foundation. Pp. 115-145.

Hilldring, John H. March 30, 1959. Interview with Forrest C. Pogue, transcript no. 42, GCMRL.

Hobby, Oveta Culp. August 28, 1963. Interview with Forrest C. Pogue, transcript no. 69, GCMRL.

Hoffman, Paul. October 19, 1960. Interview with Forrest C. Pogue, transcript no. 112, GCMRL.

Hogan, Michael J. 1998. *A Cross of Iron: Harry S. Truman and the Origins of the National Security State*. New York: Cambridge University Press.

Hollis, Sir Leslie C. April 25, 1961. Interview with Forrest C. Pogue, transcript no. 71, GCMRL.

Husted, Stewart W. 2007. *George C. Marshall: Rubrics of Leadership*. Army War College Foundation Press.

Isaacson, Walter and Evan Thomas. 1986. *The Wise Men: Architects of the American Century*. New York: Simon and Schuster.

Ismay, Hastings. October 18, 1960. Interview with Forrest C. Pogue, transcript no. 40, GCMRL.

James, D. Clayton. 1975. *The Years of MacArthur*, vol. II. Boston: Houghton Mifflin.

Kennan, George F. February 17, 1959. Interview with Forrest C. Pogue, transcript no. 104, GCMRL.

Kettl, Donald F. 2004. *System Under Stress: Homeland Security and American Politics.* Washington, DC: Congressional Quarterly, Inc.

Lee, Ulysses. 1966. *Special Studies: United States Army in World War II: The Employment of Negro Troops.* Washington, DC: US Government Printing Office.

Lovett, Robert A. August 10, 1960. Address at George C. Marshall Memorial Dinner.

———. August 28, 1973. Interview with Forrest C. Pogue, transcript no. 120, GCMRL.

Lubetkin, Wendy. 1989. *World Leaders, Past and Present: George Marshall.* New York: Chelsea House Publishers.

Luke, Jeffrey S. 1991. "New Leadership Requirements for Public Administrators: From Managerial to Policy Ethics." In James S. Bowman (ed.), *Ethical Frontiers in Public Management*, 158-182. San Francisco: Jossey-Bass.

MacArthur, Douglas. January 3, 1961. Interview with Forrest C. Pogue, transcript no. 75, GCMRL.

Marshall, George C. July 25, 1949. Interview with Sidney T. Matthews, Howard M. Smyth, Maj. Roy Lemson, and Maj. David Hamilton, microfilm reel 322, GCMRL.

Marshall, George C. 1976. *Memoirs of My Services in the World War, 1917-1918.* Boston: Houghton Mifflin.

Marshall, George C. June 20, 1947. "Remarks of the Secretary of State before the graduates of the National War College."

Marshall, Katherine Tupper. 1947. *Together: Annals of an Army Wife. 2nd ed.* New York: Tupper & Love.

———. *Papers.* GCMRL, Lexington, VA.

McLellan, David S. and David C. Acheson, eds. 1980. *Among Friends: Personal Letters of Dean Acheson.* New York: Dodd, Mead & Company.

McCloy, John J. March 31, 1959. Interview with Forrest C. Pogue, transcript no. 65, GCMRL.

Mertins, Herman. March 28, 2005. Interview with Gerald M. Pops. Pinehurst, NC.

Miller, Merle. 1974. *Plain Speaking: An Oral Biography of Harry S. Truman.* New York: Tess Press.

Mosley, Leonard. 1982. *Marshall: Hero for Our Times.* New York: Hearst Books.

Murrow, Edward R. May 24, 1953. Interview with Marshall on "See It Now," 2nd Volume, show # 38.

———. 1951. CBS Report.

Myers, Ramon H. "Frustration, Fortitude, and Friendship." In Larry I. Bland (ed.), *George C. Marshall's Mediation Mission to China.* Lexington, VA: George C. Marshall Foundation.

Nathan, Otto, and Heinz Norden (eds.). 1960. *Einstein on Peace.* New York: Simon and Schuster.

Nelsen, John T., II. February, 1993. *General George C. Marshall: Strategic Leadership and the Challenges of Reconstituting the Army, 1939-1941.* Strategic Studies Institute, US Army War College.

Nelson, Otto L., Jr. 1946. *National Security and the General Staff.* Washington, DC: Infantry Journal Press.

Neustadt, Richard E. and Ernest May. 1986. *Thinking in Time: The Uses of History for Decision-Makers.* New York: Free Press.

Northouse, Peter G. 2004. *Leadership: Theory and Practice, 3rd ed.* Thousand Oaks, Calif.: Sage Publications.

Osborn, Frederick H. February 18, 1959. Interview with Forrest C. Pogue, transcript no. 52, GCMRL.

Pace, Frank. April 1, 1959. Interview with Forrest C. Pogue, transcript no. 42, GCMRL.

Parrish, Thomas. 1989. *Roosevelt and Marshall: Partners in Politics and War.* New York: William Morrow and Company.

Parton, James. 1986. *Air Force Spoken Here: General Ira Eaker & the Command of the Air.* Bethesda, MD: Adler & Adler Publishers.

Pasco, Merrill. November 11, 1997. Interview with Richard DeMartino, GCMRL.

Pawley, William D. November 19, 1962. Interview with Forrest C. Pogue, transcript no. 85, GCMRL.

Poch, Martin C. September 14, 1960. Interview with Forrest C. Pogue, transcript no. 6, GCMRL.

Pogue, Forrest C. with Gordon Harrison (ed.). 1963. *George C. Marshall: Education of a General, 1880-1939.* Lexington, VA: George C. Marshall Research Foundation.

Pogue, Forrest C. 1966. *George C. Marshall: Ordeal and Hope, 1939-1943.* New York: Viking Press.

Pogue, Forrest C. 1973. *George C. Marshall: Organizer of Victory, 1943-1945.* New York: Viking Press.

Pogue, Forrest C. 1987. *George C. Marshall: Statesman, 1945-1959.* New York: Viking Press.

Pops, Gerald M. and Thomas J. Pavlak. 1991. *The Case for Justice: Strengthening Decision Making and Policy in Public Administration.* San Francisco: Jossey-Bass.

Powder, James W. October 19, 1959. Interview with Forrest C. Pogue, transcript no. 60, GCMRL.

Pratt, John Lee and (Colonel) George. April 25, 1962. Interview with Forrest C. Pogue, transcript no. 41, GCMRL.

Price, Harry Bayard. 1955. *The Marshall Plan and Its Meaning.* Ithaca, NY: Cornell University Press.

Priest, Dana and Anne Hull. "Soldiers Face Neglect, Frustration at Army's Top Medical Facility." *Washington Post,* February 18, 2007, A1.

Ridgway, Matthew. February 26, 1959. Interview with Forrest C. Pogue, transcript no. 21, GCMRL.

Riesman, David. 1950. *Lonely Crowd: A Study of the Changing American Character.* New Haven, CT: Yale University Press.

Robertson, Walter. September 6, 1962. Interview with Forrest C. Pogue, transcript no. 107, GCMRL.

Roosevelt, Eleanor. March 17, 1958. Interview with Forrest C. Pogue, transcript no. 87, GCMRL.

Rusk, Dean with Richard Rusk and Daniel S. Papp. 1990. *As I Saw It.* New York: W. W. Norton & Co.

Seidman, Harold. 1970. *Politics, Position, and Power: The Dynamics of Federal Organization.* New York: Oxford University Press.

Sexton, W. T. May 23, 1958. Interview with Forrest C. Pogue, transcript no. 38, GCMRL.

Shames, Benjamin. August 17, 2005. Interview with Gerald M. Pops, Chautauqua, NY.

Sherwood, Robert E. 1948. *Roosevelt and Hopkins: An Intimate History.* New York: Harper and Brothers.

Smith, Paul. July 7, 2004. Interview with Gerald M. Pops, Kingwood, WV.

Smith, Truman. October 5, 1959. Interview with Forrest C. Pogue, transcript no. 16, GCMRL.

Smith, Walter Bedell. 1950. *My Three Years in Moscow.* Philadelphia: Lipincott.

———. July 29, 1958. Interview with Forrest C. Pogue, transcript no. 88, GCMRL.

Southerland, John. "Gen. Marshall Told Me." *US News & World Report* November 2, 1959, 50-56.

Spaatz, Carl. July 24, 1959. Interview with Forrest C. Pogue, transcript no. 64, GCMRL.

Stark, Harold R. March 13, 1959. Interview with Forrest C. Pogue, transcript no. 54, GCMRL.

Stayer, M.C. January 20, 1960. Interview with Forrest C. Pogue, transcript no. 34, GCMRL.

Steelman, John R. November 5, 1958. Interview with Forrest C. Pogue, transcript no. 118, GCMRL.

Stevenson, Adlai. April 30, 1958. Interview with Forrest C. Pogue, transcript no. 100, GCMRL.

Stimson, Henry L. 1940-1945. *Diary.* Yale University Library. New Haven, CT.

Stoler, Mark A. 1989. *George C. Marshall: Soldier-Statesman of the American Century.* New York: Simon and Schuster.

———. 1998. "Why George Marshall? A Biographical Assessment." In Larry I. Bland (ed.), *George C. Marshall's Mediation Mission to China.* Lexington, VA: George C. Marshall Foundation.

Taylor, Maxwell D. July 16, 1959. Interview with Forrest C. Pogue, transcript no. 86, GCMRL.

———. 1972. *Swords and Plowshares.* Toronto: W. W. Norton & Company.

Thomas, Cora. March 10, 1961. Interview with Forrest C. Pogue, transcript no. 50, GCMRL.

Thorne, Christopher. 1978. *Allies of a Kind.* London: Hamilton.

Timberman, Thomas S. August 21, 1959. Interview with Forrest C. Pogue, transcript no. 14, GCMRL.

Time Magazine. January 3, 1944. "Man of the Year."

Treadwell, Mattie E. 1954. *The Women's Army Corps, United States Army in World War II.* Washington, DC: US Government Printing Office.

Truman, Harry S. November 14, 1960. Interview with Forrest C. Pogue, transcript no. 70, GCMRL.

Truscott, Lucien. March 21, 1959. Interview with Forrest C. Pogue, transcript no. 78, GCMRL.

Uldrich, Jack. 2005. *Soldier Statesman Peacemaker: Leadership Lessons from George C. Marshall.* New York: Amacom Books.

US Army Chief of Staff. 1943. *Biennial Report to the Secretary of War.* Simon and Schuster.

———. 1945. *Biennial Report to the Secretary of War: General Marshall's Report: The Winning of the War in Europe and the Pacific, July 1, 1943 to June 30, 1945.* Washington, DC: Center of Military History.

US Congress, House of Representatives, Committee on Foreign Affairs. 1948. *United States Foreign Policy for a Post-War Recovery Program: Hearings.* 80th Congress, 1st and 2nd sessions. Washington, DC: Government Printing Office.

Van Wart, Mongomery. 2005. *Dynamics of Leadership in Public Service: Theory and Practice.* Armonk, NY: M. E. Sharpe, Inc.

Watson, Mark S. 1950. *United States Army in World War II: The War Department: Chief of Staff: Prewar Plans and Preparations.* Washington, DC: US Government Printing Office.

Wedemeyer, Albert C. 1958. *Wedemeyer Reports!* New York: Henry Holt and Company.

Wehrle, Edmund S. 1998. "Marshall, the Moscow Conference, and Harriman." In Larry I. Bland (ed.), *George C. Marshall's Mediation Mission to China.* Lexington, VA: George C. Marshall Foundation.

Wilson, Charles McMoran. April 20, 1961. Interview with Forrest C. Pogue, transcript no. 82, GCMRL.

Wing, Richard C. October 20, 1959. Interview with Forrest C. Pogue, transcript no. 7, GCMRL.

Yu Shen. 1998. "The CCP's Views on the Marshall Mission." In Larry I. Bland (ed.), George C. Marshall's Mediation Mission to China. Lexington, VA: George C. Marshall Foundation.

Zhang Baijia. 1998. "Zhou Enlai and the Marshall Mission." In Larry I. Bland (ed.), George C. Marshall's Mediation Mission to China. Lexington, VA: George C. Marshall Foundation.

INDEX

Acheson, Dean, 4, 67n3, 68n14, 76, 89,
133n5, 137, 146, 149-150, 152,
153, 162, 165, 226, 248, 249, 259,
288, 300, 301; compared to
Marshall, 178; on Marshall traits,
64, 75, 87, 187, 301; Marshall
actions at State, 148-149, 223-
224; on MacArthur removal, 163;
opposed partition, 156; speech on
ERP, 152
accessibility and openness, 70, 79-80,
193; to media and public, 191,
198; Roosevelt's aversion to
openness, 190
accuracy, 15, 57, 63, 65, 69, 75, 246;
advice to youth, 304-303; in
agency decision process, 186, 223;
in cabinet meetings, 158; in
communications with Congress,
195; in the field, 170, 188; on
MacArthur's removal, 164; in
negotiation, 145, 151, 198; in
recording history of War
Department, 228, 295-296
achievement, 5, 73, 74, 77, 121, 147,
165, 201n16, 229, 287; in Berlin,
155; in China, 140; at Ft. Benning,
41; in WW I, 36; in WW II, 131-
132
acting chief of staff, Marshall as, 47,
100, 179
Advisory Committee on Negro Troop
Policies, 270
advocacy, 75, 93; for air power, 92; of
CCC, 42; of China peace, 144; of
citizen-soldier concept, 277-278;
of cross-channel invasion, 184; of
ERP, 197; of merit criterion, 271;
of NDA, 205; to Congress, 97-

101; 189, 200; of troop activity,
250; of unified command, 187; of
war preparedness, 6, 97, 98, 107.
See also Congress
air forces, 1, 57, 91, 92, 170, 180, 186,
205, 209, 211, 212; need to
increase, 94; Marshall's support
of, 120, 132, 214, 220-221, 241,
286, 292
air power, 6, 46, 53, 55, 92, 131, 132,
179, 196, 217, 220, 234; air and
naval power, 105
Alexander, Field Marshal (Sir) Harold,
122
allied command structure, 112, 169,
215-217
aloofness, 54, 79, 81, 86
ambition, 40, 48, 66, 69, 131, 132, 170
American Expeditionary Forces (AEF),
13, 33, 34, 37, 47, 166, 204, 205
American Red Cross (ARC), 1, 7, 40,
84, 158-161, 300
Andrews, Lt. Gen. Frank M., 46, 55,
94, 95, 208, 234
anger, 65, 75, 76, 87-88, 104, 157;
control over, 87, 195; and
decision-making, 57; directed at
problem, 256; lack of, when
disciplining, 24; over
mistreatment of troops, 256; with
technical regulations, 78, 104,
184-185, 195, 256; with war's
effect on children, 289. *See also*
temper
Anglo-American unity, 108, 165
anti-aircraft, 59, 181, 246
Arcadia conference, 108, 112, 169,
187, 216-217, 219, 220
Argentia, 108, 112, 180, 289

administrative effectiveness, 1;
and Marshall, 84; and expansive
view of public service, 301; as
knowledge acquisition, 51;
MacArthur and military ethics,
163; of mastering tasks and duties,
284-285; in military officer
training, 236; and professionalism,
199; role in public leadership, 89;
of segregated Negro units, 265;
and virtues, 302-303
European Recovery Program (ERP).
See Marshall Plan
Executive Order 9082, 212

fairness, 57-60, 67, 121; core element
in ethical leadership, 11, 52, 53; in
decisions advancing civil rights,
281; and interpersonal relations,
81; and morale, 292-293; in
negotiations, 141; in officer
selection, 102; opportunity to be
heard, 57; in organizational
dealings, 302; reputation for, 70;
re success in WW II, 293
faults, 14, 51; fault-finding, 147; of
Marshall, 85, 87, 89
field combat commands, 25, 29, 55, 59-
60, 73, 101-102, 177, 214, 247,
272, 278, 301; age limitation
policy, 60, 101-102; appointment
to, 55, 66, 81, 101-102, 239-240,
244-245, 249, 264; deference to
by headquarters, 59, 122, 163,
170-171, 173-174, 184-185;
discretion of, 172; functions of,
12, 35, 39, 235-236, 239; morale
as a command function, 253; use
of national guardsmen in, 292;
promotion dependent upon, 29;
removal from, 240, 257; without
formal authority, 24, 250, 285
field officers, 34, 142, 170, 172, 174,
184, 237, 244, 252-254; balance
needs of field and headquarters,
35; dislike of headquarter officers,
66; Marshall as field tactician, 28,
29, 44, 45, 48; integration of, 238;
as obstacles to planning, 34;

priority of, 173; rotation of, 59,
177, 255
First Infantry Division, 33, 55, 58, 171
five-star rank, 73
focus on goals, 57, 168, 177, 183-184,
302
Forrestal, James, 156, 191, 248, 300
Fort Benning, Georgia, 15, 40-41, 80,
86, 87, 191, 216, 239, 252, 284,
286; beautification of, 255; import
of Marshall's time at, 42; nature
of instruction at, 41, 179, 219,
235, 243, 244; social life of
officers, 41, 79, 83, 136; talent at,
48, 120, 208, 233; meeting and
courting Katherine Tupper Brown,
41
Fort Leavenworth, Kansas, 28, 29, 30,
48, 184, 238, 240, 284; Army staff
college, 26-27, 285; infantry and
cavalry school, 26, 83; students
taught, 49n5, 51; skills acquired
at, 194, 233-234
Fort Moultrie, South Carolina, 42, 45
Fort Reno, Oklahoma Territory, 26,
250, 284
Fort Screven, Georgia, 42-43, 45
France, 43, 78, 91, 101, 150-151; 173,
236; AEF in, 204-205; ally of US
in WW II, 46, 55, 94, 106, 180,
216; breakdown of local authority,
137; and Brussels treaty, 155;
invaded in 1940, 98; ERP
participation, 226-227, 231n18;
occupying German zone, 154; and
cross-channel assault, 113, 122,
184; with Pershing in, 55.
Franco, Francisco, 155-156
free speech, 8, 79, 276, 277
Freeman, Douglas Southall, 13, 134
French Committee of National
Liberation, 128
frugality, 20, 84

Gardner, John W., 17, 23, 24, 203
General Headquarters (GHQ),
abolished and staff transferred to
OPD, 212; debate and study of,
100-101, 208-209, 211; wartime
operations center, 100, 205

ABOUT THE AUTHOR

Gerald Pops is professor of public administration in a masters program preparing future public administrators at West Virginia University at Morgantown, a scant twenty-five miles from the birthplace of George C. Marshall. Earlier in Professor Pops' career, he was an Air Force lawyer and a legislative analyst with the California legislature. During his teaching career, he has been a visiting professor at the Georgian Institute of Public Affairs in Tbilisi, Georgia, a visiting scholar at Virginia Tech's Center for Public Administration and Policy, and a two-time Fulbright scholar in Hungary and the Republic of Georgia. He is also designated a Marshall Scholar by the George C. Marshall Foundation.

His wide-ranging set of interests has led to a variety of publications in journals and monographs within the fields of public administration, public ethics and leadership, administrative law, labor relations and conflict resolution, and public policy. Most recently, his work has concentrated on the subjects of ethical leadership and the career of George C. Marshall as an exemplar of ethical leadership. Earlier books include *The Case for Justice: Strengthening Decision Making and Policy in Public Administration*, the co-authored *Applying Standards and Ethics in the 21st Century* for the American Society for Public Administration, and *Emergence of the Public Sector Arbitrator*.

LaVergne, TN USA
24 January 2010
171020LV00003B/51/P